THE FESTIVE
FAMULARO
KITCHEN

A80
LB89.9-3

THE FESTIVE FAMULARO KITCHEN

Great Combinations of Food
Elegant Meals with Italian Flavor
and International Flair

JOE FAMULARO
& LOUISE IMPERIALE

New York

ATHENEUM

1977

Library of Congress Cataloging in Publication Data

Famularo, Joseph J
The festive Famularo kitchen.
Includes index.
1. Cookery, Italian.   2. Cookery, International.
I. Imperiale, Louise, joint author.   II. Title.
TX723.F34   641.5'945   76-30498
ISBN 0-689-10750-1

Copyright © 1977 by Joe Famularo and Louise Imperiale
All rights reserved
Published simultaneously in Canada by McClelland and Stewart Ltd.
Manufactured by American Book–Stratford Press, Inc.
Designed by Kathleen Carey
First Edition

FOR

all the mothers, fathers, grandmothers, and grandfathers in every walk of life who cook for and feed their children with love and care, and especially for our parents, Mamma Angela and Papa Joe. Their kitchen was home, home was their kitchen, and they knew its meaning to a happy, healthy, and secure family.

"Man is a cooking animal; the beasts have memory, judgment, and all the faculties and passions of our own mind in a certain degree, but no beast is a cook."

JAMES BOSWELL

ACKNOWLEDGMENTS

T HIS book is the work of many people. To begin with, all members of our family with whom we've shared, and continue to share, so many meals have played a role (and still do) in shaping the format, the color, the combinations, and the spirit of much of the food presented between these covers.

Second, we wish to express our thanks to all our friends for sharing food and food ideas, in their homes and in ours. Their desire to please us and our desire to please them have usually meant better, more exciting food. We're indebted to so many, but special thanks to Diana Buchanan, Donald Cameron, Jean Ducas, Betty and John Hettinger, Jerry Huven, Helen Kurros, Lady Fiona and Captain Michael Lowsley-Williams, Hedy and Sam Lanham, Alice and Walter McAdams, Joan Muessen, Alixe von Nagel, Al and Mildred Panariello, Tommi Parzinger, Ben Piazza, Vera Robinson, Felicia Roosevelt, Harvey Smith, Joyce and Ken Volk, and Jane and Victoria Walsh.

A very special thank-you to Craig Claiborne for writing about our food and for his encouragement and kind evaluation of our "ability to write recipes"; to Marylin Bender and Rita Reif, also of the *New York Times* for their good deeds and kind words; to Jane Bacon Ellis, food and wine editor of *House & Garden,* and her two daughters Claire and Kate (we'll cook for them anytime); to Bernie Kinzer for his willingness and patience as food critic; to Karen Lippert for the fastest-flying and most dedicated ten fingers on any typewriter; to Mrs. Keri Galuppo for her touch of editing the Italian phrases herein; and to Dorothy Parker, our editor *molto simpatica.*

And once again, but not finally, we say thank you to Louise's husband, John, and to their daughter, Susan, a true pair of tasters who never complained about overstretched stomachs as they tasted two versions of the same pastry, pasta, and pizza; beef rolls, pork rolls, and veal rolls; a little onion, more onion, and a little more onion; and too sweet, not sweet enough, and, oh, just-right food.

Joe Famularo
Louise Imperiale

FOREWORD

I N the spring of last year, we had the good fortune to be visiting friends in San Roque, Spain, a few miles from Gibraltar. One day, we left early in the morning on a two-hour drive to Jerez de la Frontera, where the celebration of *la feria* was taking place. The countryside at that time of year was splendid. We had breakfast along the way.

The tour of Jerez and the talk of the palomino grape and the Albariza soil, neither of which is found anywhere else in the world, was the best first course before our main meal at *la feria*. After much walking, visiting, eating, drinking, buying, and talking, we were happy and peaceful as we watched the sun set on this countryside dotted with Roman ruins and thought about returning to our temporary home.

As we entered the front door, Fiona, our hostess, said there would be twenty-four or twenty-five of us for a simple supper in about forty minutes. My God, I thought, what could she possibly pull together at this late hour? It was one of the best meals we ever had. Unquestionably luxurious, but to us it was superior for its simplicity. We had thin, thin slices of Scottish smoked salmon, smoked turkey, and bread and lots of ice-cold champagne. And beautiful iced caviar with lemon juice. Great combinations of food. On that evening, the idea for this cookbook was born.

The combinations of food are infinite; perhaps this is one reason why it's such fun playing the cooking game. Classic flavor combinations, such as tomato and basil, are age-old. Most people know this combination best in two forms: sliced fresh tomatoes with finely chopped basil and fresh tomatoes and basil in a sauce for pasta. But why not fresh tomatoes and basil for soup?

People accept most traditional combinations without question because they learned to like them at an early age; because they remember tasty things with nostalgia, and that usually produces a good feeling; and because they simply like and enjoy them. Think of bread and butter, ice cream and sugar cones, strawberries and cream. Think of bacon and eggs, peaches and almonds, lamb and garlic, pork and apples. And what about Stilton cheese with a glass of port or fruit and nuts with Madeira or sherry?

We can talk about today's *après*-ski supper or yesterday's *après*-theater dinner, yet one of our earliest and most appreciated food combinations was an *après*-school snack prepared by our grandmother every winter's day promptly at 3:15 P.M.: thick slices of freshly baked Italian bread covered with butter, put in the oven to combine the butter and bread, piping-hot to the touch. And with it a full cup of hot milk laced with a teaspoonful of real adult coffee. Oh, *Nonna*, we miss you.

Another *après*-school picnic took place around our big kitchen table. French fried potatoes were always a preteen favorite, especially when drowned in catsup. One day, at the age of eleven, precocious Joe announced that they were being served with mustard. The lesson: For the sake of a surprising good taste, ignore the obvious and combine flavors without the prompting of tradition. As Roy Andries de Groot suggested in a recent *Esquire* article, try a wild mushroom bouillon with *pasatelli* or a sturgeon *potage* with tiger lily buds. (If you can't find tiger lily buds, we suggest zucchini flowers.)

We still smile in happy reminiscence of sister Mary's and brother Jerry's sandwiches made of thin slices of Mamma Angela's homemade bread filled with fried green Italian peppers (be sure to add salt) and Swiss cheese—delicious. On alternate nights, just before going to sleep, there were sisters Bea's and Louise's banana sandwiches, served in bed. Can you believe it? Bananas and bread after escarole *in broda*, pasta, baked red snapper, and fruit. Dear Dottore Freud, *buona notte!*

Cooking and eating are our hobbies. Joe cooks every weekend in his country house, Tara North—a restored Greek revival house of 1840 vintage—near Pawling, New York, and Louise cooks all week long for her husband John and daughter Susan. We tend to translate everything in life into food terms. We may start talking about the weather, a television program, a new book or play, but our conversation always ends up in the kitchen—and it doesn't matter to whom we're talking.

It's not easy to describe the beginnings of our interest in food. Can having been breast-fed have anything to do with it? Can having both parents, both grandparents, brothers and sisters, aunts and uncles and cousins passionately interested in food account for it? One event easily marks one of our first memorable meals, at a time when both of us were not ten years old. Mamma Angela, with the help of Papa Joe, cooked for a week, preparing a feast to end all feasts. Our eldest brother and his friends were coming from college in South Carolina, and our parents believed that some of the best cooking in the United States is accomplished in the Deep South. (There is a community of thinking between Americans in the south of the United States and Italians in the south of Italy—their affinity, for instance, for the combination of pork fat and beans.) For this meal, our parents produced china and linen we had never seen before. Sausage meats were hung and dried; pasta was made and stored; cherries were submerged in brandy; peppers were stuffed and put away in covered containers. We couldn't believe what we were seeing. A magnificent banquet table was set for twelve. We were to be fed early (some leftover pasta, probably) and put out of sight.

About four hours before the celebration of the Feast of the Homecoming of the Eldest Son and His Esteemed Friends from the Noteworthy State of South Carolina, we started to ask Mamma Angela and Papa Joe, "What will happen if they don't come?" We were scolded and hushed, but we posed the question again. Mamma's response was *"State zitti, andate a studiare!"* ("Be quiet; go study").

This line of questioning had started at about 3:30 on the afternoon of the big event; it continued until well after 8:00, an hour and a half past their expected arrival. The phone rang, Angela spoke gently to her eldest son, and tears rolled down her cheek. All of them were still in South Carolina; they would be detained for several days. At 8:30 P.M., Mamma Angela, Papa Joe, and their five younger children sat down and enjoyed all feast and saints' days—and Christmas, too—in this one sitting. There was little conversation. We ate, we ate, and we ate.

For us, cooking is contentment. It satisfies a deep-rooted psychological need for immediate gratification. Think about the long-term objectives facing each of us: gaining an education, deciding on a lifework, following a career, raising a family, educating children, and so on. Years can roll by before it's possible to evaluate the degree of success or failure. People need little things in which to succeed on a daily basis: enjoying a good story, helping a neighbor, preparing a good meal for family and friends and for oneself.

Cooking is procedural, but it can also be creative. And because the work is done basically with one's hands, it provides fulfillment. In the food columns of newspapers, magazines, and books, one sees Aunt Tillie's Pepper Relish, Uncle Bob's Grilled Pheasant, Miss Minnie's Chocolate Cake. Or one hears about Paula's pasta sauce, Dougie's bread, or Miranda's mousse. All this represents personal achievement and satisfaction.

No one is suggesting that there is anything wrong with committee actions or group dynamics, but in our view, they don't meet *individual* psychological needs. Usually, home cooking is more an individual than a team effort. And accenting unique personal accomplishment these days is important because so many people suffer the grind of life as a cog of the wheel. Anne Willan, a first-rate cook and teacher, is known to enjoy the risk of making a soufflé for her important parties and admits to appreciating the applause it brings her as a cook—a great short-term success experience.

One can only guess how many years ago ape became man, but most authorities are of the opinion that the change took place because of a shortage of food above ground. It seems the ape was forced to leave his tree-swinging skyscraper habitat and move into the basement to search through the grassland for his daily grub. As he evolved into Homo sapiens, he learned speech and the uses of fire, and his forefeet became hands—hands for homecrafted creations, hands for home-baked foods, hands made for better living. We believe that better living all starts in the family kitchen, and the more hands there, the better.

There are two specific reasons for this cookbook. First, to help give readers a greater awareness of the possibilities in the combinations of food in the hope that they will go on to discover new ones. Some discoveries happen by accident: others, by sheer innovation. With years of cooking around our waistlines, we recently learned, for example, the advantage of adding lemon to certain chocolate dishes (see our Chocolate Cream Meringue Pie, page 407). On another occasion, we were in the midst of preparing to fill crepes with zucchini slivers and heavy cream when we realized we were out of cream. (Yes, that happens to us, too. How can we forget the message of Simone Beck, who pleads, "*Always* read through the end of the recipe before beginning to cook, even before shopping.") We substituted sour cream, and the result was delicious. We forgot to put the sliced tomatoes with basil on a recent buffet table, and that handy leftover started us on a tomato and basil soup. Pork and apples are delicious, but pork can be great in combination with many other foods, such as pears (see Index).

Second, we wanted to bring together a group of excellent recipes, many of which have been handed down for several generations, reworked, revised, and constantly tested. This cookbook isn't only *us*; it's one big family cookout. It can't be an all-Italian book because we cook and eat in so many ways. We like *cannoli* with ricotta, but we also like English plum pudding flamed with Jamaica rum. We dine frequently on lasagna in the family style, but we also like shell steaks with green peppercorn sauce. We adore a salad of fresh arugola but will switch happily to one made of sliced fresh beets, celery, truffles, and walnut halves. We like to dream about how to change a dish, and this is a joy in cooking for us.

Purists will admonish us, but what this world needs least of all these days is another cookbook of classical recipes. We don't know what the classical preparation for flank steak is (if there is such a thing); the only thing we're sure of is that every recipe we've read on stuffing a flank steak calls for meat. Meat in meat, meat on meat, meat alongside meat bores us as a steady routine. When we pick up a flank steak, our thought is: What will we do with it this time? Stuffing it with eggplant (someone's always stuffing eggplant, why not eggplant stuffing something) is simply delicious (see page 228). True classical techniques cannot be tampered with. After all, 4 tablespoons of flour will thicken 2 cups of liquid to a certain thickness only, as will 1, 2 or 3 tablespoons; but why a steak coated with black pepper only? Why not green peppercorns? If *pesto* is as good as it surely is, why not find other uses for it beyond pasta? We enjoy improvisation in the kitchen. Our guess is that you do, too, and we hope this volume will add to that enjoyment.

We remember what Dashiell Hammett once said to Lillian Hellman: "Young writers can't understand that one writer grows out of other writers." This surely applies to the world of cooks. Our originality and innovation go only so far; and we won't wait until an acknowledgment page to sing praises to our many inspirations, including Craig Claiborne, Julia Child, and James Beard.

We believe good living is the enjoyment of eating, drinking, and being with others; we love to share good food with good friends. Caring about what you put on your table can only enrich your life. When our table is set, beckoning with well-prepared food, a wonderful, warm feeling comes over us. This feeling must have been common to all members

of our family. We remember particularly one of our great-aunts, Zia
Maria Giuseppe, who, if living today, would be 105 years old. When any
relative or friend visited her, she rarely showed off a new coat or dress or
a piece of parlor furniture. Instead, she would lead you to her shiny new
refrigerator. At the end of a long, dramatic pause, she would throw open
the door and glowingly, happily, contentedly remark, *"Che bellezza!*
Guarda tutta la roba—la frutta, la salsiccia, il formaggio, i spinacci, i
broccoli—tutte queste cose buone per cucinare e mangiare" ("What a
beautiful sight! Look at all these lovely things—the fruit, the sausage,
the cheese, the spinach, the broccoli—all these good things to cook and
eat").

CONTENTS

THE FESTIVE FAMULARO KITCHEN

((1))

Angela's Artichokes and Other Appetizers, Hors d'Oeuvres, and First Courses

IN one way or another, all dictionaries (and cookbooks, too) define the appetizer or hors d'oeuvre as a small portion of food, hot or cold, served before a meal or before the main part of a meal, and designed to stimulate the appetite. Compared with what it was in colonial times in America, however, we think it's fair to say that the hors d'oeuvre has come a long way. Hors d'oeuvres in a log cabin? This may sound incredible, but custom thrift and downright self-preservation helped make the appetizer a daily ritual. In those early times, food supplies were not always assured, and hunger was a constant specter. Storms, droughts, fires, Indian raids and warfare helped to establish the hors d'oeuvre. Leftover meats, fish, game, fruits, vegetables—almost anything edible was put up in crocks and barrels and salted, pickled, smoked, corned, or preserved in lard. Such food served as emergency rations when there was no main dish to be had. Often it was served as a first course at dinner. Today's *oeufs en gelée* and *pâté en croûte* can hardly be called rations, and yesterday evening's first course of *dodine de dinde farcie* (a turkey pâté) suggests the transition from stagecoach to Concorde, gastronomically speaking.

Appetizers and hors d'oeuvres can be of meat, fish, fruit, eggs, and vegetables. Typical of the fish hors d'oeuvres might be shrimps, caviar, oysters, smoked salmon, or herring. Appetizers can be pâtés, kabobs, bouchées, or bite-sized meatballs; or they may be anchovies, asparagus tips, artichokes, or multifaceted antipastos. The combinations are limitless, and we'll mention some to stimulate the palate: snails and garlic: crab meat in a mousseline sauce; sweetbreads in puff pastry: fried oysters with horseradish sauce; Brie surrounded by a *couronne* (a crown of yeast bread); bay scallops with lime juice (Peruvian ceviche); cubed lamb in a sweet-and-sour sauce, wrapped in fresh lettuce leaves; mussels in a vinaigrette sauce; cucumbers in sour cream; quiche combinations; almonds deep-fried in butter and salted; eggs stuffed with liver pâté; *pâté maison* with sour gherkins; a hot cheese fondue made with Neuchâtel wine and Gruyère; leeks stuffed with shrimp; a game pâté in a pastry crust; and pheasant with Cognac in a terrine.

Every nation has its own appetizers. The combinations in *antipastos* are endless. Not only Italy but every country has its version of antipasto. In Italy and in America, one of the best-known, best-tasting before-pasta dishes is tissue-thin prosciutto combined with honeydew, Saratoga, or canteloupe melon or with figs. Antipastos include many varieties of fish, vegetables, and meat. The imagination can go wild with great combinations as sausages are mingled with squid, beans with broccoli, scallions with scampi, anchovies with artichokes, limas with lettuce, fennel with fungi, cucumbers with cauliflower, ricotta with radishes, olives with onions. We favor a combination of avocado slices, freshly roasted red peppers, artichokes hearts, and other foods in our antipasto.

In addition to antipasto, Italy loves two more: *spiedini*, which is a kind of sandwich of Teleme cheese and prosciutto dipped in an egg batter, fried in olive oil, and served with an anchovy sauce. An interesting version of this is presented by La Scala, a restaurant in Los Angeles. It is called *Mozzarella marinara*, but it isn't really made of mozzarella; Telema cheese is used because it melts smoothly (American mozzarella becomes stringy, as you know). La Scala breads and fries the Teleme and serves it atop a fresh tomato and basil sauce. This dish is similar to *Mozzarella in carrozza*, a Neopolitan cousin to *spiedini* made with a tomato sauce.

Taramasalata is the classic Greek appetizer of cod roe mixed with bread, olive oil, egg yolks, onion, and parsley.

The appetizers, hors d'oeuvres, and first courses in France are truly limitless. *Larousse Gastronomique** devotes thirty-four double-columned pages, in small print, to hors d'oeuvres. It includes an abbreviated recipe for the French version of Lithuanian *varéniki* (a ravioli-type pasta filled with a mixture of onion, beef, and beef kidney fat, chopped, browned, salted, peppered, and bound with béchamel sauce, then poached and served with butter). *Larousse* also includes *valesniskis polonais* (an unsweetened crepe filled with a mixture of cream cheese, butter, salt, pepper, and nutmeg, deep-fried, drained, arranged on a napkin, then sprinkled with salt, and garnished with fried parsley). Everyone knows about the famous *saucisson chaud*, heavy with garlic and served with white beans. Not so well known is the *petit feuilleté au Roquefort* served at the Château de Riell, which is near Prades in the south of France; this hors d'oeuvre is a small, light, almost veneer of *feuilleté*, covered with a light sauce of Roquefort whipped with a bit of cream and herbs. In our country, Le Périgord in New York has made two hors d'oeuvres famous: a mousse of pike with a sauce Nantua (made of mixed, diced vegetables with crayfish, moistened with Cognac, white wine, and fish velouté and seasoned with herbs, butter, and tomatoes) and a *terrine de canard* (a duck forcemeat molded in a terrine, pierced with pistachios, and trussed with truffles). And if any combination of tastes is great in first courses, it has to be that of *filet de canard au poivre vert* (slices of duck breast in a sauce of cream and green peppercorns) served at La Marée in Paris.

Caviar

Caviar is the most expensive of all foods, and perhaps for that reason, it sits on the throne of the epicurean world. In spite of a shrinking supply of sturgeons' eggs, the demand for caviar grows steadily, and the price grows along with it. More and more people are becoming caviar lovers, and they are deadly serious about their caviar's quality, service, and accompaniments. An important occasion—there's caviar! Caviar—there's an important occasion! But where does caviar really belong on the gastronomical chart? We smile at a story we once heard about Fernand Point. He did not serve caviar—not because he didn't like it, but because it was too easy to "make" and to serve. He had more fun creating a

* Prosper Montagné, *Larousse Gastronomique: The Encyclopedia of Food, Wine, and Cookery,* ed. Charlotte Turgeon and Nina Froud (New York: Crown Publishers, Inc., 1961).

mousse de truite or a *terrine de grives*. We're inclined to agree with Monsieur Point. Nevertheless, the fact that exquisite caviar is a *natural* food is no reason to exclude it from the epicure's menu.

The consensus among those who know is that the Malossol beluga caviar is the most elegant, the most expensive. (The Caspian Sea is the home of the beluga sturgeon, and the meaning of Malossol is "lightly salted.") Caviar spoons (which resemble turn-of-the-century iced-tea spoons) are considered chic by the jet set, but the important question is not what spoon to use but what to serve with the caviar. We have a strong point of view about this. We see no value in a sprinkle of fresh onions; in our opinion, this destroys the delicate taste of the caviar. We'll never understand the eggs mimosa touch; combining two kinds of eggs does not necessarily enhance the glory of either, much less the taste. (Nevertheless, some of the world's best restaurants present their most expensive caviars in this style.) We believe a touch of lemon juice is the only accompaniment necessary for caviar. Our reason is simple: the lemon complements the oil (what little there may be) in the caviar. We suggest you serve lemon wedges. (Be sure to remove the seeds—not to be fancy, but to be very practical.) And need we add that caviar and smoked salmon make one of the world's greatest combinations.

Oysters

An oyster lover goes as mad over his oysters as a caviar lover does over *his* delicacy. The first known oyster farm was founded in southern Italy in 102 B.C. by Sergius Aurata, but food historians have written of the oyster in the American Indian, Greek, Celtic, and Roman cultures. Italy has always been known for its methods of maintaining oysters but we're told the largest oyster farm in the world today is in France.

High-quality oysters are best eaten raw, in their own juices combined with a dash of fresh lemon juice. When one considers the *marennes blanches et vertes* and the *belons* of France, the Whitstables and Colchesters of England, the bluepoints of Long Island, the Malpeques of Canada, the Chincoteagues and the Lynnhavens of Virginia, the Japanese Kumamotos and the small Olympias of the Pacific Coast, is it any wonder that we want to pause before the main dish to tempt the palate with such an appetizer? (And what a pity that as children we didn't know that edible oysters are not pearl producers; we would have spared ourselves many disappointing moments.)

Smoked Salmon

One of the world's great delicacies is smoked salmon. It transcends national borders; its acceptance as a great food is almost universal. But as popular as it is in European countries, it still is relatively unknown in some areas of the United States. We believe the best we've tasted was served in Spain (San Roque), and *that* salmon came from Scotland. Connoisseurs debate the superiority of Scotch versus Nova Scotia salmon; we prefer the Scotch variety, but Nova Scotia salmon (with or without caviar) is excellent. Just be sure you get the least salty salmon.

Smoked salmon is a delight served tissue-thin on thin slices of dark pumpernickel with butter and fresh-ground pepper. It combines elegantly with capers, horseradish sauce, and sliced onions. Friends of ours in Pawling, Betty and John Hettinger, serve thin, thin slices of smoked salmon with caviar, lemon wedges, dark bread, and jiggers of ice-cold Russian-made vodka. There is almost no greater combination of food. We are partial to a smoked salmon mousse that we often serve at home for good friends. We love it in the fall of the year, when a fire is welcome even though the nasturtiums are still blooming wildly in the garden.

Olives

No one seems to be able to determine the olive's origin in history, but olives are mentioned in the Bible and in Egyptian, Greek, and Roman writings. But everyone agrees that one of the most beautiful sights in the world is the olive tree, with its gnarled trunk and gray-silver shawl, sweeping in the Mediterranean wind.

When we were growing up, we thought that green olives were American and black ones Italian. There may be some truth to this notion, but the fact is that the green olives are those that are picked unripe; the black ones are those that are left to ripen on the tree. Jars of black olives have only recently gained in popularity in American grocery shops. The jars usually seen contain green olives neatly stacked and dotted with pimientos or almonds. However, in the international markets of larger American cities, one always finds barrelfuls of black olives and green ones, too. We learned always to reach in and sample one or two before buying. If a grandparent whispered "*sono amare*" (they're bitter), that meant the olives hadn't been in brine long enough.

In fact, most olives are bitter but lose this unpleasant taste when they're pickled.

The olive is underutilized in American cooking, and we wonder why this is so. We're satisfied to push the olive as an elegant hors d'oeuvre. Serve a simple bowlful of black olives in magnificient combination with olive oil, garlic, and a sprinkle of oregano.

Melons

It is only recently that American supermarkets have learned the important marketing technique of displaying an opened melon atop a pyramid of unopened ones. There is no better way to judge the quality of this fruit without tasting it. It does help, though, to test the ends for ripeness: put the weight of both your thumbs on the stem end, and press gently; softness indicates ripeness, but beware if it is *too* soft. We also lift melons to our nostrils and sniff for fragrance. But the true test is to cut open and taste. We used to love watching the vendor stab a watermelon, as a champion swordsman might, cut a 1-inch square deep into it, and pull the piece out for us to taste.

Figs

We were surprised to hear that some fig trees in California are over a hundred years old; we didn't know they lived that long. Figs predate the Bible, were loved by the Romans and all other Europeans, and were brought to America by the Spaniards, the French, and Grandfather.

When we were growing up, our grandfather had a fig tree in a pot on a fire escape in New York City. More than once Grandmother said that his fig tree came first, his cats and kittens came second, and she came third—in that order—for tender loving care. At times, it was easy to agree with her. We always ate the figs raw, at their peak of ripeness and softness.

In the rich province of Emilia-Romagna in Italy is Parma, famous for its Parmesan cheese. It is equally famous for its ham; Parma hogs are fed on the same whey used to make Parmesan cheese. This ham is rarely salted, and it is dried slowly in the open air. A great combination: Parma ham and fresh, sweet, juicy figs.

There is an abundant literature devoted to the do's and don'ts of first courses. We add only these suggestions: If you've labored hard and diligently to present a good meal, don't overkill with heavy hors d'oeuvres that clog the palate and dull the appetite. Stay with black olives, curried walnuts, or prosciutto and roasted pepper canapés. If your group isn't too large, consider serving the first course with a cocktail or apéritif. We enjoy bringing in the Madeira Mold with Liver Pâté en Gelée (page 3) and serving it on individual plates to 6, 8, or 10 guests or presenting the whole Soufflé Roll with Crab Meat (page 37) and slicing and serving it on individual plates.

Artichokes

When artichokes are exposed to air, the process of discoloration sets in. A stack of artichokes discolored to the point of blackness is a disagreeable sight. Select bright green ones, and don't assume that largeness is an indication of tenderness, for "good things come in small packages," even where artichokes are concerned. One excellent way of testing for freshness is to cut off a piece of the stem; if the cut is white and somewhat juicy, the artichoke is young and fresh. We store artichokes in a plastic bag in the refrigerator, but only for a short time.

We find that enameled ironware works best for cooking artichokes, particularly if the vessel has a cover, but a stainless steel pan works well, too. We generally prefer carbon knives, but they spell disaster in preparing artichokes because they will discolor the artichokes; so we always turn to stainless steel knives.

The usual ways to prepare artichokes for cooking are to keep them whole, quarter them, or make artichoke hearts. To cook them whole, remove and discard the tough outer leaves, especially if they are discolored. Cut off the stem so that it is flush with the bottom of the artichoke. (Make this a straight cut so that the vegetable stands easily.) Lay the artichoke on its side, and cut off the top third with a straightaway cut. To cook them in quarters, follow all the steps for cooking them whole, and then cut them in quarters. Then use a sharp knife to remove the furry "choke" portion just above the heart. To make artichoke hearts, remove the stem flush with the bottom, and then cut away all the green leaf parts. Do not remove the "choke" at this point; it's easier to do that after the heart is cooked.

When you clean and prepare artichokes, be sure to have handy a bowl of cool water to which you've added 1 or 2 tablespoons lemon juice. You will have to dip the artichokes into this mixture to prevent discoloration as you work along. After they are pared (or "turned") and trimmed, it is very important to rub them with lemon juice and cover them with salted water.

ANGELA'S STUFFED ARTICHOKES

⅓ pound sausage links,
  pepperoni, ham, or prosciutto
1 teaspoon olive oil
1½ cups fresh bread crumbs
2 tablespoons fresh parsley,
  chopped (or 1 teaspoon dried)
2 cloves garlic, minced fine
3 eggs
¼ cup milk
6 tablespoons olive oil

Salt
Pepper, ground fresh
6 large artichokes
½ cup fresh tomatoes, peeled,
  drained and crushed (or
  canned plum tomatoes,
  drained and chopped coarse)
4 cups water
2 cloves garlic, whole

Cut the meat into small pieces or slices. In a small skillet, heat 1 teaspoon oil, and cook the meat for about 5 minutes, shaking the skillet and stirring. Drain the meat, and transfer it to a mixing bowl. Add the bread crumbs, parsley, and minced garlic, and toss well.

Beat the eggs together with the milk and 2 tablespoons olive oil. Add this to the meat and bread crumb mixture. Add salt and pepper to taste, and stir to blend.

Using a sharp knife, cut the stem off each artichoke to make a flat base. Pull off a few of the tough outer leaves. Cut off about ½ inch of the top of each artichoke, and open the top with your fingers. Invert the artichokes on a flat surface, pressing down on each one to open its leaves.

Divide the filling into 6 equal parts. Turn each artichoke on its base, and stuff the center first; then add some filling between the leaves more or less at random. (Be sure to push the stuffing down as you add it.)

Select a casserole large enough to hold the artichokes snugly in one layer. (If they do not fit close together in the casserole, tie each one around the center with string to help retain the shape.) Arrange the artichokes in the casserole, and spoon an equal amount of the tomatoes on top of each. Pour the water around them, and add the whole garlic cloves to the water. Sprinkle the artichokes with the remaining 4 tablespoons olive oil. Cover the casserole tightly, and bring the sauce to a boil. Reduce the heat, and simmer until the artichoke bottoms are tender (45 minutes to 1 hour). (To test for doneness, pull off an outside leaf; if it comes off easily, the artichokes are done.)

Remove the artichokes from the casserole with a slotted spoon. Do not serve any of the cooking liquid. Serve one artichoke per person as an appetizer. This dish can also be served as a vegetable on a dinner plate, in which case serve half an artichoke per person.

COLD EGGPLANT AL PANARIELLO

CAPERS AND ANCHOVY   SERVES 6

TO PREPARE THE EGGPLANT:
> *2 small eggplants (about ¾ pound each)*
> *Salt*
> *½ cup olive oil (approximately)*

Cut the ends off each eggplant, but leave it unpeeled. Stand each eggplant on end, and cut it lengthwise into the thinnest possible slices. Salt each slice lightly, lay the slices flat in a colander, and allow them to drain for 20 to 30 minutes. Dry each slice with a paper towel or tea towel.

TO PREPARE THE SAUCE:

> *½ cup olive oil*
> *4 tablespoons red wine vinegar*
> *1 anchovy*
> *2 cloves garlic, chopped fine*
> *4 tablespoons fresh parsley,*
> *chopped fine (or 2 teaspoons dried)*

> *2 tablespoons shallots, chopped fine*
> *2 tablespoons capers, drained*
> *Pepper, ground fresh*

In a large skillet, heat 2 tablespoons olive oil, and sauté the first batch of slices slowly on both sides, until they are cooked through. (To be sure the eggplant is cooked, insert fork tines into a slice. You can feel if it is still raw.) Don't worry if the edges of some slices char, but don't allow the entire side of a slice to blacken (not only because of the taste but because it will be more difficult to roll). Eggplant absorbs lots of oil, so don't add more oil until you are ready to sauté the next batch of slices. As you remove each slice, roll it, and set it aside to cool.

Combine the oil and vinegar, add the anchovy, and mash it until it dissolves in the sauce. Add the garlic pieces, parsley, shallots, capers, and freshly ground pepper to taste. (No cooking is necessary for this sauce.)

Serve 2 or 3 eggplant rolls on individual plates, and spoon the sauce over them. Or arrange all the rolls on a large platter, pour the sauce over them, and serve.

Anchovies

There must be main dishes of anchovies, but we don't know of any. We consider the anchovy a great companion to many other foods. It sits in every antipasto we've ever seen in Italy, Spain, or France. It has found its way into Scandinavian smorgasbords and into the cuisines, haute and peasant, of every European country. It appears in appetizers and in sauces, in egg dishes and in vegetable dishes. It is omnipresent in spite of the fact that its home is mostly the Mediterranean. It is wonderful to think of Mrs. Bridges "downstairs" larding meat with anchovies for hungry appetites "upstairs." We have no idea why Victorians used anchovies instead of salt, but we appreciate their appreciation of this versatile silver-and-blue two-inch darling of the sea.

One of the most famous anchovy dishes is the Piedmontese specialty known as *bagna cauda:* A sauce made of anchovies melted with butter and oil serves as a dip for fresh celery stalks, pepper slices, carrot lengths, and so on. In other parts of Italy, anchovies are fried, then combined with tomatoes and truffles. And of course, who has ever seen a real Italian pizza minus anchovies?

Mushrooms

Select mushrooms that are firm, clean, and unblemished (there should be no gray spots). It is better to buy them loose than prepackaged, even though they may cost a little more that way. Our experience with buying prepackaged mushrooms has not always been satisfactory. As is the case with packaged strawberries, the top layer is often for show, with lower layers degenerating in quality. And besides, it's fun to reach into the oval baskets and handpick each mushroom.

We don't peel mushrooms. We wipe or lightly brush them with a dampened tea towel or paper towel. We trim the stem ends and reserve them (usually in the freezer) for soups and stocks.

Mushrooms can be combined with bread crumbs, egg, and more crumbs, and French fried. They can be dipped in cream sauces and perched on toast. The uses of mushrooms in great combinations *en brochette* would fill a book because mushrooms combine so well with all meats and vegetables. When they are *à la grecque,* they are joined by olive oil and herbs. And in our kitchens, they have been stuffed with everything but the kitchen sink.

ANTIPASTO

AVOCADO AND RED PEPPERS   SERVES 8

TO ROAST THE PEPPERS:

10 large red bell peppers

With a damp cloth, wipe the peppers clean. Place them on a flat tray, and broil them slowly, under a low flame, until the skins are charred on all sides. Then put the peppers in a brown paper bag, and set them aside to cool for about 10 minutes. Shake the bag back and forth to help loosen the skins. When the peppers are cool enough to handle, peel off the skins, and remove the seeds. Cut the peppers into strips, and set them aside.

TO PREPARE THE OIL DRESSING:

½ cup olive oil
¼ cup white wine vinegar
2 cloves garlic, minced fine
1 teaspoon fresh basil, chopped
(or ½ teaspoon dried)

1 teaspoon dried oregano
1 teaspoon salt
Pepper, ground fresh

Put all the ingredients in a small bowl, mix them well, and allow them to stand for about 30 minutes.

TO ASSEMBLE THE ANTIPASTO:

3 avocados

1 head Bibb or Boston lettuce

10 artichoke hearts, cooked and halved (see page 9)

1 cup chickpeas

1 cup fresh mushrooms, sliced thin

1 cup green vinegar peppers, seeded

5 celery hearts, halved

1/4 pound provolone cheese, sliced thin

10 anchovy filets, drained

2 large fresh tomatoes, peeled and sliced

10 scallions, whole

1/4 pound Italian salami, sliced paper-thin

Remove skins from the avocados. Cut each avocado in half lengthwise to remove the pit; then cut the halves into slices 1/2 inch thick. Set them aside.

On a large platter, arrange the lettuce leaves, covering the entire platter. Place the artichoke hearts in the center of the platter. Place the red pepper strips around the artichokes. Then arrange the chick peas, mushrooms, vinegar peppers, celery hearts, provolone cheese, anchovy filets, and tomatoes; place the scallions on top of the tomatoes. Place the avocado slices and salami around the outer edge of the platter.

Pour the dressing all over the antipasto, and serve with slices of fresh Italian bread.

Cabbage

A split in a cabbage is a sign of its maturity; so is a strong cabbage odor. Tender and young cabbage does not smell so strong and is usually tightly packed. Choose the younger head of cabbage for it is tastier and more tender. We remove the outer leaves (there is less waste on a younger head because fewer outer leaves usually have to be removed), cut the head in quarters, and soak the pieces in salted cool water for 15 to 20 minutes.

BIRDS OF SAVOY CABBAGE

BACON AND ONION

SERVES 8

8 leaves savoy cabbage, from
  outside of head
8 slices bacon
1 pound pork butt, chopped fine
  by hand
2 onions, chopped fine
2 tablespoons fresh parsley,
  chopped fine (or 1 teaspoon
  dried)
2 tablespoons orange zest,
  chopped fine

1 cup celery, chopped
1 teaspoon salt
2 eggs
3 tablespoons soy sauce
¼ cup tomato purée
1½ cups Rich Beef Stock (see
  page 46)
2 teaspoons brown sugar

Remove whole leaves from the cabbage. With a knife, trim and shape them so that they are all of approximately equal size (6 by 8, or 7 by 7, inches). Blanch them in boiling salted water for 3 minutes. Remove them carefully, and dry them with a tea towel or paper towels. Arrange the leaves on a flat surface.

In a large skillet, cook the bacon until crisp. Remove the bacon, and set it aside to drain. Pour off half the bacon fat from the skillet. Add the pork, onion, parsley, orange zest, celery, and salt to the remaining fat, and sauté them for 15 minutes. With a slotted spoon, transfer the sautéed ingredients to a bowl. Allow them to cool.

Beat eggs and soy sauce together, and mix this with the sautéed ingredients. Divide the mixture among the 8 leaves, placing an equal amount in the middle of each leaf. Add 1 slice of bacon to each leaf. Then pick up the end of the leaf that is closest to you, and fold it over the filling.

Pick up the right side of the leaf, and fold it over to the left. Pick up the left side, and fold it over to the right. (If you're left-handed, you will probably reverse these steps.) Roll the folded cabbage over completely, fold side down. (It is not necessary to fasten these rolls with toothpicks, skewers, or string if the seam is on the bottom of the bird.)

Butter a shallow, ovenproof baking dish or pan liberally. Place the birds in the dish. Mix the tomato purée and stock, and pour this over the rolls. Sprinkle brown sugar over all.

Bake the birds in a preheated 400-degree oven for 45 minutes to 1 hour, or longer if necessary. Baste the cabbage rolls several times while they are baking. To test for doneness, insert a fork into the cabbage roll to see if it feels tender. Be sure the cabbage is cooked. (It won't hurt to overcook these birds slightly because some cabbage leaves can be tough and stringy.)

This dish may be served either as an appetizer (1 roll per person, serving 8) or as an entrée (2 rolls per person, serving 4).

WALNUTS, TOASTED AND CURRIED

BUTTER AND CURRY   SERVES 6 TO 8

> 2 tablespoons butter
> 1 teaspoon salt
> 1 tablespoon curry powder
> ½ pound walnut meats

Combine the butter, salt, and curry powder in a pie plate, and heat the mixture in the oven at 325 degrees until the butter is melted.

Add the walnut meats, and toss them (using a wooden spoon or rubber spatula) so that all are covered with the curried butter.

Heat thoroughly in a preheated 325-degree oven for about 15 minutes. Serve hot.

CRAB MEAT CANAPES

CRAB MEAT AND CREAM CHEESE   SERVES 6 TO 10

> 6 ounces cream cheese
> 8 ounces crab meat
> 1 tablespoon mayonnaise
> ½ teaspoon Worcestershire sauce

> Salt
> 36 bread or cracker rounds
> Paprika

Beat the cream cheese until it is soft. Add the crab meat, mayonnaise, Worcestershire sauce, and salt, and mix thoroughly. (If mixture is not to be used immediately, store it in the refrigerator.)

Spread the bread or cracker rounds with the crab meat mixture. Sprinkle a dash of paprika on top of each round. Broil the rounds for several minutes, until they are hot and bubbly, and serve immediately.

Another excellent way to serve this dish is to combine the ingredients for the spread, put them in a chafing dish, and heat the mixture slowly. Serve crackers or thin toast slices separately, and allow people to serve themselves.

Crepes

Crepes may well have been one of the first food combinations. Can't you see that thin pancake cooking on a hot stone (not in a temperamental crepe pan)? Whether this is accurate history or not, there's no question about the universal appeal of crepes today. They have many names and forms, including *blinis, tortillas, pannekoeken,* or *palacinta.* There are good reasons for this popularity. Crepe dough is inexpensive and easy to prepare. Crepes can be made in advance; when wrapped in a tea towel, they can be stored in the refrigerator for 3 or 4 days. They freeze and unfreeze beautifully; in most cases, they can be filled and frozen, ready to be put into a hot oven. They are perfect in combination with leftovers, including cooked vegetables, meats, fish, sauces.

The basic crepe is easy to make, and our version of it follows. Depending on how you plan to fill and serve the crepes, you can create many new tastes by adding fine herbs, saffron, onion, and so on to the basic dough ingredients. As for fillings, there is no end to the possibilities. Crepes challenge the inventiveness of cooks, for who has yet said the final word on filling the crepe? We've given recipes for some that we particularly enjoy. We hope you will, too.

CREPES

EGGS AND FLOUR   MAKES ABOUT 24 CREPES

1 cup all-purpose flour   *1 cup milk*
  Healthy pinch of salt   *3 tablespoons melted butter,*
4 eggs   *cooled*
1 cup water

Sift the flour with the salt into a bowl and make a well in the center of the mixture. In another bowl, beat the eggs well; then add them to the flour. Beat the mixture with a whisk until smooth.

Stir in the water, milk, and melted butter, and blend well. The mixture should resemble heavy cream or be just a touch lighter in texture. If you think the batter is too thick (the size of the eggs you use will determine the thickness), add more milk or water, 1 tablespoon at a time. Allow this mixture to stand for at least 1 hour (it can stand for as long as several hours). Just whisk the batter well before you use it.

Butter a hot 5- or 6-inch skillet or crepe pan. (We use a folded paper towel for this. Fold the towel in half about four times, brush it against a stick of butter, and rub it around the skillet. Repeat this procedure for each crepe.) Add some batter, and rotate the skillet so that the batter thins out and completely covers the bottom. Be sure you add enough batter to get a slight edge of crepe (less than ¼ inch) coming up the side of the skillet; this edge is handy in turning the crepe. It's important to figure out a standard amount of batter to be used for each crepe (2 tablespoons, half of a ⅓-cup measure, a full or half-full ladle, or whatever.) Use the first two or three crepes as trial runs. Then decide which quantity and measuring utensil work best, and use them for each crepe. (We usually have to discard the first crepe—not always, but *almost* always. We don't like waste, and this is about the only food we ever toss out.)

Cook each crepe for 1 or 2 minutes, until edge and bottom brown. (Often, the crepe will form little bubbles to tell you when it is "set.") Loosen the crepe edge with a knife or spatula, and turn the crepe by hand. (The crepe is hot, to be sure, but it gives us great pleasure to perform this step by hand. And besides, we think it works best.) Cook the other side for about 10 seconds, and remove the crepe from the skillet by loosening the edge (as you did to turn it) and picking it out by hand. Place the finished crepes on a flat plate; they stack extremely well. (Do *not*—repeat, *do not*—layer wax paper or anything else between crepes.) Cover the stacked crepes with a clean tea towel to help keep them warm, fresh, and ready to be filled.

CREPES FILLED WITH CHICKEN CURRY

CHICKEN AND CURRY

One leftover that combines well with crepes is Chicken Curry with 14 Condiments (page 158). Our recipe is for 12 people, and we always make that amount even if there are only 8 or 9 for curry because we know that leftover curry freezes well. Because crepes also freeze well, crepes with chicken curry are easy to assemble.

Fill the center of each crepe with several spoonfuls of curry, roll the crepe and place it, seam side down, in a baking dish. When all the crepes are rolled, spoon just a little of the sauce over them, and heat them in a preheated 400- to 425-degree oven until the curry mixture is heated through and bubbling.

Serve with just one of the condiments listed in the master recipe: chutney—a great combination. Or serve fried apples, which are quite delicious with the hot curry crepes. Also serve lemon wedges, for a few drops of fresh lemon juice over the heated crepe gives it sparkle.

CREPES FILLED WITH CHICKEN BREASTS IN CHAMPAGNE SAUCE

FOIE GRAS AND CHAMPAGNE

SERVES 6 TO 7

Halve the recipe for Chicken Breasts Supreme in Champagne Sauce (see page 154). Follow the directions but before cooking the chicken, cut the chicken breasts into ½-inch strips; then sauté them in the hot butter for 3 or 4 minutes (as if you were stir-frying them). (With 6 half breasts, there should be enough strips to fill 12 to 14 crepes.)

Place the crepes on a flat working surface, and arrange the strips of cooked chicken in the center of each crepe. Cut the foie gras in tiny squares (as in the basic recipe), and sprinkle all but a few of the pieces in equal amounts over the chicken. Add 2 scant tablespoons sauce to each crepe, roll the crepe, and put it in a baking dish, seam side down.

When all the filled crepes are in the baking dish, add the remaining sauce, but cover only the middle third of each crepe with it. The remaining few pieces of foie gras should now be strewn over the sauce as a decorative touch. (If you decide to use truffles instead of foie gras, treat the truffles in the same way. Glaze the crepes under a broiler for 5 minutes and serve quickly.)

CREPES FILLED WITH SHRIMP AND GARLIC

GARLIC AND OLIVE OIL   MAKES 12 FILLED CREPES

Halve the recipe for Scampi: Uno, Due, Tre (page 210). Cut the sautéed shrimp into ¼- or ½-inch pieces, and put them in a bowl instead of on a serving platter. Add the sauce and parsley to the bowl. Mix well, and place 1 generous tablespoon of this filling in the center of each crepe. Roll the crepes, and place them, seam side down, in a baking dish.

In a saucepan, combine 1 cup tomato sauce (page 128) and 1 cup Béchamel Sauce (page 100), and mix well. Heat the sauce to the boiling point. Pour 1 cup sauce over the crepes, and put the remaining sauce into a small serving bowl.

Glaze the crepes under the broiler for about 5 minutes, until the sauce bubbles and the crepes brown slightly. Serve them immediately, and pass the bowl of sauce.

CREPES FILLED WITH SMOKED SALMON MOUSSE

HORSERADISH AND CREAM

Here is an excellent use for leftover Smoked Salmon Mousse à la Tara North (page 28). Simply place 1 or 2 tablespoons of the mousse in the center of each crepe. Sprinkle a few drops of lemon juice over the mousse. Roll the crepes, and put them, seam side down, on individual plates or a large serving platter (no heating required). Decorate with watercress.

TO PREPARE THE SAUCE:

    1 cup heavy cream, whipped
    1 tablespoon fresh horseradish, grated
      (or 2 tablespoons commercially prepared horseradish)
      Healthy pinch of salt

Fold these ingredients together, and blend them well. Put the sauce in an attractive bowl, and serve it with the crepes.

CREPES FILLED WITH SLICED MUSHROOMS IN WHITE WINE SAUCE

MUSHROOMS AND FRESH TOMATOES   SERVES 6 TO 8

1 pound fresh mushrooms
Juice of 1 lemon
2 cups fresh tomatoes (see Note)
2 to 3 cups White Wine Sauce
  (see page 99)

½ teaspoon dried thyme
Salt
Pepper, ground fresh
12 to 16 crepes

Wipe the mushrooms clean with a damp paper towel or tea towel. Remove the stem ends, and cut the mushrooms (including the remaining stem parts) into very thin slices. Place them in a bowl, pour the lemon juice over them, and toss them well.

Blanch, core, and peel the tomatoes. Cut them into slices ½ inch thick (or thinner); then cut each slice into ½-inch cubes (or smaller).

In a heavy saucepan, bring the wine sauce to a boil; then remove it from the heat. Reserve 1 cup of the heated sauce. Combine the remaining sauce, raw mushrooms, tomato cubes, thyme, and salt and pepper to taste. (Do *not* cook this mixture.)

Fill each crepe with one generous tablespoon of the mixture and roll. Reheat the reserved 1 cup of sauce. Serve the crepes, and pass the extra sauce in case someone wants more.

Note: You must use *only* fresh tomatoes for this recipe. We've tried substituting canned or frozen tomatoes, but they simply do not have the texture to complement the raw mushrooms and the silky wine sauce.

CREPES FILLED WITH COQUILLES BEATRICE

SCALLOPS AND FENNEL   MAKES 12 FILLED CREPES

Prepare the recipe for Coquilles Beatrice (page 36) with the following exceptions: Use ½ pound bay scallops instead of 1 pound. After the scallops have cooked in the wine mixture, cut them into the thinnest possible slices. Mix the slices with the sauce, and put one generous table-spoon of this mixture in the center of each crepe. Roll the crepes, and put them, seam side down, in a baking dish.

Mix the parsley and bread crumbs, and sprinkle the crumb mixture over all the crepes. Put ¼ tablespoon butter on each crepe, and sprinkle the bacon bits over all.

Glaze the crepes under the broiler for a few minutes or until they are lightly browned. Serve them quickly, while they are hot.

CREPES FILLED WITH POACHED SEA BASS AND ROUILLE

SEA BASS AND ROUILLE   SERVES 6

Rouille is traditionally served with fish soups such as bouillabaisse and *bourride*, but we see no reason why it shouldn't be adapted to other uses. We think it is an unusual accompaniment to the somewhat neutral crepe in this recipe.

1 pound sea bass filets	*1 recipe Rouille (see page 94)*
Juice of ½ lemon	*2 tablespoons fresh parsley,*
Court bouillon (see page 23)	*chopped*
12 crepes (see page 18)	*6 lemon wedges*

COURT BOUILLON

2 cups water	*1 small fish head or any bones*
¼ cup dry white wine or dry	*from white fish*
vermouth	*3 peppercorns*
1 small onion, chopped fine	*½ teaspoon salt*
1 celery stalk, sliced fine	*1 parsley sprig*
1 small carrot, chopped fine	

Combine court bouillon ingredients in a 2 quart heavy saucepan and bring to a boil. Lower heat and simmer for 30 minutes. Strain through 2 layers of cheesecloth. Double, triple, or quadruple recipe and freeze remainder for future use.

Wash the filets, and cut them into strips from 1 to 4 inches long (but *not* longer) and place them in a bowl. Add the lemon juice, and turn the strips in the bowl so that they all come in contact with the lemon juice.

Bring the court bouillon to a boil, and put the fish pieces in it. Poach the fish until it is just tender (less than 5 minutes, depending on the thickness of the fish). Do *not* overcook the fish. If the fish pieces break, don't worry. With a slotted spoon, transfer the fish pieces to a bowl.

Place the crepes on a flat surface, and "butter" each one with some of the *rouille*. (Remember that the *rouille* is probably one of the spiciest sauces you've eaten, so spread it *thin*.) Place a piece of fish in the center of each crepe, and roll the crepe.

Put the rolled crepes in a baking pan, seam side down, and cook them in a preheated 425-degree oven for 10 minutes. Sprinkle the crepes with freshly chopped parsley, serve them with lemon wedges, pass the remaining rouille in a small bowl.

Spinach

We like to buy fresh spinach in bunches, often with the small roots still attached. The leaves should be straight and their color a rich forest green. (If the leaves are too large and curled, they'll be tough.) We carefully pick over the bunches, throw away any wilted or parched leaves, and wash the spinach at least three times. (Sand has an uncanny way of lodging in spinach leaves.) We use warm water first because it seems to do away with the sand faster, but we return to cool water for all subsequent washings.

A simple yet great combination is cooked spinach with butter, salt, and pepper. An even better one is spinach with garlic, olive oil, and a touch of red pepper flakes. In our kitchens, spinach is used in combination with ricotta in manicotti or for making ravioli in *minestra* (a beef stock with pieces of beef or a chicken stock with pieces of boiled chicken and undercooked spinach). Spinach with Béchamel Sauce (see page 100) appears in many variations with eggs, fish, and so on. There are spinach rings, spinach molds, spinach soufflés, and spinach timbales in various combinations with butter, nutmeg, rice, tomatoes, peppers, eggs, and Parmesan cheese. And spinach is great with Hollandaise Sauce (see page 95). In this chapter, we combine spinach and Parmesan cheese in an airy soufflé and wrap it in crepes.

CREPES FILLED WITH A SPINACH AND CHEESE SOUFFLE

SPINACH AND PARMESAN CHEESE   MAKES 8 FILLED CREPES

¼ cup milk, cold
3 tablespoons all-purpose flour
¾ cup milk
 Healthy pinch of nutmeg
 Salt
 Pepper, ground fresh
4 egg yolks

½ cup grated Parmesan cheese
1 tablespoon butter
1 cup spinach, cooked, drained,
 and chopped
5 egg whites
8 crepes

Combine the cold milk and flour, and set the mixture aside. In a saucepan, scald ¾ cup milk, add the flour mixture to it, and cook this until it thickens. Add the nutmeg, and salt, and pepper to taste. Remove the saucepan from the heat, and allow the mixture to cool for 4 or 5 minutes.

Add the egg yolks, one at a time, to the cooled sauce mixture, blending each one in well. Add the cheese, and blend well. Set the mixture aside.

In a small pan, melt the butter, and add the spinach. Blend the heated spinach into the eggs and cheese.

Whip the egg whites until they form stiff peaks. Fold about one-third of the egg whites into the mixture of eggs, cheese, and spinach; then fold in the remaining whites. (Do *not* overmix.)

Place the 8 crepes flat on a buttered cookie sheet (use two cookie sheets if necessary). Spoon equal amounts of the soufflé mixture onto the center of the crepes. Bake the crepes in a preheated 400-degree oven until the soufflé is puffy and browned.

Roll the crepes, and serve them with a sauce. They are especially good with Sauce Bâtarde (see page 102).

EGGS IN ASPIC IN THE TARA NORTH STYLE

FOIE GRAS AND ASPIC   SERVES 8

TO PREPARE THE ASPIC:

4 *cups Rich Chicken Stock (see page 49)*
Salt and 12 peppercorns, crushed (optional)
¾ *cup dry white wine (or ½ cup dry vermouth plus ¼ cup water)*

2 *envelopes unflavored gelatin*
2 *eggshells, crushed by hand*
2 *egg whites, beaten until foamy*

Taste the stock, and add some salt and the crushed peppercorns if you think it needs more seasoning. Add the wine or vermouth and water, gelatin, eggshells, and egg whites, and bring the mixture to a boil, whisking constantly, and follow the directions for clarifying stock (see pages 45–46). There should be about 4½ cups of clear aspic. Set it aside to cool.

TO POACH THE EGGS:

8 *eggs*
1 *teaspoon white vinegar*
Salt
Pepper, ground fresh

Put the containers you will use as molds in the refrigerator (or the freezer) to chill them. (If you have any, use the small, oval tin molds, made in France, for *oeufs en gelée*. Or you may use small porcelain ramekins or glass bowls; they should not be over 3 or 4 inches wide and, preferably, should have a slightly rounded bottom, which makes a prettier mold. We think consommé cups have an excellent shape for molds.)

Fill a large skillet about three-fourths full with water. Bring the water to a boil over high heat, and add the vinegar. Lower the heat, and add 3 or 4 eggs (more might stick together, so do them in two batches). (Slip each egg into the water from a cup, saucer, or directly from the shell. We prefer to use a saucer because it lets us get a look at the yolk intact.) Poach the eggs for 5 minutes. (The aim is to cook the egg white yet keep the yolk fairly soft—somewhere between the consistency of heavy cream and mayonnaise.) Remove the eggs with a slotted spoon, and place them on a tea towel or several layers of paper towels. Carefully pat the eggs dry, and allow them to cool somewhat. Then trim off the excess egg white, leaving about ½ inch of white around each yolk. Salt and pepper the eggs to taste.

TO ASSEMBLE:

    32 fresh tarragon leaves
    8 teaspoons mayonnaise, preferably homemade
    8 thin slices of foie gras, with truffles if possible (see Note)

Spoon enough aspic into each chilled mold to make a layer about ¼ inch thick at the bottom. Chill the molds until this layer is set.

On top of the chilled aspic in each mold, arrange 4 tarragon leaves in the shape of a four-leaf clover. Add a cool, trimmed egg to each. Then add 1 teaspoon mayonnaise to each egg, spread it over the egg very carefully. (Use a small rubber spatula for this so that you won't puncture the egg.) On top of each egg, lay a slice of foie gras. Again carefully, spoon in more aspic, covering the foie gras. (The aspic should be somewhat thickened; if it is too liquid, it will break up the mayonnaise or shift the egg.) Chill the molds well until the aspic is set.

Unmold the eggs onto individual plates, and serve. (Do *not* garnish with, or unmold onto, lettuce leaves. The mold should sit alone on an attractive plate, with possibly a single sprig of watercress.) Pass slices of homemade Melba toast and butter.

Note: The foie gras slices should be about 2 inches square and ¼ inch thick, or cut them thinner from a block of foie gras weighing 100 grams (3 ounces). Foie gras is packed with and without truffles. We prefer to use the foie gras with the truffles because it makes a tastier dish— although a trifle more expensive.

MUSSELS IN GARLIC BUTTER IN SHELLS OR RAMEKINS

GARLIC AND BUTTER   SERVES 6

3 dozen mussels, fresh (see Note)
½ pound butter, softened
1 tablespoon oregano
2 tablespoons fresh parsley, chopped (or 1 tablespoon dried)
2 medium-size onions, chopped fine
6 cloves garlic, chopped fine

2 tablespoons lemon zest, chopped fine
Juice of 1 lemon
½ teaspoon crushed red pepper (or 6 drops Tabasco)
1 teaspoon salt
Pepper, ground fresh
2 tablespoons Marsala (optional)

TO PREPARE MUSSELS:
Wash and scrub the mussel shells thoroughly. (A small, hard-bristled brush is helpful here. We think the brush method is easier than the French method of scraping mussels clean.) Remove the "beard" by pulling it out. Soak the mussels for about 30 minutes in enough salted water to cover them. (Some mussels contain sand, and the soaking helps to rid them of it.)

TO PREPARE THE GARLIC BUTTER:
Cream the softened butter. Using a rubber spatula, work the oregano, parsley, onions, garlic, lemon zest, lemon juice, red pepper, salt, pepper to taste, and Marsala (if you wish) into the butter. Mix until all the ingredients are well blended.

Shuck the mussels. Discard half of each shell, keeping the mussel in the half that is more level and will hold more of the garlic butter. Add 1 dollop of the butter mixture to each mussel shell. Put the filled mussel shells on a baking tray, and store them in the refrigerator until you are ready to heat and serve them.

At least 10 or 15 minutes before serving time (and as much as 1 hour before), remove the mussels from the refrigerator. Then, when you are ready to serve them, bake them in a preheated 450-degree oven for 10 to 12 minutes, or until the butter sauce bubbles.

Serve the mussels piping hot (6 shells per person). If some of the sauce has spilled into the baking tray, spoon it over the shells after they are on their serving plates.

Note: Canned mussels may be used if you wish. Drain the mussels, and discard the liquid. Place 6 mussels in each of 6 large shells or ramekins. Divide the butter mixture equally among them. Refrigerate and/or bake as directed.

SMOKED SALMON MOUSSE A LA TARA NORTH

LEMON AND CREAM   SERVES 12

¾ *pound smoked salmon*
 2 tablespoons butter
 3 tablespoons all-purpose flour
¾ *cup Rich Fish Stock (see page 50)*
 2 tablespoons lemon juice
 1 cup fish aspic
½ *teaspoon white pepper*

¾ *cup heavy cream, whipped*
 3 small sprigs celery leaves
 3 thin carrot slices, cut into 5-pointed stars
 3 pieces green pepper, cut into oval leaf shapes
 Fish aspic, for cubes (optional)

FISH ASPIC

 2 cups Rich Fish Stock (see page 50)
 2 egg whites
 2 crushed egg shells
¼ *cup cool water*
 1 tablespoon gelatin, unflavored

Cut the salmon into thin slices (or buy it sliced thin), and cut the slices into ¼-inch pieces. Grind or beat the pieces until they form a thick paste. This is very easy to do in a food processor such as a Cuisinart.

(However, we've tried shredding the salmon with the pastry blender attachment of a regular electric mixer, and it works well.) Set the salmon paste aside.

In a small saucepan, melt the butter. Beat in the flour with a wire whisk, and cook over low heat for 2 minutes. Add the stock slowly, add the lemon juice and keep whisking until the sauce is smooth and very thick (only a couple of minutes). Allow it to cool.

Now prepare the fish aspic. Combine the stock, egg whites, and egg shells in a 1 quart saucepan. In a small bowl or cup combine the water and gelatin and blend them until the gelatin is dissolved; add the gelatin mixture to the saucepan. Bring this mixture to a boil, stirring every 2 minutes. As soon as it reaches a boil, lower the heat (if necessary, remove pan from heat to prevent mixture from overflowing) and simmer gently for 15 to 20 minutes until the liquid becomes clear. The egg whites absorb the impurities and will form a crust as they simmer; they will crack and you'll be able to see the liquid through the crack. It is not necessary to stir once the mixture is simmering. Line a fine strainer with a double layer of cheesecloth that has been put in cold water and wrung out. Pour the mixture through the dampened cheesecloth. Allow the mixture to cool but *not* set.

Add the cooled sauce to the salmon paste and beat these together until you have a smooth paste that looks like thick, orange mayonnaise. Add ¾ cup of fish aspic, which should be liquid and cool, and pepper. Then fold in the whipped cream. (Do *not* beat it in.) Oil a 6-cup charlotte mold lightly with peanut or vegetable oil (do not use olive oil). Transfer the mixture to the charlotte mold, and refrigerate it until firm, at least 3 to 4 hours. (This mousse can be made the day before it is served.)

On a saucer, arrange the celery leaves, carrot stars, and pepper cutouts in a floral bouquet pattern. Very slowly pour or spoon ¼ cup liquid fish aspic over and around the pattern (the aspic should be about ¼ inch deep and 3 or 4 inches across.) Refrigerate this for about 3 or 4 hours to set the vegetable decoration in the aspic, and keep it in the refrigerator until you are ready to use it.

Put a hot towel around the mold to help loosen the mousse, and turn the mousse out onto a silver or glass tray or platter. (Alternatively, you can dip the mold into warm water to loosen the mousse, but watch carefully so as not to dissolve the mousse.) Loosen the floral decoration mold by putting a hot towel under the saucer and running a knife around under the edge of the aspic. When it is loosened, slide the decoration off the saucer and onto the top of the mouse. If you have two nasturtium blooms, arrange them on the side of the platter and serve.

Before serving the mousse, you may wish to add cubes of fish aspic, prepared beforehand, in this way: Make several cupfuls of fish aspic, and allow this to set in a square glass baking dish. Dice it by running a knife down the aspic at ½-inch intervals, then turning the dish and running the knife down the aspic in lines perpendicular to the first cuts. Lift these cubes out with a spatula and arrange them around the base of the mold; serve several cubes with each slice of mousse.

A must with this mousse is toasted bread thins. Remove the crusts from thin slices of bread, cut the slices into thirds, and dry them out in a preheated 200-degree oven for 30 minutes or longer.

CLAMS AIOLI IMPERIALE

LEMON AND OLIVE OIL   SERVES 4

24 *littleneck clams*	1 *small carrot, chopped fine*
5 *cloves garlic, minced*	4 *tablespoons olive oil*
2 *tablespoons shallots, minced fine (or onion)*	½ *cup fresh bread crumbs*
2 *stalks celery, chopped fine*	1 *teaspoon salt*
2 *tablespoons fresh parsley, chopped fine (or 1 tablespoon dried)*	*Pepper, ground fresh*
	3 *tablespoons lemon juice*

With a stiff brush, scrub clam shells well. Soak the clams in cold, salted water for about 3 hours.

Under cold running water, wash each clam separately; discard any that are broken or opened. Shuck the clams, and reserve the juice for another use. (Clam juice is an excellent substitute for fish stock.)

Combine the garlic, shallots (or onion), celery, parsley, carrot, oil, bread crumbs, salt, and pepper to taste, and mix well. Pour a little lemon juice on each clam, and top each with some of the bread-crumb mixture. Place the dressed clams in a baking pan, and broil them until lightly browned (3 to 5 minutes).

Serve immediately.

Madeira

No kitchen cupboard is complete today without a bottle of Madeira, and this probably was so in the past, too. It is known that after George Washington's death, a good supply of Madeira was found in his wine cellar. The wine has many excellent qualities, one being that it keeps well for months after the bottle has been opened. In the following recipe, it adds a distinct and pleasant tang to the aspic. Our Madeira Mold with Liver Pâté en Gelée is a versatile recipe because it can be served as an hors d'oeuvre or as a luncheon entrée. Either way, it's beautiful to look at and delicious to eat.

MADEIRA MOLD WITH LIVER PATE EN GELEE

MADEIRA AND THYME   SERVES 8 TO 20

TO PREPARE THE ASPIC:

6 cups Rich Chicken Stock or broth, cold, fat completely removed (see page 49)
½ cup onion, chopped
2 tablespoons unflavored gelatin
1 teaspoon fresh tarragon, chopped fine (or ½ teaspoon dried)

2 egg whites, beaten
2 egg shells, crushed
Salt
Pepper, ground fresh
4 tablespoons Madeira, preferably Sercial type (see Note)

In a saucepan, combine all the ingredients except the wine, and cook them over high heat, stirring frequently, until the mixture begins to boil. Then lower the heat, and simmer the mixture for approximately 15 minutes. It is important *not* to disturb the simmering liquid. (As egg whites cook, they will rise to the top of the liquid and look like foam. Do *not* stir or move the pan. As the mixture continues to simmer, the foam will crack. Do *not* be concerned about this.)

Strain the liquid, foam, and entire contents of the saucepan through several layers of cheesecloth. (To do this, place a strainer over a clean pan or bowl, and line the strainer completely with several layers of cheesecloth. Choose a strainer large enough to sit on the pan or bowl; the larger the mesh, the more quickly the liquid will pass through it.) The combination of egg whites, eggshells, and straining will produce a clear aspic. Add Madeira at this point. Stir the mixture, and set aside.

TO PREPARE THE PÂTÉ:

3 slices bacon, cut into 1-inch pieces
1 pound chicken livers, washed in cold water, drained, and dried
½ cup onions, chopped
½ cup Madeira, preferably Sercial type (see Note)
½ cup heavy cream
1 teaspoon fresh thyme, chopped fine (or ½ teaspoon dried)
Juice of 1 lemon
¼ pound butter (1 stick), softened
Salt
Pepper, ground fresh

In an 11- or 12-inch skillet, sauté the bacon until it is crisp. Remove the bacon pieces with a slotted spoon, and set them aside to drain on a paper towel or paper napkin.

Add the chicken livers and onion to the skillet, and cook them for about 5 minutes, or until the livers are brown on the outside and pink inside. (Do *not* overcook, but keep the heat medium to high.) Remove the chicken livers and onions from the skillet, and set them aside.

Add the Madeira to the skillet, and deglaze the pan over high heat, until the sauce thickens slightly (which it will do quickly) and has a syrupy appearance. Add the cream, and bring the mixture to a boil, stirring frequently. Remove the skillet from the heat immediately. Combine the bacon, liver, onions, and cream sauce in a bowl. Add the thyme, lemon juice, butter, salt and pepper to taste.

Put this mixture in a blender, and blend it until smooth. With a rubber spatula, empty the contents from the blender container into a clean bowl. (You may have to do this in two or three batches, so repeat the process until all the pâté mixture is smooth and blended.) Set it aside.

TO ASSEMBLE THE MOLD:

8 small leaves fresh basil (or mint)

You will have enough aspic and pâté to make two 9-inch-round molds, and round cake pans, 9 by 1½ inches, are ideal. Teflon pans are excellent, and so are the non-Teflon variety. Teflon pans do not need to be oiled, but non-Teflon pans should be lightly oiled with peanut or vegetable oil to ease the removal of the mold. (Do *not* use olive oil.)

Pour one-fourth of the aspic liquid into each pan, and refrigerate until the aspic sets. Take the pans out of the refrigerator, and decorate the center of each mold with the basil leaves (or mint).

Carefully add half of the pâté mixture to each pan. Use a rubber spatula to spread the pâté as evenly as possible over the aspic, but do *not* go to the edge of the pan; leave a border of aspic approximately ½ inch wide. Gently pour one-fourth of the remaining aspic over the pâté in each pan, and return the pans to the refrigerator until the top layer of aspic is also set.

Loosen the edge of the aspic mold in each pan with a knife. Set the pan in warm (*not* hot) water for only a couple of seconds, until the mold loosens. (Watch this step *very* carefully; you do *not* want the aspic to melt.)

Place a plate or silver tray (larger than 9 inches) over the top of each cake pan, and invert them. You will be pleased at how your mold glistens and how well your leaf decoration shows throught the aspic. This dish will keep in the refrigerator for several days.

One mold will serve 8 or 10 as a first course; two molds will feed 20 or more if served as a spread on pieces of toast or crackers, which makes this dish appealing cocktail party fare.

Note: Sercial is the driest of the Madeira wines. Although this type of Madeira is produced on the island of Madeira—out in the Atlantic Ocean between Africa and Portugal—it is made from the once imported Riesling grape.

PROSCIUTTO WITH ROASTED PIMIENTOS

PROSCIUTTO AND ROASTED PEPPERS   SERVES 6 TO 10

4 roasted peppers, cut into strips   *Pepper, ground fresh*
(see page 13)   *2 tablespoons butter*
2 tablespoons olive oil   *8 thin slices white bread*
1 clove garlic, halved   *8 thin slices prosciutto*
Salt

Combine pepper strips, olive oil, garlic, and salt and pepper to taste;
allow mixture to stand for 1 hour. Discard garlic cloves. Carefully butter
each slice of bread, and lay the slices on a flat surface. Arrange 1
prosciutto slice on each piece of bread so that as little of the meat as
possible hangs over the edge. Then arrange the pepper strips to cover the
prosciutto, again with as little overhanging as possible. Trim the crusts
on all four sides, cutting through the prosciutto and peppers to make
clean edges. Cut each slice in thirds.

Arrange these on a silver tray or decorative platter, and serve. If you
make these ahead of time (and you can), cover the platter with a tea
towel to help keep bread from drying out.

BEEF BALLS WITH THREE SAUCES

ROSEMARY AND CREAM   MAKES 50 TO 75 BEEF BALLS

TO PREPARE THE BEEF BALLS:
1 pound top round or sirloin, fine   *1 teaspoon salt*
ground   *Pepper, ground fresh*
2 slices white, French, or Italian   *1 egg*
bread, soaked in ½ cup milk   *¼ cup heavy cream*
and squeezed almost dry   *1 tablespoon butter*
4 tablespoons butter, softened
1 tablespoon dried rosemary (see
Note)

In a large mixing bowl, combine the ground beef, moist bread, butter,
rosemary, salt, and pepper to taste, and mix them well. (If you have a

meat grinder, put this mixture through the fine blade. You can also mix by hand or use a large wooden spoon to blend these ingredients as well as you can.)

Beat the egg and cream together, and blend them into the meat mixture. Shape the tiny meatballs (which should be the size of large grapes) with your hands. Grease a baking tray with 1 tablespoon butter, and arrange the meatballs on the tray. Bake them in a preheated 400-degree oven for 20 minutes, or until they are nicely browned. (Test for doneness by eating one. Do *not* overcook them.)

With a slotted spoon, remove the beef balls from the baking pan, and keep them warm. (Don't use a slotted spatula because meatballs may roll off.)

TO PREPARE THE MUSTARD CREAM SAUCE:

⅓ *cup sour cream*
⅓ *cup heavy cream*
⅓ *cup mustard (made with ⅓ cup water and 3 tablespoons English-type dry mustard)*
Salt

Combine these ingredients, and blend them well. No cooking is required for this sauce.

Prepare the Hot Sweet-and-Sour Sauce according to the directions on page 41 and the Brown Sauce according to the directions on page 93.

Place the warm meatballs in an attractive bowl or chafing dish. Put a toothpick in each one, or put a quantity of small sticks or tiny skewers on a plate or in a glass, and let people spear the meatballs themselves.

The most attractive and practical way to serve the sauces is to put them in three bowls arranged on a single tray and placed next to the meatballs. And remember, the Sweet-and-Sour Sauce and the Brown Sauce should be served hot.

Note: When you are ready to add the rosemary, we suggest that you rub the dried leaves between your hands. This gives them a finer texture and releases more flavor.

COQUILLES BEATRICE

SCALLOPS AND WHITE WINE   SERVES 6

1 pound bay scallops
6 tablespoons dry white wine
   (or 3 tablespoons dry vermouth and 3 tablespoons
   water)
6 tablespoons clam juice
1½ teaspoons lemon juice
1 small onion, chopped fine
½ teaspoon dried fennel
1 teaspoon salt

2 tablespoons cornstarch,
   dissolved in ¼ cup water
½ cup heavy cream
3 tablespoons fresh parsley,
   chopped (or 1 tablespoon
   dried)
½ cup bread crumbs
3 tablespoons butter
2 slices bacon, fried until crisp,
   crumbled

Wash the scallops in cool water. Set them aside.

In a saucepan, combine the wine, clam juice, lemon juice, salt, onion, and fennel, and bring the mixture to a boil. Add the scallops, lower the heat, and simmer for 5 minutes. (Do *not* overcook the scallops.) With a slotted spoon, remove the scallops and onion pieces, and divide them equally among 6 buttered baking shells or ramekins. Set them aside.

Add the dissolved cornstarch and cream to the cooking liquid in the saucepan. Pour this over the scallops and onions.

Mix the chopped parsley and bread crumbs, and place equal amounts of the crumb mixture on top of the scallops. Put ½ tablespoon butter and some bacon bits on top of each shell. Place the shells (or ramekins) on a baking tray, and bake them in a preheated 450-degree oven for 10 minutes. (Be sure the mixture is bubbling before you remove the shells from the oven.)

Serve very hot.

SOUFFLE ROLL WITH CRAB MEAT

SHALLOTS AND SOUR CREAM   SERVES 8 TO 12

TO PREPARE THE SOUFFLÉ ROLL:

4 tablespoons butter	*Pinch of white pepper*
½ cup all-purpose flour	*1 pint milk*
Pinch of salt	*5 eggs, separated*

Butter a jelly-roll pan (approximately 15 by 10 by 1 inch) and line it with wax paper. Butter the wax paper, sprinkle it lightly with flour, shake out the excess flour, and set the pan aside.

In a small saucepan, melt the 4 tablespoons butter. Blend in the ½ cup flour and just a pinch each of salt and white pepper. (The filling is salty, so don't use more than a pinch here.) Add the milk slowly, and bring the mixture to a boil, stirring constantly with a wire whisk. Cook for 1 minute over medium heat; then set aside to cool.

In a small bowl, beat the egg yolks, and add about ½ cup of the milk mixture. When this is well combined, add it to the milk mixture remaining in the saucepan, and heat this sauce for 1 or 2 minutes. (Do *not* allow it to boil.) Remove the sauce from the heat, and set it aside to cool. (The sauce will cool more quickly if you whisk it every few minutes or if you rub the bottom of the saucepan with a sponge dipped in cold water.)

In the meantime, whip the egg whites until they stand in peaks. (Do *not* overwhip the whites. If you do, they will become dry and will not blend well with the sauce.) Fold the whites gently into the cooled yolk sauce, and pour the soufflé mixture into the jelly-roll pan, using a rubber spatula to get all the mixture out of the saucepan and to spread it evenly in the baking pan. Bake the soufflé in a preheated 400-degree oven for about 20 minutes, or until it is lightly browned.

Spread a clean tea towel on a flat surface (where you have some room to maneuver), and turn the soufflé out onto it; the wax paper will peel off easily.

TO PREPARE THE FILLING:

2 tablespoons butter

4 tablespoons shallots, chopped
fine

6 ounces cream cheese, softened

½ cup sour cream

12 ounces crab meat, shredded

Pepper, ground fresh

Salt (optional)

2 tablespoons fresh tarragon,
chopped fine or 1 tablespoon
dried

In the top of a double boiler (the water in the bottom pan should be hot but not boiling), melt the butter, and add the chopped shallots; then add the cream cheese and sour cream. Stir and blend these ingredients over very low heat until they reach the thickness of spreadable whipped cream. Add the crab meat, pepper, salt (if you wish; remember that the crab meat and sour cream are salty) and 1½ tablespoons fresh tarragon or ¾ tablespoon dried. It is *not* necessary to cook this mixture; the heat from the double boiler will soften it so that you can spread it easily.

Spread the mixture evenly on the soufflé. Roll the soufflé, keeping the roll as tight as you can, and transfer it, seam side down, to an attractive serving platter. (Save a little filling, and streak it across the top of the roll. Sprinkle a dash of fresh or dried tarragon over the streak.) Serve the soufflé roll warm, and slice it at the table.

Swiss Chard

At Easter time, the northern Italians bake their spinach pie, and the southern Italians assemble their *pizza rustica* (see our Pizza Rustica Colomba, page 353). Fortunately, both have gained widespread popularity in the United States. Spinach is a beautiful green vegetable and is used in many Italian dishes, but we think that Swiss chard is great, too. It has an earthy, peasant quality, and it's easy to grow.

We discard the large, overgrown leaves and use the smaller ones, and we dote on the stems. We peel the stems (as if destringing celery stalks), cut them into 1- or 2-inch lengths, and cook them with the greenery.

Swiss chard is especially good when cooked with garlic and olive oil. And it gives a special personality to our Italian Bread Roll alla Verdura (see page 349). Here is our Torta di Verdura, which also includes about two links of Angela's Homemade Pork Sausage (see page 260). By the way, we make this *torta* anytime, not just at Easter.

TORTA DI VERDURA
(Swiss Chard, Sausage, and Ricotta Pie)

SWISS CHARD AND RICOTTA

SERVES 8 TO 12

TO PREPARE THE PASTRY:

3 cups all-purpose flour
½ teaspoon salt
¾ cup butter, very cold, cut into
  ¼-inch pieces (see Note 1)

¼ cup shortening, very cold, cut
  into ¼-inch pieces (see Note 1)
1 egg yolk
4 tablespoons ice-cold water

Place the flour, salt, butter, and shortening in a large bowl, and blend them with your fingertips or a pastry blender until the mixture is crumbly and looks like coarse meal. (The pastry arm of a heavy-duty electric mixer works with this chore.)

In a small bowl, beat the egg yolk and water. Add this to the flour mixture, and mix until the dough is pulled together. (You may have to add a few more drops of water to achieve the proper consistency, but do *not* overmix the dough.)

Flour your hands, and quickly shape the dough into a flattened ball. Wrap it in wax paper, and refrigerate it for 30 minutes or longer.

TO PREPARE THE FILLING:

½ pound Italian sausage links
  (see Note 2)
1 to 2 tablespoons olive oil
  (optional)
1 cup onions, chopped fine
2 cups cooked Swiss chard, with
  as little liquid as possible,
  chopped (see page 38)

1 cup Parmesan cheese, grated
1 cup ricotta
4 eggs, lightly beaten
  Salt
  Pepper, ground fresh

Remove the sausage from the casing and crumble it. In a large saucepan, sauté the meat in olive oil (if necessary) until it is browned (8 to 10 minutes.) Remove the meat with a slotted spoon, and set it aside.

Sausage will render a fair amount of fat, so remove all but 2 tablespoons of it from the pan, and reserve it for another use. In the remaining 2 tablespoons of fat, sauté the onions until they begin to turn color (about 5 minutes). Remove the pan from the heat, add the cooked Swiss chard, and mix it with the onions. Then add the Parmesan cheese, ricotta, eggs, and sausage meat, and mix well. Add salt and pepper to taste.

TO ASSEMBLE THE TORTA:

1 egg white, beaten

Divide the pastry in half. Return half to the refrigerator, and roll out the other half to fit a 10-inch pie plate. Brush the bottom and sides of the pastry with the beaten egg white (reserve a small amount to brush the top crust). Add the filling to the pie. Then roll out the other half of the pastry, and cover the pie with it, working as quickly as you can, but taking time to make a decorative edge. With a small, sharp knife, make small, attractive cuts in the center of the crust so that steam can escape during the cooking. If you wish, make decorative shapes with leftover pastry, but don't go overboard. Keep it simple; the pie itself is beautiful to look at. Brush the remaining egg white on the pastry (this will give it a warm, golden glow when it is done). Bake the *torta* in a preheated 400- to 425-degree oven for 30 to 40 minutes. The torta will turn a rich golden color when it is done.

Note 1: Both the butter and the shortening must be cold before they are cut. An easy way to prepare the butter is to cut a stick lengthwise into quarters and then cut these lengths into tiny squares. To prepare the shortening, measure it, remove it from the measuring cup, and cut it into tiny pieces. Put the butter and shortening back into the refrigerator until you are ready to make the dough because they must be cold. (We like to dice the butter and shortening on wax paper and leave the dice on the paper when we put them back in the refrigerator.)

Note 2: Of course, we hope you will use homemade sausage, but it is not absolutely necessary. You shouldn't have difficulty finding good Italian pork sausage in most butcher shops or supermarkets. Still, homemade is better.

Avocado

Like the pineapple (or almost any fruit), the avocado has a magnificent design: It is pear-shaped; its smooth flesh is a beautiful pale green; and at its center is one very large seed. We believe one of the prime joys of life is slicing an avocado in half and opening it.

One pound of avocado contains 58.6 grams of fat, which makes it a dieter's horror. Nevertheless, this American tropical fruit with its Mexican, West Indian, and Guatemalan varieties has many uses in salads, soups, and appetizers. In this chapter, we present it in great combination with a sweet-and-sour-sauce.

COLD AVOCADO HALVES WITH HOT CHINESE SWEET-AND-SOUR SAUCE

SUGAR AND VINEGAR   SERVES 6

3 whole avocados	*1 tablespoon butter*
½ cup water	*2 tablespoons white vinegar*
2 tablespoons sugar	*2 tablespoons catsup*
2 tablespoons lemon juice	*½ teaspoon salt*
1 tablespoon soy sauce	*Pepper, ground fresh*

Cut the avocados in half. Remove the pits but not the skin.

Combine all the remaining ingredients in a small saucepan, and bring them to a boil. Fill each avocado cavity with sauce, dividing it equally among the 6 halves.

This appetizer should be eaten while the avocado is cold and the sauce is hot, so serve it immediately.

TOMATO ASPIC IN FRESH TOMATOES WITH CAVIAR

TOMATOES AND CAVIAR   SERVES 8

TO PREPARE THE TOMATOES:
>   *8 medium-size fresh tomatoes*
>   *Salt*

Wash the tomatoes, and core them by cutting out the stems. (We core the tomatoes first to make them easier to peel.) Blanch the tomatoes quickly, and remove the skins, being sure not to puncture the tomatoes in the process. Widen the opening of each tomato by cutting away more at the stem end. Scoop the pulp out of the insides of the tomatoes, and put them in a measuring cup; add the pieces cut away in widening the core openings. Salt the inside of each tomato, and turn it over to drain.

TO PREPARE THE ASPIC:

3½ cups fresh tomatoes (or fresh tomatoes and canned plum tomatoes, including liquid)
1 small onion, chopped coarse
4 stalks celery, including leaves, chopped coarse
2 tablespoons fresh mint, chopped (or 1 teaspoon dried)

Juice of 1 lemon (approximately 2 tablespoons)
1 tablespoon sugar
1 teaspoon salt
1 bay leaf
2 tablespoons unflavored gelatin
½ cup cool water

To the reserved pulp and tomato pieces, add enough fresh or canned tomatoes to make 3½ cups. Combine the tomatoes, onion, celery, mint, lemon juice, sugar, salt, and bay leaf. In a large saucepan, bring these ingredients to a boil, and simmer them for 30 minutes.

Strain this mixture through several layers of cheesecloth, and discard the pulp; you should have 3½ cups hot tomato liquid. Dissolve the gelatin in the cool water, and add it to the hot tomato liquid, stirring well to dissolve it completely. You should now have 4 cups of tomato-gelatin liquid. Pour this aspic mixture into a glass or ceramic dish or bowl, and refrigerate it until it is almost set.

TO ASSEMBLE:

8 tablespoons caviar
8 lettuce leaves
8 sprigs fresh mint
1 recipe Horseradish Cream Sauce

Turn the empty tomato shells right side up, and pat them dry, inside and out. Carefully spoon 1 tablespoon of caviar into each tomato; pat the caviar lightly with the back of the spoon, spreading it over the inside bottom of the tomato.

When the aspic is almost set, spoon some of it into each shell, piling it as high in the tomato as you can. Garnish with a small sprig of fresh mint and place each tomato on a lettuce leaf. Serve with Horseradish Cream Sauce (page 102).

PEPERONI SOTT'ACETO, IMBOTTITI
(Stuffed Vinegar Peppers)

WALNUTS AND ANCHOVIES   SERVES 6 TO 8

15 vinegar cherry peppers, hot or
   sweet
2-ounce can anchovies, undrained
   and chopped fine
6 walnut meats, chopped fine
1 cup fresh bread crumbs

1 tablespoon fresh parsley,
   chopped fine (or 1 teaspoon
   dried)
1 garlic clove, chopped fine
6 tablespoons olive oil

Core each cherry pepper by carefully cutting out the stem with a small, sharp knife. Remove the seeds from the peppers. The best way to do this is to insert your index finger into the pepper and scrape them out. Be sure to keep the peppers whole. Set them aside.

In a medium-size bowl, mix all the other ingredients except 1 tablespoon olive oil. Fill each pepper with some of this mixture.

In a large skillet, heat the remaining 1 tablespoon olive oil. Add the peppers, stuffed end facing upward, and sauté them for 3 or 4 minutes.

Transfer the peppers to a serving platter. If you are not going to use them right away, they can be stored in the refrigerator in a large container; they will keep for 3 or 4 weeks. Remove them from the refrigerator about 1 hour before serving to allow them to reach room temperature. They may also be added to an antipasto or served as a condiment with baked pork chops, sliced roast or boiled beef, or plain sautéed veal scallops. They are great in combination with slices of Smithfield ham.

((2))

The Savories: Stocks, Soups, and Sauces

THE STOCKS

We've always enjoyed the Alexandre Dumas expression *"faire sourire le pot-au-feu,"* which translated loosely means, "make the pot smile." We would add *faire heureux le pot-au-feu* ("make the pot happy"), for this is the way our stockpots feel as they simmer. And so do we. A world of thanks goes to our good friend and a great cook, Alice Divine Loebel, who extended our appreciation of the simmering stockpot. Quite honestly, we couldn't cook or live without it. Alice wanted two old gate-posts she found buried in the brush near our country house in Pawling, New York; we wish we had more to give her.

Our families were, and still are, old-fashioned about stock. There was always something simmering on the back of the stove at our grand-parents' homes. Grandmothers—and grandfathers, too—didn't always agree on every stock-making technique, but they did say it was necessary to break or crack the bones because a cracked bone freed *la gelatina* ("the gelatin").

There are good canned broths (and we have to admit to the use of bouillon cubes), but there is something truly special about a good, rich, homemade stock. For one thing, it's not so salty as bouillon cubes. You may not notice this at first, but try making a soup with bouillon cubes and then with homemade stock. If you've used bouillon cubes, you'll be thirsty three hours later.

But you must remember that *le pot-au-feu qui rit ou qui est heureux* simmers for several hours; good stock *cannot* be made quickly. Making stock requires more patience and time than skill, yet stock lovers will debate techniques (e.g., stove top versus overnight slow oven, salt or no salt, and parsley sprig versus parsley stem). Because the task of making stock is somewhat time-consuming, we strongly suggest making it in large quantities; we believe in freezing stock.

Stock is the essence extracted from meat and bones by slow simmering. Strained, defatted, and clarified, beef stock becomes beef bouillon. Further reduced by cooking, beef bouillon becomes consommé. Cooked some more, it's double consommé; and eventually, when there is little left to cook, it becomes meat glaze.

Bones are essential to good stock; also, the proportion of bone to meat is important. We like our stock best when it is approximately 50 percent bone, 50 percent meat. For a bouncy brown stock, it is necessary to use meat with connective tissues because these contain the gelatin. Marrow bones are also a requirement, and they should be cut and split into small pieces; the more surface area exposed, the more essence and nutritional value will be extracted.

Finally, it is important to know how to clarify stock. It's really very simple. Here is the way we do it.

HOW TO CLARIFY STOCK

It's easy to clarify meat, poultry, game, and fish stocks by simmering them with egg whites. There are two schools of thought, however, regarding the use of eggshells: Yes, they are necessary; no, they are not. We crush them and throw them in just because we believe the eggshell is one of the most beautiful and wonderful things on earth; therefore, it must have the power to improve the clarification.

For 1 quart of liquid, first beat the whites from 2 eggs until they form soft peaks, crush the shells with your hands, and add both to the liquid to be clarified. Bring the mixture to a boil, whisking constantly, until it reaches the boiling point. Then stop whisking, and turn down the heat to the lowest possible simmering point. In 10 to 15 minutes, the egg whites will become meringuelike. (You'll recognize this stage easily, for who hasn't boiled a cracked egg and seen well-formed foam on the surface of the water?) Whatever fat and foreign matter may have been present in the stock will now have been captured by the mystical, magnetic powers of the egg white (and the eggshell). The liquid below will be clear and beautiful. Just strain the stock carefully through several layers of cheesecloth.

A RICH BEEF STOCK

BEEF AND VEGETABLES   MAKES ABOUT 2 QUARTS

A PRELIMINARY STEP:

> 2 *pounds beef shank* (*meat and bones*)
> 1 *pound chicken parts* (*particularly necks, backbones, and, if possible, feet*)
> 1 *pound beef bones*
> 1 *pound veal bones*

In a large saucepan, combine these ingredients, cover them with water, bring this to a rapid boil, and boil for 3 minutes. Remove this from the heat, and pour off the water. (Try to do this without removing the meat and bones. But if you must remove them, do so with a large slotted spoon and fork.) If you have removed meat and bones, put them back into the same saucepan.

TO PREPARE THE STOCK:

> 4 *quarts water*
> 2 *leeks, including green parts, washed carefully to remove sand and chopped coarse*
> 2 *medium-size onions, washed, but not peeled, and chopped coarse*
> 2 *large stalks celery, including leaves, washed and chopped coarse*
>
> 2 *large carrots, scrubbed clean but not peeled, chopped coarse*
> 2 *sprigs fresh thyme* (*or ½ teaspoon dried*)
> 6 *sprigs fresh parsley* (*or 1 teaspoon dried*)
> 1 *bay leaf*
> 12 *peppercorns*
> 3 *teaspoons salt*

Add all these ingredients to the saucepan containing the meat and bones. Bring them to a boil, and simmer, uncovered, for at least 3 hours. Taste for salt and pepper, but *do not* add any more at this time if you intend to freeze the stock for future use. (We find that when we use a fundamental stock after it has been frozen, the seasoning always needs to be adjusted. So wait until then to add more salt and pepper.)

Next, strain the stock, using a large wooden spoon to squeeze as much juice as possible out of meat and vegetables. If the strainer is large enough (and it should be), place a small, flat plate over the meat and bones, and push down on them to extract the juices.

Refrigerate the stock overnight. The fat will solidify, and defatting will be easy. (We dare you to try removing the fat in one piece; but you can do it in two or three pieces without any difficulty.) Then use a paper towel to wipe any remaining fat from stock bowl. Sometimes, the top of the stock will show tiny fat specks. Place a paper towel directly over the stock, and pat gently. Then lift the towel; all the fat specks will come with it.

If you are going to use some of the stock within the next 3 days, you can keep it in the refrigerator. Freeze the rest (or all) in ½-cup, 1-cup, and 2-cup amounts, to use as needed. Fill plastic containers with the stock, and freeze them overnight. Then transfer the blocks of frozen stock to large plastic bags, labeling these accordingly. When you need ½ cup or 2 cups of Rich Beef Stock (as you surely will if you use the recipes in this book), simply open the freezer door, reach in, and pull out the quantity you need.

Stock will keep in the freezer indefinitely. But once you make this delightful, rich, full-bodied stock, you'll find that it won't last long.

A RICH BROWN STOCK

BEEF AND VEGETABLES   MAKES ABOUT 2 QUARTS

Follow the directions for preparing A Rich Beef Stock, but with these exceptions:

Do not boil the meat and bones for 3 minutes. Instead, put the meat and bones in a large baking pan, and brown them in a preheated 475- to 500-degree oven for 20 to 30 minutes. Reduce the heat to 425 degrees, add the chopped onions and carrots, and brown them for an additional 30 minutes.

Transfer the browned meat, bones, and vegetables to a large saucepan, and pour off the fat from the baking tray. On top of the stove, deglaze the baking pan, using several cups of water (from the 4 quarts you'll add later). Pour this liquid into the saucepan. Then add all the other ingredients (the remaining water, leeks, celery, thyme, parsley, bay leaf, peppercorns, and salt).

Follow the remaining steps of the basic recipe, including defatting, freezing, and packaging.

A RICH VEAL STOCK

VEAL AND VEGETABLES   MAKES ABOUT 2 QUARTS

A PRELIMINARY STEP:

2 *pounds veal bones (not too*
  large)
2½ *pounds veal shank, cut into*
  cubes as if for stew (or any
  inexpensive veal pieces that
  are not too fatty)
1 *calf's knuckle*

2 *medium-size onions, washed*
  but not *peeled and chopped*
  coarse
2 *large carrots, scrubbed clean,*
  but not *peeled, and chopped*
  coarse

Place the meat and bones in a large baking tray or pan. Brown them in a preheated 475- to 500-degree oven for 20 to 30 minutes. Reduce the heat to 400 degrees, add the carrots and onions, and bake them for an additional 30 minutes.

TO PREPARE THE STOCK:

4 *quarts water*
2 *large stalks celery, including*
  leaves, washed and chopped
  coarse
2 *leeks, including green parts,*
  washed carefully to remove
  sand and chopped coarse (see
  page 56)

2 *cloves garlic, chopped coarse*
2 *sprigs fresh thyme (or ½*
  teaspoon dried)
6 *sprigs fresh parsley (or 1*
  teaspoon dried)
2 *bay leaves*
12 *peppercorns*
1 *tablespoon salt*

Transfer the meat, bones, and vegetables to a large saucepan, and pour off the fat from the baking pan. On top of the stove, deglaze the baking pan, using 2 or 3 cups water (from the 4 quarts). Pour this liquid into the saucepan. Add the remaining ingredients, and bring the mixture to a boil. Lower the heat, and simmer the stock, uncovered, for 4 hours or longer, until the liquid is reduced by half.

Strain, refrigerate, defat, package, and freeze the stock according to the instructions on page 47.

A RICH CHICKEN STOCK

CHICKEN AND VEGETABLES   MAKES ABOUT 2 QUARTS

1 *pound veal bones, preferably marrow*

3 *pounds chicken parts (wings, necks, gizzards, feet, hearts, backs, and other bones)*

3 *quarts water*

2 *leeks, including green parts, washed carefully to remove sand and chopped coarse*

2 *medium-size onions, washed, but not peeled, and chopped coarse*

2 *large stalks celery, including leaves, washed and chopped coarse*

2 *large carrots, scrubbed clean but not peeled, and chopped coarse*

½ *pound mushrooms (see Note)*

2 *sprigs fresh thyme (or 1 teaspoon dried)*

6 *sprigs fresh parsley (or 1 teaspoon dried)*

12 *peppercorns*

1 *teaspoon salt*

In a large saucepan, combine the veal bones, chicken parts, and water, and bring this to a boil. Skim off the foam. Add all the other ingredients, and bring the stock mixture to a boil again. Lower the heat, partially cover the saucepan, and simmer the stock for at least 2 hours. Strain, refrigerate, defat, freeze, and package the stock according to the instructions on page 47.

Note: Leftover trimmed stem ends are excellent for use in stock. Whenever we prepare mushrooms for another recipe, we freeze the stem trimmings just for this purpose.

A RICH FISH STOCK

FISH AND VEGETABLES   MAKES 2 QUARTS

3 tablespoons butter

3 tablespoons vegetable oil (or olive oil)

2 leeks, including green parts, washed carefully to remove sand and chopped coarse (see page 56)

2 medium-size onions, washed, but not peeled, and chopped coarse

2 large stalks celery, including leaves, washed and chopped coarse

2 large carrots, washed, but not peeled, and chopped coarse

1 quart dry white wine

3 quarts water

4 pounds fish heads and bones

2 bay leaves

¼ teaspoon dried fennel

6 sprigs fresh parsley (or 1 teaspoon dried)

12 peppercorns

1 teaspoon salt

In a large saucepan, melt the butter together with the oil. When they are hot, add the leeks, onions, celery, and carrots, and cook them for about 10 minutes, or until the onions are a pale yellow.

Then add the wine, water, and fish heads and bones, and bring the liquid to a boil. Foam will accumulate on the surface, and this should be removed. Add the bay leaves, fennel, parsley, peppercorns, and salt. Stir all the ingredients well, and simmer the stock, partially covered, for about 2 hours, or until the liquid is reduced by half.

Strain, refrigerate, defat, freeze, and package the stock according to the instructions on page 47.

THE SOUPS

Soup, from Latin *suppa*, is *sapid*, from the Latin *sapidus* ("tasty"). Like bread, it is, without question, one of the world's most popular foods. Soup and bread, together or singly, can help trace the development of people and their cultures. We'll never understand the origin of the expression "in the soup" (in an unfortunate predicament) because for us "in the soup" can only imply a most fortunate situation. Molière must have understood the importance of soup, for in *Les Femmes Savantes*, he wrote: *"Je vis de bonne soupe et non de beau langage"* ("I live by good soup and not by fine words").

Food and eating styles have certainly changed, and surely to everyone's advantage and good health; but at times, we revel in the thought of beginning a meal with the four soups that Carême served Britain's Prince Regent, later King George IV, on January 15, 1817, at the Brighton Pavilion:*

> "Le Potage à la Monglas"—a creamy brown soup, flavored with Madeira and made with foie gras, truffles and mushrooms.
>
> "Le Garbure aux Choux"—a rich flavorful vegetable broth, country style, full of shredded cabbage.
>
> "Le Potage de Orge Perlée à la Crécy"—a bland pink puree of pearl barley and carrots.
>
> "Le Potage de Poissons à la Russe"—a fish soup, "Russian style," made with sturgeon.

These were followed with four fish dishes, four "grosses pieces or pieces de resistance," 36 entrees, 5 "assiettes volantes," 8 majestic set pieces, 4 roasts of game and poultry, 32 entremets—no point in going on for we're just getting into the meal and we've sure you have the idea.

We would be happy to settle for reveling in what Roy Andries de Groot imagined Mrs. Bridges serving almost 100 years later to King Edward VII (and please remember that Escoffier is given credit for reducing Edward's meals from fifteen courses to five):

> Two "soupes"
> Sturgeon's Head garnished with Tiger Lily buds à la Chinoise, and a Bouillon of Wild Mushrooms with Passatelli a la Bolognese†

At ceremonial dinners, when two soups are on the menu, one is thick and the other clear. This is the way all cookbooks classify soups. *Consommé* is a clear soup; and a beef consommé is a meat stock, strength-

---

* Reay Tannahill, *Food in History* (New York: Stein & Day, 1973), page 337.

† Roy Andries de Groot, "Mrs. Bridges Surpasses Herself," *Esquire*, January 1975, p. 105.

ened with nonfatty chopped beef and aromatic vegetables, and clarified with egg whites, and cooked to the point of tastiness. The thick soups are generally classified as *purée, cream,* or *velouté;* they are thickened with the puréed vegetables or with roux, rice, tapioca, bread, or cream and egg yolks. Clear soups can be liquid or jellied (hot or cold), and either way, they give a prestigious touch to a formal dinner. But in our opinion, thick soups are more in vogue today because they can be served as a main course if accompanied by bread, a salad, and cheese or fruit. In this way, they can be the center of a simple but complete meal. Almost all our soup recipes in this chapter are in the thick category, but we have also included the classic recipes for beef and chicken consommés.

BEEF CONSOMME

BEEF AND VEGETABLES   MAKES ABOUT 7 QUARTS

TO COOK THE BONES:

5½ to 6 pounds rib and shin bones, cut into 1½-inch lengths and split in half
3 pounds chicken parts (necks, backs, hearts, livers, gizzards, and feet), cut into 1½-inch lengths

9 quarts cold water
1 tablespoon salt

In a very large stockpot, combine all these ingredients except the salt, and slowly bring the mixture to a boil. Lower the heat to maintain a simmer. Skim the surface of the liquid to remove the foam (coagulated albumen); repeat this procedure whenever necessary. Add the salt, and simmer slowly for 2½ hours.

TO COOK THE BEEF:

5½ *pounds lean beef round,*
boned, in 1 piece, and tied like
a filet or pot roast (with
kitchen string)

1 *pound leeks, well washed and*
cut into 1½-inch lengths (see
page 56)

1 *pound carrots, scrubbed clean,*
but not peeled, and cut into
½-inch lengths

2 *turnips, well washed, but not*
peeled, and cut into 1-inch
cubes

2 *stalks celery, including leaves,*
cut into 1-inch lengths

1 *medium-size onion, washed*
but not peeled, and stuck with
2 *whole cloves*

1 *large clove garlic, halved*

4 *sprigs fresh parsley (or 2*
tablespoons dried)

2 *sprigs fresh thyme (or 1*
teaspoon dried)

Add the beef to the stockpot, and bring the mixture to a boil again. Skim off the foam. Add all the vegetables and herbs, and simmer this slowly for 4 hours. Strain the mixture through a fine sieve, and allow it to cool, preferably overnight in the refrigerator. Remove all the fat (see instructions on page 47).

TO ENRICH AND CLARIFY THE CONSOMMÉ:

2½ *pounds ground round beef, as lean as possible*

1 *pound chicken backs, cut into 1-inch pieces*

1 *carrot, scraped and cut into ¼-inch cubes*

1 *leek, well washed and cut into thin slices (see page 56)*

2 *egg whites, lightly beaten*

In a very large stockpot, combine the ground round, pieces of chicken backs, and strained, defatted stock. (You'll have 7 to 8 quarts of stock.) Add the diced carrot and sliced leek. Then add the foamy egg whites. Bring this just to the boiling point. Then lower the heat, cover the pot, and simmer gently for 1 hour.

Strain the consommé through a colander lined with several layers of cheesecloth. Again, allow the consommé to cool in the refrigerator; and again, remove any trace of fat.

You will have approximately 7 quarts of consommé. What you don't use immediately can be frozen. If it has jellied, heat it slowly until it is liquid enough for you to measure out 2 quarts (which we assume you'll want to use at once). Freeze the remainder (see page 47). (We know you'll enjoy it later.)

TO FLAVOR THE CONSOMMÉ:

> *2 quarts consommé*
> *4 tablespoons instant tapioca*
> *1 cup Madeira*
> *4 tablespoons shallots, chopped fine*

While the consommé is liquid but cooled, add the tapioca, and let the consommé sit, covered, for at least 30 minutes. Then simmer the consommé over medium heat for 15 minutes. Add the wine and shallots, and cook it for an additional 30 minutes. Strain the consommé through a cheesecloth-lined colander. You will surely have prepared one of the finest and tastiest consommés. However, taste it before serving, and if it needs a touch of salt, add some. Then, of course, you will have to garnish the consommé. The garnishing of a consommé is important, and here are some spectacular examples:

> julienne mushrooms sautéed in butter with chervil
> julienne sweet potatoes and diced fresh tomatoes
> poached vermicelli and fresh green peas
> pearl barley with celery cooked in stock
> julienne carrots and leeks cooked in stock
> profiteroles filled with foie gras
> julienne sorrel and chervil cooked in butter
> small ravioli with chervil leaves
> beef marrow cut into small, uniform pieces
> julienne truffles
> royales made with asparagus and with beets, cut
>   into hearts, diamonds, cubes, stars, or rosettes

CHICKEN CONSOMME

CHICKEN AND VEGETABLES   MAKES ABOUT 8 QUARTS

TO COOK THE BONES:

Follow the directions for Beef Consommé (see page 52).

TO COOK THE MEAT:

Add 2½ pounds of boned ground beef round and a 5- to 6-pound chicken instead of 5½ pounds beef. Follow the instructions for Beef Consommé (see page 53).

TO ENRICH AND CLARIFY THE CONSOMMÉ:

Follow the procedure for Beef Consommé (see page 53).

TO FLAVOR THE CONSOMMÉ:

Add 1 cup sherry instead of 1 cup Madeira, and follow the instructions for flavoring Beef Consommé (see page 54).

And now, here are some spectacular garnishes:

> truffled chicken quenelles and chervil leaves
> profiteroles filled with foie gras and chervil leaves
> julienne chicken breasts and sorrel leaves
> slivers of mushrooms and truffles
> julienne lettuce and leeks
> royales of chicken, spinach, and tomato purée
> green asparagus tips and tarragon leaves

The combinations used in soups are endless. The classic *Potage Saint-Germain* (a purée of fresh peas) has become our Cool, Green, Green Pea Soup, brightened with a hint of mint. *Consommé en tasse a la moelle* (an essence of beef accented with marrow) appears as our Beef Consommé garnished with tiny cubes of marrow. And if only there were space, we'd add an oxtail broth; a *garbure* made with cabbage, chestnuts, and sausage; and our version of the *Potage Ambassadeur* served at Le Périgord in New York, a purée of fresh peas combined with sorrel, chervil, and rice. Well, there just isn't room, but here are some of our favorite savory soups.

VICHYSSOISE VERTE
(Asparagus and Leek Soup)

ASPARAGUS AND LEEKS   SERVES 8

2 cups leeks (about 4 leeks)   Salt
4 tablespoons butter   Pepper, ground fresh
2 cups potatoes, peeled, and cut   1 to 2 cups light cream
   into ½-inch cubes   4 tablespoons fresh chives,
2 cups asparagus, cut into   chopped
   ½-inch pieces
1½ quarts Rich Chicken Stock
   (or broth) (see page 49)

Cut the leeks in half lengthwise, and wash them well, separating the leaves with your fingers as you rinse them under cool running water, to remove any sand. Drain the leeks, and cut them crosswise into thin slices.

In a large saucepan, melt the butter, and sauté the leeks very lightly. Dry the potato cubes, add them to the saucepan, toss them with the leek pieces, and sauté them for 3 to 4 minutes. Add the asparagus pieces, stock, and a little salt and pepper. Bring this mixture to a boil; then simmer it gently for 30 to 40 minutes or until the vegetables are tender. Put the contents of the saucepan through a food mill, or rub it through a fine sieve. (Or you can purée it in batches in a blender, but do *not* overblend it.) Return the puréed mixture to the saucepan, and add the cream to achieve the desired thickness. Adjust for seasoning.

This soup may be served hot or cold. Sprinkle ½ tablespoon chopped chives into each cup of Vichyssoise Verte.

COLD ASPARAGUS SOUP

2 cups asparagus
3 tablespoons butter
1 cup scallions, cut into ½-inch
    lengths
2 cups Rich Chicken Stock (see
    page 49)

2 tablespoons dry sherry
    (optional)
½ to 1 cup light cream
Salt
Pepper, ground fresh

Wash and clean the asparagus according to the instructions on page 302. Cut the spears, including the tips, into ½-inch lengths.

Slowly melt the butter in a heavy saucepan, add the asparagus and scallion pieces, and cook them for 5 minutes, stirring two or three times to coat the vegetable pieces with the butter.

Add the stock and sherry (if you wish), and cover the pan. Cook this over moderate heat for about 15 minutes, or until the asparagus pieces are tender. (Check a piece for doneness; if it isn't tender, cook a few minutes longer.) Remove the saucepan from the heat.

Purée this mixture in batches in a blender, or put it through a food mill. Transfer the blended mixture to a glass, ceramic, or stainless steel container, and chill it well.

When you are ready to serve the soup, add ½ cup light cream. If the soup is still too thick for your taste, add more cream. Add salt and fresh-ground pepper to taste. This soup may also be served hot.

AVOCADO SOUP

AVOCADO AND CURRY   SERVES 6

3 ripe avocados
 Salt
 Pepper, ground fresh
1 tablespoon curry powder
1 cup heavy cream
4 cups Rich Chicken Stock (see
 page 49) (or broth)

3 teaspoons fresh lemon juice
¼ teaspoon cayenne pepper
3 teaspoons chives, chopped fine
 (or fresh shallots)

Cut each avocado in half lengthwise, and remove the pit. (To do this, hold the avocado half in one hand, and force the pit out of place with the other.) With a large spoon, scoop out all the pulp, chop it coarsely, and put it through a fine sieve together with salt and pepper to taste and the curry powder. (These ingredients, including the cream, may also be combined in a blender, in batches.) If you need some liquid to help process it, add a bit of the heavy cream. Then add the cream (or the remaining cream), and blend well.

In a large saucepan, combine the stock and lemon juice, and heat this to the boiling point. In a small bowl combine 1 cup of the hot stock with 1 cupful of the avocado mixture, and blend this well. Repeat the process until all the avocado mixture has been combined. Remove the saucepan from the heat, and add the mixture of stock and avocado to the remaining stock.

Add the cayenne pepper, and heat the soup very slowly. Test for seasoning, including the amount of lemon juice. Bring the soup just to the boiling point, and serve it immediately, garnished with the chopped chives or shallots.

MINESTRA D'ORZO E PEPERONI
(Barley Soup with Peperoni)

BARLEY AND PEPERONI

SERVES 6

1 tablespoon butter
¼ pound peperoni, sliced thin,
   then cut into ¼-inch squares
2 carrots, sliced thin
. 2 stalks celery, including leaves,
   sliced thin
1 onion, sliced thin
2 small potatoes, peeled and cut
   into ½-inch cubes (no larger)

3 sprigs fresh parsley, chopped
   (or 1 teaspoon dried)
½ cup barley
2 quarts Rich Beef Stock (see
   page 46)
Salt
Pepper, ground fresh

In a large saucepan, heat the butter, and sauté the peperoni for 3 minutes. Then remove the peperoni pieces, and set them aside.

Add the carrots, celery, onions, potatoes, and parsley to the saucepan, and sauté them for 5 minutes. Then, add the barley and stock, and cook slowly for 40 to 50 minutes, or until the barley is almost cooked. Add the sautéed peperoni pieces, and cook the soup for about 10 minutes longer, or until the barley is fully cooked. Add salt and pepper to taste.

Serve the *minestra* hot.

FRESH TOMATO AND FRESH BASIL SOUP

BASIL AND TOMATOES

SERVES 6

This soup is beautiful because it combines *fresh* tomatoes and *fresh* basil. Everyone knows the beauty of fresh, sliced tomatoes with basil. We think there is every reason in the world to combine basil and tomatoes in other ways. This soup is our warm answer to a cool gazpacho.

1 link Italian pork sausage
1 teaspoon olive oil
1 clove garlic, halved
1 large leek, cut into ½-inch pieces
1 large stalk celery, including
   leaves, cut into ½-inch pieces
1 large onion, sliced thin
1 tablespoon sugar
2 pounds fresh tomatoes, cored,
   blanched, peeled, and chopped
   coarse (see Note)

3 cups Rich Beef Stock (see page
   46)
Salt
Pepper, ground fresh
Juice of 1 lemon
6 tablespoons fresh basil, chopped
   fine (see Note)

In a large, heavy saucepan (the one in which you will cook the soup), brown the sausage link in the olive oil until it is well done (about 10 minutes). Remove the sausage, and set it aside.

There should be 2 tablespoons of oil and fat left in the saucepan. If there is more, remove the excess; if there is not enough, add a bit of butter. Add the garlic pieces, and cook them until they are light brown. Press down on the garlic with a wooden spoon to extract juice, then discard it. Add the pieces of leek, celery, and onion, and sauté them for about 10 minutes. Add the sugar, tomatoes, sausage, and stock, and bring the mixture to a boil. Reduce the heat, and simmer the contents of the saucepan for about 30 minutes.

Remove the sausage, and put the tomato mixture through a food mill. (We prefer the food mill to a blender for this because a food mill will remove most of the seeds but a blender will pulverize them. And we think the whole texture of the soup is better this way.) Add salt and pepper to taste.

Cut the sausage link into the thinnest possible slices; then cut each slice into quarters, and add them to the soup. Add the lemon juice and 4 tablespoons basil, and cook the soup for an additional 2 minutes.

Serve this soup in individual bowls with a sprinkle of the remaining 2 tablespoons basil decorating each serving.

Note: If you must substitute canned tomatoes and dried basil, use 4 cups plum tomatoes and 2 tablespoons basil (reserving ½ teaspoon basil for the garnish). But we hope you won't resort to this alternative.

Broccoli

Buy broccoli with buds that are tightly closed and stalks that are dark emerald green. Cut away the coarse leaves and tough stalk parts, and always pare the stalks with a vegetable peeler.

Leeks

Leeks are an important member of the onion family and, indeed, an important member of our family. In fact, we can't do without them. We prefer the taste of the leek to that of the onion because the leek is sweeter, as a rule, and milder. The leek is probably as old as the fig, historically speaking. No one seems able to determine its origin, although we know it was grown in ancient Egypt and Rome. Its infinitely greater popularity in Europe than in the United States is difficult to understand because it is easy to grow, almost totally free of diseases and pests, and unperturbed by frost. In Dutchess County, New York, we leave leeks in the ground until Thanksgiving. They're easy to dig up, clean, and freeze.

Leeks add significantly to salads. We especially like to do with leeks exactly what the ancient Romans did: We select young, tender leeks, cut them into thin slices, and add them to any salad. *Incantevole!* And we love the flavor of leeks in stocks and soups. Try our delicious Cream of Broccoli with Leeks, which follows.

CREAM OF BROCCOLI WITH LEEKS

BROCCOLI AND LEEKS   SERVES 6 TO 8

2 cups leeks (about 4 leeks)
2 tablespoons butter
2 cups potatoes, peeled and
* cut into ½-inch cubes*
3 cups broccoli flowerettes
1½ quarts Rich Chicken Stock
* (see page 49) (or broth)*
Salt

Pepper, ground fresh
1 to 2 cups light cream
3 to 4 tablespoons fresh chives,
* chopped (or fresh parsley) (or*
* 1 teaspoon dried)*
3 to 4 teaspoons grated Parme-
* san cheese*

Cut the leeks in half lengthwise, and wash them well, separating the leaves with your fingers as you rinse them under cool running water, to remove any sand. Drain the leeks, and cut them crosswise into thin slices.

In a large saucepan, melt the butter, and sauté the leeks very lightly. Dry the potato cubes, add them to the pan, tossing them with the leek pieces, and sauté them for 4 to 5 minutes. Add the broccoli flowerettes, stock, and a little salt and pepper. Bring this to a boil; then reduce the heat, and simmer it gently for 30 to 40 minutes, or until the vegetables are tender.

Process this mixture through a food mill, or rub it through a fine sieve. (You may also purée it in batches in a blender, but do *not* overblend it.) Return the sieved mixture to the saucepan, and add cream to achieve the desired thickness. Adjust the seasoning.

This soup may be served hot or cold. Sprinkle each bowlful with ½ tablespoon chopped chives (or parsley) and ½ teaspoon grated Parmesan cheese.

BUTTERNUT SQUASH SOUP

BUTTERNUT SQUASH AND APPLES   SERVES 6

1 *pound butternut squash, peeled and diced*	2 *onions, sliced*
3 *apples, peeled, cored, and diced*	8 *soda crackers (or 1 cup white bread cubes)*
4 *cups Rich Chicken Stock (see page 49)*	2 *egg yolks*
½ *cup dry vermouth*	½ *cup heavy cream (approximately)*
1 *teaspoon fresh tarragon (or ½ teaspoon dried)*	2 *tablespoons fresh chives, chopped fine (or 1 tablespoon frozen or dried chives)*
1 *teaspoon salt*	*Paprika (optional)*
Pepper, ground fresh	

In a saucepan, combine the squash, apples, stock, vermouth, tarragon, salt, pepper to taste, onions, and crackers (or bread crumbs), and cook them for 30 to 40 minutes, or until the squash is tender. (Test the squash for doneness by piercing a piece with a fork and mashing it. If it mashes easily, it's done.) Purée this mixture in batches in a blender. Return the purée to the saucepan.

In a separate bowl, beat the yolks and cream. Add about 1 cup of the puréed soup to the yolk mixture. Blend well, and add this to the purée remaining in the saucepan. If the soup is too thick, add more cream to thin it to your taste. (You can also thin it with milk or more stock. But we think this soup is best when it is thick.) Reheat the soup, but do *not* allow it to boil. (If you do, the egg yolks will curdle.) Check the seasoning and adjust it to your taste.

Serve the soup in individual bowls. To each serving add a dollop of cream (unwhipped) topped with a few pieces of chives or a sprinkle of paprika.

A VARIATION: BUTTERNUT SQUASH SOUP WITH CURRY

BUTTERNUT SQUASH AND CURRY   SERVES 6

While the vegetables are cooking, melt 2 tablespoons butter in a small skillet or saucepan, and add 1 tablespoon curry powder. Blend this well, and cook it, stirring constantly, for 3 minutes. Add this mixture to the vegetables before you purée them. Follow the rest of the instructions for the basic recipe.

Carrots

Fresh young carrots are bright orange with just a speck of green coloring at the stem end. If the stem end has too much green, the carrot is probably overgrown and more tough than tender. Most carrots come in plastic packages, but don't be afraid to peer through the plastic to check for green ends. And don't let that stop you from grasping the carrots to check for firmness.

Carrots are almost as versatile as potatoes. They can be scraped (or not), chopped, sliced, cubed, or cut in fancy shapes. They are served hot or cold, in soups or salads, in cakes or casseroles. They can be candied or creamed, molded or minted. For centuries, they have been combined with peas, onions, or celery; with cream, butter, or sugar. We use carrots in combination meat stuffings and salads. And we think they are wonderful in soups, such as our Carrot and Tomato Cream Soup and our Potage de Poireaux et Carottes (see pages 64 and 73).

CARROT AND TOMATO CREAM SOUP

CARROTS AND TOMATOES   SERVES 4

1 *pound carrots*

4½ *tablespoons butter*

2 *cups fresh tomatoes, cored,*
blanched, and peeled (or
canned plum tomatoes)

1 *clove garlic, chopped fine*

2 *teaspoons dried oregano*

1½ *tablespoons all-purpose flour*

1 *cup Rich Chicken Stock (see*
page 49), (or Rich Veal
Stock, see page 48)

1½ *cups milk*

1 *cup sour cream*

Salt

Pepper, ground fresh

Cut off both ends of each carrot. Wash the carrots well, using a scrub brush to clean them. (There is no need to scrape or pare the carrots unless you insist; you can get them clean by scrubbing them.) Cut the carrots into thin slices, and set them aside.

In a saucepan, melt 3 tablespoons butter, and sauté the carrot slices over high heat for 5 minutes, stirring well to coat them with butter. Add the tomatoes, garlic and 1 teaspoon of oregano, and cook the vegetables, partially covered, for 30 minutes.

While the vegetables are cooking, melt the remaining 1½ tablespoons butter in another saucepan. Add the flour, blending well with a wire whisk or a wooden spoon. Add the stock, stir the mixture constantly over low heat until it is well blended and thickened (about 5 minutes), and cook it for an additional 20 minutes.

Combine the tomatoes and carrots with the stock mixture. Add the milk and sour cream, and mix until well combined. Purée this mixture in batches in a blender or a food mill. Transfer the purée to a saucepan, and slowly bring it to the simmering point. Be sure to add salt and pepper to taste.

Sprinkle ¼ teaspoon of the remaining oregano over each soup bowl before serving.

CHILLED, DILLED CUCUMBER SOUP

2 *cucumbers, peeled, seeded, and
  chopped coarse*
1 *garlic clove, chopped fine*
3 *cups Rich Chicken Stock (see
  page 49)*
1 *cup heavy cream*
3 *tablespoons fresh dill, chopped
  fine*

Salt
Pepper, ground fresh
¾ *cup sour cream*
4 *to 6 tablespoons almonds,
  chopped (or walnuts or filberts)*

Place the cucumbers, garlic, and 1 cup stock in a blender, and blend them until smooth. Pour this into a large bowl, and add the remaining 2 cups stock, cream, dill, salt, pepper to taste, and sour cream. With a wire whisk, beat well until all ingredients are combined. Refrigerate for several hours (or better still, overnight) until the soup is ice-cold. If you are serving this soup cold, it must be *ice*-cold. Add 1 tablespoon chopped nuts to each bowl, and serve. We have also served this soup hot, with the garnish of nuts, and it's good that way too. But we think of this primarily as one of the better cool summer soups, especially when cucumber and dill are fresh from the garden.

POTATO AND DILL SOUP

6 *slices bacon*
1 *onion, sliced coarse*
2 *leeks (including some of the
  green stalks, if tender), cut into
  1-inch pieces*
1 *pound potatoes, peeled and cut
  into small chunks*

1 *tablespoon fresh dill (or 1 teaspoon dried)*
5 *cups Rich Chicken Stock (see
  page 49)*
Salt
Pepper, ground fresh
1 *cup heavy cream*

In a large saucepan, cook the bacon slices until they are crisp. Remove them, and set them aside on paper towels to drain.

Add the onion and leeks to the saucepan and sauté them in the bacon fat until softened (about 5 minutes). Add the potatoes and 1 tablespoon fresh dill (or 1 teaspoon dried), and sauté for an additional 5 minutes. Add the stock, and bring the mixture to a boil. Then reduce the heat, and simmer until the potatoes are cooked (about 30 minutes, depending on the size of the chunks).

Purée the mixture in batches in a blender. Then add salt and pepper to taste, and stir in the cream. (If the soup is too thick, thin it with more cream, stock, or milk.) Heat the soup to a simmer (do *not* let it boil).

Pour the soup into individual bowls, and crumble 1 bacon slice into each bowl. If you have used fresh dill, add a dash of fresh dill to each serving. If you have used dried dill, do not use any more as a garnish; the 1 teaspoon of it in the soup is just the right amount. Instead, add a sprinkle of fresh or dried parsley. Or add nothing at all; the bacon is decorative enough.

MINESTRONE DI RISO
(Rice Soup with Dill)

DILL AND RICE   SERVES 4

½ cup rice, uncooked
2 quarts Rich Chicken Stock (or broth) (see page 49)
2 stalks celery, including leaves, chopped coarse
1 onion, chopped
2 leeks, including green parts if tender, chopped coarse
1 tablespoon fresh dill (or 1 teaspoon dried dill seed)

1 tablespoon all-purpose flour
½ cup cream
2 eggs
1 tablespoon dry sherry
Salt
White pepper, ground fresh
Fresh dill (or dried)

In a large saucepan, combine the rice, stock (or broth), celery, onion, leeks, and dill. Cover the saucepan, and bring this mixture to a boil. Lower the heat, and simmer, covered, for 30 minutes.

When the rice is cooked, mix the flour with a little cold water, and slowly add it to the rice soup; mix this well. Let the soup boil slowly for 5 minutes, stirring frequently.

Put the soup mixture through a food mill. Then return to soup to the saucepan and put it back on the heat. (Be sure to clean out all the purée from the bottom of the food mill.)

Beat the cream and eggs together in a small bowl. Add a little soup to this mixture, and stir well. Slowly add this to the remaining soup in the saucepan, and keep stirring until well blended. Add the sherry and salt and pepper to taste. Reheat the soup, but do *not* let it come to a boil. Adjust the seasonings (if necessary).

Serve this minestrone with a little fresh (or dried) dill sprinkled on top.

UNA BELLA MINESTRA
(Escarole and Bean Soup)

ESCAROLE AND BEANS   SERVES 4

½ pound dried kidney beans
2 quarts, plus 3 cups, water
3 tablespoons olive oil (see Note)
2 garlic cloves, chopped fine
2 cups fresh tomatoes, blanched, cored, peeled, and chopped coarse (or canned plum tomatoes)
1 tablespoon fresh basil, chopped fine (or 1 teaspoon dried)

1 tablespoon salt
4 stalks celery, cut into ¼-inch slices
1 large carrot, cut into ¼-inch slices
1½ pounds escarole
Pepper, ground fresh
Parmesan cheese, grated

Soak the beans overnight in water to cover (do *not* refrigerate). The next day, drain the beans, and put them in a large saucepan with 2 quarts water. Cook them over low heat for 1½ to 2 hours, or until beans are almost done. Set the beans aside.

In another saucepan, heat the oil, add the garlic pieces, and cook for 1 minute. Then add the tomatoes, 3 cups of water, basil, and salt, and cook this mixture over moderate heat for 10 minutes. Add the celery and carrot pieces, and cook for an additional 15 minutes. Add this vegetable mixture to the beans, and put the large saucepan over medium heat. Add the escarole, pushing it into the pan with a wooden spoon to immerse it completely in the soup. Cover the saucepan, and simmer the soup for 30 minutes. Add pepper to taste.

Serve this *minestra* with liberal spoonfuls of grated Parmesan cheese.

Note: The flavor of the olive oil is important in this soup, so please make every effort not to substitute any other kind of oil.

CREAM OF ESCAROLE

ESCAROLE AND THYME   SERVES 6 TO 8

1 *large head escarole (about 1*
  pound)
8 *cups Rich Chicken Stock (see*
  page 49)
2 *tablespoons fresh parsley,*
  chopped (or 1 teaspoon dried)
1 *tablespoon fresh thyme, chopped*
  (or 1 teaspoon dried)
1 *bay leaf*

2 *tablespoons butter*
2 *tablespoons all-purpose flour*
2 *egg yolks*
1 *cup heavy cream*
  Salt
  Pepper, ground fresh
  Paprika
1 *cup garlic croutons (see page 69)*

Wash the escarole leaves carefully, removing all sand; drain the leaves very well.

In a large saucepan, combine the stock, escarole, parsley, thyme, and bay leaf, and bring this to a boil. Reduce the heat, and simmer the mixture until the escarole is tender.

Remove the bay leaf. Purée the escarole mixture in a food mill or blender. (If you use a blender, fill the container only one-third full, and purée the mixture in several batches.) Return the purée to the saucepan, or pour it into a bowl.

In another saucepan, make a roux by melting the butter, adding the flour, and cooking the mixture for 2 minutes, stirring constantly until thoroughly blended. Add the escarole purée, and bring it to a boil, stirring constantly. Then reduce the heat to a simmer.

Beat the egg yolks together wth the heavy cream untl they are blended. Add ½ cup hot soup, a few drops at a time, to the yolks and cream. Add this mixture to the soup in the saucepan. Keep the soup at a simmer. (Do *not* let it boil.) Salt and pepper to taste.

Serve with a sprinkle of paprika and hot garlic croutons.

TO MAKE GARLIC CROUTONS:
> ¼ *cup olive oil*
> 2 *cloves garlic, peeled and cut in half*
> 1 *cup fresh bread cubes, crusts removed (about 4 slices)*

Heat the oil in a large skillet. Add the garlic pieces and sauté them until they are lightly browned. (Do not overcook garlic.) Remove and discard the garlic pieces. Add the bread cubes and sauté them until lightly browned, about 2 or 3 minutes on each side. Try using rye or pumpernickel bread cubes instead of white bread; they're unusually delicious.

FISH SOUP IN THE MEDITERRANEAN STYLE

FENNEL AND FISH   SERVES 8

TO PREPARE THE STOCK:
> 2 *pounds fish bones, washed well*
> 1 *medium-size onion, chopped*
>   *fine*
> 1 *carrot, sliced coarse*
> 1 *stalk celery, including leaves,*
>   *sliced coarse*

> 1 *bay leaf*
> 6 *peppercorns*
> 4 *cups water*
> 2 *cups dry white wine*
> 1½-*pound live lobster*

In a large saucepan, combine all the ingredients except the lobster. Cover the saucepan, and simmer the stock mixture for 30 minutes. Then add the lobster, cover, and boil hard for 10 to 15 minutes, or until the lobster has turned a bright red. Remove the lobster, and set it aside to cool. Strain the stock through a fine sieve, and discard the bones and cooked vegetables. Return the stock to the saucepan, and keep it warm on very low heat.

TO PREPARE THE SOUP:

½ *pound mussels, well brushed,*
beards removed
8 *very small littleneck clams*
¼ *cup dry white wine*
1 *tablespoon olive oil*
1 *clove garlic, minced fine*
½ *tablespoon saffron threads* (*see*
Note)
¼ *teaspoon thyme*

½ *teaspoon fennel seed*
1 *small chili pepper, chopped* (*or*
¼ *teaspoon dried red pepper*
flakes)
1 *tablespoon cornstarch*
1 *tablespoon Pernod*
1 *pound fish filets* (*preferably a*
combination such as flounder,
sole, and striped bass)

In a saucepan, combine the mussels, clams, wine, and 1 cup of warm stock. Cover the saucepan, and steam the shellfish (no more than 15 minutes). (If any clams or mussels refuse to open within that time, discard them.) Set aside the opened shellfish.

Remove the lobster meat from its shell and cut it into bite-size pieces (about 1 inch long; don't make the pieces any smaller).

In a small skillet, heat the oil, and add the garlic, saffron, thyme, fennel seed, and chili pepper. Cook this for 2 minutes, and set it aside.

Mix the cornstarch with ½ cup warm stock. Blend this well, and add it to the remaining stock in the saucepan.

Cut the filets into large pieces. (If the filets are small, cut them in half; if they are large, cut them into 3 or 4 pieces.) Add them to the stock, and cook them for about 5 minutes, or until they are flaky. (Do *not* overcook the filets; if you do, they will disintegrate.) Add the mixture of oil, garlic, and seasonings, lobster pieces, and Pernod.

Put an equal amount of mussels and clams into each of 8 large soup bowls. (Be sure to distribute their juices equally, too.) Ladle the soup over the mussels and clams, and serve while it is very hot.

Note: Do not substitute powdered saffron; we are never sure how much of the powder is saffron. For the real flavor, use threads.

Filberts

Cousins of the hazelnut, filberts come from all over the world. Mediterranean countries are the leading producers, but filberts are grown also in

California and in China. The name *filbert* comes from Saint Philbert, whose feast is celebrated on August 22, the time when many nut pickers start their harvest.

We learned about filberts at a very young age, for they were strung like pearls and featured at Italian feasts. In major American cities, where Italian feasts are still held, filberts on a string can be found for sale in every food stall.

Filberts should be stored in their husks in any container with a tight-fitting lid; kept in a cool, dry place, they will keep for months. When you are ready to use them, blanch them in boiling water, and rub them on a cloth to remove their reddish-brown skins. Filberts combine beautifully with chicken stock and cream in the recipe that follows. They also make a fantastic veal scallopini when sauced in hazelnut butter.

CREME ST. PHILBERT
(Cream of Filbert Soup)

FILBERTS AND CHICKEN   SERVES 4 TO 6

¼ pound butter
1 tablespoon all-purpose flour
6 cups Rich Chicken Stock (see page 49)

1 cup filberts, ground
½ cup heavy cream
¼ cup heavy cream, whipped
4 or 6 filberts, kept whole

In a saucepan, melt the butter, add the flour and cook over low heat for 2 minutes to make a roux. (A *roux* is a blend of butter and flour cooked together slowly over low heat. The slow cooking allows the starch in the flour to expand. After the butter and flour are blended, liquid is added gradually until the mixture is the thickness of heavy cream. Practically all sauces start with a roux, as do most thick soups.) Add the stock slowly; then add the ground filberts. Cook the stock mixture for an additional 15 minutes.

Remove the saucepan from the heat, and add the cream. Put the soup in a blender, and blend it until smooth.

Add a dollop of whipped cream, topped with a whole filbert to each serving of soup.

Peas

One of *Nonna's* market tests was the fingernail pea-pod press: She would hold a pea pod in her hand and press a cut into the pod with the fingernail of her thumb or index finger. If she didn't buy a pound or two of peas, it was because no moisture had appeared in the cut. But if the cut was moist, the peas were fresh and the sale was consummated. But *Nonna* would also simply pick up a pea pod, open it, and eat the peas to test for freshness. Because we frequently accompanied her on her shopping jaunts, we were often recipients of a pea or two, but it was *Nonna* who made the decision to buy or pass. (We honestly didn't know canned peas existed until we went to college.)

Pea pods should be smooth and shiny and free of wrinkles. Fresh pea pods have a bright and beautiful green color. By the way, 1 pound of unshelled peas is not a large quantity when it comes to the finished product; for 6 people, we may buy 3 pounds of unshelled peas.

Peas should be steamed or cooked in very little water. Better still, if you have very young fresh peas, cook them without water; in a small pan, melt 1 tablespoon butter, add 1 pound shelled peas, and cover them with several lettuce leaves (washed but *not* dried). Cover the pan, and cook slowly until the peas are tender. Add salt and pepper and more butter (if you wish).

Peas, like potatoes and carrots, are adaptable. They, too, can be creamed and puréed and combined with many other vegetables. One unusual combination is artichoke bottoms filled with peas. And, of course, there's pea soup. Here is our Cool, Green, Green Pea Soup.

COOL, GREEN, GREEN PEA SOUP

GREEN PEAS AND MINT   SERVES 6

1 teaspoon salt
2 cups fresh peas
3 cups Rich Chicken Stock (see
   page 49) (or 3 cups water
   and 4 chicken bouillon cubes)
1 teaspoon fresh mint, chopped
1 teaspoon fresh tarragon,
   chopped (or 1 teaspoon dried)

1 cup dry white wine
2 tablespoons butter, softened
1½ tablespoons all-purpose flour
1 cup heavy cream
   Salt
   Pepper, ground fresh
2 tablespoons fresh chives,
   chopped (or 1 teaspoon dried)

In a saucepan, bring a little water to a boil, and add the salt. (If you are going to use bouillon cubes and water, do not add salt to the cooking peas.) Add the peas, and cook them until tender, about 5 to 10 minutes. Drain the peas, and put them into a large mixing bowl. Add the stock, mint, and tarragon. Then purée this mixture in batches in a blender. Transfer each batch of purée to a large saucepan. Add the wine to the purée, and cook this mixture over moderate heat for 10 minutes, stirring frequently.

Meanwhile, combine the butter and flour on a small plate or in a cup, and blend them well. Add this to the hot soup, and slowly bring the soup to a boil. Reduce the heat, and simmer the soup until it thickens (5 to 10 minutes). (This soup may also be served hot. If that is your plan, add the cream after the soup has thickened, and heat it just to the boiling point.) Remove the saucepan from the heat, transfer its contents to a glass or ceramic bowl, and refrigerate the soup until cold.

Before serving, stir in the cream, and adjust the seasoning with salt and pepper. Sprinkle the soup with chopped chives.

POTAGE DE POIREAUX ET CAROTTES
(Leek and Carrot Soup)

LEEKS AND CARROTS   SERVES 6 TO 8

8 *large carrots*	1 *cup heavy cream*
5 *large leeks*	2 *tablespoons butter*
7 *cups Rich Chicken Stock (see*	*Salt*
page 49)	*Pepper, ground fresh*
2 *tablespoons fresh parsley,*	*Paprika*
chopped (or 1 teaspoon dried)	½ *cup sour cream*
1 *tablespoon fresh tarragon,*	
chopped (or ½ teaspoon dried)	

Wash the carrots well, using a brush to scrub them clean. (Do *not* scrape the carrots with a vegetable peeler.) Cut off both ends, and chop the carrots into ½-inch pieces.

Cut the leeks in half lengthwise, and wash them well under cool running water, spreading the leaves with your fingers as you do, to remove any sand. Then cut the leeks crosswise into ½-inch pieces. (You may use some of the tender light green part of the stalks.)

In a large saucepan, combine the stock, carrots, leeks, parsley, and tarragon. Bring this to a boil; then simmer the mixture for about 30 minutes, or until the carrots and leeks are tender.

Purée this mixture in a food mill or in batches in a blender. (Fill the blender no more than one-third full for each batch.) Return the vegetable purée to the saucepan. Add the cream, butter, and salt and pepper to taste, and reheat the soup *just* to boiling point.

Add a dash of paprika to each serving and/or ½-teaspoon sour cream.

A VARIATION: POTAGE PUREE DE CELERI
ET POIREAUX
(Cream of Celery and Leek Soup)

LEEKS AND CELERY   SERVES 6 TO 8

Substitute 1 large head celery, including the leaves, for the 8 carrots. Separate the stalks, wash them well, and cut them crosswise into ½-inch pieces. In place of the tarragon, use the same quantity of dill. Follow the remaining instructions in the basic recipe.

SOUPE À L'OIGNON BERNARD

ONIONS AND CHEESE   SERVES 6

4 *tablespoons unsalted butter*	1 *cup grated Gruyère cheese*
8 *medium-size white onions, sliced*	2 *tablespoons fresh parsley,*
thin	*chopped fine (or 1 teaspoon*
6 *cups Rich Beef Stock (see page*	*dried)*
46)	6 *pastry rounds (see Note)*
2 *tablespoons dry vermouth*	6 *scallions, sliced thin*

In a large skillet, melt the butter, and cook the onions over low heat, stirring often, until they are light brown. (Do not cook the onions over high heat; if you do, they will char.)

In a large saucepan, bring the stock to the boiling point, and add the cooked onions. Add the vermouth to the skillet in which the onions were cooked, and deglaze it over high heat, using a rubber spatula to scrape up all the bits in the skillet. Empty this liquid into the stock mixture.

Have 6 ovenproof soup bowls near your oven. Divide the cheese and parsley equally among the bowls; then fill the bowls with the mixture of stock and onions. Be sure the onions are equally distributed. Do *not* fill the bowls completely; leave about ½ inch of space at the top.

Place a pastry round over each bowl, stretching it as tightly as possible so that it overhangs the bowl by about ¾ inch. Make a piecrust edge (with a fork or whatever) and firm the pastry over the edge of the bowl. (The pastry will give somewhat, but if at all possible, it should not touch the soup. If it does, don't be overly concerned, but do work quickly in order to get the bowls into the oven.) Place the pastry-covered bowls in a preheated 375- to 400-degree oven, and bake them until crust is browned.

Garnish each bowl with 3 or 4 thin slices of scallion.

Note: A *pâté brisée* is an excellent choice here. A *pâté feuilletée* would be an elegant alternative.

PASTA E CECI

PASTA AND CHICKPEAS   SERVES 4

2 tablespoons butter
1 medium-size onion, sliced fine
½ teaspoon thyme
2 cloves garlic, chopped fine
4 fresh tomatoes, cored, blanched, peeled, and cut into 1-inch pieces (or 1-pound can plum tomatoes)
1 teaspoon salt
2 cups cooked pasta (elbows, small shells, or other small shape)

2 to 3 cups Rich Beef Stock (see page 46)
20-ounce can chickpeas
Pepper, ground fresh
6 tablespoons grated Parmesan cheese (or other Italian cheese such as Pecorino or Romano)

In a medium-size saucepan, melt the butter and add the onion and thyme. Cook for 4 to 5 minutes, or until the onion turns yellow. Then add the garlic, tomatoes, and salt, and bring the mixture to a boil. Reduce the heat, and simmer the tomatoes slowly for 15 minutes.

Meanwhile, cook the pasta according to the package directions, but be sure to remove pasta while it is still firm (*al dente*).

When tomatoes are cooked, add the stock, and cook for an additional 15 minutes. Add the cooked pasta and chickpeas, and season with pepper. Heat only until the pasta is warmed. (Do *not* overcook; if you do, the pasta will get mushy.) If the soup is too thick, add more stock to get the desired consistency. (We prefer this soup without too much liquid, but there's no reason why you can't make it soupier.)

Serve the soup, and pass the grated cheese in a small bowl. Encourage your diners to use some. Pasta e Ceci is no combination without it.

PASTA E PESTO SOUP

PASTA AND PESTO   SERVES 6

The pesto used in this soup is different from the classic pesto because it uses spinach instead of lots of basil. We think you'll like this pesto in combination with the pasta soup.

TO PREPARE THE SOUP:

1 tablespoon butter
1 onion, chopped
2 quarts Rich Beef Stock (see page 46)
1 tablespoon tomato paste

¼ pound vermicelli, broken into 2-inch pieces (or other fine noodles)
Salt
Pepper, ground fresh

In a large saucepan, melt the butter and sauté the onion for 4 to 5 minutes. Add the stock and tomato paste, and bring the mixture to a boil. Reduce the heat, and simmer it for 8 to 10 minutes. Add the vermicelli, and cook until it is *al dente* (about 6 to 8 minutes). While the vermicelli is cooking, make the pesto.

TO PREPARE THE PESTO:

4 tablespoons fresh basil, chopped
  (or 2 tablespoons dried)
2 cups fresh spinach leaves (or
  10-ounce package frozen)
3 cloves garlic, chopped coarse
4 tablespoons olive oil

2 tablespoons butter
¼ cup grated Parmesan cheese (or
  Pecorino)
½ cup pine nuts and almonds,
  skins removed

Put all these ingredients in a blender or food processor (if you use frozen spinach, thaw it first), and blend until smooth.

Season the soup and ladle it into 6 individual bowls. Then put an equal amount of pesto into each bowl. Serve immediately.

CREAM OF POTATO AND CARROT SOUP

POTATOES AND CREAM

SERVES 6

1 pound carrots
3 tablespoons butter
1 pound potatoes, peeled and
  cut into ½-inch cubes
2 medium-size onions, chopped
2 sprigs fresh thyme, chopped
  fine (or ½ teaspoon dried)
2 sprigs fresh parsley, chopped
  fine (or ½ teaspoon dried)

1½ quarts Rich Chicken Stock
  (see page 49)
½ cup dry vermouth
½ small dried chili pepper (or ⅛
  teaspoon red pepper flakes)
2 cups (approximately) light
  cream (or half-and-half)
Salt
Dash of paprika

Cut off both ends of the carrots, and wash the carrots, using a small scrub brush to get them clean. (If you prefer, use a vegetable peeler. But we think that's a waste of a good carrot.) If a carrot is blemished, cut out the bruise with a paring knife. Slice carrots as thinly as you can, but don't worry about uniform size because the carrots will be puréed.

In a large saucepan, melt the butter, and cook the carrots, potatoes, and onions for 5 minutes, stirring to distribute the butter over all the vegetables. Add the thyme, parsley, stock, vermouth, and chili pepper, and bring the mixture to a boil. Reduce the heat, and simmer the mixture for 30 minutes, or until potatoes and carrots are cooked. Remove the saucepan from the heat, and allow the mixture to cool for a few minutes. Purée the mixture in small batches in a blender. (Or if you prefer, use a food mill.) Add the cream to the purée, and blend well. (If you want a thicker soup, add less cream; if you want it thinner, add more. We prefer the consistency of this soup to be somewhat thicker than that of vichyssoise.) Add salt to taste, and reheat the soup just to boiling point.

Add a dash of paprika to each bowl of soup, and serve.

LENTIL SOUP WITH PROSCIUTTO

PROSCIUTTO AND LENTILS   SERVES 8 TO 12

1 pound dried lentils
6 tablespoons butter
⅓ pound piece prosciutto (a butt
   end is ideal)
2 medium-size onions, chopped
   coarse
2 carrots, sliced fine
1 clove garlic, chopped coarse

3 quarts (approximately)
   Rich Chicken Stock (see
   page 49)
½ teaspoon thyme
1 bay leaf
Salt
Pepper, ground fresh

Check the dried lentils carefully to remove any foreign matter such as tiny stones or pebbles. To do this, put the lentils in a colander (we prefer the flat type to the round type for this), and swirl the lentils around by hand. Then wash them several times by holding the colander under running water. (Be sure that each and every lentil is bathed.)

In a large saucepan, melt 2 tablespoons butter, and add the piece of prosciutto, onions, and carrots. Cook this mixture until the onion begins to turn golden. Then add the lentils, garlic, stock, thyme, and bay leaf, and bring the mixture to a boil. Reduce the heat, and simmer for 1 hour or longer, until the lentils are soft and millable.

Remove and discard the bay leaf. Remove the prosciutto, and cut it into tiny pieces (less than ½ inch square) or into the thinnest possible julienne strips (1½ inches long by 1/16 inch wide). Set this aside.

Purée the lentil mixture in a food mill. (We think this soup is especially elegant if put through a very fine sieve; that gives it a smooth, silky texture.) Return the puréed soup to the saucepan, add the prosciutto pieces, and bring this to the boil. Add the remaining 4 tablespoons butter. As soon as the butter is blended, adjust the seasoning. (Remember, the prosciutto is salty and peppery, so be sure to taste the soup *before* adding any extra salt or pepper.) Thin the soup to the desired consistency by adding more stock.

Serve immediately. A fresh green salad (with an oil and vinegar dressing) is a marvelous accompaniment to this soup. And homemade rye bread is bliss, too.

Haddock

Haddock is adaptable. Cover a filet of haddock with bread crumbs and herbs, and fry it. Stuff haddock with a forcemeat of mussels, oysters, or anchovies, and bake it with onions and mushrooms. Haddock appears in soufflés, quenelles, and bouillabaisses. And, of course, haddock is smoked.

Many fish from all over the world are called haddock, but the one we know by that name is of North Atlantic origin. Although it tastes a bit like cod, it has its own distinctive flavor. We especially like it in this good, tasty chowder, which we call A Good Fish Chowder.

A GOOD FISH CHOWDER

SALT PORK AND HADDOCK

SERVES 6

3 to 4 pounds haddock (see Note)
2 cups water
2 ounces salt pork, cut into ⅛-inch pieces
2 medium-size onions, diced
2 large potatoes, peeled and cut into ½-inch cubes

1 cup celery, including leaves, sliced thin
1 teaspoon salt
Pepper, ground fresh
4 cups milk
2 tablespoons butter

Ask your fishmonger to skin the fish; remove its backbone, head, viscera, and tail; filet the fish; and give everything but the viscera to you. Wash the fish, bones, and the rest in cool water. Cut the filets into 2- or 3-inch pieces, and set them aside. Chop or cut the backbone into 2- or 3-inch pieces, and put them in a saucepan; add the head, tail, and 2 cups water.

Bring this to a boil; then simmer it for 5 minutes. Drain the liquid, and set it aside. Discard the head, tail, and bones.

In a large saucepan, render the salt pork, and cook the pieces until crisp. Remove the salt pork pieces, and reserve them. Sauté the onions and potatoes in the hot salt pork fat, stirring frequently, until they begin to turn yellow (about 15 minutes). Then add the celery, salt, and pepper to taste.

Measure the reserved cooking liquid, and add boiling water to make 3 full cups of liquid. Add this to the potato mixture, and cook it for 15 minutes more, or until the potatoes are almost done. (Do *not* overcook the potato cubes.) Add the pieces of filet, milk and butter, and simmer the soup for an additional 5 to 10 minutes, or until the fish is flaky.

When you serve the chowder, sprinkle some diced salt pork into each individual bowl.

Note: If you can't get fresh haddock, use two 1-pound packages of frozen filets. Thaw the filets in 1 cup clam juice and 1 cup water, and bring them to a boil in this liquid. (Do *not* cook the filets any longer; they will cook further later on.) As soon as the liquid boils, remove the fish. Measure the cooking liquid, and add more water (if necessary) to make the 3 cups needed for this chowder, and follow the rest of the instructions.

SOUP IN THE CHINESE STYLE

SHRIMP AND EGG   SERVES 4

4 eggs	8 fresh shrimps (or frozen)
1 teaspoon sugar	1 teaspoon lemon juice
1 teaspoon salt	2 teaspoons soy sauce
3 tablespoons dry sherry	8 leaves fresh spinach
5½ cups Rich Chicken Stock, completely defatted (see page 49)	

Beat the eggs, and add the sugar, salt, sherry, and 1¼ cups stock. Put this mixture into the top part of a double boiler. Cover the egg mixture, and steam it over simmering water for approximately 15 minutes, or until it forms a custard. Set this custard aside.

Meanwhile, bring about 2 cups water (just enough to cover 8 shrimps) to a boil. (The best way to do this is to put the shrimps into a saucepan, cover them with water, remove them, and bring the water to a boil.) Add the lemon juice and shrimps, and cook until the shrimps turn pink (only a few minutes). (Do *not* overcook the shrimps; if you you do, they will shrivel and get tough.) Remove the shrimps from the liquid, and slice them in half lengthwise. (Do this by laying a shrimp on its side and running a sharp knife through it.) Put 4 shrimp halves into each of the 4 soup bowls.

Then bring the remaining 4¼ cups stock and soy sauce to a boil. While the stock is heating, stack the spinach leaves, and slice them into pieces ¼ inch wide. Add the spinach slices to the boiling stock, and cook them for 2 minutes.

Turn the custard out onto a platter, and cut it into 1-inch squares. Gently put 2 squares of custard into each soup bowl. Add the soup with the spinach leaves to the bowls, and serve.

SORREL SOUP

SORREL AND CHERVIL   SERVES 6

4 tablespoons butter	2 tablespoons cornstarch,
24 leaves sorrel, chopped fine	dissolved in ¼ cup water
3 tablespoons fresh chervil,	1½ cups milk, scalded
chopped fine (or 1 tablespoon	3 egg yolks
dried)	½ cup heavy cream
4 cups Rich Chicken Stock (see	Salt and pepper to taste
page 49)	

In a large saucepan, heat the butter, and sauté the sorrel leaves for 4 to 5 minutes. Add the chervil and stock, and bring the mixture to a boil. Then add the cornstarch mixture, and cook for 3 to 5 minutes, stirring constantly, until the soup thickens. Add the milk, stir the mixture well, and set it aside.

In a small bowl, combine the egg yolks and heavy cream, and beat them with a fork until well mixed. Add about 1 cup of the sorrel mixture to the yolks and cream, and quickly mix well. Add this to the contents of the saucepan, bring the soup just to the simmering point, season to taste, and serve it hot.

TOMATO AND CUCUMBER SOUP, COLD OR HOT

TOMATOES AND CUCUMBERS   SERVES 6 TO 8

3 tablespoons butter
1 small clove garlic, halved
2 medium-size onions, chopped
   coarse
3 tablespoons all-purpose flour
6 fresh tomatoes, skinned and
   chopped coarse (or 3 cups
   canned tomatoes)
3 cucumbers, peeled and chopped
   fine

3 cups Rich Chicken Stock (see
   page 49)
1 cup heavy cream
Salt
Pepper, ground fresh
6 leaves fresh basil, chopped fine
   (or 1 teaspoon dried)

In a saucepan large enough to hold all the ingredients, melt the butter, and cook the garlic pieces for 1 minute. Add the onions, and cook them over low to moderate heat, stirring frequently with a wooden spoon, and cook them until they are light brown. (Do *not* scorch the onions.) Add the flour, mix well, and cook 1 minute, stirring constantly.

Then add the tomatoes and cucumbers, and stir to blend all the ingredients. Add the stock, and simmer the mixture for 30 minutes.

Remove from the heat, and blend well in batches in a blender or food processor. (Do this a few cupfuls at a time, and pour each blended batch into a large bowl.) When all the mixture has been blended, add the cream and salt and pepper to taste. Refrigerate the soup until ice-cold. Or reheat the soup if it is to be served hot.

Serve the soup in a large bowl or in individual bowls and garnish it with a sprinkle of the fresh basil.

Note: Do try to use freshly ground pepper (rather than the ready-ground kind); it will give this soup an extra kick.

ZUPPA DI PISELLI E POMODORI
(A Soup of Peas and Tomatoes)

TOMATOES AND PEAS   SERVES 6

2 tablespoons butter

2 tablespoons olive oil

½-pound piece of prosciutto (see Note)

1 cup onions, chopped coarse

1 carrot, sliced thin

1 clove garlic, minced

2 sprigs fresh thyme, chopped fine (or 1 teaspoon dried)

2 cups fresh tomatoes, cored, blanched, peeled, and chopped coarse (or canned plum tomatoes)

4 cups Rich Chicken Stock (see page 49) (or Rich Veal Stock, see page 48)

2 cups fresh peas (or frozen)

Pepper, ground fresh (optional)

In a large saucepan, heat the butter and olive oil. Add the whole piece of prosciutto (or its equivalent), and brown it over medium heat (about 10 minutes). Add the onions and carrots, and brown them, too (another 10 minutes). Add the garlic, thyme, tomatoes, and stock, and simmer the soup for 30 minutes. (Maintain the simmer; this mixture should not be cooked at a raging boil.) Add the peas, and continue to cook the soup only until the peas are tender (5 to 10 minutes).

Because prosciutto and other ham products are salty, no additional salt has been suggested here; but add some if it suits you. In any case, you may want to add a dash of freshly ground black pepper.

Remove the meat, and cut it into ½-inch squares. Return the bits of prosciutto (or other ham) to the soup, and mix them with other ingredients. Now the soup is ready to be served.

Note: Some Italian delicatessens sell end pieces of prosciutto. They are ideal for this soup, and they cost less. A piece of Smithfield or country ham about ½ pound in weight will work well also. In a pinch, boiled ham will be all right.

WATERCRESS AND POTATO SOUP

3 cups potatoes, peeled, and cut into ½-inch pieces	*4 tablespoons butter*
3 cups Rich Veal Stock (see page 48) (or Rich Chicken Stock, see page 49, or 1½ cups of each)	*1½ cups milk, scalded*
	4 egg yolks
	1 cup heavy cream
	Salt and fresh-ground pepper to taste
3 bunches fresh watercress	

In a saucepan, combine the potatoes and stock, and boil the potatoes until they are cooked (about 20 minutes). (Cover the saucepan to keep the stock from boiling away.)

Wash the watercress; then spin it dry, or pat the leaves with a tea towel. Set aside 8 small branches to be used as a garnish. Chop the remaining watercress coarse, including the stems. Set aside one-third of the chopped watercress. In another saucepan, melt the butter, and add the remaining two-thirds of the watercress. Cover the saucepan, and cook the watercress for about 12 minutes, or until tender.

Combine the potatoes and stock with the cooked watercress, and purée the mixture in a blender or in a heavy-duty mixer (using a wire whip). (You can also use a food processor; if you do, follow the manufacturer's directions for blending cooked vegetables.)

Put the purée in a saucepan, add the milk, and mix well. Combine the egg yolks and cream in a small bowl, and mix well with a fork. Add this to the purée. Add salt and pepper to taste. If the soup is too thick for your taste, thin it by adding more milk or cream. Adjust the seasoning.

Divide the uncooked chopped watercress equally among 8 bowls. Pour soup into each bowl, and garnish it with 1 small branch of watercress.

The hot soup and the raw crunchy, chopped watercress make an interesting combination.

SOUPE AUX HARICOTS BLANCS

WHITE BEANS AND CELERY   SERVES 6

6 tablespoons butter
1 tablespoon olive oil
4 stalks celery, including leaves,
   sliced thin
2 carrots, sliced thin
1 small onion, sliced thin
8 cups Rich Chicken Stock (see
   page 49)
2 cups dried white beans, cooked
6 slices French bread, 1 inch
   thick, oven-toasted

1 cup Emmental cheese (or
   Gruyère or Parmesan cheese),
   grated
Salt
Pepper, ground fresh
1½ tablespoons fresh parsley,
   chopped fine (or 2 teaspoons
   dried)
1½ tablespoons fresh chives,
   chopped fine (or 2 teaspoons
   frozen)

In a large saucepan, heat 3 tablespoons butter and the oil. Add the celery, carrots, and onion, and stir the vegetables with a wooden spoon to coat them with the butter and oil. Cover the saucepan, and cook the vegetables for about 10 minutes, stirring frequently so that you don't burn the vegetables, particularly the onions.

Add the stock, and cook the mixture, covered, for about 30 minutes over medium heat, or until the vegetables are tender. Add the cooked beans, and simmer the soup for several minutes more. Add salt and pepper to taste. (Freshly ground pepper is a *must* with this soup.)

Butter each slice of bread, using ½ tablespoon of the remaining butter for each. Arrange grated cheese on each slice of bread. Place 1 slice of bread in each soup bowl, and pour the hot soup over it. Mix the parsley and chives, and sprinkle ½ tablespoon of the herbs over each serving.

WHITE NAVY BEAN SOUP IN THE ITALIAN STYLE

WHITE BEANS AND LEEKS   SERVES 8

3 cups leeks
1 cup celery stalks, including
  leaves, sliced
6 tablespoons butter
2 quarts Rich Beef Stock (see page
  46) (or Rich Veal Stock, see
  page 48)
1 teaspoon dried oregano
5 cups cannellini beans (2 20-ounce
  cans), drained (or white navy
  beans soaked overnight and
  cooked until tender)

Salt
Pepper, ground fresh
1 cup light cream (optional)
4 tablespoons fresh parsley,
  chopped
4 teaspoons grated Parmesan
  cheese

Cut the leeks in half lengthwise, and wash them well, separating the leaves with your fingers as you rinse them under cool running water, to remove any sand. Drain the leeks, and cut them crosswise into thin slices.

In a large saucepan, melt the butter, and sauté the leeks and celery until they are tender (5 to 10 minutes), stirring frequently so that they do not brown. Add the stock and oregano, and heat the mixture just to the boiling point. Reduce the heat, and simmer until the leeks and celery pieces are almost cooked (5 to 10 minutes). Add the cannellini beans (or precooked navy beans), and salt and pepper to taste, and cook only until the beans are heated through.

If you wish, you can purée this soup by processing it through a fine sieve or food mill or in a blender (in batches). Then return the puréed mixture to the saucepan, add the cream and reheat. (Use more cream and/or stock to obtain the desired thickness.)

Fill the soup bowls, garnish the soup with the chopped parsley and grated Parmesan cheese, and serve it very hot.

MUSSEL SOUP IN THE ITALIAN STYLE

WHITE WINE AND MUSSELS   SERVES 6

4 pounds fresh mussels
4 tablespoons olive oil
2 cloves garlic, halved
1 cup dry white wine
2 tablespoons butter
1 large onion, chopped
2 stalks celery, including leaves,
  sliced fine
2 sprigs fresh parsley, chopped (or
  1 teaspoon dried)

1 cup tomato purée
1 teaspoon oregano
1 quart Rich Fish Stock, including
  liquid from mussels (see page
  50) (or clam broth)
Salt
Pepper, ground fresh

Wash and scrub the mussels thoroughly. (A small, hard-bristled brush is helpful for this.) Remove the "beards" by pulling them out, and soak the mussels for about 30 minutes in enough salted water to cover them. (Some mussels contain sand, and soaking helps to rid them of it.)

In a large saucepan with a tight-fitting cover, combine the cleaned mussels, oil, garlic, and wine. Cover the pan and boil the mussels for 5 minutes, or until most (or all) of the shells are opened. Transfer the opened mussels to a large bowl or another saucepan, and set them aside. (There are two schools of thought about mussels that don't open when steamed: Discard them, or pry them open with a knife. We suggest you toss out the unopened ones. The knife process is risky and can cause cuts; it is also time-consuming.) Strain the cooking liquid through a sieve lined with several layers of cheesecloth to be sure you remove any remaining sand, and measure it by the cup.

In another saucepan, melt the butter, and sauté the onion, celery, and parsley until the onion turns golden. Add the tomato purée and oregano. Add the stock (or clam broth) to the strained mussel liquid to make 1 quart of liquid; add this to the vegetables and tomatoes. Simmer this broth for 5 minutes. Then add the opened mussels, still in their shells, and cook another 2 to 3 minutes until the soup is piping hot. Add salt and pepper to taste.

Serve Mussel Soup in the Italian Style in large bowls with lots of crusty Italian bread.

ZUCCHINI AND CORN SOUP

ZUCCHINI AND CORN   SERVES 6

4 *ears fresh corn (or 1 cup frozen*
  or canned corn)
2 *tablespoons olive oil*
4 *tablespoons butter*
1 *large onion, chopped fine*
2 *cloves garlic, chopped fine*
4 *fresh tomatoes, peeled, and*
  chopped fine (or 2 cups canned
  plum tomatoes)
4 *cups very thin zucchini, unpeeled,*
  cut into 1-inch slices (see Note)

4 *cups Rich Beef Stock (see page*
  46)
3 *tablespoons fresh basil, chopped*
  fine (or 1 tablespoon dried)
1 *small dried hot chili pepper (or*
  ½ teaspoon red pepper flakes)
Salt
3 *tablespoons grated Parmesan*
  cheese

Shuck the corn, and drop the cobs into boiling salted water; cook them for 7 minutes. Remove the corn cobs from the water, and cool them. Then cut the kernels off the cobs, and set them aside.

In a large saucepan, heat the oil and butter, and add the onion and cook slowly until the onion is softened and begins to turn light brown. Add the garlic, and continue to cook 2 minutes, stirring frequently.

Add the tomatoes, zucchini, stock, basil, and chili pepper, and simmer this mixture until the zucchini slices are tender. (Use a fork or a slotted spoon to take out a piece and test it for doneness. Do *not* overcook zucchini; we think it tastes best undercooked, probably because we prefer the *al dente* texture.) Just before the zucchini is done, add the corn. Taste, and adjust the salt. (Do *not* add black pepper; the chili pepper will produce quite a bite by itself.)

Serve the soup in individual bowls or a large tureen. Sprinkle ½ tablespoon Parmesan cheese over each bowl, or sprinkle all the cheese over the soup in the tureen. Zucchini and Corn Soup is especially good in combination with hot, buttery corn sticks or corn bread.

Note: If the zucchini are large, slice off the ends, cut the zucchini in half lengthwise, and cut each half in half lengthwise again. You now have quarters of zucchini in long strips. Cut out seeds by running a paring knife down the length of each strip (as if you were removing the meat from a slice of canteloupe, but not cutting as close to the skin). Cut the seeded zucchini strips into 1-inch pieces.

MINESTRONE SOUP IN THE FAMILY STYLE

ZUCCHINI AND LIMA BEANS   SERVES 8 TO 10

TO PREPARE THE BREAD BALLS:

1 cup bread crumbs

¼ cup plus 2 tablespoons grated
Parmesan cheese (see Note)

1 tablespoon fresh parsley,
chopped fine (or 1 teaspoon
dried)

1 teaspoon dried oregano

1 egg, lightly beaten

¼ cup milk

Salt

Pepper, ground fresh

Mix all these ingredients in a medium-size bowl; when they are well
blended, make tiny balls (no larger than 1 inch in diameter). (You
should have about 20 of these tiny bread balls.) Set the bread balls aside
until you are ready to add them to soup.

TO PREPARE THE SOUP:

3 tablespoons olive oil

2 tablespoons butter

2 small potatoes, peeled, and
chopped into ½-inch cubes (or
smaller)

2 cloves garlic, chopped fine

2 medium-size onions, chopped
fine

4 large tomatoes, cored, blanched,
peeled, and diced (or 2 cups
canned plum tomatoes)

6 cups Rich Beef Stock (see page
46)

3 small zucchini, unpeeled and
sliced thin (about 2 cups)

2 cups fresh peas, shelled (or
10-ounce package frozen)

2 cups fresh lima beans, shelled
(or 10-ounce package frozen)

4 stalks celery, including leaves,
sliced fine

2 carrots, sliced thin

2 fresh cherry peppers (or 1 dried
chili pepper)

2 tablespoons fresh basil (or
1 teaspoon dried)

2 tablespoons fresh parsley (or
1 teaspoon dried)

Salt

Pepper, ground fresh

Grated Parmesan cheese

In a deep saucepan (large enough to hold all the ingredients), heat the
olive oil and butter. Add the potato cubes, and cook them for 5 minutes. Then add the garlic and onions, and cook the mixture 2 minutes
longer.

Add the tomatoes, stock, zucchini, fresh peas, fresh lima beans, celery, carrots, cherry peppers (or chili pepper), basil, and parsley. Cover the saucepan, and cook the stock and vegetables over low heat, stirring frequently, for 40 minutes, or until the lima beans are tender. (If you use frozen limas and peas, add them 20 minutes after you add the other vegetables.) Do *not* overcook the vegetables; they should be *al dente*. About 10 minutes before the vegetables have finished cooking, add the bread balls.

The tomatoes and zucchini will release a good amount of liquid, so the 6 cups of stock should provide enough liquid. However, if you prefer a thinner soup, add more stock to achieve the desired consistency. Add salt to taste, and use pepper freshly ground from a mill, an important complement to the various fresh vegetables in this soup.

Put some grated Parmesan cheese in a bowl, and encourage people to help themselves. A tablespoon of Parmesan cheese added to this soup makes a tasty combination.

Note: If you prefer, you can flavor the bread balls with ¼ cup finely diced ham or with 3 slices bacon, fried crisp and crumbled.

ZUCCHINI SOUP IN THE COUNTRY STYLE

ZUCCHINI AND ONIONS   SERVES 6

3 tablespoons olive oil
1 clove garlic, halved
3 medium-size potatoes, peeled and cut into ½-inch cubes
1 onion, sliced thin
2 stalks celery, cut into ½-inch pieces
2 tablespoons fresh parsley (preferably flat Italian type), or 1 teaspoon dried)
1 teaspoon oregano
6 cups Rich Beef Stock (see page 46)

1 large fresh tomato, cored, blanched, peeled, and cut into ½-inch chunks (or ½ cup canned plum tomatoes)
1 pound small zucchini, washed, unpeeled, and cut into ¼-inch slices
2 teaspoons salt
Pepper, ground fresh
6 teaspoons grated Parmesan cheese

In a large saucepan, heat the oil and brown the garlic halves; then discard the garlic. Add the potatoes, stir to coat them with the oil, and cook them for about 5 minutes. Add the onion, celery, parsley, and oregano, and cook this mixture until the onions are softened or turn yellow.

Add the stock, tomatoes, zucchini slices, and salt, and bring the soup to a boil. Reduce the heat, and simmer the soup until the zucchini slices are tender. (Do *not* overcook the zucchini slices; they should be *al dente.*)

Pour the soup into individual bowls and sprinkle freshly ground pepper and 1 teaspoon Parmesan cheese over each serving. If you are serving the soup in a tureen, sprinkle pepper and all the Parmesan cheese over it. Serve hot.

THE SAUCES

Sauces, which can take hours to prepare, are capable of taking all the fun out of cooking for family and friends. Because the preparation of sauces is time-consuming, it can be the major problem when you are pulling together a meal. In years past, we've been known to exclaim, "Well, that's the last dinner for twelve people this year!"—and that time of year was March or April.

The answer to this problem—and the way to restore happiness to your cooking hours—is to make sauce bases in quantity and freeze them in small packages for future use. This is the way large, efficient restaurants do it. Don't think for a moment that the sauce chef concocts a sauce every time one is needed; he or she may pull a sauce together just before serving it, but usually any variety of sauce can be made quickly if the sauce base (the *mother sauce*) has been made ahead of time.

And so this is the way to handle sauce preparation at home. For example, from the mother sauce known as *espagnole*, or *brown sauce*, come other sauces such as *poivrade*, *Périgourdine*, or *Bordelaise*. Madeira sauce also is made from a concentrated sauce espagnole by adding to it Madeira, stock, butter, and other ingredients. The mother sauce for white sauces is called *velouté*. It is made from a roux (butter and flour) that is cooked long enough to eliminate its raw-flour taste but not long enough to lose its white color. The liquid is a white stock of chicken, veal, or fish. If milk is used, the sauce becomes a *béchamel*. If the velouté is reduced until it is really thick and heavy cream is added to give it the desired consistency, it becomes a *sauce sûprème*. Another basic is tomato sauce, and from it comes many other sauces, too. Then there are egg yolk and butter sauces, the best known of which is probably *hollandaise*.

In this chapter we've included some of the sauces you'll need as you prepare various combinations of food presented in this book. Although many of them appear in other cookbooks and there are classic recipes for them, we have improvised when we felt it necessary to add a special touch here or there. Of course, there simply isn't room to include all sauces, but we want to mention a few unusual ones. *Agrodolce* is an Italian sweet-and-sour sauce usually not found in Italian restaurants in this country. It is served with rabbit, hare, and braised meats. *Agradolce* is made from the juices of the cooked meat, brown sugar, vinegar, capers, raisins (or sometimes currants), chocolate (yes, *chocolate*), and crystallized orange, lemon, or grapefruit peel. Pine nuts or almonds may also be added. *Gribiche* is made of oil, vinegar, hard-boiled egg yolks, salt, pepper, capers, and chopped gherkins. It is usually served with fish and shellfish. A famous sauce used with game is *grand veneur*. This is a venison gravy mixed with a poivrade sauce and combined with red currant jelly and cream.

It is a pleasure to reach into the freezer and pull out 1 cup of brown sauce or 2 cups of all-purpose velouté. From the former, it is easy to whisk up a sauce Madeira, or from the latter, a Sauce Sûprème. Double, triple, or quadruple our recipes for Brown Sauce and Velouté Sauce, and freeze them by cupfuls or in even smaller amounts. You won't regret it.

BROWN SAUCE

BEEF STOCK AND HAM

MAKES ABOUT 8 CUPS

8 tablespoons butter

¾ pound Danish canned ham, cut into small cubes (or American boneless boiled ham) (see Note)

½ pound fresh mushrooms, chopped fine

2 carrots, scraped and sliced thin

2 onions, sliced thin

1 teaspoon dried thyme

½ cup all-purpose flour

8 cups Beef Stock (see page 46)

1 bay leaf

½ cup tomato purée

½ cup dry red wine

Salt

Pepper, ground fresh

4 teaspoons butter (optional)

4 teaspoons all-purpose flour (optional)

In a large saucepan, melt the butter, and add the ham, mushrooms, carrots, onions, and thyme. Cook over medium heat, stirring frequently, until the ingredients are almost dry and starting to brown.

Sprinkle this mixture with the flour, and cook, stirring constantly, until the flour starts to darken. Add the stock, stirring rapidly with a wire whisk. When the mixture is thickened and smooth, add the bay leaf. Cover the saucepan, and cook, stirring occasionally, for about 1 hour.

Add the tomato purée, wine, and salt and pepper to taste. Cook, covered, for 45 minutes longer, stirring occasionally. Then strain the sauce.

For a thicker sauce, blend 4 teaspoons butter with 4 teaspoons flour, and add it, bit by bit, stirring with the whisk, until the sauce reaches the consistency you want.

Leftover Brown Sauce freezes well.

Note: Kentucky or Virginia ham can also be used in this sauce, but reduce the amount to ½ pound.

ROUILLE

Traditionally, rouille is made with a mortar and pestle and we hope you'll work the rouille this way; however, you can achieve a sauce in a blender.

8 cloves garlic, chopped fine
2 teaspoons red pepper flakes,
  cut fine (or dried chili peppers)
1 teaspoon salt

1 cup bread crumbs, soaked in ½
  cup water and squeezed dry
  (see Note)
½ cup olive oil

If you are using a mortar and pestle, work the garlic pieces, the red pepper flakes or chili pepper pieces, and the salt into a paste. Then work in the bread crumbs and combine them until they are thoroughly mixed. Add the olive oil, a tablespoonful at a time, until you achieve a smooth paste.

If you are using a blender, combine the garlic pieces, pepper flakes, salt, and bread crumbs in the blender. Blend for only a few seconds, check that the mixture is smooth enough, and then add the oil, a tablespoonful at a time.

Sieve the rouille before serving.

Note: Italian and French bread have more body than American sliced bread. Although we prefer you use fresh Italian or French bread, we'd rather you use stale bread of this type than the white sliced bread. You can make the crumbs in a blender. If you don't have a blender, cut or tear the bread in pieces.

A VARIATION:

We have improvised with our rouille making and find the following *pas mal:* To two cups of aioli sauce, add 2 teaspoons of red pepper flakes (or dried chili peppers, crushed fine) and ½ teaspoon saffron powder. (Because red pepper flakes are extremely fiery, you may want to start with one teaspoon of pepper flakes and add all or part of the second teaspoonful as you desire.)

HOLLANDAISE SAUCE

BUTTER AND EGG YOLKS   MAKES ABOUT 1½ CUPS

2 tablespoons white vinegar   5 or 6 egg yolks, depending on size
4 tablespoons water   of eggs
1 teaspoon salt   1 cup melted butter
1 teaspoon white pepper, ground   Juice from ½ lemon
   fine   (approximately 1 tablespoon)

In the top pan of a double boiler, combine the vinegar, water, salt, and pepper. Over *direct* high heat (it's all right here to have the water in the bottom pan at a fast boil), reduce the vinegar and water mixture by half, keeping the pan uncovered.

Remove the top pan from the heat, add the yolks to it, and whisk immediately. Set the top over, but somewhat out of, the bottom of the double boiler, so that the boiling water is not against the base of the top pan. The object here is to produce thickened egg yolks, not cooked eggs. When the yolks are well mixed and somewhat thickened, take the top pan off the heat.

Gradually add the butter, whisking constantly, until the sauce is as thick as you wish it to be. Test for seasoning and add more salt if needed. Add the lemon juice, a few drops at a time, and check sauce for its lemon taste.

To keep hollandaise warm while you are putting the finishing touches to other things, put the top of the double boiler containing the sauce in a pan of warm water. (Do *not* keep the top pan over the bottom of the double boiler unless you discard the hot water and replace it with lukewarm water.)

If the hollandaise is too thick, just whisk in a teaspoonful or tablespoonful of hot water (or more if necessary), to obtain consistency you want. If the sauce is too thin, put a teaspoonful of water in a dry, warm bowl. Add a tablespoon of the thin sauce and beat hard with a wire whisk. Add another spoon of sauce and beat. Repeat this until all the thin sauce has been incorporated. If there is separation of the sauce (and we recognize that this can happen), add a teaspoon or a tablespoon of *hot* water and whisk the sauce until it is smooth.

A BUTTER AND CREAM SAUCE

BUTTER AND CREAM   MAKES ABOUT 2 CUPS

1 cup dry white wine (or ¾ cup   2 cups heavy cream
dry vermouth mixed with ¼   1 cup butter (2 sticks), softened
cup water)   Salt
¼ cup champagne vinegar (or   Pepper, ground fresh
white vinegar)   Few drops fresh lemon juice
½ cup shallots, chopped fine

In a medium-size saucepan, combine the wine (or vermouth), vinegar, and shallots. Boil this mixture vigorously over high heat for about 5 to 10 minutes until only about 1 teaspoon of the liquid is left. (Do *not* scorch the shallots). Then add the heavy cream, and again boil the sauce vigorously until it is thick enough to coat a spoon (8 to 10 minutes).

Take the pan off the heat, and add the butter, little by little, and keep working the butter into the sauce until it is completely absorbed. Season with salt and pepper to taste, and add those few drops of lemon juice to finish it off.

The French call this delicious sauce *beurre blanc*. Serve it with poached or baked fish, steamed broccoli, or baked zucchini lengths. A great combination is 2 tablespoons of this sauce with a baked potato.

MOUSSELINE SAUCE

HEAVY CREAM AND HOLLANDAISE SAUCE

3 parts Hollandaise Sauce, warm (see page 95)
1 part whipped heavy cream, cold

Keep the whipped cream in the refrigerator until you are ready to use it. Combine the two ingredients just before you are ready to use or serve the sauce. You can make any quantity you need, but keep the 3-to-1 proportions. For example, use ¾ cup hollandaise to ¼ cup whipped cream, 1 cup hollandaise to ⅓ cup whipped cream, 1½ cups hollandaise to ½ cup whipped cream, and 3 cups hollandaise to 1 cup whipped cream.

BEARNAISE SAUCE

2 tablespoons dry white wine (or dry vermouth)
2 tablespoons tarragon vinegar (or white vinegar)
⅓ cup fresh shallots, chopped fine

1 cup Hollandaise Sauce (see page 95)
1 tablespoon fresh tarragon, chopped fine (or 1 teaspoon dried)

In a small saucepan, combine the wine, vinegar, and shallots. Cook this mixture over medium heat until all but 1 teaspoon of the liquid (approximately) has evaporated. (Be careful not to cook away all the liquid and burn the pan. This *has* happened to us, usually when we've walked away to work on something else.)

Stir this cooked-down mixture into the hollandaise sauce; then stir in the fresh tarragon. (If you use the dried tarragon, put it in the palm of one hand; then rub both hands over the bowl or pan containing the hollandaise sauce. This crushes the dried herb and seems to release more flavor.)

CHORON SAUCE

2 tablespoons butter
1 fresh tomato, blanched, cored, peeled, seeded, and cut into ½-inch cubes
1 tablespoon tomato paste, fresh (or canned)
1 cup Béarnaise Sauce (see above)

In a small skillet, melt the butter, add the tomatoes and tomato paste, and cook this mixture for about 5 minutes, making sure that it reaches a boil. Combine the tomato mixture with the Béarnaise.

VELOUTE SAUCE

CHICKEN STOCK AND BUTTER   MAKES ABOUT 2½ CUPS

> *4 tablespoons butter*
> *½ cup all-purpose flour*
> *3 cups Rich Chicken Stock, scalded (see page 49)*
> *(or Rich Veal Stock, see page 48)*

In a medium-size pan, melt the butter, and add the flour to it. Stir and blend with a wire whisk or wooden spoon, and cook over medium heat for about 2 minutes. Slowly add the scalded stock, and keep whisking. Allow the sauce to simmer for about 20 minutes.

CURRY SAUCE

CURRY AND VEGETABLES   MAKES 2 TO 2½ CUPS

> *6 tablespoons butter*
> *1 clove garlic, chopped fine*
> *1 celery stalk, chopped fine*
> *1 small carrot, chopped fine*
> *1 medium-size onion, chopped*
> *fine*
> *3 tablespoons all-purpose flour*
> *3 tablespoons curry*
> *3 sprigs fresh thyme (or ½*
> *teaspoon dried)*
>
> *3 sprigs fresh parsley (or ½*
> *teaspoon dried)*
> *2½ cups Rich Chicken Stock*
> *(see page 49)*
> *1 teaspoon fresh lemon juice*
> *Salt*
> *Pepper, ground fresh*

In a large skillet, melt 4 tablespoons butter, and cook the garlic, celery, carrot, and onion, stirring frequently, until the onion begins to change color. Sprinkle the flour over the vegetables, stir well, and cook over medium heat for about 5 minutes.

Add the curry, thyme, and parsley; then add the stock, and stir to blend all the ingredients. Bring this mixture to a boil, lower the heat, cover the skillet, and allow the mixture to simmer for 25 to 30 minutes, or until the vegetables are well cooked. Check the mixture several times while it is cooking, and stir it well.

Put this mixture through a fine sieve, and press the vegetables against the sieve with the back of a large spoon or with a pestle to extract as much juice as you can from them. (You can also put the mixture in a blender, but the texture is better if you sieve it.) Add the remaining 2 tablespoons butter, 1 teaspoon lemon juice, and salt and pepper to taste.

WHITE WINE SAUCE

FISH STOCK AND CREAM   MAKES ABOUT 3 CUPS

½ cup mushrooms, chopped (see
  Note 1)
1 teaspoon shallots (or onions),
  chopped fine
6 tablespoons butter
¼ cup all-purpose flour
1 tablespoon lemon juice

½ cup dry white wine
3 cups Rich Fish Stock (see page
  50) (see Note 2)
1 cup heavy cream
Salt
Few drops lemon juice

In a medium-size saucepan, combine the mushrooms, shallots (or onions), 1 tablespoon butter, lemon juice, and wine, and bring this mixture to a boil. Reduce the heat, and simmer until almost all the liquid has evaporated (about 10 minutes).

Add 3 tablespoons butter and the flour, and combine these thoroughly with the other ingredients. Then add the stock, and cook the sauce until it is well blended and thickened. Add the cream, and cook the sauce until it is reduced by one-fourth.

Add the remaining 2 tablespoons butter and salt to taste. A few drops more of lemon juice adds the final touch to this sauce.

Note 1: This is an excellent time to use those trimmed stem ends you've been keeping in the freezer.

Note 2: In preparing this sauce, use the fish stock if the sauce is to be used for fish and shellfish dishes. But use Rich Chicken Stock (page 49) or Rich Veal Stock (page 48) for their appropriate recipes (e.g., use chicken or veal stock to prepare the white wine sauce called for in Veal Birds in White Wine, page 277.)

BECHAMEL SAUCE

FLOUR AND MILK   MAKES ABOUT 2 CUPS

2 tablespoons butter   *Pinch of salt*
4 tablespoons all-purpose flour   *Pepper, ground fresh*
2 cups milk, warmed
1 bouquet garni: 1 bay leaf,
  1 celery stalk, 1 sprig parsley,
  1 piece carrot, ¼ onion

In a medium-size saucepan, melt the butter. Add the flour, and stir with a wire whisk until the butter and flour are blended and smooth. Cook over low heat for about 2 minutes. Then slowly add the warm milk, and continue stirring until blended. Add the bouquet garni, and cook over low heat for about 15 minutes.

Put the sauce through a fine strainer, and season to taste with salt and pepper.

MORNAY SAUCE

SWISS CHEESE AND BÉCHAMEL SAUCE   MAKES ABOUT 2½ CUPS

2 cups Béchamel Sauce (see above)
4 egg yolks, lightly beaten
½ cup Swiss cheese, grated or cut into tiny pieces

In a saucepan, combine all the ingredients, and cook the sauce over a low heat, stirring constantly with a wire whisk. (As the sauce heats, the cheese will melt, of course, so it's important to keep the wire whisk moving.) When the cheese is thoroughly blended and the sauce is smooth, continue to cook the mixture only until it is hot enough for your purpose. Then remove the saucepan from the heat, and serve the sauce.

AIOLI

GARLIC AND OLIVE OIL   MAKES ABOUT 1 CUP

Aioli is a very thick sauce, almost a solid mass; we think it is heavier than mayonnaise, which it resembles. Because its foundation is of garlic and olive oil, it is basically in the style of Provence. One could almost call it *Friday sauce*, because in the south of France it is made religiously every Friday and served with eggs, carrots, potatoes, and many kinds of fish.

6 cloves garlic	*1 teaspoon lemon juice*
2 small egg yolks	*Salt*
1 cup (approximately) olive oil	*Pepper, ground fresh*

Crush the garlic in a mortar and pestle, making it as smooth as possible. (This can also be done in a blender, but the sauce will be tastier if you use a mortar and pestle.) Add the egg yolks, and combine these two ingredients completely. Then add the olive oil, a drop at a time (more or less), and lemon juice, a couple of drops at a time, until all the oil and lemon juice have been added and the sauce has thickened. Season with salt and pepper. (You should end up with a sunshiny "mayonnaise," redolent of garlic.)

We can think of many uses for this fabulous sauce. For example, drop a spoonful in soup or a dollop on broiled fish filets, or mix some into potato salad in place of regular mayonnaise.

BARBECUE SAUCE

GINGER AND GARLIC   MAKES ABOUT 2 CUPS

2 cloves garlic, chopped fine
2 tablespoons fresh ginger, peeled and chopped fine
1 cup soy sauce
½ cup dry sherry
½ cup catsup

Combine all these ingredients, and mix them well. Coat the meat (spareribs, roast pork, and so on) liberally with the sauce, and allow it to marinate for several hours.

Baste the meat frequently as it grills or broils, making sure to coat it on all sides.

HORSERADISH CREAM SAUCE

HORSERADISH AND CREAM   MAKES ABOUT 1 CUP

½ cup heavy cream, whipped   2 tablespoons fresh lemon juice
2 tablespoons horseradish, grated   ½ teaspoon fresh mint, chopped
2 tablespoons mayonnaise   (or healthy pinch of dried
1 teaspoon dry mustard   mint)

Combine all these ingredients by folding them into the whipped cream one at a time. Continue to fold the mixture until it is well blended.

SAUCE BATARDE

LEMON AND EGG YOLKS   MAKES ABOUT 2 CUPS

10½ tablespoons butter, softened   2 egg yolks
2½ tablespoons all-purpose flour   4 tablespoons heavy cream
1 cup water, almost boiling   2 tablespoons lemon juice
1 cup milk, scalded   Salt and pepper

In a saucepan, melt 2½ tablespoons butter over moderate heat; add the flour, and blend well.

In another saucepan, mix the water and milk, and keep this mixture at the boiling point. Pour it slowly into the flour mixture. Keep stirring until the two are blended, and cook over low heat until the sauce thickens (about 5 minutes). (Be sure to stir the sauce constantly.)

Blend the egg yolks and heavy cream, and add about ¼ cup thickened sauce. Then blend this mixture with the sauce remaining in the saucepan, and heat the mixture. (But do *not* let it boil.)

Add 2 tablespoons lemon juice and salt and pepper to taste. Finally, add 8 tablespoons butter, blend, and serve.

A REMOULADE SAUCE

MAYONNAISE AND HERBS   MAKES 1¾ CUPS

1½ *cups mayonnaise*
4 shallots, chopped fine
1 tablespoon anchovy paste
3 tablespoons pickled water-
melon rind (or sweet or dill
pickle), chopped fine
1 tablespoon fresh parsley,
chopped fine (or ½ teaspoon
dried)
1 tablespoon fresh tarragon,
chopped fine (or ½ teaspoon
dried)

1 tablespoon capers, chopped
fine
1 tablespoon Dijon mustard
2 tablespoons catsup
2 tablespoons fresh lemon juice
1 teaspoon sugar
1 or 2 tablespoons heavy cream
(optional)

Combine all these ingredients, and refrigerate the mixture for several hours. If you wish to thin this sauce, add heavy cream (by the table-spoon) to achieve the desired consistency. Mix again.

Use this sauce over hard-boiled eggs, with cold chicken, or to "butter" sandwich bread. The watermelon rind (or pickle) provides the sweet-sour taste.

((3))

Pastas, Their Sauces, and the Versatile Egg

THE PASTAS AND THEIR SAUCES

Until we were teen-agers, we didn't know that pasta could be bought in a grocery store. In our home, in the homes of aunts and uncles, grand-mothers and grandfathers, *paisanos* galore, the wooden pole dripping with pasta *asciutta* was as permanent a piece of furniture as the kitchen table. If it was not a wooden pole, there were white tablecloths, dusted with flour, covering every available flat surface one could find, including beds, filled to their edges with pasta *fatta in casa* "made at home"). Manicotti on Mondays, *tagliatelle* on Tuesdays, *maruzze* on *Mercoledi*, gnocchi on *Giovedi*, vermicelli on *Venerdi*, spaghetti on *Sabato, e ditalini* on *Domenica*. Literally, we had some pasta in some form or shape each day, and all of it was made at home.

Nor did we know of the existence of the pasta machine until col-lege days were over and Hammacher Schlemmer, the specialty depart-ment store in New York, advertised it in the *New York Times*. By that time, we were in our twenties.

Like the family's cleavers that cut across many chicken necks, the family pasta board received special care and safekeeping. Ours, made by an Italian carpenter, was quite thick and heavy and measured approximately 4 feet square. It was never washed. On it were rolled sheets and sheets of pasta, each sheet lightly folded over and cut into noodle strips. We noticed at an early age that neighbors and relatives compared and sized up pasta boards with as much concern and care as they did pasta quality.

It would take pages to list *all* the kinds of pasta. We think most pasta types will fit into one of these four general groupings:

String pastas: best known, of course, is spaghetti; but *spaghettini* (thin spaghetti) and vermicelli (thin, thin spaghetti) seem to be gaining in popularity in this country. There's also *capellini, fedelini, spaghettoni,* and so on.

Ribbon pastas: best known are probably fettucine or perhaps lasagne. There's also *fettucelle* (a narrower fettucine), *margherita* (a noodle rippled along one side), *margheritine* (a smaller *margherita*), and so on.

Tubular pasta (better known as macaroni): Tubular forms can be ribbed, plain, grooved, pierced, ridged; the best known is probably *ziti* or rigatoni.

Fancy-shaped pastas: This is the type that amuses us most; its designs are without number. There are little cupids (*amorini*), little rings (*anelli*), and ribbed rings (*anellini rigati*). What we call bows are butterflies (*farfalle* to the Italians), and of course, they come in all Italian sizes: tiny butterflies (*farfallette* and *farfalline*) and big butterflies (*farfalloni*). Believe it or not, there are more elbows than butterflies in the Italian markets: *bucatini, perciatelli, maccheroncelli, mezzanelli, mezzani.* Then there are the ribbed elbow varieties, and so on. Jack Denton Scott, in his book *The Complete Book of Pasta,** lists pasta names. We believe it's the most comprehensive list of pastas we've ever seen.

We're happy to see a return to homemade foods. More and more people seem to be baking from scratch, and from what we hear and see, almost every one is trying his or her hand at pasta making. Recipes for pasta are plentiful in cookbooks, and in the last ten years, entire books have been devoted to the art of making and cooking pasta. We've seen

* Jack Denton Scott, *The Complete Book of Pasta: An Italian Cookbook* (New York: William Morrow & Company, 1968).

thousands of recipes on pasta making, and it's surprising how many differences there are. It seems redundant to add to the literature, but we've included several of our pasta recipes because we know they work and like the way they work. Basically, we use more eggs than other recipes call for; we use less water but add olive oil. Our *pasta fresca all'uovo* (egg noodles) and *pasta verde* (green noodles), both in this chapter, are delicious.

HOW TO USE A PASTA MACHINE:

We have a pasta machine, and we think it is a helpful tool and easy to use. All the pasta machines we've seen are fitted with smooth rollers that will produce several thicknesses of *sheet* (which is what pasta dough is called when it has been rolled out, whether by hand or by machine). A knob can be turned to widen or narrow the opening between the smooth rollers. (Our machine has six settings.) Cutting rollers, which can be attached to the machine, slice the sheet to the noodle width of your desire. Pasta machines are usually fitted with 2 mm. and 6 mm. cutting rollers. (The two cutting rollers are attached to the machine in a single piece.) Additional rollers of 1.5 mm., 4 mm., and 12 mm. width are also available. Only one pasta width may be cut at a time.

As simple as pasta making may be with and without a pasta machine, it nonetheless requires some time. Even though we store homemade pasta, we run out of it quickly. We think commercially produced pasta in the United States is good, and not long ago we realized one reason why: Pasta is manufactured in this country by American families of Italian ancestry (Ronzoni, Buitoni, and so on). These pasta producers are extending the range of their products monthly; we can't go by the supermarket's pasta shelves without finding something new for *brodo* or a spicy sauce. The combinations of pasta and sauce are many, as are the stuffings for tubular pastas. Meat and ricotta stuffing for ravioli, manicotti and *cannelloni* are well known. (Some authorities say that stuffed pasta is called *ravioli* only when it is stuffed with ricotta, eggs, and other cheeses. If pasta is stuffed with other fillings, such as salami or sausage, then they should be called *agnolotti*.) There are many imaginative fillings for *conchiglie* (large shells) and *tufoli* (tubes a little smaller than manicotti shells) made of spinach, beef, pork, poultry, veal, or cheeses. One of our favorite manicotti stuffings combines ricotta, Parmesan, and Fontina d'Aosta cheeses with almonds, wine, cream, onions and chicken.

The classic method for making manicotti shells is to prepare pasta, and cut it into rectangles approximately 4 inches square. We enjoy that greatly, but our manicotti pancakes are easy to make; they do not require boiling. They are prepared and cooked like crepes and are handled in approximately the same manner. They are delicate; they freeze magnificently; they are easy to handle.

Gnocchi, one of the more interesting pastas, should be as well known in this country as are spaghetti and macaroni, but unfortunately, they are not. They are popular in northern Italy, where they are made with a maize flour (polenta) or from potatoes. Gnocchi are not boiled; they are poached in boiling water. As soon as they rise to the top, they are removed from the water and dressed in a number of ways. They can be combined with spinach, ricotta, Parmesan cheese, butter, tomato sauce, meat sauce, chicken livers, or vegetable sauce. In this chapter we present our version of Gnocchi alla Romana and Potato Gnocchi, a favorite of ours.

No one questions the versatility of this Italian national dish, which is now becoming one of America's major eating habits. Just look at the space provided by supermarkets for pasta products. Like Italians, Americans are learning to recognize pasta's affinity for almost every imaginable food. Among the great combinations, surely, are pasta with garlic and olive oil, pasta with tomatoes and basil, pasta with butter and cheese, and pasta with meat and mushrooms. The sauces for pasta can be made in every conceivable form; the best-known combinations appear in *pesto*, marinara, and Bolognese. Fish sauces, better known in Italy than in America, can be delicious and deserve greater recognition here. Red and white clam sauces are on some American menus, but they often are tasteless. In this chapter we offer one of our favorite white clam sauces and a favorite lobster sauce. And we think a fabulous combination with garlic and olive oil is fresh ginger pieces.

By the way, here is how we like to serve our pasta and sauce. Homemade pasta absorbs liquid faster than commercially made pasta. We always add 3 or 4 tablespoons of butter to our pasta as soon as it is drained. We then add a little more than half the amount of sauce, and mix it well with the pasta. The remaining sauce is spooned over the pasta after it has been divided into individual plates.

Cooking pasta is one of the more imaginative parts of Italian cooking; it is lighthearted and reflective of the Italian people. Looking at a bowl of pasta is like looking at the whole of Italy; one sees sunshine and laughter, vivid colors and strong scents, opera stagings and mellifluous chatter. Italians enjoy eating pasta, and perhaps this is why it is eaten daily.

MANICOTTI WITH CHICKEN AND ALMONDS

ALMONDS AND FONTINA CHEESE   SERVES 6

12 *manicotti pancakes (see page*
   120)
2 *chicken breasts, skinned,*
   boned, and halved
Juice of ½ lemon
3½ *tablespoons plus 1 teaspoon*
   butter
¼ *cup onion, chopped fine*
2 *tablespoons all-purpose flour*
1 *cup Rich Chicken Stock or*
   broth (see page 49)
½ *cup heavy cream*
½ *cup grated Fontina or Gruyère*
   cheese

Salt
Pepper, ground fresh
3 *tablespoons blanched almond*
   slivers
1 *tablespoon dry vermouth*
1 *small egg*
1 *cup ricotta*
6 *tablespoons Parmesan cheese*
3 *tablespoons fresh parsley,*
   chopped fine
½ *teaspoon lemon zest, chopped*

Prepare the pancakes and have them ready.

Place the chicken breasts in a bowl, and add the lemon juice. Toss well, and let stand for 10 to 15 minutes.

Melt 1½ tablespoons butter in a saucepan, and add the onion. Cook, stirring, until the onion is softened. Sprinkle with the flour, and cook for 2 minutes, stirring with a wire whisk.

Slowly add the stock or broth, stirring rapidly with the whisk. When thickened and smooth, add ¼ cup cream. Simmer about 10 minutes, stirring occasionally. Then add the Fontina or Gruyère cheese and salt and pepper to taste. Stir to blend, and set aside.

Meanwhile, melt 1 teaspoon butter in a small iron skillet (or some other suitable oven pan), and add the almonds in one layer. Place in a preheated 350-degree oven, and bake, shaking the skillet and stirring the almonds until they are golden brown. Remove, and allow to cool. (Do *not* turn the oven off.)

Drain the chicken pieces, pat them dry, and sprinkle them with salt and pepper to taste. Melt 2 tablespoons butter in a skillet, and add the chicken. Brown on both sides quickly (about 3 or 4 minutes), and remove. Add the vermouth to the skillet, and cook about 30 seconds, stirring. Pour these drippings into a bowl.

Cut the chicken into ½-inch cubes, and add to the bowl. Add the cheese sauce, almonds, remaining ¼ cup heavy cream, egg (if the egg is large, use only half of it: beat the whole egg and measure it by teaspoons or tablespoons), ricotta, 4 tablespoons Parmesan cheese, and chopped parsley. Blend this well with a fork or whisk.

To assemble, spoon an equal amount of the chicken mixture down the center of each manicotti pancake; roll to enclose the filling.

Select a baking dish large enough to hold the rolled manicotti in one layer. Spoon enough sauce into the dish to cover the bottom. Then arrange the filled manicotti over the sauce, and cover with a second layer of sauce. Reserve the remaining sauce.

Cover the dish with foil, and bake at 350 degrees for 15 to 20 minutes, until piping hot and bubbling. Sprinkle with the remaining 2 tablespoons Parmesan cheese, and run briefly under the broiler to glaze. Sprinkle with the lemon zest, and serve hot. Pass the remaining sauce in a separate bowl.

Basil

Basil is an herb that was largely unpopular in the United States until the last two decades, when the pizza craze helped it become better known. In the south of France, it has always been the queen of the herb world.

Pistou in Provence and *pesto* in Piedmont depend on several cupfuls of basil. There are at least half a hundred varieties of basil, but we know sweet basil best because of its fabulous affinity for garlic and tomatoes. If you haven't yet grown basil, you should. A flowerpot will do, but if you give it space in the garden with lots of sun and air, one plant will sprout enough leaves to last all summer! We grow a dozen plants. Basil grows easily, profusely. It looks good and smells beautiful. It's versatile and freezes superbly. Pick it now, and eat it later.

Pick, wash, and dry leaves. Fill a 1-pint plastic container, or make *pesto* when the basil is fresh, and freeze it in small cubes or by the half cupful. A half cup will sauce 1 pound of spaghetti.

Mario Buatta, well-known New York designer, always asks for a bowl of fresh basil, even when he orders steak. Perhaps it is for the reason given in *The Great Herbal* (published in 1526): "Basil taketh away melancholy and maketh merry and glad."

PASTA E PISELLI ALL'ANGELA
(Pasta Shells with Peas)

BASIL AND PEAS   SERVES 4

3 tablespoons olive oil
1 large onion, chopped fine
1 large garlic clove, chopped fine
2 cups fresh tomatoes, cored,
  blanched, peeled, and chopped
  coarse (or canned plum
  tomatoes)
3 cups fresh peas, cooked 5 to 7
  minutes (or frozen peas, cooked
  according to package directions)
½ pound pasta shells, preferably
  occhi di lupo ("eyes of wolf"),
  Cirio brand, made and packaged in Naples (or 1-inch
  macaroni shells manufactured
  domestically)

10 leaves fresh basil, washed,
  patted dry, and chopped fine
Salt
Pepper, ground fesh
½ cup (approximately) grated
  Parmesan cheese

In a 2-quart saucepan, heat the oil, and sauté the onions until they begin to soften and turn color. Add the garlic, and cook 2 minutes longer. Add the tomatoes, and cook slowly for 10 minutes.

While the tomatoes are cooking, cook the peas and the pasta; drain both. When the tomatoes have cooked 10 minutes, add the peas and pasta. Then add the basil, salt, and pepper, and bring to a boil. Remove from the heat, and serve immediately with the grated Parmesan in a separate bowl.

This dish is a cousin of the great combination *pasta e fagioli,* more commonly known as "pasta fasool." If you want to make the "fasool," use 3 cups canned *cannellini* beans (white navy beans) instead of the peas; these are packaged by all the Italo-American food manufacturers and can be found in almost every supermarket. The "fasool" can also be frozen. You can also substitute fresh lima beans for the peas. Black-eyed peas fit well, too.

GNOCCHI ALLA ROMANA

BUTTER AND PARMESAN CHEESE   SERVES 6

¼ *cup butter*	2 *cups milk, scalded*
¼ *cup all-purpose flour*	2 *egg yolks*
¼ *cup cornstarch*	¾ *cup grated Parmesan cheese*
½ *teaspoon salt*	*Butter*

Melt ¼ cup butter, and when it is bubbling, add the flour, cornstarch, salt, and milk. Cook for 3 minutes, stirring constantly.

Add the egg yolks and ½ cup cheese. Put this mixture into a buttered shallow pan, and cool it. Then turn it on a board and cut it in squares, diamonds or strips. Place this on a buttered ovenproof platter, put a bit of butter on it, sprinkle with the remaining cheese, and brown in a hot oven (400 degrees) for about 15 minutes, or until heated through.

LASAGNE IN THE FAMILY STYLE

CHICKEN AND SAUSAGE   SERVES 8 TO 12

TO PREPARE THE SAUCE:

2 tablespoons olive oil
4 links Italian sausage
4 chicken thighs
1 whole chicken breast, split, skin
  removed
1 small onion, chopped fine
1 garlic clove, chopped fine
2-lb.-3-oz. can Italian plum
  tomatoes, sieved (or 4 cups fresh
  plum tomatoes, peeled, seeded,
  and chopped)

1 tablespoon fresh or frozen basil,
  chopped (or ½ teaspoon dried)
1 teaspoon salt
  Pepper, ground fresh

In a large saucepan, heat the oil, and cook the sausage over medium heat for 10 minutes or until brown. Add the chicken, and brown on all sides (about 5 minutes). Remove the sausage and chicken, and set aside. Add the onion and garlic, and sauté until lightly browned. Add the tomatoes, basil, salt and pepper to taste. Let it come to a fast boil; then lower the heat, and simmer for 30 minutes. Add the sausage, and simmer another 30 minutes. Add the chicken, and cook 30 minutes more. (Altogether, the sauce does not need to cook more than 1½ hours to 2 hours.) When done, remove the chicken and sausage. Allow to cool enough to remove the chicken bones. Cut the chicken into ½-inch cubes, and keep them warm. Cut the sausage into thin slices, and keep them warm.

TO PREPARE THE PASTA:

2½ cups all-purpose flour
3 eggs, beaten lightly
½ teaspoon salt
1 tablespoon vegetable oil (or olive oil)
¼ cup warm water

In a medium-size bowl, add 2 cups flour, make a well in the center, and add the eggs, salt, oil, and water. Mix well.

Transfer the dough onto a floured board and knead, adding the reserved ½ cup flour if necessary, for about 15 minutes. Roll the dough into a ball, cover it with a bowl or tea towel, and let it rest for 15 minutes. Roll the dough into a cylinder about 6 or 7 inches long, and slice it into ½-inch pieces. Flatten pieces slightly with a rolling pin.

Pass the dough through the plain rollers of a pasta machine a few times. It is important to dust the dough with flour to prevent it from sticking. Turn the dial down a few notches to narrow the opening, and pass the dough through the rollers again. Keep changing the dial setting until the desired thickness is obtained. You will need about 12 strips of pasta to fill a 12-by-9-by-3-inch baking pan with 4 layers of pasta. The sheets of pasta should be 4 inches wide and 12 inches long (long enough for the baking pan). If the sheets are longer, you can cut them, and you obviously will need fewer of them.

In a large saucepan, bring 3 quarts water to a boil. Add 1 teaspoon salt. Boil rapidly. Add 3 sheets of pasta, and cook for 5 minutes, or until tender. Have another large saucepan ready with a colander placed on top of it. Carefully empty the boiling water and pasta from the first saucepan through the colander into the second saucepan, catching the cooked pasta in the colander. Run the cooked pasta under cold water. Use the same hot water to cook the remaining pasta, 3 sheets at a time. Repeat until all the pasta is cooked.

The pasta will be firm enough to handle with your hands. Lay the cooked sheets on a clean tea towel, and pat them dry before you assemble the lasagne.

TO PREPARE THE FILLING:

2 pounds ricotta, whole or skim milk

2 eggs, lightly beaten

1 teaspoon salt

2 tablespoons parsley, chopped fine

4 tablespoons grated Parmesan, Romano, or Locatelli cheese

½ pound of mozzarella, cut in ¼-inch cubes

Pepper, ground fresh

Put the ricotta, eggs, salt, parsley, grated cheese, and mozzarella into a large bowl; pepper liberally, and mix well. Set filling aside.

TO ASSEMBLE:
> *Tomato sauce with chicken and sausage pieces*
> 12 *sheets cooked pasta*
> *Ricotta filling*
> 4 *tablespoons grated Parmesan, Romano, or Locatelli cheese*

In a baking pan, approximately 12 by 9 by 3, spoon some of the tomato sauce over the bottom of the pan; spread the sauce to cover thinly. Arrange 3 sheets cooked pasta over the sauce. Add a layer of the ricotta mixture (use one-third of mixture), add one-third of the chicken cubes and sausage slices, sprinkle 1 tablespoon grated cheese, and add more sauce overall. Cover this with 3 pasta sheets, and repeat procedure to make another layer. Do this again for the third layer, and cover the top with the remaining 3 pasta sheets. Cover with sauce and the remaining tablespoon of grated cheese. Bake in a moderate oven (350 degrees) for 30 minutes, or until the sauce is hot and bubbling.

This dish freezes extremely well and may be frozen after it is completely assembled. Wrap it well for freezing; when you are ready to use the lasagne, no thawing is necessary. We cover it with aluminum foil and bake it for 1 hour or more, first covered and then, after 45 minutes, uncovered, until the lasagne is heated through and the sauce is bubbling.

FEDELINI (THE FAITHFUL) WITH CLAM SAUCE

CLAMS AND GARLIC   SERVES 4 TO 6

Fedelini, which means "the faithful," is one of the thinnest of the rope or string pastas; it's thinner than vermicelli. When you make your pasta, roll it out as thin as possible, then roll it lightly in folds about 4 inches wide, starting with the edge closest to you. When the circle of pasta is so folded, cut into the thinnest slices possible. Cook as you would Egg Noodles in the Homemade Style (see page 119).

5 dozen littleneck clams (or 3
7½-ounce cans of minced
clams)
2 large cloves garlic, chopped fine
½ cup olive oil
1 carrot, scraped, cut lengthwise
in 6 pieces and chopped very
fine
4 tablespoons butter
½ cup scallions (or onions),
chopped fine

1 cup clam juice (in addition to
cooking liquid or liquid from
canned clams)
1 cup dry white wine
Pinch of red pepper flakes
Salt
8 sprigs parsley, stems removed,
chopped fine
1 pound homemade fedelini

Scrub the clams thoroughly with a stiff wire brush, rinsing them several times. Soak clams in cool fresh water for 30 minutes or longer to remove any sand in the clams. Remove the clams by hand from the bowl or pan in which you soaked them. (Sand will have sunk to the bottom; draining would stir the water and give you some sand with your clams.) Place the clams in a heavy, covered saucepan, along with half the garlic pieces and about 4 tablespoons olive oil. Cover, and cook (i.e., steam) over medium heat until the clams open (10 to 15 minutes). Do *not* overcook. Discard any clams that have not opened. When you separate the clams from their shells, catch all the juice you can (for the sauce). Cut the clams in half or in thirds. Set clams and clam juice aside.

In a large skillet, heat the remaining oil and the butter. Add the carrot pieces, and sauté them for about 5 minutes. Add the scallions and remaining garlic pieces, and cook for several minutes, until they begin to brown lightly. Add all the juice from the cooked fresh clams (or from the canned clams), the additional 1 cup clam juice, and the white wine. (Don't forget the extra clam juice; it's important. We keep a bottle of clam juice handy in case we need more. We use less oil and more juice than traditional white clam sauce recipes call for. You can see the pasta through our sauce.) Do *not* add the clams yet, but put in the red pepper flakes. Boil for 10 or 15 minutes to allow most of the wine to cook off. Add salt, and adjust red pepper seasoning. (Don't make it too hot, or you won't taste the clams).

Just before you are ready to serve it, add the clams and parsley to the cooked pasta. Bring the sauce to a boil, and sauce the pasta. We believe our sauce is especially good because the carrots add a hint of sweetness to the taste and because the carrot and parsley colors are very attractive in combination with the clams and pasta.

COD CON CONCHIGLIETTE
(Merluzzo with Tiny Pasta Shells)

CREAM AND PEPPER   SERVES 4 TO 6

One distinguishable aroma in Paddy's Market (see page 130) is the smell of salted codfish. Actually, it seems to be the characteristic aroma of every Italian market, wherever it may be. *Baccala* (dried codfish) is another food we grew up with; childen had to eat it on Christmas Eve, or there would be an empty sock at the mantle the next morning. (By the way, one wonderful stocking stuffer item used by Grandpa Cerabone was fresh fruit: beautiful oranges, pears, and so on.) Even these days, Christmas Eve doesn't seem quite complete to us without *baccala*. Codfish was boiled and then dressed with dried red-hot peppers sautéed in olive oil; some relatives cooked it with raisins and onions. The smell of *baccala* permeated the house for quite awhile. It always had to be soaked overnight; and on such nights, almost every hour on the hour, we heard one parent saying to the other, *"Cambia l'acqua del baccala"* ("Change the water in which sits the codfish").

1 *piece salted dry codfish, about ¾*	2 *tablespoons butter, softened*
to 1 pound	*Pepper, ground fresh*
2 *cups milk (approximately)*	1 *cup heavy cream*
1 *small garlic clove*	1 *pound* conchigliette (*or*
4 *tablespoons olive oil*	*equivalent tiny pasta shells*)

In a large-enough pan or bowl soak the codfish for at least 24 hours. Change the water frequently, or the fish will be too *salato*. (Note that this recipe does *not* call for salt.)

Drain the codfish, and put it in a covered, ovenproof pan or dish. Add enough milk so that the fish is just barely covered. Put the garlic clove in with the fish and milk, cover the pan or dish, and bake in a preheated 350-degree oven for 25 to 30 minutes, or until the fish is tender.

Drain the fish, discard the milk, but reserve the garlic clove. Remove the bones and skin from the cod, and discard. (Be sure *all* bones are removed.) Flake the fish. (It's easy to do this with your hands.) Purée the cod and garlic clove in a food processor (e.g., a Cuisinart or a blender), adding the oil a little at a time, then the butter, and then the pepper. Be liberal with the pepper; it adds considerably to the taste. Then add the heavy cream until you've achieved a smooth, creamy mixture. Do *not* overbeat.

Cook the *conchigliette* according to the package directions, but not beyond the *al dente* point. Combine the cod-cream sauce with the *conchigliette*, toss well, and serve on a large platter, in a large bowl, in individual bowls, or on individual plates. Sprinkle some freshly ground pepper overall.

FUSILLI CON FUNGHI
(Spaghetti Twists with Mushrooms)

DRIED MUSHROOMS AND EGGPLANT   SERVES 4 TO 6

½ cup dried mushrooms, tightly
  packed (see Note)
½ cup olive oil
1 dried chili pepper, whole
1 medium-size eggplant, ends
  removed, cut into ½-inch cubes
1 garlic clove, chopped fine
2 cups fresh tomatoes, blanched,
  cored, peeled, and diced (or
  canned Italian plum tomatoes)
2 tablespoons fresh parsley,
  chopped (or 2 teaspoons dried)

1 tablespoon fresh basil, chopped
  (or 1 teaspoon dried)
Salt
Pepper, ground fresh
1 pound fusilli (spaghetti twisted
  like a corkscrew)
2 tablespoons butter, softened
  (optional)
6 tablespoons grated Parmesan
  cheese (optional)

Put the dried mushrooms in a small bowl, cover them with lukewarm water, and let stand for about 30 minutes.

In a large skillet, heat the olive oil, add the dried whole chili pepper, and cook until the pepper becomes crisp. Remove, and set aside. In the same skillet, sauté the eggplant cubes on all sides for 15 minutes. Stir them frequently, and don't be alarmed at how much oil they absorb. Add the garlic pieces, and sauté for 2 minutes.

Add the tomatoes, parsley, basil, and salt and pepper to taste. Crush the crisp chili pepper, and add that, too. (The easiest way to do this is to hold the chili pepper in your hand over the skillet. Rub your hands together, crushing the pepper.)

Drain the mushrooms, and cut them into small pieces. Add them to the skillet. Bring this mixture to a boil, lower the heat, and cook for 30 minutes, or until eggplant cubes are tender. Check sauce for seasoning, and add more salt if you need it (we doubt that you'll want to add more pepper).

While the sauce is cooking, boil 6 or 7 quarts of water in a large saucepan. Add salt, and cook the *fusilli* according to package directions, being sure not to overcook them. Drain the *fusilli* when properly done, and return them to the saucepan in which they were cooked. If you wish, add 2 tablespoons softened butter, and stir with the *fusilli*. Add the sauce, and combine well with the *fusilli*.

Serve on individual plates or in one large bowl or serving platter. (Some people like Parmesan cheese with this; add it if you wish. We think the flavor is delicate, and the cheese is too strong for the mushrooms.)

Note: This dish should be prepared with the Italian-type dried mushrooms found in Italian, French, and other specialty grocery shops. You may use fresh mushrooms, but it won't taste quite the same. If you use fresh mushrooms, slice enough to make 1 full cup.

CAVATELLI FATTI A MANO
(Pasta Shells Made by Hand)

MAKES 1 POUND

EGGS AND FLOUR   SERVES 3 TO 4

2½ *cups all-purpose flour*
2½ *teaspoons baking powder*
1 *teaspoon salt*
1 *egg, lightly beaten*
½ *cup warm water*

In a medium-size bowl, sift 2 cups flour with the baking powder. Make a well in the center, and add the salt, egg, and a little water at a time. Mix well. Transfer the dough to a floured board, and knead for 10 minutes adding reserved flour if necessary. Roll into a ball, cover with a bowl or tea towel, and let rest for 15 minutes.

Divide the dough into 9 or 10 pieces, and roll each piece into an 11- to 12-inch cylinder, rather like a long French bread. Then cut each cylinder into ½-inch pieces. Dust the pieces with flour, and with your thumb, press down firmly on the piece of dough and roll it away from you over your thumb. This action will produce the shell-like form.

The pasta should be cooked within 1 hour of making it. Sauce it according to your fancy.

EGG NOODLES IN THE HOMEMADE STYLE

MAKES ABOUT 2 POUNDS

EGGS AND FLOUR   SERVES 6 TO 8

> *6 eggs, lightly beaten*
> *3½ cups all-purpose flour*
> *1½ teaspoons salt*
> *2 tablespoons olive oil*
> *2 tablespoons lukewarm water*

Into a large bowl, put 3 cups flour. Make a well in the center, and add the eggs, salt, oil, and water. Mix well. Transfer the dough onto a floured board, and knead, adding the reserved flour if needed. Knead for 10 minutes or until the dough becomes firm and satiny-looking. Roll the dough into a ball, cover it with a bowl or tea towel, and let it rest for 15 minutes.

Roll dough into a cylindrical form about 12 inches long, and slice it into 1-inch pieces. Flatten each piece with a rolling pin; then dust each piece with a little flour. Pass the dough through the plain rollers of a pasta machine a few times. Turn the dial down a few times, and pass the dough through again. Remember to dust the dough with flour to prevent it from sticking. Keep changing the dial setting (to make the opening narrower) until desired thickness of dough is obtained.

Once you've made sheets of pasta, you'll have to cut them into noodle sizes (unless you are making large sheets for lasagna). Now run the pasta (after flouring it again very lightly) through the appropriate cutting roller for the desired width. Have a long, clean wooden pole (the handle of a broom works well here) ready, and hang the noodles on it to dry (2 or 3 hours or overnight).

When the noodles are thoroughly dried, lift them carefully from the pole or slide them off. Cook in boiling salted water until *al dente* (about 5 minutes). Sauce in any way you wish.

Noodles can be stored (in a cardboard box with cover) in a cool dry place for 3 to 4 weeks, or even longer.

MANICOTTI SHELLS (PANCAKES)

MAKES 12 PANCAKES

EGGS AND FLOUR

SERVES 3 TO 4

3 eggs
1 cup water
1 cup all-purpose flour
Salt to taste
Melted butter

Break the eggs into a bowl, and beat with a whisk. Stir in the water. Add the flour gradually, stirring with the whisk. Add the salt, stir, and let stand for 30 minutes.

Heat a 7- or 8-inch crepe pan or small Teflon skillet over moderate heat, and brush lightly with melted butter. Add about 3 tablespoons of batter, and tilt the pan this way and that until the batter covers the bottom. (The crepes should be quite thin but substantial enough to handle.) Cook about 35 seconds on one side; then turn the crepe, using a spatula or your hands, and cook on the other side briefly (2 or 3 seconds). Slide crepe out of the pan.

Repeat this process until all the batter is used, brushing the skillet lightly with butter if necessary before each pancake is made.

Shells or crepes can be made 1 or 2 days in advance and refrigerated, or weeks in advance and frozen. Stack them on foil or freeze paper and wrap them well.

PASTA VERDE IN THE HOMEMADE STYLE
(Green Noodles *alla casalinga*)

MAKES ABOUT 1½ POUNDS

SPINACH AND EGGS

SERVES 6

3½ cups all-purpose flour	1½ teaspoons salt
3 eggs, lightly beaten	½ cup spinach, cooked, drained,
2 teaspoons olive oil	and puréed

Into a large bowl, put 3 cups flour; make a well in the center, and add the eggs, oil, and salt. Mix these ingredients a little, and add the spinach. Mix well. Transfer the dough onto a floured board, and knead, adding the reserved flour if needed, for about 15 minutes. Roll dough into a ball, cover with a bowl or tea towel, and let rest for 15 minutes.

Roll the dough into a cylindrical form about 12 inches long, and cut it into 1-inch pieces (as though you were cutting French or Italian bread). Dust each piece of dough with flour, and flatten a little with a rolling pin. Pass the dough through the plain rollers of a pasta machine a few times. (It is important to keep dusting the dough with flour to prevent it from sticking.) Turn the dial down a few notches to narrow the opening, and pass the dough through again. The strips will be much longer. Keep changing the dial setting downward until the desired thickness of pasta is obtained. Have a long, clean wooden pole ready, and hang the noodles on it to dry (2 to 3 hours or longer).

When thoroughly dried, lift pasta carefully from pole or slide it off, and cook *al dente* in boiling salted water (about 5 minutes). This should be served, of course, with a sauce.

Fontina D'Aosta

There are American imitations of this great Italian cheese, but they do not measure up to the original. (Fontina, as a cheese name, is protected in Italy but is not protected in the United States.) The real Fontina comes from the Val d'Aosta, a mountainous area just south of Switzerland. It looks like Swiss Gruyère and tastes like Gruyère or Emmental. It has a rather light brown crust and comes in large wheels, like Swiss cheese, but it doesn't have the fretwork of holes. Don't settle for the imitation; buy the *real* Fontina d'Aosta.

TIMBALLO DI FETTUCINE
(Baked and Molded Fettucine)

FONTINA CHEESE AND CREAM   SERVES 6 TO 8

TO PREPARE THE FETTUCINE:

1 pound fettucine or homemade   *1 cup heavy cream*
   noodles (see page 119)   *1 pound Fontina cheese, cut into*
3 tablespoons butter   *small pieces*
¼ cup grated Parmesan cheese   *Freshly ground pepper*

Cook the fettucine or homemade noodles in boiling salted water to the *al dente* point, and drain them. Put them back in the pan in which they were cooked, and add the butter, Parmesan cheese, heavy cream, Fontina cheese, and fresh-ground pepper.

TO PREPARE THE BAKING DISH:

4 tablespoons butter
½ cup fine bread crumbs
1 egg

Butter well an oval ovenproof casserole (approximately 9 by 14 by 2, preferably clear glass). Add ¼ cup bread crumbs, and tilt the baking dish back and forth to cover the entire surface of the dish with crumbs. Empty the extra crumbs onto a sheet of wax paper. Beat the egg well in a small bowl, and pour it into the crumbed baking dish. Tilt the dish again to cover all the crumbs with the egg. Add the remaining ¼ cup crumbs, and tilt to cover the surface completely. Turn out and discard excess crumbs.

With a rubber spatula, transfer all the pasta, scraping the sides and bottom of the pan, into the double-crusted baking dish. Place in a preheated 350-degree oven, and bake for 15 minutes, or until heated through. (If the baking dish is clear glass, you'll be able to see the crust turn a golden brown, and you'll know it's ready.) Remove from the oven, and allow to sit for 10 to 15 minutes.

Then turn the *timballo* out onto a large oval platter, and garnish with a fresh sprig of parsley. This is a very handsome and tasty dish.

Ginger

This edible root is deeply rooted in history. Almost every known civilization—Indian, South Asian, Chinese, Arabic, Roman, Greek—has used it in many ways. Its tuber resembles an iris root. It has a paper-thin, light brown skin that can be peeled off with a parer. It freezes well, grates well, slivers well. Probably its most popular use is in gingerbread or cookies. Is there any shape anywhere that has not been gingerbreaded? The famous ginger essence is also found in ale, beer, and wine.

It is one of the most exciting flavors, and we enjoy its use. We feature it here in a sauce for pasta, but look for it in other combinations, too: Chicken Chinoiserie (see page 160), one of our favorites and simple to cook; Beef, Stir-Fried, with Peppers and Onions (see page 230); Leg of Lamb à l'Orange (see page 290); and a delicious Purple Plum Chutney (see page 379).

A SPECIAL AND QUICK SAUCE FOR VERMICELLI

GINGER AND GARLIC   SERVES 4

There is no tomato in this sauce. It is a variation of the classic *aglio e olio* (garlic and olive oil) sauce. The fresh ginger is the unusual ingredient in this recipe.

½ cup olive oil
½ carrot, scraped and chopped in
  very small pieces
4 cloves garlic, chopped in very
  small pieces
2 tablespoons fresh ginger,
  chopped in very small pieces
1 scallion or small onion, chopped
  in very small pieces

1 teaspoon dried oregano
1 teaspoon salt
½ teaspoon red pepper flakes
½ cup dry vermouth
1 pound vermicelli
1 cup water
2 tablespoons butter
  Grated Parmesan cheese

Heat the oil in a large skillet or a 1-quart saucepan. When the oil is hot, add the carrot pieces, and cook for about 3 minutes. Stir often. Then add the garlic, ginger, onion, oregano, salt, red pepper flakes, and vermouth. Cook for about 5 minutes. Add the water. Stir well, and reduce the heat to as low as possible.

Now cook the vermicelli according to the package directions, but be sure the pan is quite large and that the water is at a rolling boil before you add the pasta. If the directions do not call for adding salt to the water, add 1 teaspoon salt anyway *after* the water has reached a rolling boil. Do not break vermicelli in two or in pieces; add it to the water full length, as taken out of the package. As soon as the pasta is in the pan, use a large wooden fork to immerse it in water. Stir the pasta into the boiling water until it is completely covered. Keep stirring gently but frequently. Constantly test for doneness by pulling out a strand or two with a large wooden fork, running it under cold water quickly, and tasting it immediately. Discard the strand if not cooked *al dente*, test again in 10 or 15 seconds, and repeat the process if necessary. Do not leave the range or stove, or your pasta will be *stracotto* ("overdone").

As soon as the pasta is cooked, remove the saucepan from the heat, and immediately drain it into a colander. Shake the colander quickly, and return the pasta to the empty pan in which it was cooked. Mix quickly with the butter, add three-fourths of the sauce, and mix again.

Serve this immediately in individual plates or bowls or on one large serving platter. Add the remaining sauce, a spoonful over each serving, or pour all the sauce over the pasta on the large platter. Serve grated Parmesan cheese separately. We never serve pasta unless everyone is *a tavola*. People wait for pasta; pasta waits for no one.

COZZE CON PASTA VERDE
(Mussels with Green Pasta)

LEMON AND OLIVE OIL   SERVES 4 TO 6

48 to 54 fresh mussels
1 garlic clove, halved
1 cup dry white wine
1 pound Pasta Verde in the
　Homemade Style (see page
　121)
2 tablespoons butter
⅓ cup olive oil
¼ cup fresh lemon juice

Juice from steamed mussels
3 medium-size fresh tomatoes,
　not too ripe, cored, blanched,
　peeled, seeded, and chopped
　into ½-inch pieces (canned
　tomatoes are not to be substi-
　tuted)

Wash the mussels with a stiff brush, remove beards, and cover with water. Let them stand for 3 to 4 hours, changing the water several times to get rid of the sand. Drain them, and put them in a large, covered saucepan. Add the garlic pieces and the wine. Cover the pan, and steam the mussels over low heat until the shells open. Discard any unopened ones. Remove the mussels from their shells, being careful to capture all the juice (for the sauce). Discard the shells.

Cook the pasta until it is *al dente*. Drain it, and return it to the saucepan in which it was cooked. Add the butter, olive oil, lemon juice, and juice from steamed mussels. Also add half of the mussels and half of the fresh tomatoes, and toss the pasta well.

Empty the mixture of pasta and sauce into a large bowl or platter, or divide for individual servings. Arrange the remaining mussels and tomato pieces on top of the pasta. The cool tomato pieces, uncooked, contribute to a wonderful combination of textures and tastes.

LOBSTER AND WHITE WINE IN A
FRESH TOMATO SAUCE

LOBSTER AND WHITE WINE   SERVES 4

4 tablespoons butter
2 cups cooked lobster meat, cut
    into ½-inch pieces
4 tablespoons olive oil
2 small garlic cloves (or 1 large
    garlic clove), chopped fine
¼ cup shallots (or onions or
    scallions), chopped fine
½ cup dry white wine (or 5 table-
    spoons dry vermouth mixed
    with 3 tablespoons water)
1 tablespoon tomato paste (or
    2 tablespoons tomato purée)
2 tablespoons fresh basil, chopped
    fine (or 1 teaspoon dried)
1 teaspoon dried oregano

1 teaspoon zest of lemon peel,
    chopped fine
6 large fresh tomatoes (about
    2 pounds) cored, blanched,
    peeled, seeded, and cut into
    ½-inch cubes to make approxi-
    mately 4 cups (or 4 cups canned
    plum tomatoes with a little
    liquid)
Salt
Pepper, ground fresh
2 tablespoons shallots, chopped
    fine
1 tablespoon fresh parsley,
    chopped fine (or 1 teaspoon
    dried)

In a large, heavy enameled skillet or a large saucepan, heat the butter.
Add the lobster pieces, and cook them quickly over high heat for about
1 minute, stirring frequently. Using a slotted spoon, transfer the lobster
pieces to a small bowl, and set aside.

In the same skillet or saucepan, heat the olive oil. Add the garlic and
shallots, and cook them until they turn golden (about 5 minutes), being careful not to let them brown. Pour in the wine (or the vermouth-
and-water combination), and cook for another 5 minutes so that the
liquor can cook away.

Remove from the heat, and add the tomato paste or purée, basil,
oregano, and lemon zest. Mix this well; then add the fresh or canned
tomatoes, and cook for about 15 minutes. (During this time, the
tomato sauce should be quickly brought to a boil, then simmered over
lowered heat.) Remove the pan from the heat, and add the lobster meat
and salt and freshly ground pepper to taste. Stir well. Transfer the
sauce to the top pan of a double boiler, and keep it warm while you
are cooking the pasta. Do *not* overcook the tomato sauce; that is, keep
it warm in this fashion for *only* 10 to 15 minutes.

Combine the chopped shallots with the parsley and sprinkle over the lobster sauce after it has been spooned over the pasta. This recipe yields enough sauce for 1 pound of pasta. We prefer it with vermicelli or *spaghettini*.

A QUICK TOMATO SAUCE WITH MARSALA

MARSALA AND BACON   SERVES 4

4 cups fresh plum tomatoes,   1 garlic clove, chopped fine
  blanched, stems and skins   4 slices bacon, cooked and
  removed (or canned plum   crumbled
  tomatoes)   Salt and freshly ground pepper
2 tablespoons butter   ½ cup Marsala
2 small onions, chopped fine   ½ teaspoon dried oregano

Put the tomatoes through a food mill. Do *not* use a blender. (A food mill will purée and get rid of the seeds; a blender chops the seeds along with the tomatoes.)

In a large skillet or medium-size saucepan, melt the butter, and cook the onion until it is soft. Add the garlic, tomato purée, and crumbled bacon. Then add salt and freshly ground pepper to taste. Boil this sauce hard for 4 minutes. Add the Marsala and oregano, and cook for another 4 minutes.

Toss half of the sauce with cooked vermicelli or other pasta. Add the remainder of the sauce by spoonfuls on top of the pasta, and serve immediately. This recipe yields enough sauce for 1 pound of pasta.

FETTUCINE GALLINA
(Homemade Noodles with Chicken and Two Sauces)

PARMESAN CHEESE AND CREAM   SERVES 4 TO 6

TO PREPARE THE FETTUCINE:
  1 pound Egg Noodles in the Homemade Style (see page 119).

Make the noodles, and set them aside until you are ready to boil them. (You can substitute ½ pound commercially prepared egg noodles, but the homemade ones will taste much better.)

TO PREPARE THE CHICKEN:

4- to 5-pound chicken, including neck, gizzard, and heart
2 celery stalks, including green leaves, sliced coarse
1 carrot, sliced thin
1 medium-size onion, stuck with 2 cloves

1 teaspoon salt
10 peppercorns, bruised (or ground fresh)
½ cup dry vermouth (optional)

Wash the chicken, and put it in a covered saucepan. (The saucepan shouldn't be too much larger than the chicken.) Add the neck, gizzard, and heart. Add the celery, carrot, onion, salt, peppercorns, and dry vermouth (if you wish), and cover with water. Bring this to a boil; then lower the heat, and simmer for 40 to 50 minutes, or until the chicken is cooked. (Do *not* overcook the chicken.) Transfer the chicken to a bowl or plate to allow it to cool, but boil the stock rapidly to let it cook down. As soon as you can handle the chicken (the sooner, the better), remove all the meat. Discard the skin and other fatty parts, but return all the bones to the boiling stockpot. Cut the chicken pieces into chunks of 1 to 2 inches, and set aside. Reduce the stock to about 2½ cups.

TO PREPARE THE TOMATO SAUCE:

2 tablespoons butter
1 tablespoon olive oil
2 or 3 large ripe tomatoes, cored, blanched, peeled, and chopped coarse (or 2 cups canned plum tomatoes)

1 small onion, chopped fine
½ teaspoon dried oregano
Salt
Pepper, ground fresh

Heat the butter and olive oil in a skillet. Add the onion, and cook until it is softened. Add the tomatoes, oregano, and salt and pepper to taste. Cook for about 10 minutes, and set aside. You will have about 2 cups of sauce.

TO PREPARE THE VELOUTÉ SAUCE WITH GARLIC:

2 tablespoons butter	1 egg yolk
1 large garlic clove, chopped very fine	¾ cup heavy cream
4 tablespoons all-purpose flour	Pinch of red pepper flakes
2 cups stock from cooking the chicken	

Melt the butter in a saucepan. Add the garlic pieces, and cook until they begin to turn golden. Do *not* allow them to brown. Add the flour, and cook for about 2 minutes. Slowly add the chicken stock, and cook over low heat for about 20 minutes. In a small bowl, beat the egg yolk, cream, and red pepper flakes. Add about ½ cup of the hot stock sauce to this mixture, beat well, and then add this cream sauce to the stock sauce in the pan. Keep the sauce warm. You will have about 2 cups of sauce.

TO ASSEMBLE:

Cooked noodles	¾ cup grated Parmesan cheese
3 tablespoons butter	4 tablespoons scallions (including light green, tender part), chopped fine
2 cups velouté sauce with garlic	
2 cups tomato sauce	
Meat from the chicken	

Cook the noodles to the *al dente* point. (Please do *not* overcook the noodles, homemade or "store-boughten.") Drain them, and return them to the saucepan in which they were cooked. Add 1 tablespoon butter to the noodles. (Use the other 2 tablespoons butter to butter a baking dish.) With the aid of a rubber spatula, add half the velouté sauce to the noodles. Transfer half of this mixture to the baking dish. Add half the tomato sauce and all the chicken pieces. Add the remaining noodles, and cover with the remaining tomato sauce. Top with the remaining velouté sauce. Sprinkle the cheese and chopped scallions overall, and bake in a preheated moderate oven (350 to 375 degrees) for 20 to 25 minutes, until the entire dish is well heated and the top is lightly browned.

POTATO GNOCCHI

POTATOES AND NUTMEG   SERVES 3 TO 4

5 *Idaho potatoes*   ½ *cup grated Parmesan,*
¼ *teaspoon salt*   *Romano, or Locatelli cheese*
¼ *teaspoon grated nutmeg*   1½ *cups all-purpose flour*
2 *egg yolks, room temperature*

Bake the potatoes in a preheated 350-degree oven for 1 hour. Skin the
potatoes, and put them through a food mill or mash them. Put the
mashed potatoes into a large bowl.

In another bowl, mix the egg yolks, salt, nutmeg, and ½ cup of grated
cheese; mix well. Combine with the mashed potatoes. Add the flour, a
little at a time, until a dough forms and holds together. The dough
should be soft but firm enough to roll.

On a floured board, roll small amounts of dough into small cylinders;
cut each cylinder into ½-inch pieces. Take each piece, and press it
(and roll it) against a cheese grater. This gives the gnocchi a nice design and texture.

Drop the gnocchi gently into 4 quarts boiling salted water, and cook
for 5 minutes. Drain, and top the gnocchi with the desired sauce.

RED SNAPPER SAUCE FOR ROTELLE

RED PEPPERS AND ONIONS   SERVES 4 TO 6

Paddy's Market, which extends from 34th Street to 42d Street on Ninth
Avenue, in New York City is a true paradise for shopping. Empty grape
crates, orange rinds, and double-parked vehicles clutter the area. People
from all over the city go there for the beautifully fresh produce. The
freshness of foods marketed there satisfied our grandparents, and they
continue to satisfy us. Among the vegetable stalls, international herb-
and-spice shops, and specialty meat stores are a half-dozen fish markets.
We dare anyone to find fresher fish or greater variety. Red snapper
filets, fresh as can be, inexpensive as you could want, are the basis for this

refreshing pasta sauce, which we like to spoon over *rotelle* ("little wheels"). They're not hard to find on supermarket shelves.

3 tablespoons olive oil
1 large red pepper, cored, seeded, and cut into ½-inch cubes
1 medium-size onion, sliced fine
1 garlic clove, chopped fine
6 anchovy filets
3 cups fresh tomatoes, cored, blanched, peeled, seeded, and chopped into ½-inch pieces (or canned plum tomatoes, sieved)
Plenty of pepper, ground fresh

1 pound red snapper filets, washed, dried, and cut into 1- to 1½-inch squares
1 teaspoon lemon juice
1 pound rotelle macaroni
2 tablespoons butter
6 sprigs fresh Italian parsley, stems removed, chopped fine

In a heavy saucepan, heat the olive oil, add the red pepper, onion, garlic, and anchovies, and cook for 5 minutes, stirring frequently. Use a wooden spoon or rubber spatula to dissolve the anchovies.

Then add the tomatoes, sprinkle liberally with freshly ground pepper (this sauce should have a spark or two), and cook for an additional 10 minutes. Add the red snapper and lemon juice, and cook until the fish is tender and flaky. This will not take long, so you'll have to keep your eye on it. Test a piece of fish with a fork for doneness.

While the sauce is cooking, cook the *rotelle* according to package directions but not beyond the *al dente* point. Drain the pasta, and return it to the saucepan in which it was cooked. Add the butter, and mix well. Put the pasta on a large serving platter, or on individual plates; add the sauce, and serve. Garnish with parsley.

SEA SCALLOPS IN A MARINARA SAUCE

SCALLOPS AND TOMATOES   SERVES 4 TO 6

1½ to 2 pounds sea scallops
Juice of ½ lemon
4 tablespoons olive oil
1 clove garlic, chopped fine
2 medium onions or 1 large
onion, chopped fine
4 cups fresh tomatoes, cored,
blanched, peeled, seeded, and
chopped into ½-inch pieces
(or canned plum tomatoes,
sieved)

1 tablespoon fresh parsley,
chopped (or ½ teaspoon
dried)
1 tablespoon fresh basil,
chopped (or ½ teaspoon
dried)
Salt
Pepper, ground fresh
1 teaspoon sugar
½ cup white wine (optional)
Grated Parmesan cheese

Wash the sea scallops, put them in a bowl with the lemon juice, and allow them to stand at room temperature for 15 minutes. Drain and dry them, and set aside.

In a large saucepan, heat the oil. Add the garlic and onion, and sauté them until they begin to take on a light brown color (this takes only a few minutes). Add the tomatoes, parsley, basil, salt, and freshly ground pepper to taste, sugar, and wine (if you wish). Mix well, and bring to a boil. Lower the heat, and let the sauce simmer, uncovered, for approximately 20 minutes.

Add the scallops, and simmer, still uncovered, for about 15 minutes, until the scallops are tender. (Do *not* overcook them, or they will toughen.) Test with a fork; the best way to test for doneness and tenderness is to taste a scallop.

Serve over pasta. But first mix one-third of the sauce with the pasta, and then pour the remaining sauce over the pasta, whether it's all on one large platter or served in individual dishes. Pass the Parmesan cheese separately. (Remember, not everyone likes cheese on fish sauces.)

SPAGHETTI PRIMAVERILE
(Spaghetti with spinach, mushrooms, and cream)

SPINACH AND MUSHROOMS   SERVES 2 TO 3

4 cups fresh spinach leaves,   *1 cup heavy cream*
*   shredded*   *Salt*
½ pound mushrooms   *Pepper, ground fresh*
*   Juice of 1 lemon*   *½ pound spaghetti*
4 tablespoons butter   *4 heaping tablespoons grated*
1 clove garlic, chopped fine   *   Parmesan cheese*
2 tablespoons Marsala

Cook the shredded fresh spinach in boiling salted water until it is tender. Drain well, and set aside.

Wipe the mushrooms with damp kitchen toweling, and cut off stem ends. Slice thin, add lemon juice and mix well.

Melt the butter in a skillet, and add the garlic and Marsala. Cook for 3 minutes; then add the sliced mushrooms. Cook an additional 5 minutes. Add the heavy cream, and bring the mixture to a boil. Add some salt, then pepper liberally. Remove from heat.

Cook the spaghetti (or other pasta) *al dente*, according to the package directions. Drain the pasta, and return it to the pan in which it was cooked. Add the spinach and mushroom mixture to the pasta.

Put the dressed spaghetti in individual serving plates, and top each with Parmesan cheese. (Serves 2 or 3 as a main dish; more as a side dish.)

TOMATO SAUCE WITH MEAT IN THE FAMILY STYLE

TOMATOES AND BEEF   SERVES 6 TO 8

1 tablespoon olive oil
1 small carrot, chopped fine
1 garlic clove, chopped fine
1 small onion, chopped fine
1 pound ground chuck, good
   quality
6 cups fresh or canned tomatoes
   (including pulp and liquid),
   put through food mill to
   remove seeds

1 tablespoon fresh basil,
   chopped fine (or ½ teaspoon
   dried)
1 tablespoon tomato paste
½ cup red wine, good quality
   (optional)
1 teaspoon sugar
1½ teaspoons salt
   Pepper, ground fresh

In a heavy saucepan, heat oil. Cook carrot for 2 minutes. Add onion and garlic, and cook over high heat for 3 minutes. Add ground meat, and cook over high heat until the red color disappears (about 5 minutes). Add wine (if you wish), and sugar.

Add tomatoes, basil, tomato paste, salt, and freshly ground pepper to taste; lower heat to moderate, and bring to boil. Simmer for 1½ hours, and stir frequently (every 10 minutes or so).

Note: If you are using fresh tomatoes, skin them first by plunging them into boiling water and removing skin with aid of a paring knife. Whether you use fresh or canned, Italian plum tomatoes are preferable to others because they have more pulp than liquid and they just are tastier. If by chance, tomatoes are thick and pulpy but lack sufficient liquid content (this almost never happens), add up to ½ cup water to get the consistency of sauce you want.

SALSA TARTUFATA (A TRUFFLED SAUCE)

TRUFFLES AND WHITE WINE   SERVES 4

4 tablespoons butter

3 chicken livers, washed, picked
over, dried, and cut into ¼-inch
cubes

3 chicken gizzards, washed,
trimmed, dried, and cut into
¼-inch cubes

3 chicken hearts, washed,
trimmed, dried, and cut into
¼-inch cubes

½ cup dry white wine

2 cups fresh tomatoes, cored,
blanched, skinned, seeded, and
chopped into ½-inch pieces
(or canned plum tomatoes,
sieved)

Salt

Pepper, ground fresh

2 truffles, sliced very thin and
cut into thinnest strips possible
(see Note)

Grated Parmesan cheese
(optional)

In a skillet, heat 3 tablespoons butter, and sauté the chicken livers, gizzards, and hearts until they are lightly browned. Transfer the chicken organs to a plate, and keep them warm.

Add the wine to the skillet, and with a rubber spatula, deglaze the pan completely over high heat. Then add the tomatoes and salt and pepper to taste, and cook for 5 minutes. Add the chicken pieces to the tomato mixture, and cook an additional 5 minutes over low heat. Add the truffles and any truffle juice you have, and cook for 2 minutes. Stir in the remaining 1 tablespoon of butter, and blend it in well.

Sauce your cooked pasta, and serve immediately. This sauce can be used with a variety of string pastas, such as *spaghettini, vermicelli, fedelini, and fettuccelle* (a narrower version of fettucine). Pass the grated Parmesan if you wish.

Note: If you use canned truffles, drain them and reserve the juice for the sauce.

THE VERSATILE EGG

Today, we think of eggs in terms of their great importance in kitchens all over the world; eggs are a staple and versatile food. But through the ages, the egg has meant many other things: It possessed magical power, was responsible for good or bad fortune, was (and still is) the symbol of fertility, was connected with various forms of witchcraft (if you see a neighbor or friend turn an empty eggshell upside down and break it with a spoon, who knows why?), and Mother Egg was responsible for birth and rebirth in all its forms.

We've never once run out of eggs; we never inventory them and always buy them automatically. We couldn't cook without them. Eggs combine magnificently with other foods and are responsible for performing culinary miracles. They whip into Italian zabaglione, French mayonnaise, and American baked Alaska. They are indispensable as lightening, thickening, binding, and enriching agents. They are necessary for cutlets, fritters, and custards; in garnishings, salads, and dressings: in sauces and soups. They clarify liquids. They become main dishes. They scramble, fry, boil, poach, and bake. And oh, yes, they pickle.

In addition to this remarkable versatility, the egg is special because it can be turned into a meal on only a few minutes' notice. Eggs, prepared in any way, served with salad, cheese, and fruit will be welcomed by any guest expected or otherwise.

Famous combinations bring eggs together with herbs, cheese, and crab meat in the various omelet forms. Our own joy-of-cooking-with-no-notice usually translates eggs into a *frittata*. A *frittata* with vegetables, meat, fish, or cheese or combinations of these, is healthful, satisfying, and easy to make. It has lots of eye appeal, too. We've presented a six-egg *frittata* with peas, but you can substitute approximately the same amount of any other food for the peas. Try, for example, a 10-egg *frittata* with spinach, or a 6-egg *frittata* with broccoli. The combinations are infinite, and we hope you'll invent some of your own.

FRITTATA DI PISELLI
(Omelet of Peas)

PEAS AND EGGS   SERVES 4

2 tablespoons olive oil
1 tablespoon butter
1 small onion, sliced fine
1 small garlic clove, chopped fine
6 eggs
¾ cup fresh or frozen peas, cooked
  (or canned peas, if you must)

6 fresh basil leaves, chopped fine
  (or ½ teaspoon dried)
2 tablespoons grated Parmesan
  cheese
Salt
Pepper, ground fresh

In an 8-inch omelet pan, heat the oil and butter. Add the onions, and sauté them until they are lightly browned. Add the garlic, and cook for 2 minutes longer.

Put the eggs in a bowl, and beat them well. Add the peas, basil, cheese, and salt and pepper to taste, and mix well. Pour this egg mixture into the skillet, and cover the pan. Cook until the *frittata* is set on the bottom side. (This will take several minutes.) Take a 9- or 10-inch plate, set it bottom side up over the skillet, and turn the *frittata* over onto it. Slip the *frittata* back into the skillet, and cook this side for several minutes until browned. *Frittata* can be served hot or cold. Cold *frittata* makes a good sandwich filling.

FRITTATA DI SPINACHIE
(Omelet of Spinach)

SPINACH AND EGGS   SERVES 6

3 tablespoons olive oil
1 tablespoon butter
1 large onion, sliced thin
1 garlic clove, chopped fine
10 eggs
½ pound fresh spinach, washed,
  dried, and chopped fine (about
  1 cup)

⅓ cup grated Parmesan cheese
1 tablespoon fresh tarragon,
  chopped fine (or ½ teaspoon
  dried)
Salt
Pepper, ground fresh

In a heavy 10-inch iron skillet or other ovenproof skillet, heat the oil and butter. Add the onion slices, and cook them until they begin to brown. Add the garlic, and cook 2 minutes longer.

Beat the eggs in a large bowl until they are blended. Add the spinach, cheese, tarragon, and salt and pepper to taste, and mix well. Pour this mixture into the skillet, and cook it for several minutes on the stove top until the eggs begin to set in the bottom of the skillet. Then place the skillet in a preheated 350-degree oven, and bake it for about 10 minutes, until the *frittata* is set. To brown the top, put under the broiler for 1 or 2 minutes.

This *frittata* can also be completed on top of the stove. Turn it over onto a platter that is larger than the skillet, and slip it back into the skillet to cook the other side. (Be sure you can handle the weight of the skillet; remember, this *frittata* calls for a larger skillet than is required by the six-egg *frittata*.) Serve the *frittata* from the skillet. It cuts like a pie and is delicious with a salad and cornbread.

FRITTATA DI BROCCOLI
(Omelet of Broccoli)

BROCCOLI AND EGGS   SERVES 6

Eliminate the spinach. Use 1½ cups cooked chopped broccoli, and sauté it after the onion and garlic have been sautéed. Cook the broccoli just until it heats through and is covered with oil, butter, onions, and garlic. Follow the rest of the procedure.

FRITTATA CON GRANCHIO
(Omelet with Crab Meat)

CRAB MEAT AND EGGS   SERVES 6

Eliminate the spinach. Add 1 cup cooked, cubed crab meat (or shrimp) after the garlic is cooked, and sauté until heated through. Then add the beaten eggs, and follow the rest of the procedure. You may wish to substitute dill for the tarragon.

FRITTATA DI CIPOLLE
(Omelet of Onions)

ONIONS AND EGGS   SERVES 6

Eliminate the spinach, and increase the onion slices to 2 cups. Sauté them until lightly browned. Then add the eggs. All other ingredients remain the same, as does the cooking procedure.

FRITTATA DI PEPERONI
(Omelet of Peppers)

PEPPERS AND EGGS   SERVES 6

Eliminate the spinach. Wash and dry 4 medium-size peppers (2 red, 2 green). Core them, remove seeds, and chop them into ½-inch cubes. Sauté them for 3 minutes before adding the onion. Follow the rest of the procedure.

FRITTATA CON PROSCIUTTO
(Omelet with Prosciutto)

PROSCIUTTO AND EGGS   SERVES 6

Eliminate the spinach. Add ½ cup diced prosciutto, and sauté with the onions to get the most from the fine fat flavor of this ham. Eliminate the tarragon, and be careful of how much salt and pepper you add.

FRITTATA CON SALSICCIA
(Omelet with Sausage)

SAUSAGE AND EGGS   SERVES 6

Eliminate the spinach. Heat the oil and butter, and sauté 3 links Italian sausage, sliced thin, until well done. Then add the eggs. Eliminate the tarragon, and substitute ½ teaspoon dried oregano.

FRITTATA CON PEPERONI SOTT'ACETO
(Omelet with Pickled Peppers)

VINEGAR PEPPERS AND EGGS   SERVES 6

Eliminate the spinach and tarragon. If sweet peppers are used, use 2 cups chopped vinegar peppers; (if hot peppers are used, use ¼ to ½ cup, depending on your taste for hotness). Sauté peppers with onions before adding garlic pieces. If hot peppers are used, eliminate pepper.

Vinegar peppers sautéed in this way make a delicious and unusual *frittata*. Cut into tiny squares, it can be served as an hors d'oeuvre.

Horseradish

A horseradish plant in a garden is a lovely sight, but its practical use comes from its thick taproot. Horseradish is often grated for use as a condiment in dips, spreads, and sauces. In our Frittata "Rafanata" in the Italian style, it is grated for use in an omelet. This Frittata may also be served in wedgelike slices with a variety of meats, notably roast beef, or cut into squares and served piping hot as an hors d'oeuvre.

FRITTATA "RAFANATA" IN THE ITALIAN STYLE

HORSERADISH AND PARMESAN CHEESE   SERVES 4 TO 8

½ *cup vegetable shortening,*
  melted

1 *cup grated fresh horseradish*
  (rafano)

1 *cup grated Parmesan cheese*

1 *small potato, peeled and grated,*
  raw

2 *eggs, well beaten*

1 *teaspoon baking powder*

Heat the shortening in a 7½-inch skillet. Mix all the other ingredients in a bowl. With your hands, shape the mixture into a ball. Put into the hot shortening. (Be very, very careful to lay it in gently; hot shortening can splatter.) Flatten the mixture with a wooden spoon to the approximate size of the skillet. (Shortening will come up the sides of the skillet, and that is what is supposed to happen.)

Over low heat, cook each side until it is well done (approximately 5 minutes). When one side is brown (edges will begin turning deep brown although top will remain off-white or pale cream), remove the pan from the heat, and pour off and reserve as much of the shortening as you can without damaging the shape of the "pie."

Press a plate that is larger than the skillet against the skillet, and quickly turn over the omelet onto the plate. Put the shortening back into the skillet, and slowly slip the omelet back in. Cook it another 4 or 5 minutes, or until this side is also browned.

Then decide which side is better looking, and serve that side up. This *frittata* can be eaten cold, but the flavors are more fragrant and tastier if it is served hot.

EGGS BAKED IN RICE POCKETS

ANCHOVIES AND EGGS   SERVES 4

2½ *cups chicken stock or broth*
2 *tablespoons butter, softened*
1 *cup uncooked rice*
1 *cup fresh tomatoes, cored,*
  blanched, peeled, and chopped
  coarse
1 *tablespoon tomato paste*
1 *large garlic clove, chopped*
  very fine
1 *bay leaf*

4 *whole eggs, at room*
  temperature
4 *anchovy filets, well washed,*
  rinsed, dried, and cut in half
  lengthwise
2 *tablespoons grated Parmesan*
  cheese
1 *tablespoon fresh parsley,*
  chopped fine (or ½ teaspoon
  dried)

In a medium-size, covered saucepan, bring the stock and butter to a boil. Add the rice, stir well, and bring to a boil again. Cover immediately, and lower heat as much as possible, to keep liquid barely simmering. With the cover on, cook the rice 12 to 15 minutes, or until it is tender. Do *not* overcook, or rice will get mushy, rice grains should be independent of each other and should not stick together.

While the rice is cooking, combine the tomatoes, tomato paste, garlic, and bay leaf in a skillet, and bring to a boil. Simmer, uncovered, for 10 minutes, stirring frequently. Discard bay leaf.

Put the cooked rice in a 7 by 10 by 2-inch baking dish (not too deep); with a spoon, create 4 "pockets," each large enough and deep enough to hold an egg. Spoon the tomato sauce over the rice, putting a little into each pocket. Break the eggs, one at a time, into a saucer, and slip an egg into each pocket. Crisscross two anchovy halves over each egg. Sprinkle with Parmesan cheese and parsley, and bake in a preheated 325-degree oven for approximately 15 minutes, or until the eggs are set.

The baking dish should be brought to the table and the eggs and rice spooned onto individual plates.

BAKED EGGS FOR BREAKFAST

BUTTER AND CREAM   SERVES 4

> *8 eggs*
> *4 tablespoons butter*
> *½ cup heavy cream*
> *Salt and freshly ground pepper*

These eggs are best baked (2 to a dish) in individual au gratin dishes (approximately 6 inches wide and 1 inch deep). Put 1 tablespoon butter in each dish, and place them in a preheated 325-degree oven. Allow the butter to melt; Then remove each dish, and use a rubber spatula to spread the butter so that it covers the bottom of the dish.

Add 2 eggs to each dish, and spoon 1 tablespoon heavy cream over each egg yolk. Sprinkle with salt and pepper to taste. Return the dishes to the oven, and bake for approximately 10 minutes, or until the whites set. Serve at once.

Eggs cooked in this way, *sur le plat* ("on the plate"), can be combined in many ways with other foods (sausages, country ham slices, and so on). One of our favorite combinations is to add several tablespoonfuls of sautéed mushrooms to the bottom of each dish after the melted butter has been spread and just before the raw eggs are added.

((4))

A Whole Chicken, en Casserole, en Croute; Quail and Quince, and Other Gossamer Poultry and Game Preparations

POULTRY

Chicken, like bread, potatoes, and rice, can be eaten every day with interest. The term *chicken* includes everything from a spring chicken weighing only 1½ pounds to a fat hen weighing as much as 6 pounds. The chicken is truly omnipresent; it is the most popular food bird in the world, and it is cooked and served in hundreds of ways. Simon and Howe, in their *Dictionary of Gastronomy*,* tell us that the earliest mention of the domestic fowl occurred in a passage by a Greek author, circa 570 B.C., about the same time that Aesop was admonishing the foolish milkmaid: "Don't count your chickens before they are hatched."

Poultry culture is a fine art today, but it is not without its critics. The average fowl, before it reaches our supermarkets, passes through battery-fed operations that have little or no resemblance to the way they were fed and cared for in the barnyards of yesterday.

A chicken of first quality can make an elegant preparation—if you

* André L. Simon and Robin Howe, *Dictionary of Gastronomy* (New York: McGraw-Hill Book Company, 1970).

can find it! A first-quality chicken should be well fed. It should also be fresh-killed and not frozen, although quick-frozen poultry is better than the cold-storage variety. When we were growing up, the roasted chicken we had for Sunday dinner was slaughtered early Sunday morning. Our mother, Angela, and our grandmother, Beatrice, were the executioners. Their meat cleavers were kept in special places and scrupulously cared for. The bird(s) were picked up early Sunday morning from the family butcher or from a *paisano* who raised them in his barnyard in Long Island or New Jersey. It may be difficult for you to imagine this, but the bird was axed on a New York City windowsill.

You may not have a handy chopping block, but you can try to find an honest butcher who sells freshly killed poultry. When you find him, hold onto him. Is freshly killed chicken more expensive? Yes. But, then, isn't filet mignon more costly than chuck?

Braised or boiled, poached or pan-fried, chicken lends itself to many compatible combinations. And for those who prefer their chicken uncooked, there's the Japanese *torisashi*: thin slices of uncooked chicken breast with angel's-hair servings of radish, lemon, and scallions, and horseradish and soy sauce.

To *poach* poultry is to simmer it gently in stock or water. The stock is usually chicken or veal, but diluted beef stock may also be used. The usual procedure calls for cleaning and trussing the bird and rubbing it with a piece of lemon; we almost always let the bird sit in water with the juice and rind of half a lemon for 15 minutes or so. The bird (which may be larded, depending on the recipe you're following) is then put in a large saucepan and covered with stock or water (in which case it makes its own stock). The liquid is brought to a boil, and then the heat is lowered to achieve a slow, gentle simmer until the bird is cooked. (To test for doneness, prick the chicken with a fork or knife. The juice that comes forth should be clear and light pink.)

Poaching is a popular way to prepare poultry, and there are endless combinations.

Poach a chicken, and serve it covered with a velouté sauce combined with a thick tomato purée (the proportions should be approximately 1 cup of velouté and ¼ cup of tomato purée, depending on the thickness of both sauces). We combine poached chicken pieces and velouté and tomato sauces with homemade fettucini in our Fettucine Gallina (see page 127).

Partially cook rice in chicken or veal stock, mix it with a cut-up truffle, and stuff a chicken. Then poach the bird until it is cooked, and serve it with mushrooms cooked in thickened chicken stock sauce (use the liquid in which the chicken was poached, flavored with 1 tablespoon of Madeira).

Poach a chicken, and while it is cooking, add a variety of vegetables to cook, too (carrots, onions, celery, turnip chunks, and so on). Serve it with chicken stock enriched with a roux plus egg yolks, cream, and 2 or 3 tablespoons of chopped fresh parsley, basil, thyme, or tarragon. Add ¼-inch cubes of peeled fresh tomatoes.

Poach a chicken, and serve it with a curry sauce.

One of the more famous poached birds is French; it is a chicken *à la demi-deuil* ("in half-mourning"): under its skin, it's studded with sliced black truffles, and then the whole chicken is bathed in a sauce suprême.

Poach a chicken with vegetables, put it in a casserole, and cover it with a pâté *brisée* according to our recipe A Whole Chicken en Casserole, en Croûte, in this chapter.

To *braise* a chicken is to brown it all over, then cook it slowly, covered, in a braising liquid until it is tender. This method is generally used for poultry that is large (and therefore older). The braising liquid may be water or stock prepared in advance, but red or white wine, a marinade, and vegetables are almost always added.

Poach a bird, about 5 pounds in weight, with onions, carrots, celery, and herbs until it is almost tender. Cook the bird in the oven with butter, garlic, red wine, and bacon. Add some stock and herbs. When the bird is done, cut it in serving pieces, and serve it with the vegetables and a thickened sauce.

Cut a chicken, and brown the pieces in butter with onions. Finish cooking, covered, with a curry sauce.

Brown chicken pieces in butter, and ignite them with Cognac. Then cover them with onions, garlic, juniper berries, and heavy cream, and cook in your oven or Dutch oven until almost done.

During the last few minutes of baking, add some chopped truffles or mushrooms, or both.

Famous ways to braise ducks are *a l'orange* or *aux figues* (with figs).

An interesting way to braise chicken was developed by the chef Luigi Strazzoli. He braises pieces of boned chicken with shallots, mushrooms, and artichokes in white wine laced lightly with sherry. This Roman specialty, named for the Seven Hills, is called *Pollo dei Sette Colli* ("Chicken of the Seven Hills").

To *sauté* poultry is to brown it, whole or in pieces, in butter, oil, or some other fat. The procedure is similar to braising, but the cooking time is much shorter. Older poultry is braised; younger poultry is sautéed. The sautéeing is done quickly and usually with small pieces of meat, although spring chickens can be halved, somewhat flattened, and sautéed.

Sauté chicken pieces in oil and butter, and then deglaze the pan with a *duxelles* sauce combined with chopped prosciutto and some tarragon. This sauce is then served over the browned chicken pieces.

Brown a whole chicken by sautéeing it in butter and adding onions to cook along with it. Remove the chicken, deglaze the pan with vinegar, and boil the liquid down. Then add a thickened brown sauce, heat well, and pour all over the chicken.

There's chicken cacciatore ("hunter's style"); chicken sautéed with herbs, shallots, and white wine; chicken sautéed with olives, mushrooms, anchovies, and parsley; chicken sautéed tarragon or truffles; chicken sautéed with morels or other mushrooms; chicken sautéed with paprika and potatoes.

We find that chicken breasts and thighs are excellent for buying, cooking, serving, and freezing. Chicken thighs are meaty, as are breasts, and are considerably less expensive than most meats (it seems to us that only the more expensive cuts of beef, for example, can be sautéed, and we hope we've chewed on our last piece of pan-fried chewy supermarket slabs of sinewy steak). Chicken thighs and breasts sauté quickly and can be brought easily from stove top to tabletop; one of their best features is their ability to freeze and reheat.

Two of our sauté recipes in this chapter are for Chicken Thighs in an Herbed Cream Sauce and Chicken Parts in the 28 West Style. There are several others. Our chicken breasts are sautéed in Chicken Breasts Suprême in Champagne Sauce. And without question, one of the simplest, best-tasting, and most elegant in Suprême de Volaille aux Truffes: chicken breasts stuffed with mozzarella and truffles and sautéed in butter.

The Chinese, and now other peoples as well, sauté or stir-fry their chicken in a wok. A great combination of food that brings together celery and walnuts with chicken is Chicken with Walnuts in the Chinese Style.

Roasting poultry or game can be done in two ways: in an oven or on a spit over a naked flame. Poultry is well roasted when pure white juice flows out of the bird's body; if there are red traces, the poultry is not perfectly cooked. Winged game, however, should give out a pinkish liquid. Poultry and game should be trussed and barded to protect the delicate breasts from browning too quickly. Barding (tying a piece of fat around the bird or meat) also helps to keep the drier parts of the bird—its breast, for example—moist. Spit-roasted poultry and game should be basted frequently with fat; it is the fat that produces a rich browning. In spit roasting, allow the juices to run into a pan. The fat in the juice will rise to the top, and you can brush it on the roast. Chickens may be roasted in combinations of dressings, stuffings, vegetables, and fruits.

WHOLE CHICKEN EN CASSEROLE, EN CROUTE

CARROTS AND CREAM   SERVES 6 TO 8

This is a spectacular one-dish meal to bring to the table. It is quite simple to make. Although many of the ingredients are in the traditional chicken pot pie, this presentation is tastier because of the enriched white wine sauce and considerably more dramatic in appearance, with the whole chicken enveloped in a steaming piecrust as it is set on the table. Whole carrots stuffed in the bird's cavity add just the right panache.

TO PREPARE THE CHICKEN AND STOCK:

3- to 4-pound whole
chicken, including the neck,
gizzard, and heart

3 chicken breasts, with bone in,
skin removed, halved to make 6
pieces

1 onion, chopped coarse

7 carrots (1 sliced thin, 6 kept
whole)

1 celery stalk, sliced thin

1 tablespoon fresh tarragon,
chopped (or 1 teaspoon dried)

1 bay leaf

3 sprigs parsley (or 2 tablespoons
dried)

½ teaspoon black pepper, ground
fresh

1 cup dry vermouth

2 quarts water (approximately)

Wash the chicken, neck, gizzard, and heart, and put all in a saucepan just a little larger than the chicken, and deep enough to hold more ingredients. Add the chicken breasts, but do *not* add the liver.

Add all the other ingredients. Pack the chicken breasts and other items as tightly together as you can so that about 2 quarts of water will cover the contents. Cover the pot, and bring to a boil. Reduce the heat, and keep at a simmer.

The chicken breasts should be done in 10 to 15 minutes. Do *not* over-cook them. Remove the chicken breasts, and bone them. Add the breastbones to the chicken stockpot, and continue to cook for another 30 or 40 minutes, until the whole chicken is done. Put the boned chicken breasts aside.

While the whole chicken is simmering, test the whole carrots for done-ness; when they are *al dente*, remove them from the simmering pot even if the whole chicken requires additional cooking. Set the whole carrots aside.

Remove the whole chicken when done, and keep it whole. Be careful when removing it from the pot. (A good way is to lift it with a large wooden spoon inserted in its cavity.) Set it aside. If there are parsley, celery, carrot slices, or other pieces of vegetables clinging to the chicken, remove them, and put them back into the pot.

Turn up the heat, and boil the stock rapidly for another 30 minutes. Strain the stock. You will need 5 cups, but don't be concerned if there's more; you can always freeze it for another use or use it to thin the sauce later in this recipe. The stock will be tastier, however, if you cook it down to at least 6 cups.

TO PREPARE PÂTE BRISÉE:
2 *cups all-purpose flour*
¼ *pound butter*
3 *tablespoons vegetable shortening*
½ *teaspoon salt*
5 *tablespoons iced water*

Before measuring flour, cut butter and shortening into very small pieces, and put them on a plate or a piece of wax paper and into the freezer for 5 or 10 minutes. They must be cold, but *not* frozen, before they are mixed with the other ingredients.

Combine flour, salt, butter, and shortening in a large mixing bowl, and work with a pastry blender (or fingertips) until mixture resembles coarse meal. (Do *not* overblend; if you do, the butter and shortening will begin to melt.)

Add several ice cubes to a 1- or 2-cup container. Add water, and stir rapidly with fork or spoon to "ice" water. With a measuring tablespoon, quickly add 5 tablespoons of iced water to meal mixture; then quickly gather the dough into a ball with several hand movements, as if you were molding an oversized meatball. (This shouldn't take more than several seconds.) If some of mixture or dough will not adhere, add a few drops of iced water to nonadhering bits of dough to complete ball. Knead ball two or three times, and sprinkle lightly with flour. Wrap in tin foil or wax paper, and refrigerate for at least 30 minutes (more if possible).

TO PREPARE THE SAUCE:
4 *tablespoons butter*   2 *egg yolks*
8 *tablespoons all-purpose flour*   1 *cup heavy cream*
5 *cups chicken stock (from*   *Salt to taste*
  cooking the chicken)   *Juice of* ½ *lemon*

Melt the butter in a saucepan, and stir in the flour to make a roux. Stir the roux for 3 minutes. Do *not* let it brown. Add the chicken stock, stir frequently, and bring to a slow boil. Cook for 2 or 3 minutes, and then remove from the heat.

In a small bowl, combine the egg yolks and cream, and beat them until smooth. (Beating with a fork is sufficient, or use a hand egg beater or wire whisk if you wish.) Slowly add about ½ cup of the stock mixture. Mix this well, and return it to the larger saucepan of stock. Mix until smooth, and return to heat for several minutes. The mixture should be thick enough to coat a spoon. If it is too thick, add additional stock; if too thin, add *beurre manié,* and simmer until thick enough. Salt to taste, and add the lemon juice. Set aside.

TO ASSEMBLE:

1 whole chicken, cooked
6 chicken breasts, cooked
6 carrots whole, cooked
5 cups cream sauce (approxi-
mately)

1 recipe pâté brisée, uncooked
Several sprigs fresh parsley

Place the whole chicken in an uncovered casserole about 9 inches in diameter and 4 inches deep. Place the chicken on its neck end with legs and thighs facing upward; the chicken's back should lean against one side of the casserole. Add the chicken breasts to the bottom of the casserole, and use them to hold the leaning chicken in place. (The reason for the leaning chicken is that when it is covered with crust and baked, the outline of whole chicken will be visible and quite beautiful to look at. There is something terribly voluptuous about chicken. Place the carrots in the cavity opening so that about half of the carrot lengths protrude from it. Add the cream sauce to the casserole.

Remove the ball of dough from the refrigerator, and place it on a lightly floured surface. Roll it out as quickly as possible, and check each roll of dough to be sure it is not sticking to the surface. Flour both top and underside lightly to prevent sticking. Continue to roll to required size (approximately 14 inches if casserole is 9 inches in diameter), and place it over the filled chicken casserole immediately. As you place the pastry over the casserole, tear the pastry to allow the carrots to stick out. (Do this with your hands.) Be sure to hook the pastry over the edge of the casserole by making one of several pastry edges (stand-up, fork flute, fluted, or rope). If you cannot put the casserole into the oven immediately, place it in the refrigerator to keep the pastry from melting. (However, remember that the contents of the casserole are warm, and the pastry won't hold for long, even in the refrigerator.) There is no need to prick the pastry because steam can escape through the pastry at the carrot points.

Cook the casserole in the middle of a preheated 400-degree oven for 35 or 40 minutes, until the pastry is nicely browned. Remove it from oven. Add several sprigs of fresh parsley by lodging them between the carrots. Serve immediately.

Run a knife through the center of the pastry to cut it in half. Cut half the pastry into thirds, and remove them to a serving plate. This will allow you to serve breasts and sauce easily and also to cut into one side of the whole chicken. Be sure to serve at least 4 or 5 tablespoons of sauce with the chicken and pastry and add 1 whole carrot from the cavity as a side vegetable. Add a piece of parsley to each individual serving.

CHICKEN WITH WALNUTS IN THE CHINESE STYLE

CELERY AND WALNUTS   SERVES 4 TO 6

1½ *pounds chicken breasts*
  Juice of ½ lemon
2 *tablespoons soy sauce*
2 *tablespoons cornstarch*
1 *teaspoon salt*
1 *teaspoon sugar*
2 *teaspoons dry sherry (or dry*
  white vermouth or rice wine)
2 *cups celery, cut into ¾-inch*
  squares

1 *cup onions, cut into ½-inch*
  squares
1½ *cups bamboo shoots, cut into*
  ¾-inch pieces
12 *water chestnuts, sliced tissue*
  thin
6 *tablespoons peanut oil*
½ *cup chicken stock*
1½ *cups walnut meats*

Wash the chicken breasts in cool water. Bone and skin them; cut them in half. Trim off all fat. Poultry scissors or a sharp paring knife is excellent for this. This dish calls for pure white chicken meat, so be fastidious in cleaning and preparing it. Without drying them, put the chicken pieces in a bowl. Add the lemon juice, stir the chicken in it, and set aside for about 10 minutes.

Then dry the chicken pieces with paper towels or a tea towel. (We find it easy to lay a tea towel on a flat surface, put the chicken pieces on half of it, fold over the other half, and pat the pieces dry.) Flatten the chicken pieces as completely as possible, and with a sharp knife, cut them into ¾-inch lengths; then cut the lengths into ¾-inch squares.

In a large bowl, add the soy sauce, cornstarch, salt, sugar, and sherry (or vermouth or rice wine); stir well until fully combined, and then add the chicken pieces. Move the chicken around in the bowl to cover the pieces with the sauce. Set this aside while you prepare the vegetables.

Wash the celery stalks well. If the stalks are stringy, use a potato peeler to scrape the outsides, thereby destringing them. If the stalks are too wide, cut them in half lengthwise. An interesting effect is achieved by adding a few pieces with leaves and slicing the stalks on the bias (rather than straight across). Combine the celery pieces with the cubed bamboo shoots and onion pieces and the water chestnuts (cut in the thinnest possible slices), and put them all into a bowl.

This dish is best prepared by using two woks. If woks are not available, ordinary large skillets are almost as good. Add 3 tablespoons peanut oil to each wok or skillet, and heat until sizzling. If the oil begins to smoke, turn down the heat, but keep the oil very hot. Vegetable oil may be substituted for the peanut oil, but *do not* use olive oil, butter, or margarine (their flavors are too pronounced). Cook the vegetables first by putting them all in the wok. Stir frequently (using a pair of chopsticks, a wooden spoon, or a pancake spatula) until the vegetables are browned somewhat at the edges but still crisp.

As soon as you begin to cook the vegetables, add the chicken and its marinade to the other wok or skillet. The chicken will cook quickly (in 1 or 2 minutes). Be sure to stir the chicken pieces so that all cook quickly and evenly. Add the stock to the chicken, and remove the wok or skillet from the heat.

The vegetables should be cooked by now. Remove them with a slotted spoon, and put them into the wok or skillet holding the chicken. Quickly sauté the walnut meats in the remaining hot oil in which the vegetables were cooked (this should take only 30 seconds to 1 minute). Add the walnuts to the chicken and vegetables, and heat over very high heat for 1 minute or less. Serve immediately.

CHICKEN BREASTS SUPREME IN CHAMPAGNE SAUCE

CHAMPAGNE AND FOIE GRAS   SERVES 6 TO 8

TO PREPARE THE SAUCE:

3 tablespoons butter   *⅔ cup dry champagne*
3 tablespoons all-purpose flour   *1 cup heavy cream*
2 cups Rich Chicken Stock (see
*   page 49)*
2 tablespoons fresh tarragon,
*   chopped fine (or 1 teaspoon*
*   dried)*

In a medium-size saucepan, heat the butter slowly, and add the flour. Stir with a wire whisk until well blended. Add the chicken stock and tarragon, and bring the mixture to a boil. Add the champagne, and simmer as slowly as possible for about 30 minutes. Add the heavy cream, and simmer for another 10 minutes.

TO PREPARE THE CHICKEN:

6 whole chicken breasts or 12 half   *2 tablespoons butter*
*   chicken breasts*   *2 tablespoons shallots, chopped*
Juice of 1 lemon   *   fine*
Salt   *One 2-ounce can foie gras (or*
Pepper, ground fresh   *   one ½-ounce truffle, sliced fine)*

Place the can of foie gras in the refrigerator.

Wash the chicken; remove the skin, gristle, and bones. Use poultry scissors or a sharp paring knife to cut away any remaining pieces of fat or bone. After washing them again, put chicken breasts in a bowl, add the lemon juice, and let stand for 10 to 15 minutes. Drain the chicken, and dry with a paper or tea towel. Salt and pepper to taste.

Heat the butter in a large skillet, and add the chicken. Sauté until done on both sides (10 to 15 minutes on each side). Transfer chicken breasts to a platter, and put them in a warm oven, but do *not* cook further. Add the shallots to the skillet, and cook until they are soft.

Add 1 or 2 cups sauce to the skillet. Over moderate to high heat, deglaze the skillet, and add every drop from the skillet to the champagne sauce.

Arrange the chicken on the platter, and add the sauce by pouring it over the meat. There will be quite a bit of sauce because this dish is meant to be served with rice or pasta. (Our preference is a small amount of buttered noodles mixed with parsley or more tarragon.) Put the pasta (or rice) on the platter first, and top with the chicken pieces. Add the slices of truffles over all. If using foie gras, cut it into tiny squares and add all but a few pieces over the chicken before adding the sauce. The remaining few pieces of foie gras should be strewn over the sauce as a decorative touch. If you grow fresh tarragon, add a 4- or 5-inch stem of it, too.

CHICKEN STEW IN THE FRENCH STYLE

COGNAC AND SHALLOTS   SERVES 8

Two 2½- to 3-pound chickens
Juice of 1 lemon
Salt
Pepper, ground fresh
6 tablespoons butter
6 slices bacon
¼ cup French brandy or Cognac
½ cup shallots, chopped
4 tablespoons all-purpose flour
2 cups chicken stock
2 cups dry white wine (or 1 cup dry vermouth and 1 cup water)
1 bouquet garni wrapped in cheesecloth (1 bay leaf, 12 peppercorns, several sprigs of parsley, several sprigs of thyme or 1 teaspoon of each dried, and 1 celery stalk, including leaves, chopped)

8 carrots, scraped and kept whole
3 large raw potatoes, peeled, cut in half and each half cut into 6 pieces
1 pound mushrooms, wiped lightly with a tea towel or paper towel and kept whole (trim just enough of the stem ends to freshen)
Sprig of fresh parsley (or ½ teaspoon dried)

Cut both chickens into serving pieces, and wash them. (We remove most of the skin from the breasts, thighs, and backs but leave it on the drumsticks because a little chicken fat adds to the flavor.) Put the undried pieces into a large bowl, and add the lemon juice. Allow the chicken to rest in the lemon juice for 10 to 15 minutes.

Brown the bacon slices in a skillet. Remove, drain on paper towels, and set aside.

Take the chicken pieces out of the lemon juice, and place them on a tea towel. Pat them dry, and salt and pepper them well. Sauté them in 4 tablespoons butter, 4 or 5 pieces at a time, depending on the size of the skillet; when the pieces are well browned on both sides, transfer them to a large, covered casserole. Add the Cognac, ignite it, and watch it burn away.

Leave only 2 tablespoons bacon grease in the skillet, and sauté the shallots in it for 5 minutes, stirring frequently with a wooden spoon. Sprinkle the flour over the shallots, blend well with the spoon, and cook an additional 2 minutes. Then add the stock, and stir continually as the sauce thickens. Add the wine, and stir until blended, which means that the bottom of the skillet is well scraped and deglazed. Add the sauce to the casserole.

Combine the bouquet garni ingredients in a bowl or on top of a chopping board or work counter so that you'll know how large a piece of cheese-cloth you'll need. (We usually use a double thickness of cheesecloth.) Add the bouquet garni, whole carrots, and potatoes to the casserole.

Put the casserole in a moderate oven (375 degrees), and bake for 30 minutes. In the meantime, melt 2 tablespoons butter in a large skillet, and sauté the mushrooms over high heat for 5 minutes. Remove with a slotted spoon, and add to the casserole. Test the chicken and vegetables for doneness, and carefully stir all the ingredients. Return the casserole to the oven, and cook until the chicken is tender and the vegetables slightly underdone (approximately 10 minutes).

Just before serving, crumble the bacon slices over the contents of the casserole, and sprinkle ½ teaspoon dried parsley overall. Or throw on a fresh parsley sprig for a refreshing touch of bright green. Or turn chicken stew out onto a large platter, and sprinkle bacon and parsley overall.

This stew may be made a day or two ahead of time, or it may be frozen for several months. It is beautiful not only because of its taste and fragrance, but also because of the free time it gives you to sit with your guests or family. A wonderful accompaniment is a simple salad of arugola with an oil and vinegar dressing.

CHICKEN THIGHS IN AN HERBED CREAM SAUCE

CREAM AND TARRAGON   SERVES 6

TO PREPARE THE CHICKEN:

12 *chicken thighs*
  Juice of ½ lemon
3 *carrots, ends removed, sliced*
  thin
3 *celery stalks, including leaves,*
  sliced thin
2 *leeks, well washed, sliced thin*
1 *medium-size onion, chopped*
  coarse

2 *sprigs fresh parsley (or ½*
  teaspoon dried)
2 *sprigs fresh tarragon (or ½*
  teaspoon dried)
1 *bay leaf*
12 *whole peppercorns*
1 *teaspoon salt*

Wash the chicken thighs in cool water, and cut away all or most of the skin on each thigh. Put thighs in a bowl (no need to dry them), and add the lemon juice. Move the thighs around in the bowl to cover each piece with juice, and let stand for 10 to 15 minutes.

Transfer the chicken thighs to a heavy saucepan, and cover them with approximately 4 cups cold water. Add the carrots, celery, leeks, onion, parsley, tarragon, bay leaf, peppercorns, and salt. Bring this to a boil, and let it simmer for about 30 minutes, or until the chicken thighs are tender.

Remove chicken thighs with a slotted spoon, and keep them warm. Remove peppercorns, bay leaf or any pieces of vegetables clinging to the chicken, and toss these back into the stock. Cook stock down at a vigorous boil for another 15 to 20 minutes. Strain, and measure 3 cups stock. Discard the vegetables after extracting as much juice from them as you can by pressing them firmly against the strainer. Excess stock may be stored in the refrigerator for a few days; freeze if you intend to keep longer. (If by chance you end up with less than 3 cups, add water.) Set the stock aside.

TO PREPARE THE SAUCE:

6 *tablespoons butter*
6 *tablespoons all-purpose flour*
3 *cups chicken stock (from*
  cooking chicken thighs)
2 *cups heavy cream*

In a saucepan, melt 4 tablespoons butter, and add the flour. Blend well with a wire whisk, and then slowly add the 3 cups stock. Keep stirring as you cook for 15 minutes. Pour the heavy cream into the thickened sauce, and slowly bring it to the boiling point. Remove from the heat, and add the remaining 2 tablespoons butter. Adjust salt seasoning.

Arrange the chicken thighs on a serving platter, and add just enough sauce to cover them. Put the remaining sauce in a bowl or pitcher or sauceboat. Sprinkle a bit of tarragon over the creamed thighs, and serve immediately.

This dish should be served with boiled potatoes, rice, noodles, grits, cornbread or cornsticks, or something else that will absorb the sauce. And pass the sauce!

CHICKEN CURRY WITH FOURTEEN CONDIMENTS

CURRY AND APPLES   SERVES 12

TO PREPARE THE CHICKEN AND THE STOCK:

Two 4- to 4½-pound chickens,	*1 bay leaf*
including necks and viscera	*1 sprig fresh parsley (or ½*
2 celery stalks, chopped coarse	*teaspoon dried)*
12 peppercorns	*1 tablespoon salt*
2 carrots, chopped coarse	*3 whole cloves*
1 onion, chopped	*1 cup dry vermouth (optional)*

Wash the chickens, and put them into a large kettle. Add the necks and gizzards, but save the livers for another use. Cover the chickens with cool water, and add the other ingredients. Bring to a boil, and simmer for 45 minutes, or until the chickens are tender. Remove the chickens from the kettle, and set aside to cool. Keep the kettle on the heat to cook the stock down. As soon as the chicken is cool enough to handle, bone it, and put the *bones* back into the stockpot. Discard the skin.

Cut the chicken meat into 1-inch cubes, and set aside. Boil the stock rapidly, and cook down for 1 hour. Strain the stock, and discard all bones, vegetables, and herbs.

TO PREPARE THE SAUCE:

2 tablespoons vegetable oil

8 slices bacon

½ cup celery stalks, including leaves, sliced thin

½ cup onion, chopped fine

3 garlic cloves, chopped fine

½ cup all-purpose flour

1 cup applesauce

¼ cup curry (more if desired)

6 tablespoons tomato paste

2 tablespoons sugar

2 tablespoons lemon juice

2½ cups chicken stock

2 to 3 cups light cream

In a large saucepan, sauté the bacon slices in the vegetable oil until they are well done. Remove them with a slotted spoon, put them on a paper towel to drain, and set them aside. (They will be crumbled later, put in a bowl, and serve as one of the condiments.)

Add the celery, onion, garlic, and flour, and cook for 5 minutes. Stir constantly.

Then add the applesauce, ¼ cup curry powder, tomato paste, sugar, lemon juice, and stock, and cook for 45 minutes. Stir frequently, and taste for desired curry strength. (We usually add more by combining curry powder with 1 or 2 tablespoons of leftover stock and adding this to the sauce.) The curry sauce should have bite, as if you had added chili powder or a dash of Tabasco.

Measure sauce to see how many cups you have. For each cup of sauce, add 1 cup light cream. Bring this to a boil, add the chicken pieces, and heat through. Thin, if you wish, with either more light cream or stock. Place in a serving dish (we like to use a shiny, tin-lined copper kettle or a large decorative platter or bowl) and set it in the center of the table, surrounded with bowls or saucers of the following condiments:

1. crumbled bacon pieces
2. chopped onion
3. chopped fresh green pepper
4. small chunks of fresh pineapple
5. raisins
6. shredded coconut
7. sliced bananas (tossed in lemon juice to prevent darkening)
8. crushed peanuts (use a rolling pin)
9. chopped fresh tomatoes (cored, blanched, peeled, and cut into small squares)

10. chopped dates (pits removed)
11. Chutney 1 (see page 378)
12. Chutney 2 (see page 379)
13. whole preserved kumquats
14. diced apples (tossed in lemon juice to prevent darkening)

We serve this curry with a base of rice, and our guests help themselves to any or all of the condiments. A teaspoonful of each atop the curry is the way we do it, but the chutneys go on the side. We've tried many different wines with curry, and we still think ice-cold beer is best. There is no greater combination with curry.

CHICKEN CHINOISERIE

GARLIC AND GINGER   SERVES 6

3 chicken breasts, boned and
skinned, halved to make 6
pieces
1 garlic clove, chopped fine
2 tablespoons fresh ginger,
chopped fine

3 tablespoons soy sauce
3 tablespoons rice wine (or dry
vermouth)
¾ cup cornstarch (approximately)
½ cup peanut oil

Remove the skin, cartilage, and all fat from the chicken breast halves, and wash them under cold water. (A pair of scissors is a good utensil to help remove the skin and fat and trim the breasts.) Dry the pieces of chicken, and put them in a clean bowl.

Add the garlic, ginger, soy sauce, and rice wine to the bowl, and mix well by moving breasts around in the bowl. Marinate at least 30 minutes, but no more than 3 hours (the chicken seems to toughen after that). Keep the bowl covered with a cloth, plastic wrap, or foil to keep the chicken from drying.

Heat the peanut oil in a skillet large enough to hold all 6 breast halves in one layer. Oil should be *hot* but not burning. While the oil is heating, perform the next step quickly.

Place the cornstarch on a plate close to the cooking unit. Stir the chicken breasts to be sure each piece gets its share of the marinade, garlic, and ginger pieces, and coat each piece liberally with cornstarch.

Go from the cornstarch plate to the skillet with the hot oil in one step; repeat with the rest of the chicken pieces.

Fry the chicken breast halves 2 minutes or less on each side, depending on thickness of the meat. Use wooden or metal tongs to turn the chicken, and keep the heat as high as you can without burning the oil. You will be pleasantly surprised at how fast the chicken breasts will cook and brown. These breasts should be served within a few minutes of being browned.

STUFFED CHICKEN IN THE PERSIAN STYLE

HONEY AND APRICOTS   SERVES 6

TO PREPARE THE CHICKEN:

> 4- to 5-pound roasting chicken
> Juice of 1 lemon

Wash the chicken well in cold water. Place it in a pan, cover it with water, add the lemon juice, and let it stand for 10 to 15 minutes. Remove the chicken from the water, dry it well, and set it aside.

TO PREPARE THE STUFFING:

2 tablespoons butter	*1 cup chicken stock*
1 medium-size onion, chopped fine	*¼ cup honey*
½ cup bulgar (see Note)	*½ cup dried apricots, chopped fine*
1 teaspoon cinnamon	*Salt*
	Pepper, ground fresh

In a covered saucepan, heat the butter, and sauté the onion for about 5 minutes, stirring frequently. Add the bulgar, and cook an additional 5 minutes. Then add the cinnamon, stock, honey, apricots, and salt and pepper to taste. Bring this to a simmer, keeping the heat as low as possible. Cover the saucepan, and cook for another 5 minutes, just barely simmering. Remove the saucepan from the heat, and allow it to stand for 45 minutes, or until the bulgar (or rice) has absorbed the liquid. (Do not remove the cover during this time.) Then stuff the chicken with this mixture, and roast it in a moderate oven (350 to 375 degrees) for 1½ hours or longer, until the chicken is done.

TO BASTE AND GLAZE THE CHICKEN:
2 tablespoons butter
¼ cup honey
½ teaspoon salt
Pepper, ground fresh
⅓ cup sesame seeds

Heat the butter and honey until it is combined. Brush this mixture over the chicken every 10 minutes while it is roasting. Do *not* add the sesame seeds until the last 10 minutes of roasting. At that point, mix the salt and pepper with the sesame seeds, and sprinkle the seeds all over the chicken. Place chicken on a large platter and bring it to the table and carve it there.

Note: You can substitute rice for the bulgar (cracked wheat), but try to use the bulgar. It is obtainable in many shops across the country, particularly in large cities. You can order it by mail from Middle Eastern Food Center, 380 Third Avenue, New York, New York 10016. Bulgar has other uses; a particularly good one is a refreshing salad, à la Alma Sotel, in combination with diced fresh tomatoes, chopped parsley, oil, vinegar, salt, and pepper.

CHICKEN THIGHS IN THE GUMBO STYLE

OKRA AND PLUM TOMATOES   SERVES 8

12 chicken thighs
Juice of ½ lemon
½ cup all-purpose flour
1 teaspoon salt
Pepper, ground fresh
4 thin slices bacon
1 quart chicken stock
2 tablespoons butter
*2 medium-size onions, chopped
fine*
*2 green peppers, seeded, sliced,
and chopped into ¼-inch pieces
(see Note)*

1 hot chili pepper, fresh or dried
*2 cups fresh plum tomatoes
(canned plum tomatoes are
acceptable)*
1 garlic clove, chopped fine
*3 ears fresh sweet corn (or 1 cup
frozen or canned corn kernels)*
4 full tablespoons rice, uncooked
*1 cup fresh okra, chopped in
1-inch pieces (or one 10-ounce
package frozen okra)*

Remove the skin from the chicken thighs, and wash the chicken in cool water. Put the thighs, still wet, in a large bowl, and add the lemon juice. Set aside for 10 to 15 minutes.

In the meantime, combine the flour, salt, and pepper in a brown paper sack or a plastic bag (approximately 11 by 14 inches). Dry the chicken thighs with paper towels or a tea towel, and put them in the bag. Hold the opening of the bag closed with one hand and the bottom of the bag with the other, and shake it vigorously to coat the thighs. This is an easy and neat way to flour chicken parts, but be careful not to let the bag pop out of your hands.

Fry the bacon slices in a large skillet until well done. Place them on paper towels to drain, and set them aside to cool.

Brown the chicken thighs on both sides in the bacon fat, and when each piece is done, place it in a large, flameproof casserole or saucepan. (Whichever you choose, it should have a cover.) Add the chicken stock, cover the cooking utensil, and cook the chicken thighs until tender (25 to 30 minutes.)

After you cover the chicken pot, you can start preparing the vegetables. Melt the butter in the same saucepan or skillet in which the chicken was browned. Add the onion, green pepper, and chili pepper. Cook for several minutes until the onion is soft. Add the tomatoes and garlic. (If you use fresh tomatoes, be sure to core and peel them and chop them coarse.) Cook 1 minute, and set aside.

When the chicken thighs are half cooked (after approximately 15 minutes of cooking), add the mixture of onion, pepper, tomato, and garlic to the chicken thighs and stock. Then add the rice. Three minutes later, add the okra. When all these ingredients are cooked, and the chicken is nearly done, crumble the bacon slices and add them, along with the corn kernels. Boil for 1 or 2 minutes and serve piping hot.

We serve this chicken dish with very hot bread, buttered or herbed. An excellent way to do this is to cut a loaf of Italian or French bread in half, butter it liberally, and run it under the broiler until butter is melted and the edges of the bread are toasty brown. Leftover biscuits or rolls also make a good accompaniment. One of our favorite breads with this dish is a piping-hot skillet of freshly made corn bread. Cook the corn bread right in the iron skillet; cut in wedges like a pie; and heap on the butter.

Note: Instead of bell peppers, we use Italian fryers; they're better tasting.

CHICKEN IN THE BURGUNDY STYLE

ONIONS AND RED WINE   SERVES 4

2 chicken breasts, halved to
  make 4 pieces
4 chicken thighs
4 tablespoons oil
4 tablespoons butter
¼ pound salt pork, kept whole
6 small onions, chopped coarse
3 shallots, chopped coarse
2 garlic cloves, chopped fine
2 tablespoons all-purpose flour

1 tablespoon fresh marjoram
  (or ½ teaspoon dried)
2 bay leaves
1 teaspoon fresh thyme (or ½
  teaspoon dried)
Salt
Pepper, ground fresh
2 tablespoons brandy
1½ cups good quality red wine
½ pound mushrooms, sliced thin

Wash the chicken pieces in cool water, dry them well, and set them aside.

In a large skillet, heat the oil and butter, and sauté the salt pork with the onions, shallots, and garlic for 5 minutes. Transfer this to a 3-quart casserole. In the same skillet, brown the chicken pieces on both sides. Transfer them to the casserole, and add the flour, marjoram, bay leaves, thyme, salt and pepper to taste, brandy, and wine. With a large wooden spoon, move the chicken pieces around in the casserole to mix with the other ingredients. Bake in a preheated 350-degree oven for 30 minutes.

Add the mushrooms to the casserole, and cook for an additional 10 minutes, or until the chicken is done. Adjust the salt and pepper to taste, and serve piping hot, with lots and lots of French bread.

CHICKEN PARTS IN THE 28 WEST STYLE

ONIONS AND SOUR CREAM   SERVES 4

This dish is especially good for the working person, the apartment dweller who hurries home and stops off quickly at the corner grocery (as I did when I lived at the address from which this recipe derives its title). The ingredients are easily obtained, and the dish can be made the evening before it is to be served. The chicken parts can be sautéed, the sauce can be made and poured over the chicken pieces, and this can sit in the refrigerator overnight. The next day, the chicken can be cooked an additional 35 or 40 minutes, the sour cream can be added—and there you are.

3-pound broiler, cut up into 8 pieces (or 8 chicken thighs or wings)
Juice of ½ lemon
2 tablespoons butter
1 tablespoon olive oil
4 tablespoons Cognac or brandy
2 garlic cloves, chopped fine
¼ pound fresh mushrooms, wiped clean and stem ends removed, sliced thin

2 teaspoons tomato paste (or 2 tablespoons tomato purée
3 tablespoons all-purpose flour
1 cup dry white wine (or ½ cup dry vermouth and ½ cup water)
1 cup Rich Chicken Stock or broth (see page 49)
Salt and pepper
1 cup sour cream
4 tablespoons scallions, including light green part, chopped fine

Wash the chicken pieces, put them in a bowl with the lemon juice and enough water to cover, and allow them to stand 10 to 15 minutes. Drain the chicken pieces, and dry them well.

In a large skillet, heat the butter and olive oil, and brown the chicken pieces on both sides. Put them into an ovenproof, covered baking dish. Deglaze the skillet with the Cognac or brandy, using a spatula to scrape the pan thoroughly. Add the garlic and mushrooms, and cook for 3 or 4 minutes. Then add the tomato paste or purée and flour; stir this well until all ingredients are combined. Slowly add the wine and then the chicken stock, and cook over low heat until the sauce begins to thicken. Add salt and pepper to taste, and pour this sauce over the chicken.

At this point, the baking dish may be covered and refrigerated overnight. Or cover the dish, place it in a preheated 350-degree oven, and bake it for about 30 minutes, or until the chicken is done.

Transfer the chicken pieces to a warm serving platter. Combine the sour cream with the sauce in the baking dish, and mix well. Pour the sauce over the chicken pieces, but do *not* cover them completely. Sprinkle the chopped scallions overall, and serve immediately. Wild rice is terribly good with this.

CHICKEN IN THE PORTUGUESE STYLE

PORT AND MADEIRA SERVES 6

Port and Madeira are among Portugal's best-known wines. Here they make a great combination with the chicken breasts in a lemon-tinged cream sauce.

6 *chicken breasts*	*½ teaspoon pepper*
Juice of ½ lemon	*1 clove garlic, chopped fine*
¼ cup butter	*1 cup heavy cream*
3 onions, chopped	*Salt*
½ cup port	*Pepper, ground fresh*
2 tablespoons Madeira	*½ cup Rich Chicken Stock or*
1 teaspoon salt	*broth (see page 49)*
½ teaspoon tarragon	*½ teaspoon lemon juice (or more,*
½ teaspoon nutmeg	*to your taste)*

Wash the chicken breasts, and trim them of all fat, skin, bone, and gristle. (Use poultry scissors or a sharp knife.) Put the chicken pieces in a bowl, and cover them with fresh, cool water. Add the juice of ½ lemon, and allow the chicken to stand for 10 to 15 minutes.

In a small saucepan, heat the butter, and cook the onions until they are softened. Then add the port, Madeira, salt, tarragon, nutmeg, pepper, and garlic. Cook for 5 minutes. Stir in the cream, cover the pan, and keep this sauce warm.

Drain the chicken pieces, and wipe them dry with paper towels or a tea towel. Salt and pepper the chicken breasts on both sides. In a large skillet, heat the olive oil, and sauté the chicken over high heat to brown both sides. Lower the heat, and cover the pan. Cook over very low heat for 10 to 15 minutes, or until the chicken is tender. Transfer the chicken to a serving platter, and pour off the oil from the skillet.

Add the stock or broth to the skillet, and deglaze it over high heat. Strain the stock or broth into the cream sauce. Mix this well, and add lemon juice to taste. Pour the cream sauce over the chicken breasts, and serve immediately.

You can also prepare this dish with chicken thighs, with legs, or with a whole chicken, cut up. Just watch the sautéeing time for the various cuts, so that you do not overcook them.

UCCELLETTI DI POLLO
(Rolled Chicken Breasts with Prosciutto Stuffing)

PROSCIUTTO AND MUSHROOMS   SERVES 6 TO 8

These "little birds" are often made with thin slices of beef or veal, and they are good; but we especially like these *uccelletti di pollo*.

TO PREPARE THE CHICKEN BREASTS:

> 4 *whole chicken breasts, halved to make 8 pieces*
> 1 *tablespoon lemon juice*
> *Salt*
> *Pepper, ground fresh*

Bone and skin the chicken breasts, taking care not to separate the filets from the breasts. Wash them in cool water, and put them in a bowl (it is not necessary to dry them first). Add the lemon juice, and let the chicken sit for 15 minutes. (During this time, you can prepare the stuffing.)

Remove the chicken breasts, put each one between sheets of wax paper, and pound very lightly to flatten. Remove the top sheet of paper, and salt and pepper each piece on both sides.

TO PREPARE THE STUFFING:

> 3 *tablespoons butter*
> 4 *heaping tablespoons shallots, chopped fine*
> 4 *heaping tablespoons celery, including leaves, chopped fine*
> 8 *medium-size mushrooms, chopped fine*
>
> ½ *cup bread crumbs, unflavored*
> 2 *tablespoons fresh parsley, chopped fine (or 1 teaspoon dried)*
> *Salt and pepper*
> 8 *thin slices prosciutto*

Melt 3 tablespoons butter in a skillet or saucepan, add the shallots and celery, and cook them for about 5 minutes. Add the mushrooms, and cook for another 5 minutes. Remove skillet from the heat, add the bread crumbs and parsley, and mix well. Salt and pepper, to taste, but go lightly with the salt because prosciutto is very salty.

Arrange 1 prosciutto slice on each of the 8 chicken breast halves, and divide the stuffing among them. Roll each piece, beginning with the small end. Secure the rolls with wooden skewers, 6 or 8 inches long, just as you would affix a straight pin to a piece of cloth or paper. If the ends of the roll turn up a bit, flatten it by pushing down lightly with the palm of your hand.

TO BAKE THE CHICKEN:

2 eggs
1 tablespoon vermouth
  (optional)
  1 cup flour (approximately)
1½ cups bread crumbs, unflavored
  Salt

Pepper, ground fresh
4 tablespoons butter
Few sprigs of parsley
Lemon wedges

Beat the eggs in a bowl with a fork and add the vermouth (if you wish), and the salt and pepper. Roll the bird in the flour, dip it in the egg, and coat it completely with the bread crumbs. (An easy way to do this is to put the bread crumbs in a plate or flat soup bowl and, holding the end of skewer, turn the roll until fully coated.) Use 2 tablespoons butter to grease the baking tray; dot the chicken with the remaining 2 tablespoons butter. Bake at 400 degrees for 30 minutes (longer if rolls are large). When the rolls are cooked, set them on an attractive platter or tray, lined up like birds on a telephone wire, and be sure the skewers are all on the same side. Place a few sprigs of parsley across the top, and serve with lemon wedges. A squirt of lemon on these birds is delicious. Because there is no sauce with the *uccelletti,* we recommend cold spiced peaches, whole or halved. The hot birds and the cold peaches make a great combination.

CHICKEN FERRAGOSTO

TOMATOES AND ROASTED PEPPERS   SERVES 6 TO 8

Ferragosto is the Feast of the Assumption and is celebrated on August 15th. Our recipe is an adaptation of the classic Roman one.

TO PREPARE THE PEPPERS:

1 pound sweet red peppers for roasting (approximately 4 or 5
  depending on size), cut into 1-inch squares after roasting

Follow the basic instructions for roasting peppers (page 13). You can buy roasted peppers in jars (and they're good), but we think it's so much better to prepare your own. It's really quite simple and can be done a day or even a week ahead of time. The roasted peppers should be stored in the refrigerator in a plastic or other covered container. They may also be frozen *without* mixing with oil.

TO PREPARE THE CHICKEN:

6 *whole chicken breasts, boned, skinned, and halved to make 12 pieces*
Juice of ½ lemon
3 *tablespoons olive oil*
1 *tablespoon butter*
2 *large garlic cloves, halved*

1 *chili pepper (or 1 hot Italian cherry pepper), seeded and diced*
1 *large onion, chopped fine*
4 *cups fresh plum tomatoes, peeled and skinned (or canned plum tomatoes)*
Salt

Wash the chicken-breast halves in cool water. Trim off all fat with a poultry scissors or a sharp paring knife. Without drying the chicken pieces, put them into a bowl. Add the lemon juice, stir the chicken in it, and set aside for about 10 minutes.

In a skillet, heat the olive oil and butter, and sauté garlic pieces until they are light brown. Discard garlic. Dry the chicken-breast halves with paper towels or a tea towel, and add as many as will fit into the skillet, leaving about 1 inch of space between the pieces, and cook on both sides until they are light brown. Transfer them to a flameproof casserole.

Pour the oil from the skillet, leaving just enough to coat the bottom. Add the chili pepper and onion, and cook for 5 minutes, stirring frequently. Add the tomatoes and salt to taste, and cook for 15 minutes. Pour the vegetable mixture over the chicken pieces in the casserole, and cook slowly until the chicken is done (about 15 minutes). Do *not* overcook the chicken.

Just before serving, add the roasted pepper squares to the casserole. Serve as soon as the peppers are heated through.

Truffles

We wish we could be as blasé about truffles as a friend who once sighed, "A truffle is a truffle is a truffle." We wish, too, that we could solve the mystery of the truffle: the aloof little plant can't be cultivated. We all know that there are black truffles and white ones and that specially trained dogs and pigs scent them out and dig them up. The black truffles come from Périgord, an area around Cahors in the southwestern part of France. The best period for them is January, but they are obtainable fresh from the middle of December to the end of February. The white ones come from the Piedmont area in northern Italy, and their best period is November. They are extremely expensive, and we're somewhat embarrassed to include our recipe for a salad of truffles (see page 374). We considered adding "in the *molto caro* style" (in the very expensive style) to the title of the recipe, but that would be gilding the truffle, so to speak.

In any case, we're stuck on truffles, and we're not going to engage in the white-versus-black debate. To have either is a richly rewarding experience. Their fragrance is indescribable, and inhaling the attar once will make you an addict. Our rationalization is that a small tin of truffles is no more expensive than a good bottle of wine or bourbon. We've played games with truffles, usually to find out whether a particular dish can really be made without them. Our Suprême de Volaille aux Truffes (Chicken Breasts with Truffles) simply will not do without the truffles. This is one reason why the truffle continues to be one of the necessary luxuries of our world.

SUPREME DE VOLAILLE AUX TRUFFES
(Chicken Breasts with Truffles)

TRUFFLES AND ALMONDS   SERVES 6

3 chicken breasts, halved to make
   6 pieces
Juice of ½ lemon
Salt
Pepper, ground fresh
¼ pound mozzarella (or a good-
   quality Gruyère cheese), cut
   into strips ½ to ¾ inches wide,
   2 inches long, and ¼ inch
   thick
2 tablespoons fresh parsley,
   chopped fine (or 2 teaspoons
   dried)

3 small whole black truffles (2
   sliced into 12 pieces for stuffing
   and 1 chopped fine for garnishing)
4 tablespoons butter
½ cup dry vermouth (or dry white
   wine)
⅓ cup Rich Chicken Stock (see
   page 49)
⅓ cup almond slivers

Wash the chicken breasts; skin, bone, and trim them of as much fat as possible, keeping them in one piece. Place them in a bowl, add the lemon juice, cover them with cool water, and allow them to stand for about 15 minutes. Drain them, and dry well with a clean tea towel. Place the chicken pieces on a flat surface, smooth side down, and salt and pepper the pocket right under the filet piece of the breast. (It is rarely necessary to cut a larger pocket.)

Fill each pocket with a strip of mozzarella, some parsley, and two pieces of truffle. Arrange the chicken breasts so that almost no mozzarella or other stuffing is showing, merely by patting the breasts and molding them with your hands. (The chicken will adhere by itself, so string or toothpicks are not required.)

In a large skillet, heat the butter, and sauté the chicken breasts until nicely browned on each side (5 to 10 minutes per side, depending on the thickness of the breasts). Add the vermouth or wine, and allow it to cook down for 3 or 4 minutes (it will thicken somewhat). Scrape the bottom of the skillet with a wooden spoon or a rubber spatula, and stir wine sauce. Add the chicken stock, and cover the skillet. Cook for an additional 5 minutes. Remove cover, add almond slivers, and cook 1 minute longer. Do *not* overcook the breasts.

Transfer the breasts to a serving platter, pour sauce over them, garnish with the chopped truffle, and serve immediately.

GAME

The term *game* includes wild animals and birds that are hunted both for sport and for food. In most countries, these animals and birds are protected by game laws, usually prohibiting hunting during the nesting season. However, as far as we know, rabbits are not protected by game laws, although they are considered game. In America, the principal game animals are deer, bear, rabbit, squirrel, coon, and wild boar; the most popular game birds are pheasant, duck, grouse, quail, turkey, dove, snipe, and woodcock.

Two problems with game are the gamy aroma (although to many this is its chief virtue) and the dryness of its flesh. However, both problems can be overcome, in the first case by proper hanging and the removal of certain glands and in the second case by barding (tying a piece of fat around the meat or bird when cooking it). Barding gives the meat more succulence and makes basting every 5 or 10 minutes unnecessary. It is especially important when there is an absence of natural fat, which is usually the case with game birds.

Game, the trophy of the hunter, fares well in great combinations of epicurean delight. Capons, turkeys, ducks, geese, pigeons, pheasants, and squabs, like chicken, may be roasted in combinations of dressings, stuffings, vegetables, and fruits. Roast pheasant has an affinity for juniper berries; guinea hen graces herself with grapes in the French combination, *pintadeau aux raisins; caneton aux citrons* dovetails duck with lemon. The English combine their Aylesbury duck with red currant jelly and prove to the world why Aylesbury, famous for its lace, is famous for its duck, too. We present a venison pie that we call Venison Cubes en Croûte and a delicious deer loin combination Loin of Venison Roasted with Chestnuts. Butter and herbs combined with wild duck appear in A Salmi of Wild Duck. Another great combination is Roast Duckling with Sauerkraut; the special ingredient is juniper berries. Wild rabbit, which we fry in a Southern way, is combined with wine and tarragon.

GRILLED TURKEY BREAST IN SHERRY
WITH ROSEMARY

ROSEMARY AND SHERRY   SERVES 6 TO 8

3- to 4-pound turkey breast	*8 tablespoons butter, melted*
2 cups dry sherry	*Salt*
2 tablespoons dried rosemary	*Pepper, ground fresh*

This is best prepared with a frozen turkey breast, which should be allowed to thaw. The breast should be in one piece and completely boned. Remove the skin, if any. Cut the breast into 1-inch-thick slices; cut the slices into 1-inch strips, and cut those into 1-inch cubes. Put the turkey cubes in a flat pan or on a large platter. They should be in one layer if possible. Pour the sherry overall.

Put the rosemary leaves in a mortar, and crush them with a pestle until they become powdery. (You *can* do this by rubbing the leaves between your hands, but you'll do a better job with a pestle.) Sprinkle this over the turkey pieces, and toss. Marinate for at least 2 to 3 hours, or longer if you like.

Put the turkey pieces onto individual skewers (one skewer per guest) or on several large skewers (which you'll be able to serve on a large platter). Brush well with melted butter, and salt and pepper to your taste. These turkey cubes are especially good grilled over an open fire, but they can also be done under an oven broiler. Turkey is often somewhat dry, so be sure to baste with melted butter often during the grilling process. Use more butter if you need it.

It is also possible for the turkey to absorb the sherry completely. Don't be concerned; this is supposed to happen. But if there is any sherry marinade left, use it to brush the turkey cubes as they are grilling.

Goose

In Germany, there is a popular saying, *Eine gute gebratene Gans ist eine Gabe Gottes* ("a fine roast goose is a gift from God"). Throughout central Europe, the goose is placed higher on the gastronomical ladder than the turkey. This has been true in England, too, from before Queen Victoria's reign to the present day. In fact, the goose reigned supreme in the days of Queen Elizabeth I. It is traditionally served on Michaelmas Day (September 29), the anniversary of a great naval victory won by the English against the Spaniards, and is the essential part of a Christmas dinner. The British roast goose is usually stuffed with onions and sage, a great and ancient combination. Yet, it is France that produces more goose by-products than any other country. Foie gras, of course, is one of the best and most renowned.

In these days of unisex, it's worth noting that at a quick glance, it's not easy to tell a goose from a gander. When either the male or the female is trussed and ready for the oven, the appellation *goose* is applied indiscriminately. Perhaps at that point, no one cares.

Probably one of the world's greatest combinations of food is fresh goose liver pâté perfumed with black truffles. It is superbly made in Strasbourg, Toulouse, Landes, and other parts of France.

Although it is universally agreed that the most delicate part of the goose is its liver, there are other specialties, particularly from the Toulouse goose, that are excellent. *Confit d'oie* is a rich and delicious confection of goose preserved in its own fat and aspic; it combines brilliantly with onions, lentils, potatoes, kidney beans, cabbage, or peas; it is, in our opinion, the key ingredient in cassoulet.

On the Atlantic coast of France, near La Rochelle, there's a restaurant called Le Soubise. Its proprietor, Madame Benoit, prepares a great combination of foods, *Pigeonneaux Fermiers*. She starts with plump young pigeons slit down the back, with the breastbones removed. They are stuffed with a mixture of fresh duck liver, pigeon liver, diced pork, chopped black truffles, garlic, shallots, thyme, and parsley. Then they are tied, spread with goose drippings, and surrounded by carrots, turnips, and *jambon de campagne*. In Paris, a specialty at the former restaurant of Michel Guérard, Le Pot au Feu, was *Le Ragoût Fin du Pot au Feu*, a combination of *coquillettes*, foie gras, sweetbreads, duckling, and truffles in a mushroom sauce. And recently, a friend described a new combination served in the south of France called *Filets Gourmands d'Oie Fraîche*, which is thin strips of breast of goose marinated in red wine and olive oil and herbs, grilled quickly, and served with a *sauce bigarade* mixed with the goose juices deglazed with white wine. The bigarade sauce contained caramelized sugar, orange and lemon juices, and vinegar.

Apples

There's good reason why apple pie is archetypically American. Varieties of apples were brought here by the Dutch, English, and French, and the apple tree is known to have grown next to totem poles in many an Indian village. Because Americans consume almost as many apples as they do hamburgers and hot dogs, they should be more adept at buying better apples. Many apples are picked prematurely and spend considerable time in storage. There is nothing wrong with this, but it is the tree-ripened apple that is the succulent one. Split an apple *stem* with both thumbs and index fingers; if it is soft and juicy, the apple probably is a good one.

Apple pie and Cheddar cheese is one well-known great combination of food, but apples also have an affinity for rum, pork, sugar, raisins, celery, and countless other foods. Apples can be fried or frittered, baked or buttered, jellied or juiced, crunched or chutneyed, stewed or stuffed. We combine them here with apricots and oranges and stuff them in a goose to be roasted.

A ROASTED GOOSE WITH APPLES, APRICOTS, AND ORANGES

APRICOTS AND ORANGES   SERVES 6

TO PREPARE THE GOOSE:
> *8-pound ready-to-cook goose*
> *Juice of ½ lemon*
> *Salt*

Wash the goose in cool water, put it in a pan, cover it with water, add the lemon juice, and let it sit for 20 minutes. Remove the bird, and dry it inside and out with paper towels or a clean tea towel. Salt the cavity, and set the goose aside.

TO PREPARE THE STUFFING:

> *3 tablespoons butter*
> *1 medium-size onion, chopped fine*
> *2 celery stalks, including leaves, scraped and cut crosswise into thin slices*
> *½ cup dried apricots, soaked and cut into ¼-inch cubes (soak dried apricots in water for 2 hours)*
> *½ cup fresh oranges, skin, membrane, and seeds removed, cut into ½-inch cubes*
> *½ cup tart apples, peel and seeds removed, cut into ½-inch cubes*

> *4 cups white bread, toasted and cut into ½-inch cubes*
> *1 tablespoon fresh parsley, chopped (or 1 teaspoon dried)*
> *1 tablespoon fresh thyme, chopped (or 1 teaspoon dried)*
> *¼ pound butter*
> *1 cup chicken stock or water*
> *2 tablespoons Cognac or brandy (optional)*
> *Salt*
> *Pepper, ground fresh*

In a large skillet, melt the butter, and sauté the onion and celery until the onion is pale yellow (about 10 minutes). Remove from heat, and set aside.

In a large bowl, combine the apricot, orange, and apple pieces with the toasted bread cubes. Add the parsley and thyme, and then add the cooked onions and celery to this mixture. (Use a rubber spatula to get all the pieces out of the skillet.) In the same skillet, add the butter, chicken stock, and Cognac or brandy. Bring to a boil, lower the heat, allow the butter to melt, and deglaze the skillet. As soon as this is done, remove the skillet from the heat. Pour the liquid into the bowl, and use a rubber spatula to scrape all the drippings into the bowl. Mix well. Add salt and pepper to taste.

Fill the cavity with the stuffing, and truss the goose. (A general rule is approximately ¾ to 1 cup of stuffing for each pound of oven-ready bird.) Place the bird, breast side up, on a rack in an open roasting pan, and roast it in a preheated 325-degree oven until the leg joints move easily (about 4 hours). As the goose roasts, remove as much fat as you can from the roasting pan. Just spoon it out of the pan, and reserve it for another use (such as *confit d'oie* and cassoulet).

When the goose is cooked, transfer it to an attractive oval serving platter. Make a gravy from the drippings in the roasting pan, and serve it in a separate bowl.

Duck

Long Island duck breeders remember the month of March in the year 1873, for that was the time that nine ducks were imported from the imperial aviaries of old China. That was the beginning of what is today the world's largest duck-breeding industry. There are other ducks (Michigan, Maryland, and Boston), but the Long Island duckling appears to be the most widely available commercially dressed duck. It usually weighs 4 to 5 pounds.

In England, the favored duck is the Aylesbury; in France, the Rouennaise; in China, the white Peking duck. Mandarin ducks are magnificently colored and develop a strong attachment to their mates. If separated, they will sadden and perhaps die.

ROAST DUCKLINGS WITH SAUERKRAUT

JUNIPER BERRIES AND SAUERKRAUT

SERVES 6

TO PREPARE THE DUCKLINGS:

Two 4-pound dressed ducks, whole
Salt
Pepper, ground fresh
1 tablespoon paprika
2 garlic cloves, halved

2 onions, whole, each stuck with a clove
2 apples, unpeeled and quartered
3 tablespoons butter
½ cup dry white wine

Wash the ducks well in cool water, and dry the inside and out. Season the cavities with salt, pepper, and paprika. Stuff each with 2 pieces garlic, 1 onion stuck with a clove, 4 pieces apple, and 1 tablespoon butter. Rub the outside of the ducks with the remaining 1 tablespoon butter, salt and pepper them, and place them (breast side up) on a rack in a roasting pan. Be sure to prick the skin on the breasts and thighs to release the fat as the birds cook. Pour about ¼ cup water into the roasting pan. Roast the ducks in a preheated 350-degree oven for 2 hours, and baste them with the wine approximately every 15 minutes. When you baste them, use 1 tablespoon of wine at a time, and pour it over each duck. If the water and wine cook off completely during the roasting period, use a little more of each as you baste. When the ducks have cooked for 45 minutes, turn them over on their breasts. After an additional 45 minutes, turn them over again, breast side up.

TO PREPARE THE SAUERKRAUT:

4 cups sauerkraut
6 juniper berries, crushed
2 teaspoons caraway seeds

3 slices bacon, cooked until crisp and then crumbled
½ cup dry white wine

During the last 30 minutes of roasting, combine the sauerkraut, juniper berries, caraway seeds, bacon, and white wine in a shallow baking dish. Put this mixture in the oven, and cook for 25 minutes, or until the sauerkraut is heated thoroughly.

To serve, remove the apple and garlic pieces and the onions from the cavities, and discard. Carve the ducks into serving pieces. Transfer the sauerkraut mixture to a large serving platter, and arrange the duck pieces on top of it.

A SALMI OF WILD DUCK

BUTTER AND HERBS   SERVES 4 TO 6

Two *3-pound wild ducks* (see
Note)
Juice of 1 lemon
Salt
Pepper, ground fresh
2 *duck livers*
¼ *pound salt pork, cut into*
¼-*inch slices and diced into*
¼-*inch pieces*
3 *tablespoons butter*
Bouquet garni (*3 sprigs fresh
thyme, 3 sprigs fresh parsley, 3
sprigs fresh rosemary, tied
together*)

2 *tablespoons shallots, chopped
fine*
2 *tablespoons all-purpose flour*
3 *cups Rich Beef or Veal Stock*
(*see pages 46, 48*)
1 *cup red wine*
1 *tablespoon brandy*

Wash the ducks in cool water, place them in a large bowl, and allow them to stand in water mixed with lemon juice for about 15 minutes. Dry them well, inside and out. Salt and pepper them inside and out, and put a duck liver in each cavity.

In a skillet, cook the diced salt pork until well done. Set aside.

In a roasting pan, spread 1 tablespoon butter to coat the bottom of the pan. Put about half the cooked salt pork dice over the butter and also add half the melted salt pork fat. Place the bouquet garni in the center of the pan (the length of the bouquet should follow the length of the pan). Sprinkle two-thirds of the shallots over this; divide the remainder, and put it into the duck cavities. Put the ducks, breast side down, in the roasting pan. Roast them in this way for 20 minutes in a preheated 325-degree oven. (Do *not* turn the ducks during this time.)

In a medium-size saucepan, melt 2 tablespoons butter; when it is bubbling, add the flour, and blend well with a wire whisk. Cook this roux until it begins to darken. Add the stock slowly, whisking all the while, and then add the wine. Bring to a boil, remove from the heat, and set aside.

When the ducks have cooked for 20 minutes, remove them from the oven. Carve the ducks by cutting off the legs, wings, and breasts. Set aside. Remove the livers from the cavities, cut them into small pieces, and add them to the sauce. Skim off as much fat as you can from the roasting pan. Return the duck pieces to the pan, pour the brandy over them, and then pour the sauce overall. Sprinkle the remaining cooked salt pork pieces overall, and return the roasting pan to the oven to cook an additional 25 minutes.

Note: This recipe is for wild duck, but you can also use domestic duck (if that is your only choice). Cooking time will be 2 hours, 15 minutes for a 4½-pound domestic duck, or about 25 minutes per pound. Also, if you use a domestic duck, omit the salt pork.

ROAST PHEASANT WITH WILD RICE IN THE CHINESE STYLE

GINGER AND RICE WINE   SERVES 4 TO 6

TO PREPARE THE PHEASANT:

Two 2- to 3-pound young pheasants
Salt
Pepper, ground fresh
2 lemon slices, ¼-inch thick
2 stalks celery leaves
4 slices fat salt pork (or fatty bacon)
1 cup Rich Chicken Stock (see page 49)

Rinse the pheasants in cool water, and dry them well inside and out. Salt and pepper each bird inside and out. In each cavity, place 1 slice of lemon and 1 piece of celery leaf. Tie the legs together with string, and turn the wings under. Arrange 2 slices of fat salt pork or fatty bacon on each breast.

TO PREPARE THE MARINADE:

¼ cup soy sauce
½ cup peanut oil
½ cup rice wine (or dry sherry)
2 large cloves garlic
4 slices fresh ginger, ¼-inch thick

Combine all the ingredients to make the soy sauce marinade. Cut 2 small squares of cheesecloth, several layers thick, large enough to fit over each pheasant breast, and dip them in the marinade. Lay each cheesecloth square (they should be dripping wet) over the salt pork on each breast. Place the birds, breasts up, on a rack in a roasting pan. Pour the stock into the pan, and roast the pheasants in a preheated 350-degree oven for approximately 30 minutes per pound. (Test by inserting a fork in the thickest part of the breast; when the juice runs clear, the bird is cooked.) Baste frequently with the marinade by brushing or spooning some of it over the cheesecloth and onto the rest of the bird.

TO PREPARE THE WILD RICE:

1 cup preserved kumquats, sliced	1 teaspoon salt
½ cup rice wine (or dry sherry)	Pepper, ground fresh
2 cups wild rice, uncooked	6 cups Rich Chicken Stock (see
4 tablespoons butter	page 49)
½ cup scallions, including tender green parts, cut into ¼-inch slices	

Soak the sliced kumquats in the rice wine or sherry for about 1 hour.

Wash the wild rice well in several changes of cool water, and drain it well. In a large, covered enameled iron pan or casserole (or any other flameproof, ovenproof vessel), heat the butter, add the scallions, and cook for 2 minutes. Add the well-drained wild rice, and cook for 3 minutes over low heat, stirring frequently.

Add the salt, pepper to taste, and chicken stock, stir, increase the heat, and allow the stock to come to a boil. Drain the kumquats, and add them to the rice. Cover the rice with buttered wax paper, cover the pan, and cook in a preheated 350-degree oven for approximately 40 minutes, or until the rice is tender.

About 20 minutes before the birds are finished, do the following: Remove the cheesecloth. Baste the breasts well with the marinade. Add the marinade to the roasting pan. During the remaining cooking time, baste the birds again with the juices in the roasting pan.

When the birds are cooked, take them out of the oven, and remove the string. Transfer the wild rice to a serving bowl or platter, and serve it separately with the roasted pheasants. Or make a bed of rice on a large serving platter, and place the pheasants on top of it.

Quail

All over the world, the quail is known as a bird of passage. By the thousands, quails cross the Mediterranean in the spring to visit Europe and migrate to Africa and India in the fall. In the United States, the terms *quail* and *partridge* are used interchangeably. Many refer to this bird as the *bobwhite* because of its call. It is one of the most abundant of all the game birds, especially in the Southeast. Quail is a small bird, 5 to 6 ounces, and one quail will serve one person.

Quince

Many of us believe Eve used the apple to entice Adam, but there are others who say she used the quince. That may be the reason for the old superstition that assured love, peace, and happiness if a quince was present at the marriage banquet table. One of the earliest fragrances we remember was the smell of quince at our grandparents' home, where Grandmother Beatrice and Grandfather Giuseppe lived happily married for almost sixty years. We once questioned Grandmother about quince and happiness, and she said "slosh" in Italian, explaining that we smelled quince because she had wrapped it in fresh linen cloths and placed one in every linen and clothes drawer in the house.

We wonder why one of the earliest-known garden fruits is one of today's least cultivated. Raw quince is tart and mouth-puckering in an uncomfortable way but cooked quince is simply delicious.

QUAIL WITH QUINCE

QUAIL AND QUINCE
SERVES 4

6 quinces, wiped, quartered,
  cored, and pared
½ cup sugar
1 cup water
½ cup Madeira
4 quails, dry plucked, singed,
  drawn from the neck, head and
  neck removed, and wings
  trussed (as for squab)

4 tablespoons butter
1 cup Rich Consommé (or Rich
  Beef Stock or broth) (see pages
  52 or 46)
4 tablespoons Cognac or brandy
1 tablespoon lemon zest, chopped
  fine
Salt
Pepper, ground fresh

Arrange the quince quarters in a shallow, covered baking dish, and sprinkle the sugar over them. Add the water and Madeira, and cook in a preheated 325-degree oven for about 1½ hours. Baste frequently during cooking, and test for doneness with a fork.

While the quinces are cooking, prepare and cook the quails. Melt the butter in a large, heavy enameled saucepan with a cover. (The pan should be large enough to accommodate the 4 quail in one layer.) Brown the birds on all surfaces, and salt and pepper them to taste. Cover the pan, and bake in a preheated 375-degree oven for approximately 30 minutes.

Remove the pan from the oven, and transfer the quails to a large, warm serving platter. Keep the birds warm.

Remove as much excess fat as you can from the pan in which the birds were baked. To this pan, add the consommé or beef stock, Cognac or brandy, and lemon zest. Bring this mixture to a boil, reduce the heat, and simmer for approximately 15 minutes, stirring frequently and deglazing the pan as you stir.

While this sauce is simmering, arrange the cooked quinces around the quails. Then pour the sauce over the birds, and serve immediately.

Venison

Our recipes for venison included here are really recipes for deer meat. *Venison* used to mean any meat of any hunted animal, but today, it applies only to antlered animals (antelope, deer, elk, moose, and reindeer). Lots of deer are hunted in Dutchess County, and although we are not hunters, we are on the receiving end. Many neighbors, friends, and relatives present us with neatly butchered venison chops and roasts, and our only hope is that these meats are not from the beautiful animals we see in our open fields and lonely woods early in the morning or just after the sun has set. Young deer cooks like veal and beef; older meat usually requires a marinade. Venison chops and steaks are best cooked medium to rare. Almost anything you do with beef you can do with venison, including ground meat in the burger form. A great combination is prepared by Roger Fessaguet. Formerly with the Oustau de Beaumaniere, a famous inn near Les Baux, not far from Avignon, he is now chef at La Caravelle in New York City. His roast leg of venison is served with a *sauce poivrade.*

VENISON CUBES EN CROUTE

2½ pounds boneless venison, cut
    into 1¼-inch cubes
½ cup all-purpose flour
1 tablespoon salt
    Pepper, ground fresh
8 tablespoons butter
2½ cups Rich Beef Stock (see
    page 46)
1 cup sweet vermouth
1 tablespoon fresh rosemary,
    chopped fine (or ½ teaspoon
    dried, rubbed between the
    hands)

2 tablespoons fresh parsley,
    chopped fine (or ½ teaspoon
    dried)
12 small white onions, whole
1 pound fresh mushrooms,
    wiped clean and stem ends
    trimmed, sliced ¼-inch thick
1 cup peas, cooked
1 pastry crust (see page 150)
1 egg yolk, lightly beaten with
    1 tablespoon water
3 sprigs fresh parsley

In a plastic bag, combine the flour, salt, and freshly ground pepper, and mix well. Add the venison cubes to the bag. Hold the bag closed with one hand, and hold the bottom of the bag with the other; shake vigorously to coat the venison cubes with the flour mixture. Shake off excess flour as you remove the cubes from the bag.

In a covered, heavy saucepan or flameproof casserole, heat the butter, and brown the venison pieces on all sides over rather high heat. When all the pieces are browned (do them in batches), put them back in the saucepan or casserole, add the stock and vermouth, and bring to a boil. Then lower to a simmer, and add the rosemary and parsley. Cover the pan, and cook at a simmer for 1½ hours. Remove the cover, add the onions, cover, and cook for 10 minutes. Remove the pan from the heat, add the peas and sliced mushrooms, and mix well. The liquid should have thickened to the consistency of heavy cream; if it hasn't, transfer all the contents except the sauce to the casserole in which the dish will be baked, and cook down the liquid. Or add some *beurre manié* (a mixture of butter and flour in equal proportions, well combined) until you get the desired consistency.

Select a round casserole, approximately 9 to 11 inches wide and 2 inches deep, and add the venison mixture and sauce. Cover the casserole with a piecrust, making your preferred crust edge. Brush the top of the crust with the mixture of egg yolk and water, create a steam opening, and bake in a very hot oven (450 degrees) until the crust is nicely done and a rich golden color.

Serve with a few fresh parsley sprigs strewn over the croûte.

LOIN OF VENISON ROASTED WITH CHESTNUTS

CHESTNUTS AND ORANGE   SERVES 6

3-pound tenderloin of venison (approximately)
6 thin strips salt pork (or bacon slices)
Salt
Pepper, ground fresh
1 cup orange juice, squeezed fresh
8 tablespoons butter, softened
2 tablespoons rosemary, chopped fine (or 1 teaspoon dried, rubbed between the hands)

3 medium onions, each stuck with 2 cloves (one in each end)
2 cups canned, drained, peeled, and cooked chestnuts (see Note on page 258)
½ cup beach plum jelly (or currant or damson plum jelly)
3 tablespoons lemon peel zest, chopped fine

Arrange the salt pork strips over the loin of venison to bard it. Liberally salt and pepper the barded loin, and roast it quickly in a preheated 450-degree oven for 15 minutes. This will sear the loin and help to keep the juices in, a principle used in roasting ribs of beef and other meats.

Then lower the oven to 325 degrees, and add the orange juice, butter, rosemary, and onions to the roasting pan. Cover the pan with heavy foil, securing the edges and foil around it, and roast for an additional 45 minutes (approximately 15 minutes per pound). If your loin is larger than 3 pounds, adjust the timing. Baste with the pan juices every 10 minutes. After the loin has cooked for 20 minutes (and at a time when you are ready to baste again), add the drained chestnuts to the roasting pan. Keep it covered with the foil, and continue roasting and basting.

In the meantime, combine the jelly and 2 tablespoons lemon zest in a small saucepan, and cook until the jelly is melted. Approximately 10 minutes before the loin is finished, remove and discard the foil. Brush the melted jelly mixture all over the loin with a pastry brush, and allow to roast, uncovered, for 10 to 15 minutes to develop a glaze. Then transfer the venison to a warm serving platter. With a slotted spoon, transfer the chestnuts and the onions to the platter. Cut the onions in half.

Remove as much excess fat as you can from the roasting pan, and heat the juices directly on the stove top to cook down. If you want this to thicken faster, add some flour, and whisk quickly and constantly until you obtain the consistency you want. If you added too much flour and the sauce is too thick, thin it with warm water. Put the sauce in a serving bowl, and serve it separately.

The loin should be sprinkled with 1 tablespoon lemon zest and brought to the table in one piece. Slice and serve the loin at the table. Add half an onion and a spoonful of chestnuts to each serving, and pass the sauce.

Rabbit

It is best to eat rabbit when it is young, between 3 and 4 months old. Young rabbits have a tender, fine-textured meat, like chicken in color, and little or no gamy flavor. If you have caught the rabbit as your own game, draw, clean, and skin it immediately. We marinate it in lemon juice, as we do chicken, but for a little longer: about 30 minutes. Most wild rabbits weigh 2 to 3 pounds and can serve two to three people; they are interchangeable with domestic rabbits as far as recipes are concerned. Rabbit is fairly versatile. It can be roasted, potted, pâtéed, and boiled. It can be sautéed with paprika or curry. A great combination is with mushrooms in the chasseur and cacciatore styles. Another great combination is roasted rabbit with a mushroom sauce or a sauce in which Marsala and rosemary are brought together. We present it here in our favorite style: Southern fried with white wine and tarragon.

SOUTHERN-FRIED WILD RABBIT WITH
WINE AND TARRAGON

WHITE WINE AND TARRAGON   SERVES 4 TO 6

Two 2- to 3-pound rabbits   ¼ *cup light cream*
(wild or domestic), cut into   2 *tablespoons fresh tarragon*
serving pieces   *leaves, chopped fine (or 1*
Juice of 1 lemon   *teaspoon dried)*
Salt   ¾ *cup fine fresh bread crumbs*
Pepper, ground fresh   8 *tablespoons butter (1 stick)*
½ *cup all-purpose flour*   1 *cup dry white wine*
2 *eggs, lightly beaten*

Wash the rabbit pieces in cool water, and place them in a large bowl.
Add the lemon juice, stir to coat them, and leave them to marinate
for about 30 minutes. Remove the pieces from the bowl, and pat them
dry with a tea towel or paper towels. Salt and pepper the pieces to taste
on both sides. Put the flour, eggs, and bread crumbs in flat-type soup
bowls.

Mix the eggs with the light cream and tarragon. Flour each piece of
rabbit, shake off the excess flour, dip the piece into the egg mixture, and
dip it into the bread crumbs. Put the prepared pieces of meat in the
refrigerator, and leave them there for 30 minutes or longer.

In a large, covered skillet, melt the butter. When it is hot, brown the
rabbit pieces on all sides. (You may have to do this in batches.) When
all are browned, put them all in the skillet, pour the wine over them,
lower the heat, cover the skillet, and simmer for about 40 minutes.
Remove the cover, and cook 10 minutes more, or until the meat is
tender. If you want, you can transfer the rabbit pieces to a preheated
375-degree oven, and bake them for the last 10 minutes, or until done.

Squirrel

Squirrel, like rabbit, if caught as your own game, should be drawn,
cleaned and skinned immediately. And it should be refrigerated at once.
The scent glands under the forelegs and near the spine at the lower
back should be removed. It's easy to hunt squirrel because they're found
all over the country. But if you're timid about that, they can be bought

in many meat shops, especially in large cities, where there are butcher shops catering to European tastes.

If the squirrel is young, the white meat is especially tender. If it's young squirrel, we think it's excellent fried or broiled. If it's older, it is better stewed. Although squirrel is probably best known in the United States stewed in combination with vegetables, including onions, tomatoes, potatoes, and corn (the basis for Brunswick stew), we present it sautéed with Calvados, a fine French apple brandy.

SQUIRREL SAUTEED WITH CALVADOS

BUTTER AND CALVADOS   SERVES 6

Three 1-pound squirrels	*4 slices of bacon, cut into*
(approximately), cut into	*½-inch pieces*
serving pieces	*½ cup Calvados*
Juice of ½ lemon	*2 tablespoons butter*
⅓ cup all-purpose flour	*1 cup heavy cream, heated but*
1 teaspoon salt	*not boiled*
Pepper, ground fresh	*Paprika*

Ask your butcher to clean and cut the squirrels into serving pieces if you're not able to do so. Wash the pieces in cool water, and allow them to sit for 20 minutes in a bowl of fresh water to which the lemon juice has been added. Drain, and dry the pieces thoroughly. In a paper or plastic bag, combine the flour, salt, and pepper, and shake it to mix these ingredients. Add the squirrel pieces, hold the bag closed, and shake it vigorously to coat them well. Remove the meat from the bag, shaking off any excess flour, and set the pieces of meat aside.

In a large, covered skillet, sauté the bacon pieces until they turn color (3 to 4 minutes). Add the pieces of meat, and brown them well on both sides. Then pour in the Calvados, cover the skillet, and let the meat cook further, at a slow simmer, until tender. Test for doneness by piercing a piece of the meat with a fork. Then, add the butter, and stir it around the meat pieces. Cook 1 additional minute and then transfer the meat to a warm platter.

Add the heavy cream to the skillet, heat the cream over moderate heat (but do *not* boil), and use a rubber spatula to deglaze the pan. Pour the sauce over the meat, but do not cover each piece completely.

Garnish with several dashes of paprika, and serve immediately.

((5))

Calamari at Christmastime, a Casserole of Cream-Sherried Shrimp, More Fish, Shellfish, and a Marvelous Lobster Stew, Too

FISH

It's not easy for us to forget one of the worst train trips we've ever taken from New York City to Pawling, New York, a two-hour jaunt—and that was before the railroads went bankrupt. A Friday, the beginning of a weekend, and it was to start with a bang because eight guests were to come for dinner that evening.

Fish is fresh, fish is cheap, fish cooks quickly, and we decided on fish for dinner. We picked up our "fresh" fish in the late afternoon and caught our train, and as we sank into our coach seats, we suddenly realized that it was one of the hottest days of the summer and that the air-conditioning wasn't working. Everything was all right, odorwise, to White Plains, but by Chappaqua, our embarrassment was indescribable. By Brewster, we had nearly expired. We'll never know why we didn't discard the fish at Mt. Kisco—but what, then, were we going to eat?

The point of this story is that fish deteriorates considerably faster than meat. We had not selected strictly fresh fish. We should have checked to be sure that the eyes were bright and bulging, that the flesh was firm, that the gills were pink, and that the fish smelled of the sea.

Fish is found all over the world and is prepared in a multitude of ways. And who can say which types are superior? Salt-water or fresh-water fish? Fish from cold waters, or from warm waters? Brook trout or lake trout?

Quite frankly, we're sorry the church went soft about meatless Fridays, for as we grew up, fish in our home received the full gastronomic attention and plaudits it deserves. Fish is rich in protein and therefore rich for health.

We almost always use lemon with our fish, usually in the form of a marinade. We wash the fish or filets and put them in a bowl with some lemon juice. If we're out of lemon, we use lime, orange, or even grapefruit juice. (One way to avoid fish-smelling fingers is to rub your hands with lemon before you touch the fish. Squeeze the lemon for juice, then cut open the half rind, and rub it over your fingers and hands.)

Another good point to keep in mind is that unlike most meat, fish does not require long cooking periods. There is no tough connective tissue to break down; fish is already tender. Most fish is done as soon as it loses its transparent look and becomes white. We give it the fork test to check for flakiness: If it flakes easily as we lift it with a fork, it's cooked.

Fish translates into many great combinations. Three of the best known for filets of sole are with almonds (*amandine*), with butter (*meunière*), and laced with white wine and a hollandaise sauce (*à la bonne femme*). A famous French preparation is *quenelles*. A quenelle is a sort of fish dumpling made with butter, *panada* (a roux or bread mixture), and eggs. Its shape is almost always oval, and it can be formed in a spoon and dropped into boiling liquid or poached in a mold. It is usually served with a sauce, cream or otherwise. Bass makes a good quenelle.

Here are some great fish combinations to get the juices flowing: red snapper sprinkled with basil, thyme, and garlic and topped with a beurre blanc, all cooked *en papillote*; salmon and sturgeon baked in champagne with a *mirepoix* (a mixture of diced carrots, onions, and celery) and served with a touch of fresh tarragon; shad roe combined with a sorrel sauce; baked trout stuffed with salmon mousse; smoked haddock submerged in a brioche; skate sauced in black butter; and one of our favorites: a whiting pâté with curry.

A WORD ABOUT FISH FILETS:

Many of our fish recipes call for filets. To filet fish, clean, skin, and bone it. (By the way, a great "truc"—that is, trick—we learned from Dione Lucas is to salt your fingers to prevent the skin slipping when you have to remove it from flat fish.) But you'll be spared this task because all fish markets sell fresh fish filets and supermarkets carry frozen ones. Fish filets are mostly interchangeable in recipes, and if we suggest using filets of sole, you can use filets of bass, bluefish, flounder, haddock, hake, halibut, perch, pike, pompano, red snapper trout, and so on.

In this chapter, we've combined filets of sole with crab meat (Filet of Sole with Crab Meat) and with spinach (Sole and Lobster in the Florentine Style). One of our most elegant and best-tasting fish combinations is a turban of sole (a mold of filets filled with rice and parsley) turned out and then filled with shrimp and scallops in a white wine sauce —truly a combination for an important occasion.

FILET OF SOLE WITH CRAB MEAT

CRAB MEAT AND THYME   SERVES 4 TO 6

6 fresh filets of sole, large
  enough to roll
Juice of 1 lemon
8 tablespoons (1 stick) butter
1 carrot, sliced very thin
1 onion, sliced thin
1 celery stalk, including leaves,
  sliced thin
1 tablespoon fresh parsley,
  chopped fine (or ½ teaspoon
  dried)
1 tablespoon fresh thyme,
  chopped fine (or ½ teaspoon
  dried)

1 cup crab meat, cut into small
  pieces or shredded
½ cup heavy cream
  Salt
  Pepper, ground fresh
1 cup fish stock, strained
½ cup dry white wine
3 tablespoons all-purpose flour
½ cup milk
3 tablespoons grated Parmesan
  cheese
1 sprig fresh parsley or 2
  teaspoons fresh parsley,
  chopped (or 1 teaspoon dried)

Wash the filets under cool running water. While the filets are still dripping wet, put them in a bowl, and add half the lemon juice. Move the filets around in the bowl so that each gets some of the lemon juice.

Allow them to remain this way for at least 30 minutes at room temperature, or for several hours under refrigeration.

Melt 4 tablespoons butter in a saucepan or skillet, add the carrot slices and sauté them for about 5 minutes. Then add the onion, celery, parsley, and thyme, and cook an additional 5 minutes. Remove from the heat.

Add the crab meat and cream to the vegetable mixture, and fold all together. Salt and pepper to taste.

On a flat surface, arrange the filets, smooth side up, and spread the crab meat mixture evenly on them. Roll each filet, starting with the smaller end and rolling toward the larger end. Fasten each roll with one or two toothpicks, as necessary, and place each roll in a baking dish just large enough to hold the 6 rolled filets. We think this is an important step in the preparations because the rolled filets and the cooking liquid (the stock and wine) should cook together in a confined space. If you use a large pan, the cooking liquid will disperse and simply boil away, flavoring the pan instead of the fish.

Add ½ cup fish stock and ½ cup wine to the baking pan. Cover with buttered paper, and poach the filets in a preheated 350-degree oven for 15 to 20 minutes, or until almost done.

While the filets are poaching, make the sauce by melting 2 tablespoons butter in a small pan. Stir in the flour, blend well, and cook for 2 minutes, stirring constantly. Add remaining ½ cup fish stock and ½ cup milk, and bring to a boil. Then add the cheese and remaining 2 tablespoons butter, and simmer about 3 more minutes.

Remove the paper from the filets, and pour the sauce over them. Pour the remaining lemon juice over the filets. Bake 2 minutes longer, and then place the baking dish or pan under the broiler to brown the fish lightly and quickly.

Serve immediately in the baking pan if it's one you can bring to the table. Or serve the filets on individual platters, and sprinkle some fresh or dried parsley over each fish roll.

BAKED STRIPED BASS WITH DILL

DILL AND WHITE WINE   SERVES 4 TO 6

TO PREPARE THE BASS:

4-pound fresh whole striped bass, viscera removed, but with head and tail
Juice of 1 lemon
1 carrot, sliced lengthwise into 4 pieces and then cut into small dice

6 shallots, finely chopped
1 tablespoon fresh dill, chopped fine (or 1 teaspoon dried dill weed)
Salt
Pepper, ground fresh

Wash the bass several times in cool water. Pat it dry, and lay it on a baking tray covered with foil. (The sheets of foil should be large enough to wrap the fish.) Dot the bass with the lemon juice inside and out. Add the carrot, shallots, and dill inside and over the outside of the fish. Salt and pepper liberally inside and out, and fold the foil over to enclose the fish completely (head and tail included). Place this in a preheated 375-degree oven, and bake for about 30 minutes, or until the fish is flaky. Test with a fork. When the fish is done, open the foil. Some juice will have accumulated. This should be poured off and become part of the 2 cups stock needed for the sauce. Transfer the baked bass to a large serving platter. (We usually pick up the whole fish while it is still in the foil, place it on a platter, and roll it off the foil.)

TO PREPARE THE SAUCE:

3 tablespoons butter
3 tablespoons all-purpose flour
2 cups Rich Fish Stock (see page 50)

⅓ cup dry white wine
Salt
Pepper, ground fresh
Few drops of lemon juice

We usually make this sauce while the bass is baking. In a small saucepan, melt the butter. Add the flour, and beat well and constantly with a wire whisk for about 2 minutes. Add the stock and wine, blend well, and cook over low heat for 20 to 30 minutes. (We add about 1½ cups stock, knowing that we'll later be adding the juices from the baked fish; this works easily and well. Don't be overly concerned about the amount of stock; the sauce can be thickened, if you want, by adding beurre manié.) Stir frequently. Adjust the salt and pepper, and add a few drops lemon juice.

We do not pour the sauce over the fish. Put it in a bowl, and serve separately. Bring the whole fish to the table, filet it there, and serve on individual plates with 2 tablespoons sauce on the side.

SOLE AND LOBSTER IN THE
FLORENTINE STYLE

MARSALA AND SPINACH   SERVES 3 TO 4

TO PREPARE THE FISH:

6 fresh filets of sole   *2 tablespoons Marsala*
Juice of ½ lemon   *1 garlic clove, chopped fine*
½ cup dry white wine   *Salt*
2 tablespoons butter   *Pepper, ground fresh*
2 cups lobster meat, cut into
small pieces (see Note)

Wash the filets in cool water, and place them in a bowl. Add the lemon juice, and toss the filets in the bowl to coat them with the lemon juice. Let them stand for 30 minutes at room temperature, or longer under refrigeration.

Butter a baking pan large enough to hold 6 filets folded in half. Arrange the filets so that they do not overlap; fold filets in three if necessary. (They will have to be removed from the baking pan to a serving platter in whole pieces after they have cooked, and it's easier to do this if they're not overlapped.)

Pour the white wine over the filets first, then salt and pepper them to taste. Butter a piece of wax paper large enough to cover the baking pan, or use tin foil. Bake filets in a preheated 350-degree oven for 15 minutes, or until cooked. Do *not* overcook.

While the filets are poaching, melt 2 tablespoons butter in a saucepan or skillet. When it is hot and bubbling, add the lobster pieces, Marsala, garlic, salt, and pepper, and cook for 4 minutes, stirring frequently. Remove from the heat.

Use a spatula to remove the filets to a large serving platter (try to keep them whole). Divide the lobster by placing spoonfuls of it on top of the 6 filets. Keep them warm.

TO PREPARE THE SAUCE:

4 egg yolks	*½ cup Gruyère cheese, grated*
1 teaspoon fresh tarragon, chopped fine (or ½ teaspoon dried)	*2 tablespoons Rich Fish Stock (see page 50)*
Juice of ½ lemon	*1 cup spinach leaves, uncooked and chopped very fine*
½ cup heavy cream	*Salt*
4 tablespoons butter	*Pepper, ground fresh*

In the top of a double boiler, combine the egg yolks, tarragon, lemon juice, and ¼ cup heavy cream. Beat constantly with a wire whisk until the mixture begins to thicken. Add the remaining cream, butter, Gruyère cheese, fish stock, and chopped raw spinach, stirring constantly until all is well blended and thickened. Salt and pepper to taste.

Pour sauce over the filets and lobster, and then put your Florentine masterpiece under the broiler to toast it quickly and lightly. Serve at once.

Note: Crab meat may be substituted for lobster. Or you may use 3 large shrimps per person. Boil them until only slightly pink, and then follow the rest of the procedure.

FILETS OF SOLE BAKED IN BROWN PAPER BAGS

MUSHROOMS AND SOUR CREAM   SERVES 6

Paper-bag cookery is not new; we have read about it a lot. Yet, we have rarely seen it in the homes of friends, and we don't notice it on restaurant menus, although we remember having Pompano *en Papier* some time ago in a New Orleans restaurant (it was not presented in a very attractive way). Our version of this dish accents herbs, butter, sherry, and sour cream. They are a glorious combination, and this is a truly excellent way to prepare and present fish filets. It requires only a few minutes to prepare the bags, and the extra time is worth it—a sure way to please your guests.

6 large fresh filets of sole	6 tablespoons sour cream
Juice of 1½ lemons	1 tablespoon fresh chives,
12 medium-size mushrooms,	chopped fine (or 1 teaspoon
sliced thin	dried)
9 tablespoons butter, softened	Salt
2 garlic cloves, chopped fine	Pepper, ground fresh
2 tablespoons sherry	6 brown paper bags, 1-pound size
1 tablespoon fresh tarragon,	(see Note)
chopped fine (or 1 teaspoon	1 lemon, cut lengthwise in 6 slices
dried)	

Select absolutely fresh fish. Wash the filets in cool water, place them in a bowl, and add the juice from ½ lemon. Toss the filets in a bowl to cover them with the lemon juice, and let them stand for 30 minutes at room temperature, or for several hours under refrigeration.

Clean the mushrooms (if necessary) by wiping them with a clean tea towel or paper towel; slice them as thin as possible, after removing the stem ends. Put the sliced mushrooms in a clean bowl (preferably glass or ceramic), add the juice of ½ lemon, and toss the mushrooms to coat them with the juice. Set them aside.

Pat the filets dry, and lay them on a flat surface, smooth side up. Coat both sides of each filet with 2 tablespoons of softened butter. Salt and pepper the side facing up.

Melt another 2 tablespoons butter in a saucepan or skillet. Add the garlic, sherry, and tarragon, and cook over high heat for 4 minutes. The sauce will thicken slightly as the sherry cooks down. Stir several times with a rubber spatula while cooking.

Brush or spread this sauce over the fish by placing spoonfuls of it on each filet. Add 1 tablespoon sour cream to each filet. Divide the sliced mushrooms among the filets. Fold filets in half.

Divide 3 tablespoons butter among the 6 folded filets by placing a pat of butter on top of each. Salt and pepper each one again, and add a sprinkle of chopped chives and a few drops of the remaining lemon juice.

Spread some butter over the outside of each bag, trying to coat it as evenly as you can (but don't make a fetish of this; the bags will not burn). Open each bag wide. Using a spatula, lift each folded filet, and place it in a paper bag. Fold over the opening of each bag twice securely, thereby creating a steam bath for each filet. Set the filled bags on a baking tray with a shallow rim. (A jelly-roll pan is excellent.) Bake at 375 degrees for 25 minutes.

The buttered brown paper itself bakes nicely. It develops a transparent look and remains puffed up; as a result, it is quite attractive to bring to the table. Serve in the paper bags, but first make a cross cut in each bag with scissors or very sharp pointed knife. Or cut an elongated V shape into the top of the bag, and pull back beginning with the bottom of the V.

Serve with extra lemon wedges (seeds removed). We've never been able to understand why some three- and four-star restaurants get away with serving lemon wedges with seeds when they can be cut away or scooped out so quickly and easily.) Tiny boiled new potatoes, *un*skinned, are a wonderful combination with this. The harmony of the browns of the potatoes and the paper bags, accented by bright lemon wedges, is really satisfying to the eye, just as this delicious combination is to the stomach.

Note: You can use 10-by-15-inch parchment paper in place of the paper bags, but we think the brown bags are more attractive. (Parchment paper has a see-through quality after baking and in this particular dish looks messy because of the drippings.)

SALT COD WITH POTATOES AND ONIONS

POTATOES AND ONIONS   SERVES 6 TO 8

> 2 *pounds dried salt cod*
> 4 *large potatoes, boiled, peeled,*
>   *and cut into 1-inch cubes*
> ¾ *cup olive oil*
> 4 *onions, sliced*
> 2 *cloves garlic, chopped fine*
> 1 *bay leaf*
> ¼ *teaspoon hot pepper flakes*

> ¼ *teaspoon thyme*
> 1½ *cups dry white wine (or 1 cup*
>   *dry vermouth and ½ cup*
>   *water)*
> ½ *cup cooking liquid from cod*
>   *Fresh parsley, chopped fine*

Soak the cod in cold water overnight; change the water at least four times during the soaking (see page 116). Drain the cod, cut it into 2-inch pieces, and put them in a medium-size saucepan. Barely cover the cod with water, and simmer until tender (10 to 15 minutes). Drain the cod pieces, and transfer them to a bowl. Reserve about ½ cup of the liquid in which the cod was cooked, and set it aside.

Boil the potatoes, and set them aside until they are cool enough to handle. Peel and cube them, and set them aside.

In a large skillet, heat the oil, and cook the onion until it begins to turn color. Add the garlic pieces, bay leaf, pepper flakes, and thyme. Stir well, and cook for 2 minutes.

Then add the cod, potatoes, wine, and ½ cup cooking liquid, and cover the pan. Simmer for 20 to 30 minutes, or until the potatoes are heated through. Sprinkle chopped fresh parsley over all.

TURBAN OF SOLE WITH RICE, FILLED WITH SHRIMP AND SCALLOPS, IN A WHITE WINE SAUCE

SCALLOPS AND WHITE WINE   SERVES 10

TO PREPARE THE SHRIMP AND SCALLOPS:

1½ cups dry white wine (or 1 cup dry vermouth and ½ cup water)	1 small bay leaf
	1 pound scallops
1 teaspoon salt	½ pound mushrooms, wiped clean and sliced thin
¼ teaspoon pepper	1 pound shrimp, shelled
3 tablespoons shallots, chopped fine (or 2 tablespoons scallions or onions)	¼ slice lemon

In a medium-size saucepan, combine the wine or vermouth and water with the salt, pepper, shallots, and bay leaf. Bring to a boil, and cook over high heat for 3 minutes. Set aside.

Add the scallops and mushrooms to the wine mixture. The liquid should barely cover the ingredients; if it does not, add some water. Cover the pan, and simmer 4 minutes. Do *not* overcook. Remove the scallop and mushroom mixture to a clean bowl, and set aside. Discard the bay leaf. Let the liquid boil down to about 1¼ cups, and set aside. (This cooking liquid will be used in the white wine sauce.)

If the shrimps are frozen, cook them 1 minute less than the directions on the package suggest, and add the lemon slice to the water in the pan. They are done when they just begin to turn pink. If unfrozen, cook them with the lemon slice until they barely turn pink. Do *not* overcook; the shrimp will cook a bit more when they are added to the hot white-wine sauce. Add the shrimp to the scallops and mushrooms.

TO PREPARE THE WHITE WINE SAUCE:

3 tablespoons butter	*2 egg yolks*
4 tablespoons all-purpose flour	*¾ cup heavy cream*
1 cup cooking liquid from	*Salt*
scallops and mushrooms	*Pepper, ground fresh*
¾ cup milk	*Dash of lemon juice*

Melt the butter in a medium-size saucepan (a 2-quart pan is perfect), add flour, and mix well. Cook for about 2 minutes. Remove the pan from the burner, and slowly add the cooking liquid. Stir thoroughly, slowly add the milk, and stir again. Bring to a slow boil, and simmer for 1 minute, stirring constantly.

In a large bowl, combine the egg yolks and ½ cup heavy cream. Beat together until well mixed, and then add the thickened sauce *little by little*. Return to the heat, and cook 1 or 2 minutes. Add remaining cream and more cooking liquid if necessary to get the consistency you want. (The sauce should coat a spoon thickly.) Salt and pepper to taste, and add several drops of lemon juice. This improves the taste significantly. Do *not* add scallops and shrimp to sauce yet; it will take another 30 minutes or so to prepare and cook the fish mold. Therefore, set the sauce aside, and start to make the turban of sole.

TO PREPARE THE RING MOLD AND ASSEMBLE THE TURBAN:

½ cup milk	*2 tablespoons butter, cut in*
Butter for coating ring mold	*small pieces*
3½ pounds filet of sole	*¼ pound Fontina cheese, cut*
Salt	*into small pieces*
Pepper, ground fresh	
Approximately 1 cup cooked	
rice mixed with 2 tablespoons	
parsley and 2 tablespoons	
butter	

Heavily butter a 6-cup ring mold, and set it aside.

If time permits, wash the fish filets, and soak them in ½ cup milk. This seems to keep the fish light and bright white. If not, wash, and dry the filets. Salt and pepper each filet to taste, and arrange them in the mold so that they overlap each other and also hang over both inside and outside rings of the mold. (The inside of the mold should be completely covered with the filets.)

Fill the mold with the cooked rice (which has been mixed with parsley and butter); then turn down the ends of the filets to encase the rice. Cover the mold with tin foil.

Put the mold in a larger pan such as a roasting pan, and fill this larger pan (or bain-marie) with boiling water to cover about 1 inch of the bottom of the mold. Cook the mold in a hot oven (400 to 425 degrees) for 15 or 20 minutes. Do *not* overcook it.

While the mold is cooking, combine the shrimp, scallops, mushrooms, and white wine sauce in a saucepan so that the mixture will be ready to heat. But do *not* heat it until after the mold has been turned out.

Invert the mold on a large, ovenproof platter or silver serving piece. Hold the mold against the platter, and drain the excess liquid. (You will need a hot pad against the mold to keep your hand from burning, and the best place to do this draining is at the kitchen sink.) There is usually a fair amount of liquid in the mold, and if it is not drained, it will thin the white wine sauce, which is not what you want to happen. This sounds complicated, but it isn't. Just be sure you understand the directions. (Of course, you can capture this fish juice and reserve it for a later use.)

Now heat the shrimp, scallop, wine sauce, and pour this mixture into the center of the mold.

Cover the top of the ring and its center with pieces of Fontina cheese and butter. Put this under the broiler for a few seconds, until the cheese and butter are partially melted. (Be sure your serving platter fits into your oven.) Add a parsley sprig, and serve immediately.

BAKED FILETS OF FLOUNDER SAUCED IN SHERRY AND BUTTER

SHERRY AND BUTTER   SERVES 6

T O   P R E P A R E   T H E   F L O U N D E R :

6 filets of flounder	*1 onion, chopped fine*
4 tablespoons butter	*1 garlic clove, chopped fine*
2 tablespoons lemon juice	*½ cup water*

Wash the filets under cool water, pat them dry with a tea towel or paper towels, and set them aside.

Use 4 tablespoons butter to grease a shallow baking dish. (One that is not too large is preferable; the filets should be close together so that the juices won't run all over.) Arrange the filets in the dish; you probably will have to fold them in half in order to get all 6 in.

Pour the lemon juice and water over the filets, and sprinkle them with the onion and garlic pieces.

Cover this with tin foil or a baking dish cover, and bake in a preheated 350-degree oven for 15 minutes, or until the filets are done. (Do *not* overcook them.)

T O   P R E P A R E   T H E   S A U C E :

6 tablespoons butter	*Pepper, ground fresh*
1 cellery stalk, including tender green leaves, sliced fine	*1½ tablespoons all-purpose flour*
¼ cup dry sherry	*¼ cup milk*
Salt	*¼ cup heavy cream*

Melt 3 tablespoons butter in a saucepan, add the celery pieces, and sauté them for several minutes, but don't let them get soft.

Add the sherry, and season with salt and pepper to taste. Cover, and cook slowly for 10 to 15 minutes, until the celery is tender but *not* over-cooked.

Then add the flour, and stir well. Continue to cook over low heat, and add the juices from the fish dish, including the onion and garlic pieces. (The easiest way to do this is to remove the cooked filets from the baking pan with a spatula. Put them aside, and keep them warm.) When the sauce thickens, add the milk slowly, and bring to a boil. The sauce should be thick enough to coat a spoon. Add the cream and remaining 3 tablespoons butter, and stir well. You may prefer to strain the sauce, but we don't think this is necessary. We like the texture (visually and tastewise) of the celery and onions in the creamy sauce.

Serve this dish with glazed whole carrots: It's a great combination.

RED SNAPPER, STUFFED AND BAKED

SHALLOTS AND BUTTER   SERVES 6

TO PREPARE THE FISH:
>   1 whole red snapper, 3 to 4 pounds
>   Butter
>   Juice of 1 lemon
>   Salt
>   Pepper, ground fresh

Wash the fish several times in cool water, and dry it well. Put the fish in a buttered baking dish, and sprinkle it with lemon juice inside and outside. Salt and pepper the fish, inside and out. Allow it to stand for 30 minutes at room temperature, or longer in the refrigerator (up to 3 hours).

TO PREPARE THE STUFFING:

>   1 tablespoon butter
>   ½ cup shallots, chopped (or
>   onions or scallions)
>   ⅓ cup dry white wine
>   3 thick slices of Italian or French
>   bread, soaked in milk and
>   squeezed dry

>   ½ cup butter, melted
>   2 eggs, lightly beaten
>   2 tablespoons fresh parsley,
>   chopped fine (or ½ teaspoon
>   dried)
>   Salt
>   Pepper, ground fresh

In a skillet, melt 1 tablespoon of butter, and sauté the shallots for 3 minutes. Transfer shallots to a mixing bowl. Add the wine to the skillet, and deglaze the pan over high heat. Use a rubber spatula to scrape the skillet drippings into the mixing bowl with the shallots. Add the bread, melted butter, eggs, parsley, and salt and pepper to taste; mix well. Stuff the fish cavity.

Dot the fish with butter, and bake in a preheated 375-degree oven 30 to 40 minutes, or until the fish is done. Baste the fish several times with the pan drippings.

Note: When your fishmonger cuts the fish open, remind him that you're going to stuff it, and ask him not to cut the slit all the way to the tail end. He should make the slit from the head to the vent, leaving enough connective flesh to hold in the stuffing.

SALMON STEAKS, MARINATED AND GRILLED

SUGAR AND MUSTARD   SERVES 4

> 4 *salmon steaks, 1 inch thick*   4 *teaspoons salt*
> *Juice of 1 lemon*   ½ *cup sugar*
> 4 *tablespoons fresh dill, chopped*   4 *tablespoons Dijon mustard*
> (*or 2 teaspoons dried dill*
> *weed*)

Wash the salmon steaks, dry them well, and place them in a shallow baking pan. (A jelly-roll pan is excellent.) Line the pan with foil so that it covers the sides completely, forming a pan within a pan. The marinade for the salmon should not be allowed to seep through the foil.

In a small bowl, combine the lemon juice, dill, salt, sugar, and mustard. With a small wooden spoon, blend to make a marinade paste. Coat both sides of the salmon steaks. When both sides are completely coated, cover the steaks with another piece of foil, and weight them with another jelly-roll pan of the same size or plates or some other adequate substitute. Marinate the steaks in this fashion in the refrigerator for a *minimum* of 12 hours; we prefer to allow them to marinate overnight.

Remove the steaks from the refrigerator 1 hour before grilling time. Preheat the broiling unit, and broil the steaks approximately 5 minutes on each side. (They should be about 5 inches below the broiling unit.)

Serve with additional mustard if you wish.

FRESH FISH FILETS CON POMODORI
(WITH TOMATOES)

TOMATOES AND HERBS   SERVES 4

1 *pound fresh fish filets* (sole,
   flounder, *or whatever you*
   prefer)
   Juice of ½ *lemon*
2 *tablespoons olive oil*
1 *garlic clove, chopped fine*
1 *onion, chopped fine*
2 *cups fresh tomatoes, cored,*
   blanched, peeled, seeded, and
   chopped coarse (*or canned*
   plum tomatoes, sieved)

2 *teaspoons parsley, chopped*
   fine
1 *teaspoon fresh or frozen basil,*
   chopped fine (*or* ½ *teaspoon*
   dried)
½ *teaspoon oregano*
1 *teaspoon salt*
¼ *cup dry white wine* (*or dry*
   vermouth)
   Pepper, ground fresh

Wash the filets in cool water, put them in a bowl with the lemon juice, and allow them to stand for 15 minutes. Pat them dry, cut them into 3-inch pieces, and set them aside.

In a large skillet, heat the oil, add the garlic and onion, and brown lightly. Add the tomatoes, parsley, basil, oregano, and salt, and cook over medium heat for 15 minutes. Then add the filet pieces, wine, and pepper to taste, and cook for 5 minutes. (These pieces of fresh filets cook quickly.)

Serve on a bed of rice or with fresh, crusty Italian bread.

MOUSSE DE SOLE AUX TRUFFES
(Sole Mousse with Truffles)

TRUFFLES AND CREAM   SERVES 6 TO 8

TO PREPARE THE MOUSSE:

1½ *pounds filet of sole*
1 *cup white bread crumbs*
¼ *cup milk*
1 *cup heavy cream*
   Salt

Pepper, ground fresh
4 *egg whites*
1 *tablespoon truffle, chopped*
   fine

Wash and dry the filets. Put them through a meat grinder, using the fine blade; or use a balloon wire whisk, and shred the filets, a little at a time, until they are mashed or pulverized.

Soak the bread crumbs in the milk; if they are too moist, squeeze out some liquid. Add the crumbs to the mashed filets, and mix well. Then add the cream, and blend well. Add salt and pepper to taste.

Whip the egg whites to stiff peaks, and fold them into the fish mixture. Add the chopped truffle.

Liberally butter a mold (a glass or tin soufflé pan or ring mold will work nicely, but be sure it is ovenproof), and fill with the mousse mixture. Place the mold in a bain-marie, and bake in a preheated 350-degree oven for approximately 45 minutes, or until done.

Turn out the mousse onto a warmed serving platter.

TO PREPARE THE SAUCE:

8 tablespoons (1 stick) butter	*Salt*
2 tablespoons all-purpose flour	*Pepper, ground fresh*
1 cup Rich Fish Stock (see page 50)	*½ teaspoon lemon juice*
	Sprig of parsley
½ cup heavy cream	

Melt 3 tablespoons butter in a small saucepan, stir in flour, and blend well. Then add the fish stock, and bring to a boil. Cook slowly until the sauce thickens. Add the cream and remaining butter, a little at a time. Salt and pepper to taste, add the lemon juice, and blend well.

Serve immediately by pouring the sauce over the mousse. Now for a sprig of parsley on top of the mousse!

SHELLFISH

It has been said that to live by the sea is to live well. Shellfish admirers envy those who live close to the source of the plenitude of shrimps, lobsters, scallops, clams, and oysters.

But we can enjoy good crustaceans between seas, thanks to speedy air transportation and chefs, hosts, and hostesses who know that good seafood dishes depend on strictly fresh seafood, that even frozen seafood should be used quickly after it has thawed. Don't despair; you *can* have a delicious clambake in Kentucky.

Seafood must *not* be overcooked. In our view, this is the one cardinal sin committed by many cooks. We ourselves have seen beautiful shrimps shrivel into tough, chewy pieces because we were not paying sufficient attention. A good rule to follow is to remove the shrimps as soon as they turn pink. If you're not sure about doneness, quickly taste a piece. And don't just move the pan off the burner; you must remove the shrimps from the hot water. (Otherwise, they will go on cooking.) Live lobsters should be put into boiling water; they, too, are cooked when they turn pink.

Shellfish, like all fish, can be part of many great combinations. At the Chateau du Domaine St. Martin in Vence, France, we dined on scallops cooked in a court bouillon with carrots and parsley, served with a *beurre blanc*. They called this a Coquille Saint-Jacques à la Nage. From the Atlantic coast of France, there's *mouclade* (creamed mussels) a dish of tiny *moules* steamed as for a marinière, the juices strained and greatly reduced; heavy cream is added, together with a telling soupçon of curry powder. Then there are mussels with a sauce made from pounded lobster coral and enclosed in a crepe—an extraordinary combination.

Shrimp

Shrimp bisques and shrimp Newburg always seem to taste better in New Orleans, thanks to the creativity of the Creole cooks. Then there are shrimps rémoulade and shrimps de Jonghe (boiled in a court bouillon).

Some great combinations originated in Charleston, South Carolina. Shrimp and green corn pie, various shrimp and rice dishes, puffy shrimp puddings, shrimps sautéed in butter, shrimp paste served with hot buttered hominy grits.

In England, there are potted shrimps laden with butter, anchovy sauce, and mace. The French join mussels with shrimps (*à la Dieppoise*); the Danes lay them on sour rye bread. The scampi are sautéed in garlic and oil in Italy; and after the Japanese dip them in batter and deep-fry them, they sauce them with *dashi*. The Japanese also prepare *gosokuni* in challenge to Italy's scampi. *Gosokuni* are shrimps cooked in their shells in peanut oil, then bathed in soy sauce and sake. Harry's Bar in Venice serves *Scampi alla Carlina* (scampi cooked in butter with fresh tomatoes, capers, and small mushrooms).

Shrimps are skewered with onions, cooked with curry, dipped in dill sauce, layered with rice, doused with lemon, coated with olive oil, broiled with mustard, mixed with mayonnaise, blended with beer, baked with brandy, combined with cream, soused in spices, boiled in soup, topped with tomato sauce.

Our scampi are prepared in several minutes; we call this dish Scampi: Uno, Due, Tre ("one, two, three"). We combine shrimp with mustard and dill for Cold Shrimp for a Buffet and with almonds and cream sherry for a richer dish, A Casserole of Cream Sherried Shrimp. We also fantail them, bathe them in a special batter, and deliciously deep-fry them fast so that they may be served with two tasty sauces: one piquant, the other sweet (Fantailed Shrimp, Battered and Deep-Fried).

A CASSEROLE OF CREAM-SHERRIED SHRIMP

ALMONDS AND CREAM SHERRY   SERVES 6

This is a simple and effective dish to prepare and serve. It's perfect for a small dinner party because it can be pulled together ahead of time and go into the oven when the guests arrive. Cream, sherry, and almonds are a great combination with shrimp, and a salad of lettuce or other green vegetables with one of the oil and vinegar dressings (see page 360) is an excellent accompaniment. The creamy, rich texture of the shrimp casserole and the tartness of the salad are made for each other.

2½ pounds large fresh shrimps	1½ cups fresh tomatoes,
3 tablespoons lemon juice	cored, blanched, peeled, and
3 tablespoons olive oil	put through a food mill to
3 tablespoons unsalted butter	remove seeds and to purée
¼ cup green pepper, chopped	¾ cup cream sherry, California
coarse	variety if possible
¼ cup onion, chopped coarse	1 cup heavy cream
½ teaspoon cayenne pepper	1 cup slivered almonds,
1 teaspoon salt	blanched
1 cup rice, uncooked	Pepper, ground fresh

Shell, devein, and clean the shrimps; put them in a bowl, and add the lemon and oil.

In a medium-size casserole, heat the butter, and sauté the green peppers and onions for 5 minutes. (Do *not* brown them.) Add the cayenne pepper and salt. Then add the rice and shrimps, and mix well. Add the tomatoes, sherry, cream, and almonds, mix well, and cover.

Bake in a preheated 350-degree oven for 1 hour, or until done. Before serving, sprinkle freshly ground pepper overall.

COLD SHRIMP FOR A BUFFET

MUSTARD AND DILL   SERVES 10 TO 20

TO PREPARE THE SHRIMPS:

2 tablespoons pickling spices   *72 large shrimps (about 3 to 3½*
2 cloves garlic, halved   *pounds if frozen, more if fresh*
Juice of 1 lemon   *and unshelled)*
12 peppercorns, whole

Combine the pickling spices, garlic cloves, lemon juice, peppercorns, and enough water to cover the shrimps (you'll have to use your judgment) in a large saucepan. Bring to a boil, and cook briskly for 5 minutes. Add the shrimps, and cook until they are pink (about 5 minutes). (Do *not* overcook the shrimps, or they will shrivel and toughen.) Remove the shrimps from the liquid immediately, and let them cool.

TO PREPARE THE SAUCE:

3 cloves garlic, put through a   *1 teaspoon dill seed*
garlic press (or chopped very   *3 tablespoons Tzigane mustard*
fine)   *(see Note)*
Juice of 3 lemons   *2 teaspoons salt*
6 tablespoons olive oil   *Pepper, ground fresh*
2 tablespoons dry vermouth

In a bowl, combine all the sauce ingredients. Add the shrimps to the sauce. Toss several times, and marinate overnight.

Note: Tzigane mustard is a product of France, made and distributed by Fauchon. It is a combination of mustard, vinegar, salt, paprika, tomato, and pimiento. This combination gives a special flavor to the shrimp. We've tried this dish with other mustards with almost the same result, so if you don't have this Fauchon mustard, try a substitute.

FANTAIL SHRIMP, BATTERED AND DEEP-FRIED

MUSTARD SAUCE AND MARMALADE   SERVES 6

TO PREPARE THE SHRIMPS:

> 2½ *pounds jumbo shrimps*
> ½ *teaspoon salt*
> 2 *garlic cloves, chopped fine*

Wash and shell the shrimps in cool water, leaving their tails intact. Split the shrimps down the back, but do not cut them all the way through. Devein the shrimps, and flatten them gently, without separating the halves. Place the shrimps in a bowl, add the salt and garlic pieces, and marinate for 30 minutes or longer.

TO PREPARE THE BATTER:

> 2 *cups all-purpose flour*
> ½ *teaspoon salt*
> 1½ *tablespoons baking powder*
> ⅔ *cup vegetable oil*
> 1½ *cups cool water*

In a bowl, mix the flour, salt, and baking powder. Slowly add the vegetable oil to the flour mixture until a ball of dough is formed. (The dough will leave the sides of the bowl.) Then slowly add the water to the dough. The batter will develop a consistency resembling that of pancake batter.

TO COOK AND SERVE THE SHRIMPS:

> 3 *cups vegetable oil*
> ½ *cup dry mustard*
> ½ *cup orange marmalade*

Add to the dry mustard ½ to ⅔ cup of water, and mix thoroughly. The resulting mustard should have the consistency of heavy cream.

Heat 3 cups vegetable oil to 400 degrees. Dip one shrimp at a time into the batter, and hold the shrimp over the bowl to let the excess batter drip back into it. Deep-fry the shrimps immediately in hot oil, one at a time, until nicely browned. Transfer each browned shrimp to paper toweling.

Serve the shrimp hot, and pass the two sauces (mustard and marmalade). The idea is to pick up a shrimp by the tail or cut it with knife and fork, and dip it into both sauces.

SCAMPI: UNO, DUE, TRE

OLIVE OIL AND GARLIC   SERVES 6

3 pounds large raw shrimps	3 garlic cloves, chopped fine
½ cup olive oil	½ cup flat Italian parsley, chopped
Salt	fine
Pepper, ground fresh	

Once the shrimps are cleaned, this is one of the easiest dishes to make. It's also one of the best tasting.

Shell and devein and shrimps, and wash them carefully in cold water. Pat them dry with paper towels or a tea towel.

Heat the oil in a very large skillet, and sauté the shrimps over high heat until they turn pink (about 5 minutes). Season them liberally with salt and fresh-ground pepper (this one time you really *must* use the peppermill), remove them from the skillet, and place them on a serving platter.

Then add the garlic pieces to the remaining oil in the skillet, and sauté over high heat very quickly and briefly (less than 2 minutes). Pour this sauce over the shrimp, sprinkle all with parsley, and serve right away.

Squid

In classical times, Greek and Roman gourmets considered squid the finest fish in the sea; it was presented as a delicacy at their many banquets. Aristotle, in his *Historia Animalium,* written prior to 300 B.C., described the squid in detail. Squid is a member of the phylum of mollusks, which includes oysters and clams. Like most fish, squid is a health food; it is high in protein and phosphorus and also contains traces of calcium, thiamine, and riboflavin.

Squid had long been a favorite in Europe and in Asia. Because it abounds in Mediterranean waters, it is prepared often in Italian homes. As children, we chuckled when Grandfather, with a *calamari* (the only name for squid that we knew then) in hand, described how the *calamari's* feet (tentacles) grew out of his head.

In the United States, squid is just beginning to gain some popularity. Fish markets in large American cities, especially those markets catering to customers with European backgrounds, sell fresh squid, and supermarkets often carry frozen squid. Look for it; it's quite inexpensive and can be prepared in many tasty ways.

Pieces of squid can be washed, dried, dipped into a mixture of eggs and milk, coated with bread or cracker crumbs, and fried for several minutes on each side in very hot shortening. Squid is tasty in chowder; it can replace other fish in typical chowders that combine bacon or salt pork, onions, potatoes, milk, flour, and so on.

We offer Calamari at Christmastime, which is squid stuffed with raisins, onions, and bread. This was one of many fish dishes that traditionally adorned our family's dinner table on Christmas Eve, and we called it *Calamari Natalizi.*

HOW TO DRESS A SQUID:
Lay the squid on a flat surface in front of you, and stretch it lengthwise from left to right, tentacles to your right. With a sharp knife, cut just below the eyes; this will free the tentacles. There are ten tentacles, and in the center of them is the mouth; pull or cut it off, and discard it. Pull off whatever skin you can from the tentacles, but don't be concerned if you don't get much off. (We always use the tentacles; chopped up in stuffings is one way.) Squeeze the body, and pull the head out; the viscera will come out of the body easily. Discard all this. Now pull out the transparent center bone (the chitinous pen or quill). What remains of the squid is a sack. Wash this well, and peel off the outer skin, which is purply gray and membranelike; it pulls off easily. Wash the squid well, and keep it whole if you plan to stuff it. You can also slice it crosswise to make thin circles or cut it lengthwise. Now you are ready to follow your recipe.

CALAMARI AT CHRISTMASTIME

RAISINS AND ONIONS   SERVES 4

TO STUFF THE SQUID:

1 tablespoon olive oil *1 tablespoon grated Parmesan*
1 tablespoon butter *cheese*
½ cup onion, chopped fine *1 large egg, lightly beaten*
 Squid tentacles, chopped *Salt*
¼ cup dry white wine *Pepper, ground fresh*
1 cup fresh bread crumbs *2 pounds fresh or frozen squid*
1 tablespoon orange zest, *(about 8 medium or 12 small*
 chopped fine   *squid), whole*
⅓ cup raisins

In a skillet, heat the olive oil and butter, and sauté the onion and tentacles until they are lightly browned. Transfer them to a mixing bowl.

Add the wine to the skillet, and deglaze the pan over high heat. With a rubber spatula, scrape the skillet liquid into the mixing bowl. Add the bread crumbs, orange zest, raisins, cheese, egg, and salt and pepper to taste, and combine with the onions and tentacles. (This stuffing mixture should be fairly dry but well blended; if it is too dry, add more white wine by teaspoonfuls.)

Stuff the cleaned and washed squid a little more than half full. (Do *not* fill them more than that.) Secure with a toothpick, or sew loosely with white thread.

TO COOK THE SQUID:

2 tablespoons olive oil *¾ cup dry white wine*
2 tablespoons butter *½ teaspoon dried oregano*
½ cup onion, chopped fine *Pinch of red pepper flakes*
1 small garlic clove, chopped *(optional)*
 fine   *Salt*
2 cups fresh tomatoes, cored, *Pepper, ground fresh*
 blanched, peeled, seeds *2 tablespoons fresh flat Italian*
 removed, and chopped fine (or *parsley, chopped*
 canned plum tomatoes, sieved)

In a skillet, heat 1 tablespoon olive oil and 1 tablespoon butter. When they are hot and bubbling, add the squid, and sauté, over low heat. (The squid will enlarge as they sauté, so keep the heat low.) As the squid begin to turn color—they will become whitish, almost translucent—remove them from the skillet, transfer them to a dish, and set them aside.

In a large, covered saucepan or heavy enameled pan, heat the remaining 1 tablespoon oil and 1 tablespoon butter. Sauté the onions until they are pale yellow (about 4 minutes). Add the garlic, and cook for 1 additional minute. Then add the tomatoes, wine, oregano, red pepper flakes (if you wish—we hope you will), and salt and pepper to taste. Cook over high heat for about 5 minutes, stirring frequently. Add the sautéed squid to the tomato mixture in a single layer (if at all possible); and cover the pan. Cook the squid over low heat for about 30 minutes, or until done.

Serve on a platter garnished with chopped fresh Italian parsley.

VARIATION: POTATO AND RICE STUFFING

POTATOES AND RICE

SERVES 4

2 tablespoons olive oil	¼ cup grated Parmesan cheese
2 tablespoons butter	2 tablespoons fresh flat Italian
⅓ cup onion, chopped fine	parsley, chopped
Squid tentacles, chopped fine	1 egg, lightly beaten
1 cup rice, cooked	Salt
¾ cup raw potatoes, shredded	Pepper, ground fresh

In a skillet, heat the oil and butter, and sauté the onion until it is softened. Add the tentacles, and cook for 4 minutes, or until the onion is lightly browned. Add the cooked rice, potatoes, cheese, parsley, egg, and salt and pepper to taste. Mix thoroughly, and remove from heat. You will have almost 2 cups of stuffing for your *calamari*.

Follow the rest of the procedure for cooking the squid on the stove top.

Lobster

We remember our first trip to San Diego, California, because we ate New England lobster that was especially good and we were assured that the lobsters we had that evening were flown in from Boston that same day. And if you've dared fare on other than French food in Paris, you surely must have seen American lobsters, flown over fresh from our own

New England, offered on menus of the best restaurants. For many of us, lobster is king of the seas. Varieties in abundance are found off California and Florida waters. Most supermarkets in America feature rock lobster (frozen tails) that come from Australia, New Zealand, and South Africa; they're not only popular but delicious, too. Europe claims its own true lobsters found in North Atlantic seas, and debate continues over whether the Dublin prawn is superior to the Norwegian. We can remember a fine French friend taking us to task for not using *langouste* for the lobster we put in homemade bouillabaisse. In New York recently, we ate a delicious dish called *Langoustines Provençales* made with Dublin Bay prawns. Although they looked like the Italian scampi, they were imported from Denmark and combined with garlic, oil, and tomatoes.

Great combinations with lobster are well known: lobster *à l'Américaine,* lobster salad, lobster curry, lobster Newburg, and the Napoleonic lobster thermidor. Lobster combines with sherry, Madeira, and Cognac; with onions, garlic, and tomatoes; with butter, cayenne, and white wine; with salt, dill, and cream sauce. Lobster in lettuce-leaf folds, which is served in some Chinese restaurants, is another fabulous combination. Lobster, mushrooms, shrimp, and ham—all diced—are stir-fried, enveloped in lettuce leaves, and garnished with cubed fresh tomatoes and cucumbers. And what about grilled lobster flamed in Cognac? Or grilled Norway lobster brochettes dripping with a white butter sauce?

Boiled, sautéed, flambéed, curried, broiled, skewered, buttered, creamed, deviled—lobster in all ways rates among the best in any of the great combinations of food we know. We've presented Lobster Stew, Rock Lobster Tails in the Fra Diavolo Style, and Broiled Live Lobster Our Style, with Bourbon.

BROILED LIVE LOBSTER OUR STYLE, WITH BOURBON

BOURBON AND BUTTER   SERVES 2 OR 4

2 medium-size live lobsters
  (about 1½ pounds each) (see
  Note)
2 tablespoons olive oil
8 tablespoons butter
  Juice of 1 lemon

1 tablespoon fresh tarragon,
  chopped fine (or 1 teaspoon
  dried)
¼ cup bourbon
  Salt
  White pepper, ground fresh

Plunge the paralyzed lobster, head first, into rapidly boiling salted water, and leave it in the water for 3 minutes. Remove the lobster (which will have turned pink), even if the water has not returned to a boil within the 3 minutes. Cut each lobster in half, using a cleaver, sharp knife, or lobster shears. Place the halves cut side up, and remove the sacs located near the heads, the intestinal veins, and the spongy lung tissues.

Put the oil in a large, shallow baking pan, and place the lobster halves in the pan, cut sides up. Put 1 tablespoon butter, broken into small pieces, over each lobster half, and dot each half with lemon juice. Sprinkle the tarragon over the halves. Bake the lobsters in a preheated 450-degree oven for 10 to 15 minutes, or until the shells turn a vivid red orange.

Heat the bourbon (do *not* allow it to cook down). Add 1 tablespoon butter, broken into small pieces, to each lobster half, and salt and pepper to taste. Place the lobsters under the broiler until they are light golden color (about 3 minutes).

Remove the lobsters, pour the bourbon over them, and ignite it. Move the pan around with a swirling motion to distribute butter, lemon juice, and flaming bourbon evenly over the lobsters.

As soon as the flame goes out, place the lobster halves on individual plates. Stir the sauce in the pan to blend it thoroughly, and divide it among the halves. Don't waste a single drop of this bourbon sauce.

Note: This is a simple way to serve live lobster *if* you know how to prepare a live lobster for cooking. When you buy lobsters, choose ones that flap their tails actively (a movement that resembles an open hand closing up into a fist). To pick up a live lobster, grab it at the shoulder area or chest (the heavy part between the legs) with your thumb and middle finger. To paralyze the lobster, pick it up in the same way, and place it on a chopping board, pushing down on the body. (Or you can fold a tea towel in half and then in half two more times and use the folded towel to cover the lobster's head and claws.) Take a sharp knife, and pierce straight into the back of the lobster at the point where the chest and tail intersect (the location of the spinal cord); this will paralyze the lobster immediately.

LOBSTER STEW

GRUYÈRE CHEESE AND POTATOES   SERVES 6

1 slice bacon
4 tablespoons butter
1 large onion, chopped fine
2 carrots, cut into ¼-inch slices
3 celery stalks, including leaves,
  chopped coarse
1 bouquet garni (3 sprigs
  parsley, or 1 teaspoon dried;
  1 sprig thyme, or ½ teaspoon
  dried; 10 peppercorns; and 1
  bay leaf—all tied in
  cheesecloth)
  Two 2½-pound fresh lobsters
2 large potatoes
1 cup fresh green peas, cooked
  al dente in stock or plain
  boiling water (or 1 package
  frozen peas)

1½ cups heavy cream
1½ cups milk
½ teaspoon thyme
½ cup shredded Gruyère cheese
½ cup fresh mushrooms, sliced
  and tossed in 1 tablespoon
  lemon juice
Salt
Pepper, ground fresh
1 tablespoon fresh parsley,
  chopped (or 1 teaspoon
  dried)

Fry the bacon slice in a large, covered saucepan (you'll need the cover later on). When the bacon is done, remove it, slice it, and set it aside. Add 2 tablespoons butter to the bacon fat, and sauté the onion, carrots, and celery pieces for 10 minutes, or until the onions become golden. Add enough water to cover the lobsters (approximately 3 quarts) but do *not* add the lobsters yet. (Use less if you can; you'll have to boil this liquid down quite a bit later.) Bring to a boil, drop in the bouquet garni, cover, and simmer for 20 minutes.

Remove the cover, add the lobsters, and cook them at a good simmer, until they turn a vivid red (up to 15 minutes). Remove the lobsters, and allow them to cool so that you can handle them; remove 90 percent of the meat from the shells, and cut it into large pieces. Keep meat in several claws to add to the stew for color and decoration.

Meanwhile, reduce the liquid to 1 quart by boiling rapidly; do not cover the pan.

An excellent way to prepare the potatoes is to cook them in this stock. Peel the potatoes, cut them in half, and add them to the boiling stock. Cook them until tender, and remove them. Cool them for handling, cube them, and set them aside. Strain the lobster liquid, and discard the vegetables; reserve 1 quart of this liquid.

If you are using fresh peas, cook them in salted water in a small saucepan, drain, and set aside. (If you are using frozen or canned peas, drain them, and set them aside.)

In another large saucepan, combine the cream, milk, and 2 tablespoons butter, and bring them to the boiling point. Add 1 quart of strained lobster liquid, thyme, and Gruyère cheese. Add the lobster meat, diced potatoes, cooked fresh peas (or thawed frozen or drained canned peas), raw mushrooms, and salt and pepper to taste. Heat for 5 minutes, or until the stew is heated through and the cheese is melted.

Pour the stew into individual bowls, and sprinkle fresh or dried parsley over each serving.

ROCK LOBSTER TAILS IN THE FRA DIAVOLO STYLE

TOMATOES AND GARLIC   SERVES 8

8 *large rock lobster tails*	2 *garlic cloves, chopped fine*
Juice of ½ lemon	2 *tablespoons fresh parsley,*
4 *tablespoons butter*	*Italian flat type if possible (or*
2 *tablespoons olive oil*	1 *teaspoon dried)*
2 *onions, chopped fine*	1 *teaspoon dried oregano*
1 *green pepper, seeded and*	*Salt*
chopped fine (we prefer	*Pepper, ground fresh*
Italian-type fryer pepper or	½ *cup brandy*
cherry pepper)	
1 *cup fresh tomatoes, cored,*	
blanched, peeled, and chopped	
fine (or canned plum tomatoes,	
drained)	

In a large saucepan bring to a boil enough water to cover the lobster tails; then add the lobster and the lemon juice, and cook until the tails are almost done. Do *not* overcook them (we suggest you check the package directions carefully). Remove the tails with a slotted spoon, or drain them into a colander. (Do this quickly; you do not want the lobster to cook any longer than necessary.) With scissors or a sharp knife, cut away the membrane on the underside of the tail (lobster shears or even poultry shears are good for this). Pull the lobster meat out of the shells. (This is easily done if you start at the wide part of the tail.) Keep the shells in one piece; you will be stuffing them later. Cut the lobster meat into chunks (approximately ¾-inch cubes), and put them aside.

In a skillet or heavy saucepan, melt 2 tablespoons butter and olive oil. Add the onions and green pepper, and sauté them for 3 minutes. Add the tomatoes, garlic, parsley, oregano, and cook, uncovered, for 20 minutes. Salt and pepper to taste.

Combine the tomato mixture with the lobster chunks. Place the 8 empty shells in a baking dish, and divide the mixture among them. Use all the filling, and don't fret about piling it high or seeing some of it run over the shells into the baking dish. Cut 2 tablespoons of butter into 8 pieces, and dot each shell with a piece of it. Cook the tails in a preheated hot oven (400 to 450 degrees) for 10 minutes, until they are bubbly.

Meanwhile, heat the brandy. Just before serving, ignite the brandy, and pour it all over the lobster tails. Serve immediately.

MUSSELS IN THE HIELY STYLE

SPINACH AND WHITE WINE   SERVES 6

One of the best meals we've ever eaten anywhere was at Le Hiely-Lucullus in Avignon, France. We arrived in Avignon one Sunday morning, and it wasn't until we were *sur le pont* that we remembered the refrain we sang in fourth grade: *"Sur le pont d'Avignon, l' on y danse, l' on y danse."* A strange but a glorious feeling. After dinner Sunday evening, we went back to our hotel singing, *"Près du pont d'Avignon, l' on y mange, l' on y mange."*

Le Hiely-Lucullus is not a fancy setting; there is no garden, no *moulin*, no hilltop, no frequent visits from a movie star. It's just a large, wide-open, beautiful room on the second floor of a magnificent old building in the downtown business section of Avignon, on the rue de la République. There were no flowers on the tables, but we sat next to large windows overlooking the street; the sills held boxes filled with the brightest red geraniums. They may just as well have been on the table. Monsieur and Madame Hiely, the chef-owner and his wife, are indescribably delightful, and so is the food they serve. The *Feuilleté de Ris de Veau aux Mousserons* was exquisite; we've not had it prepared and served better before or since. Equally exquisite was a dish called *Le Gratin de Moules aux Epinards*. The Hielys were kind and gave us instructions on how to prepare it (mostly in French, with an occasional "yes," "okay," and "good"). Anyway, here is their/our version of it.

4 pounds fresh spinach (or two 10-ounce packages frozen)	*1 cup heavy cream*
	4 egg yolks
3½ tablespoons butter	*½ teaspoon saffron stems*
3½ tablespoons olive oil	*Salt*
3 quarts mussels	*Pepper, ground fresh*
1 cup dry white wine, de bon qualité, n'est ce pas?	*⅓ cup bread crumbs, plain*

Bring 2 quarts of water to a boil in a large saucepan, and blanch the spinach for 4 minutes. Drain immediately and well, and chop the spinach fine. (If you use frozen spinach, thaw it fully, drain it well, and chop it fine.)

Dry the saucepan (the one in which you blanched the spinach), and heat the butter and olive oil in it. Add the spinach, and cook it until heated through. (Do *not* cook longer than necessary.) Transfer the spinach to a shallow baking dish (one that you can carry to the table for serving). Set aside, and keep warm.

Clean the mussels (see page 27), and put them in a large saucepan with a tight-fitting cover. Add the wine, and steam them open. Be sure to strain and keep the liquid after shelling and bearding the mussels; it will be used in the sauce. Put the mussels over the spinach in the baking dish.

In a small saucepan, combine the heavy cream, ½ cup mussel liquid, and egg yolks. Cook over low heat, beating constantly with a wire whisk, until the sauce has thickened. Add the saffron stems to the sauce; salt and pepper to taste.

Pour the sauce over the mussels and spinach. Sprinkle the bread crumbs overall, and broil in the oven until a top crust is formed and the dish is bubbling (about 6 to 8 minutes). Serve immediately.

((6))

A Simple Roast Filet of Beef,
Shell Steaks, Beef Balls,
and More Beef

I N early times, the priests of Rome paid homage to their gods by burning the viscera of cattle, carefully saving the rest of the beef for their feasts. Although records of per capita consumption for the Roman elite were not kept, our guess is that it at least equaled the high figures recorded since. However, in the sixteenth century meat consumption must have dropped dramatically during the Lenten season when it was considered criminal to break the rules and regulations that strictly forbade the eating of meat. (One sixteenth-century English law put Lenten meat-eating offenders in prison for three months.) It was permissible for sick people to eat meat, but only with a doctor's prescription. There has been recognition for centuries of the importance of meat—one of our best sources of protein—to the diet.

Three generations of our family have bought most of their meat from the same butcher shop. And that butcher shop has been owned and operated by the same family for more than fifty years. It may sound trite to say "know your butcher," but it will probably pay off for you to do so; it has for us—for over fifty years. We know our butcher, and he knows

every member of our family; he wouldn't *dare* give us a bad piece of
meat. It's unfortunate that the supermarket, so convenient in other ways,
has depersonalized the butcher. In spite of their spiffy two-way automatic
communications systems, those squawk boxes rarely work. When they
do, one never knows to whom he is talking, and the request for a special
cut or fresh grind of meat falls on deaf ears. The result is usually resort-
ing to the prepackaged selections, encased in plastic.

Because we are a nation of beef eaters, we should know something
about the major cuts. Beef, unlike veal, is cut into two sides; in other
words, the carcass is cut in half lengthwise. Then each side is cut in half.
The loin, the tenderest part of the beef, comes from the hindquarters.
From it are cut the beef tenderloin, filet mignon, sirloin, and porterhouse. The flank, also from the hindquarters, produces London broil
and flank steaks. The leanest hindquarter cut is the round, and from it
come many cuts, including choice-grade rump roasts, sirloin tips, bottom
and top round (bottom for moist-cooking, top for dry), and eye round
(excellent for dry-roasting).

The forequarters produce ribs of beef, which are cut into tender
steaks and roasts; brisket of beef, which, when cured, becomes corned
beef; and chuck, which provides many cuts (of which we consume a
great deal). From the neck, the butcher provides stew meats or ground
meats. Cuts from the shoulder give us meats for pot-roasting, stewing,
and braising. *Prime ribs* or *first cut* come from the rib portion of the
forequarters and are the first three ribs closest to the short loin. The
whole rib, which contains seven ribs, is often served in restaurants and
at large buffet parties; it is usually roasted and makes an appealing dis-
play. In addition to prime ribs, there are the *center cut* (the middle two
ribs after the first cut) and the *end cut* (the remaining two ribs).

Cuts that can be roasted or broiled are usually more expensive
because these are dry methods of cooking, as compared with moist
methods (pot roasts, stews, and so on). Meats for dry-cooking should
have a high degree of *marbling* (the amount of fat actually interwoven
with the lean meat). Meats that you can dry-roast can also be moist-
cooked, but the reverse is not true. There are excellent ways to moist-cook
filet mignon, but don't attempt to cook a pot roast as you would prime
ribs. Yet many meats with little marbling (and therefore with less cost)
can make great meals. They require a little more time and an added bit
of ingenuity; see our Flank Steak Stuffed with Eggplant and our Beef
Roll Imbottito di Legumi ("filled with vegetables").

Most meat shoppers check for marbling because it is the easiest way to recognize high-quality beef. It is responsible for the natural moisture in the meat; while the beef cooks, the fat adds flavor and makes the meat juicier and tenderer. The wise meat shopper also looks for color. For beef, it should be a bright, rosy red. The U.S. Department of Agriculture has five approved grades of beef: first, prime; second, choice; third, good; fourth, standard; and fifth, commercial. If you want better-quality beef, buy only the prime and choice grades.

Boiled beef, of course, combines with other foods in a hundred ways. The famous combinations bring it together with horseradish and other piquant sauces. Stockpot vegetables, such as onions, carrots, celery, and leeks are served with slices of boiled beef, as are coarse salt, gherkins, and other pickles. An interesting way to prepare boiled beef is to coat each slice with mustard, baste with melted butter, dip in fine bread crumbs, and broil until golden. We enjoy boiled beef best when it is prepared in a traditional family style. The boiled beef, hot or cold, is cut into ¼-inch slices and placed on a large serving platter, slices overlapping. Around the slices we arrange a variety of seasonal vegetables: tomato slices, thickly sliced boiled potatoes, fresh green beans *al dente*, cooked broccoli, cauliflower, asparagus spears, or Brussel sprouts, and lots of raw green and red peppers. All are covered with an oil and vinegar dressing heavily spiked with garlic, and a lemon wedge is added for zest.

Braised beef combines excellently with other foods, spices, and herbs. The meat is browned on all sides; then a very little liquid, in which the meat will cook, is added. The browning need not always be done on the stove top; try browning the beef in the oven under the broiler. Probably the two best-known braised beef dishes are the French *boeuf Bourguignonne,* in which beef and red wine are gloriously combined, and the American pot roast, in which beef is first browned and then combined for moist-cooking with beef broth and a variety of herbs, spices, and vegetables.

A familiar braised beef combination is *carbonnades Flamande,* which follows an old Flemish custom of browning meat and then combining it with beer and onions. We make this with a piece of top round of beef (about 5 pounds) kept in one piece. We cover the beef with freshly ground pepper and broil it in the oven about 6 inches from the broiling unit until the meat is quite crisp, in fact charred just a bit. We then put it in a heavy saucepan or casserole with a cover and add the drippings, a half-dozen onions, some rosemary, and about 1½ cups stout. We simmer this for almost 2 hours, covered, until the meat is tender. We usually add 1 or 2 cups of good beef stock or broth after the meat is cooked and removed from the pan and thicken this with a beurre manié for a rich sauce.

A braised brisket of beef, larded with Cognac-soaked lardoons, then marinated and cooked with pigs' feet is another great combination, as is beef stew with a strong paprika accent. A variation of braised beef that appeals to us is our Braciola in Brown Sauce in this chapter. These beef birds (or *paupiettes* as the French call them) are easy to make and freeze exceptionally well. We add orange zest and forgo the typical Italian touch of cooking them in a tomato sauce; ours simmer in a brown sauce. But we've included a Pot Roast in the Italian Style in this chapter, which does combine the beef with tomatoes and red wine. The Pot Roast in the Oriental Style in this chapter is a great combination of beef with curry, honey, soy sauce, and ginger.

Sirloin, filets mignons, and porterhouse steaks combine perfectly with butter alone: grilled, sautéed, broiled, or roasted. But additional combinations are many, including mushrooms, anchovy filets, onions, shallots, garlic, and Bordelaise and Bercy sauces. Steak fried in oil and garnished with a tomato fondue combines *à la niçoise;* steak flattened, seasoned with salt and paprika, dipped in flour, and sautéed quickly in lard is in the Viennese style. We believe one of the simplest, tastiest, and most elegant combinations is Shell Steaks with Green Peppercorn Sauce.

A beef tenderloin, also known as *filet mignon* or *chateaubriand,* is a long, slender, boneless, cut from the loin. The eye sections of porterhouse, T-bone, and sirloin steaks contain a small part of the tenderloin (the tenderest part of the animal). Actually, we think it's not so expensive when you consider that there isn't an ounce of waste and that a small serving is sufficient. Beef tenderloin is always served rare and therefore takes little time to cook. A 3- to 4-pound tenderloin is cooked in 30 minutes. It is delicious served cold and combines with other foods and flavors in most delicate ways. For example, it can be sliced and joined with a limitless variety of freshly cooked cold vegetables and set in aspic. An entire cold filet can be set in tarragon-flavored aspic and decorated with truffles, tarragon leaves, and egg pieces. Cold filet slices can be served with sliced tomatoes and/or artichoke hearts and/or asparagus spears, with a simple oil and vinegar dressing.

Served hot, beef tenderloin may be best known as *beef Wellington,* in which it is married to foie gras and truffles. On many menus, we see *filet strips stroganoff*, in which the meat is bathed in a roux and beef stock sauce accented with sour cream. Inserting slivers of truffles into a filet, barding it, tieing it with string, and moist-cooking it in a stock flavored with Madeira produces another good combination of flavors. Our suggestion for beef tenderloin is A Simple Roast Filet of Beef, to be found in this chapter. We also bring it together with shallots and sherry in Tenderloin of Beef: Slices, Spices, and Spirits. And for real fun on a rainy, dreary Monday evening, put together the Brandied Filet Mignon Burgers.

Tournedos are small slices of filet, weighing 3 to 4 ounces apiece. In restaurants, you often see them called *medallions of beef filet*. They are always cooked rapidly, usually in oil or butter, or both. They are probably most often presented as *tournedos Rossini*: sautéed in butter, arranged on croutons, topped with a slice of foie gras; topped again with several slices of truffles, and covered with a Madeira sauce. Tournedos are combined with many familiar sauces (Béarnaise, Bordelaise, and so on), but we think they take on a new tingle when they're served with a special horseradish cream sauce.

English cooks have made famous many varieties of meat pies. One of the simple classics is the beefsteak pie, made with chunks of lean rump steak combined with seasonings (including nutmeg, onion, and parsley) and potato cubes, all covered with pastry.

A great combination of foods is found in *grenadins de boeuf*: thin slices of beef, lightly sauced with Béarnaise, joined with a heart of artichoke, and dressed in a *sauce Choron* (a tomato-tinted Béarnaise). Simpler combinations are grilled steaks with a *marchand de vin* (shallots, red wine, veal stock, parsley, lemon juice, salt, pepper, and lots of butter) or just steaks with shallots, chopped raw or sautéed lightly. There are tournedos with a *beurre Bercy* (shallots, butter, and white wine), or *filet de boeuf Périgourdine* (simply beef filet with foie gras). We enjoyed an unusual combination at Chasen's Restaurant, Los Angeles, when we dined on *steak Diane*: a filet mignon, flattened like a veal scaloppine, cooked rare over very high high heat, fired with cognac, and dressed with chives and freshly ground pepper. Also unusual in taste is *Kinderroulade*: a thin slice of beef cut from the top round; wrapped around a slice of bacon, sour pickles, carrots, and onions: and baked in its own juices and lots of red wine. But possibly the combination to outdo all others is found in the Japanese *shabu shabu*: A pot of bubbling chicken stock is shared by the diners, who, with chopsticks, plunge beef chunks, mushrooms, bamboo shoots, prosciutto pieces, and so on into the chicken stock and from there into a series of sauces, including soy and lemon, with garnishes of sesame seeds and ground chili peppers.

BRANDIED FILET-MIGNON BURGERS

COGNAC AND BUTTER   SERVES 6 TO 8

> 2 pounds filet mignon, ground   ¼ cup cornstarch
> ½ pound prosciutto, sliced tissue   4 tablespoons butter
>   thin (see Note)   Juice of 1 lemon
>   Salt   ¼ cup cognac
>   Pepper, ground fresh

Remove some of the fat (but not all) from the filet. If you have a food processor that will grind meat, grind the filet at home just before you're ready to use it. If you don't, ask your butcher to grind the filet for you. Put the ground meat into a mixing bowl.

Refrigerate the prosciutto slices until you are ready to use them. (They're difficult to cut in any case, but they will be easier to handle if they are cold.) Dice them (as best you can) into ½-inch cubes, and add to the beef.

Sprinkle with some salt, but go lightly because prosciutto is salty. Sprinkle with freshly ground pepper to taste. Mix well with your hands, and form a thick pie of the ground beef on your worktable. With a knife, divide into 6 or 8 wedges, depending on how large you want the burgers to be or how many people there are to serve, and shape into burgers.

In a large skillet, heat the butter. Meanwhile, put the cornstarch on a large, flat plate. Put the palms of your hands into the cornstarch and pat some of the powder onto each burger on its way into the skillet. You can powder all the burgers at one time and set them aside, but don't let them sit for more than a few minutes or the meat will absorb the cornstarch. Because these are filet-mignon burgers, they require little cooking. Sear them over high heat, and transfer them to a warm platter.

Deglaze the skillet with the lemon juice and cognac, scraping with a rubber spatula. Pour sauce over burgers, and serve.

Note: If you do not have prosciutto, there are two substitutes: Prosciuttino, an American-made product found in some delicatessens, is actually quite good, especially if it is combined with other foods. Not the same as the real thing, but less expensive, and tasty. Virginia or Smithfield ham can also be substituted. Use ⅓ pound instead of ½. Dice either the prosciuttino or the ham just as you would the prosciutto.

BEEF CUBES WITH CURRY AND CONDIMENTS

CURRY AND GINGER   SERVES 6

3 pounds top round or chuck, cut into 2-inch cubes
2 tablespoons vegetable oil
1 tablespoon butter or margarine
½ cup onion, chopped coarse
1½ tablespoons curry powder
1½ teaspoons salt
¼ cup crystallized ginger, chopped fine

1½ tablespoons fresh mint (or 1 teaspoon dried)
3 tablespoons flour
2½ cups Rich Beef Stock or beef broth (see page 46)
Few whole cloves, tied in cheesecloth
Pepper, ground fresh
3 tablespoons fresh lime juice
½ cup light cream

In a 3-quart casserole, heat the oil and butter, and sauté the beef cubes until lightly browned (about 20 minutes). Remove the beef, and set aside.

Leave a small amount of oil in the casserole (if not enough is left, add a little more), and sauté the onion for a few minutes. Add the curry powder, salt, ginger, and mint, and mix a little. Then add the flour, and stir until well combined. Add the beef stock very slowly, and mix well. Return the beef to the casserole, and add the whole cloves. Pepper liberally, and let come to a boil. Reduce the heat to low, cover, and simmer for about 1½ hours, or until the beef is tender.

When the beef is done, discard the cloves in the cheesecloth. Stir in the lime juice and cream, and cook about 5 minutes.

Arrange the beef cubes on a large platter, and serve with fried rice and accompaniments such as fig preserves, sliced bananas, chopped onions, raisins, shredded coconut, chopped salted nuts, crushed red pepper, sliced tomatoes, and pickles.

TO PREPARE THE FRIED RICE:

> *2 tablespoons vegetable oil*
> *1 garlic clove, halved*
> *2 cups long-grain rice*
> *5 cups Rich Beef Stock (or 5 cups*
> *boiling water and 3 beef*
> *bouillon cubes) (see page 46)*
> *Pepper, ground fresh*

In a large skillet, brown the garlic halves and rice in the oil (8 to 10 minutes). Turn off heat, and let the rice sit for 5 minutes. Discard the garlic halves. In a medium-size saucepan, bring the water and bouillon cubes to a boil. Slowly add to the rice. Cover, and cook for 20 minutes. When done, add fresh-ground pepper to taste.

FLANK STEAK STUFFED WITH EGGPLANT

EGGPLANT AND ONIONS   SERVES 6

TO MAKE STUFFING:

> *3 tablespoons butter*
> *3 tablespoon olive oil*
> *¾-pound eggplant, peeled and*
> *cut into ½-inch cubes*
> *1 cup onion, chopped fine*
> *1 garlic clove, chopped fine*
> *½ cup celery, including leaves,*
> *sliced thin*

> *½ teaspoon dried oregano*
> *1 tablespoon fresh parsley,*
> *chopped fine (or 1 teaspoon*
> *dried)*
> *1 teaspoon salt*
> *Pepper, ground fresh*
> *1 cup bread crumbs*
> *2 eggs*

In a large skillet, heat the butter and oil, and sauté the eggplant cubes for 10 minutes. (The eggplant will absorb the oil and butter; in fact, the skillet will be quite dry by the time you add the next ingredients. However, do *not* add more oil or butter. If you keep stirring the ingredients, you'll have no problem sautéeing them for the required cooking time.) Add the onion, garlic, celery, oregano, parsley, salt, and pepper, and cook an additional 5 minutes. Remove the skillet from the heat, and transfer its contents to a large bowl. Add the bread crumbs, and mix in well. Beat eggs lightly, and add to this mixture also. Mix well, and set aside.

TO PREPARE THE FLANK STEAK:

2½- to 3-pounds flank steak
1 recipe eggplant stuffing
3 tablespoons butter
3 tablespoons olive oil
2 carrots, sliced fine
1 large onion, chopped fine
1 cup fresh tomatoes, cored, blanched, peeled, and chopped fine (or 1 cup canned Italian plum tomatoes; use as much pulp without liquid as you can)

1½ cups dry red wine
¼ teaspoon dried oregano
Salt
Pepper, ground fresh
Few sprigs fresh parsley

Ask your butcher to trim the excess fat from the flank steak and make a pocket. Lay the flank steak on a flat surface, and fill the pocket with the eggplant stuffing. Secure the pocket with a 6-inch steel skewer or toothpicks, tie it with string, or sew up the opening.

Heat the butter and oil in a large, covered casserole. Cook the flank steak until it is browned all over. Add the carrots, onions, and tomatoes, and cook for 10 minutes on low heat. Add the wine, oregano, salt, and pepper, and cover the casserole. Simmer for 1¼ to 1½ hours. When the stuffed steak is done, put it on a warm serving platter.

You may use the sauce as it is, with carrot slices and so on. Or you may strain or purée it and pour it over the steak. Add a touch of fresh parsley before serving it. We think it is interesting to cut this steak in wedges, just as you would slice a pie. The stuffing is puffed up and attractive; it is somewhat firm and will adhere to the meat if you cut and serve it carefully. You can, of course, simply slice the steak, but it seems unfair for two of the servings (the two end cuts) to get far less stuffing.

BEEF, STIR-FRIED, WITH PEPPERS AND ONIONS

GINGER AND SOY SAUCE   SERVES 4

1 *pound boneless beef, such as*   2 *tablespoons fresh ginger,*
   tenderloin or sirloin   *chopped fine*
3 *tablespoons soy sauce*   3 *cups onion slices*
2 *tablespoons water*   3 *cups green pepper slices,*
1 *tablespoon sherry or rice wine*   *approximately 2 inches long*
   (*optional*)   *and ¼ inch thick* (*see Note*)
2 *tablespoons cornstarch*   6 *tablespoons peanut oil* (*or*
½ *teaspoon sugar*   *vegetable oil*)

Keep the beef in the refrigerator until the moment you're ready to use it. It's difficult to slice raw meat at room temperature. (If meat is too soft to slice fine, we put it in the freezer compartment for 15 minutes or so.) Cut the beef against the grain in ¼-inch slices; lay the slices flat, and cut again into ¼-inch strips. Try to end up with julienne beef strips, about 2 inches long and ¼-inch thick. Set the strips aside.

In a medium- or large-size bowl, combine the soy sauce, water, sherry or rice wine (if you wish), cornstarch, sugar, and ginger. Mix well until thoroughly blended. Add the beef strips, and let them marinate while you slice the vegetables.

Use medium-size onions. Put the curved side of the onion on a flat surface (root end to the left, sprout to the right), and slice ¼ inch thick. Lay slices flat, cut in half, and separate the onion sections.

Without adding oil at this point, heat the wok until it is hot. Carefully add 2 tablespoons of oil, and rotate the wok to heat oil quickly. Add the pepper strips, and stir-fry them for 2 or 3 minutes. Transfer them to another container (we use another wok placed alongside the cooking one).

Add 2 more tablespoons of oil, and turn up heat so that wok and oil are very hot. Carefully add the onions, and stir-fry them for 2 or 3 minutes. Add them to the peppers.

Again, reheat the cooking wok, add the remaining 2 tablespoons of oil, ginger, and beef strips. With a chopstick or another utensil, separate beef strips as quickly as you can. As soon as they turn pale (this will normally take only 1 minute), add the peppers and onions, and mix in with the beef strips. Stir-fry a few times over very high heat, and serve right away.

Note: In New York City, Mott Street and Mulberry Street run into each other. Mott Street is Chinatown, and Mulberry is Little Italy. In other words, we think you should use the lighter green, longish Italian fryer-type pepper. We prefer its flavor to that of the thick, heavy, dark green bell pepper, and we're sure the Italian fryer stir-fries better.

Bourbon

Many years ago, when James Beard wrote that bourbon, as a cooking spirit, isn't used half enough, we not only believed him, we took his counsel to heart. In our cooking since that time, we have found that a good bourbon whiskey leaves one of the most exciting and haunting flavors. One of our long-time favorite dishes is Shell Steaks with Green Peppercorn Sauce, and we believe good Kentucky bourbon whiskey is a key ingredient. Bourbon also makes its mark in desserts, such as Strawberry Pie in the Carolina Style and Cocoa Roll à la Bourbon where it is divinely combined with chocolate. Both recipes are in Chapter Fourteen.

Bourbon is peculiar to the United States, for this is the only country that makes it, just as Scotch whiskey is made only in Scotland and Cognac is made only in France.

Bourbon, "discovered" in the late eighteenth century, is made of corn, with a little rye and barley malt, combined with a fine limestone water. It was named for Bourbon County (first in Virginia, today also in Kentucky), which was named for the French royal family. The labels on many bottles of bourbon carry the phrase *sour mash*; this simply means that some of the undistilled liquid from yesterday's fermented mash of grain goes into today's supply. This is a "blood transfusion," if you will, a way of assuring continuity in the brew's character and flavor.

One of the most famous bourbon combinations is the mint julep. Others include bourbon flambées with cuts of beef and bananas. Bourbon is poured over ham roasts and cooked with kidneys. And we can't resist adding a touch of it to black bean soup.

SHELL STEAKS WITH GREEN PEPPERCORN SAUCE

GREEN PEPPERCORNS AND BOURBON   SERVES 4

*4 shell steaks, at least 1 inch
  thick and about 1 pound each
  (or individual filets mignons)
1 teaspoon butter
Salt
¼ cup good Kentucky bourbon
  whiskey
2 tablespoons green peppercorns,
  drained and bruised (see
  Note)*

*½ cup heavy cream
2 tablespoons Dijon mustard or
  equivalent
1 tablespoon fresh parsley,
  chopped fine*

Remove steaks from the refrigerator, remove excess fat, and let them come to room temperature.

In a large skillet, heat the butter, add the steaks, and cook them to your taste. (We think you should do this over high heat so that each side of the steak is well browned.) Remove steaks to a warm plate, and keep them warm without cooking further. Salt to taste.

Empty the skillet of excess drippings (but do *not* wash it in any way). Return the skillet to moderate heat, pour in the bourbon, and deglaze skillet with the aid of a rubber spatula. Add the bruised green peppercorns, and stir into bourbon sauce with spatula. Add the cream all at once, and blend with other ingredients; add the mustard, and blend some more. (The idea here is to add these ingredients quickly with your left hand and to stir continually with the spatula with your right hand, or vice versa.) Do *not* burn sauce.

We think it is best to serve these steaks on individual plates. Place a steak in the center of each plate, top it with a dash of chopped parsley, and add several tablespoonsful of sauce alongside the steak. Please do *not* pour the sauce over the steak. Serve *immediatamente*.

Note: Green peppercorns are packed in liquid in small bottles; you can't get a tablespoon or teaspoon in the mouths of these bottles. Remove peppercorns as best you can, drain them, and "bruise" them on a chopping board, using the flat side of a chopping utensil. Or you can put 2 tablespoons peppercorns in a handkerchief and pound them lightly with a knife handle, meat pounder, or whatever. Of course, if you have a mortar and pestle, bruise them with that.

TOURNEDOS WITH HORSERADISH CREAM SAUCE

HORSERADISH AND CREAM   SERVES 6

12 *tournedos, 3 or 4 ounces each*
   Salt
   Pepper, ground fresh
3 *tablespoons butter*
1 *cup hollandaise sauce*
1 *cup whipped cream*

1 *tablespoon horseradish, grated fresh (or 1½ tablespoons bottled horseradish) (see Note)*
Watercress

Ask your butcher not to make the tournedos larger than 4 ounces each. There are two reasons for this: Each person is served two tournedos, and the smaller tournedos look better on the plate. Salt and pepper the meat to your taste.

Heat the butter in a large skillet over high heat; sear and brown the meat quickly. This meat should stay tender; it will be ready (rare) when it has cooked 3 minutes on each side over high heat. Transfer the tournedos to a warm platter.

To make the sauce, combine the hollandaise, whipped cream, and horseradish.

Pour a small amount of sauce on part of each tournedo and the rest of it on the platter between the pieces of meat. We usually serve this on individual plates: two tournedos per person, with sauce on the side and decorated in a carefree manner with a piece of watercress.

Note: If you grow horseradish, it's easy to grate it in a food processor. You can do it by hand with an ordinary grater, but it's considerably more difficult. Horseradish was a popular item in our home as we grew up. We still remember well how all the family took turns at grating horseradish because no one could take the "tears" for long.

BEEF BALLS IN SPIRITED CREAM SAUCE

LEEKS AND CREAM   SERVES 6

TO PREPARE THE BEEF BALLS:

1½ pounds ground sirloin	½ teaspoon thyme
½ cup milk	Salt
3 slices fresh white bread, crusts removed	Pepper, ground fresh
	1 egg, lightly beaten

Break up the meat with your hands, and put it in a large bowl. Put the bread in a soup bowl, and pour the milk over it. Soak the bread as thoroughly as you can. *Without* squeezing the bread, break it into small pieces, and add it to the meat. Add the thyme, salt to taste, and a liberal sprinkle of freshly ground pepper (don't be too timid with this). Add the egg, and blend all this with your hands. When well blended, put the meat on a flat work surface, and shape it into a thick pie. With a knife, cut into 6 wedges; make 4 beef balls from each wedge. You should finish up with 24 small- to medium-size beef balls.

TO COOK THE BEEF BALLS AND PREPARE THE SAUCE:

3 thin slices bacon	1 cup Rich Beef Stock or broth
4 tablespoons butter	(see page 46)
2 cups leeks, sliced thin, using some of the pale green part	1 cup heavy cream
	1 cup sour cream
½ cup Cognac	½ cup fresh parsley, chopped fine

In a large skillet, cook the bacon slices until crisp. Remove them to a paper towel to drain, and set aside.

Add 1 tablespoon of butter to the bacon grease, and cook the beef balls. They will cook better if there is at least ½ inch of space between them. Turn them carefully so that they brown on all sides. (A small pair of wooden tongs is helpful for this.) Add more butter as necessary until beef balls are thoroughly browned. Transfer the beef balls to a covered casserole.

Add the leek slices to the skillet, and sauté them for 5 minutes. Transfer the leeks to the casserole.

Pour the Cognac into the skillet, deglaze as rapidly as possible with the help of a spatula, and pour the Cognac into the casserole. Add the stock or broth and heavy cream to the casserole. Stir gently to combine, cover, and simmer over low heat for about 20 minutes. A few minutes before serving, remove cover, and add sour cream. Stir gently, bring just to a boil, and serve.

This is a fine combination with the thinnest variety of egg noodles. Cook the noodles while the beef balls are simmering in the spirited cream sauce. Place the noodles on a large, decorative oval platter, and put the beef balls on top of the noodles. Spoon the sauce over the beef balls, but let some of the noodles show through. Sprinkle the chopped parsley over all.

BOEUF EN BROCHETTE EXTRAORDINAIRE

LEMON AND THYME　　　　　　　　　　　　　　　　SERVES 4 TO 6

1½ pounds filet of beef, cut in　*⅛ teaspoon dried hot pepper*
　1½-inch cubes　　　　　　　　*flakes*
3 tablespoons olive oil　　　　*Juice of 2 lemons*
8 tablespoons butter, melted　*Salt*
½ teaspoon dried thyme　　　*Little pepper, ground fresh*
1 tablespoon Dijon mustard

This beef filet en brochette is delicious when cooked over a charcoal grill, but it is good cooked under the broiler, too.

Divide the beef cubes between two long skewers. You should have about 16 cubes, so 8 on each skewer will work well. Because you're not filling space with mushrooms, green peppers, or onions in this particular brochette, you'll have room on the skewers for all the meat.

Combine the oil, 4 tablespoons melted butter, thyme, mustard, and hot pepper flakes, and mix well. Brush this combination on all sides of the beef cubes. Salt to taste, and add a dash of fresh-ground pepper. (Hot pepper flakes are used, but we think fresh-ground black pepper has a flavor all its own and is essential to this dish.)

This meat can be cooked in about 3 minutes per side. Brush more of the seasoned oil and butter mixture on the cubes while they are cooking. Combine the remaining 4 tablespoons of melted butter with the lemon juice. Heat this quickly, and pour over skewered meat just a second before serving.

We like to serve this brochette in two ways:

Stir-fry 1 pound snow peas in a wok, transfer them to a large decorative platter or silver tray. Place the two skewers on top of the snow peas, and serve. Pass the butter and lemon juice so that each person can pour some sauce over the beef cubes on his plate.

On a large decorative platter or silver tray, arrange 12 to 20 fresh arugola leaves in a pattern (like leaves on a branch, for instance, and place the two skewers on top of them. Pour the butter and lemon sauce over the skewered cubes; the sauce complements the greenery. Watercress can be substituted; so can tender, lovely hearts of escarole, endive, or romaine.

BRACIOLA IN BROWN SAUCE
(Beef Birds in Brown Sauce)

ORANGE ZEST AND MARSALA   SERVES 6

6 thin beef slices, each measuring about 6 by 7 inches and slightly less than ¼ inch thick
2 slices fresh orange zest
3 tablespoons butter
¾ cup onion or scallions, chopped fine
¼ cup celery, including tender green leaves, chopped fine
½ teaspoon dried oregano

Pepper, ground fresh
¼ cup fresh bread crumbs
4 tablespoons Marsala, plus ⅓ cup
¼ cup pine nuts (pignòli)
Salt
6 thin slices prosciutto
2 tablespoons olive oil
4 cups Brown Sauce (see page 93)

If the slices of beef are not thin enough, place them on a flat surface, and pound them lightly with a flat mallet or the bottom of a clean skillet.

Cut the orange zest into very thin strips (julienne), and cut the strips into very thin dice.

Heat 1 tablespoon butter, and add the onion, celery, oregano, and pepper to taste; cook, stirring, until the onions become pale yellow.

Place the bread crumbs in a mixing bowl, and add the onion mixture and orange zest. Add 2 tablespoons of Marsala, pine nuts, and salt to taste; blend well.

Spoon equal amounts of this mixture onto the beef slices, pressing it down with your fingers to help it adhere. Place a slice of prosciutto on top of each. Roll the meat, beginning with the narrower end, jelly-roll fashion, and skewer each roll or tie with string.

Melt 2 tablespoons each of butter and olive oil in a skillet, and brown the beef on all sides (10 to 15 minutes). Remove the *braciola* and pour off the fat. Add 2 tablespoons Marsala, and stir to dissolve the brown particles that cling to the bottom of the skillet.

Put the brown sauce in a casserole; add ⅓ cup Marsala and the *braciola*. Cover tightly, and simmer 1 hour or longer, until the beef is tender. Serve piping hot with rice.

BEEF ROLL IMBOTTITO DI LEGUMI
(Beef Roll with Vegetable Stuffing)

OREGANO AND PARMESAN CHEESE   SERVES 6 TO 8

TO PREPARE THE STUFFING:

2 tablespoons olive oil
2 tablespoons butter
1½ cups onion, chopped
1½ large carrots, in thin curls 1
   inch long and less than
   inch thick (use a potato or
   vegetable peeler)
¾ cup celery, including leaves,
   sliced very thin
2 garlic cloves, chopped fine

4 slices white bread, crusts
   removed, soaked in milk
¼ cup fresh parsley, chopped
   fine (or 1 teaspoon dried)
½ cup grated Parmesan cheese
1 teaspoon dried oregano
1 egg, lightly beaten
   Salt
   Pepper, ground fresh

In a skillet, heat the oil and butter. Add the onions, carrots, and celery, and cook for 6 to 8 minutes, until the onions begin to turn yellow. Add the garlic, and cook 1 minute. Transfer the mixture to a large bowl.

Squeeze the bread to remove some of the milk, but keep it fairly moist; break into small pieces, and add to the vegetable mixture. Mix in the parsley, cheese, oregano, and egg. Add about 1 teaspoon salt, and sprinkle liberally with freshly ground pepper. Mix well, and set aside.

TO PREPARE AND COOK THE BEEF ROLL:

1½ to 2 pounds round steak, cut in one large piece approximately ½ inch thick (see Note)
Salt
Pepper, ground fresh
1 tablespoon olive oil
1 tablespoon butter

⅓ cup brandy or Cognac
½ cup dry red wine
1 cup Rich Beef Stock (see page 46)
¼ cup tomato paste (or ½ cup tomato purée)
1 teaspoon dried oregano

Spread out the steak on a flat surface. Pound it with a mallet if necessary, to achieve desired thinness. Salt and pepper liberally, and spread stuffing as evenly as you can.

Beginning with the smaller or narrower end, roll the steak, jelly-roll fashion: secure it with string, toothpicks, or small skewers.

In a large, covered saucepan (a casserole or Dutch oven will do), heat the oil and butter, and brown the beef roll on all sides. Remove the pan from the heat, and quickly add the brandy or Cognac. Ignite it, and let it burn off. Then return the pan to the heat. Add the wine, stock, tomato paste or purée, and oregano. Allow the liquid to come to a boil, and simmer, uncovered, for 5 minutes. Cover the pan, and cook for 50 to 60 minutes, or until the *rollatini di manzo* is done. During the cooking, baste the beef roll every 10 or 15 minutes.

To serve, place the beef roll on a large serving platter; remove the string, toothpicks, or skewers; and slice carefully. We think it's more elegant (because it's tidier) to serve this beef roll by itself, rather than over noodles, pasta, or rice. It can be accompanied by potatoes: scalloped, *à la Chantilly,* parslied, rissolé.

Note: Ask your butcher to flatten it to about ¼-inch thickness. (If he won't do this for you, don't fret. You can do it yourself at home.)

A SIMPLE ROAST FILET OF BEEF

SHALLOTS AND BUTTER
SERVES 6 TO 8

TO PREPARE THE FILET:

> *3- to 4-pound whole filet of beef*
> *6 tablespoons butter*
> *⅓ cup shallots, chopped fine*
> *Salt*
> *Pepper, ground fresh*

Ask your butcher to trim the filet and ready it for roasting. (We like to have it tied so that it won't get out of shape.)

Allow the butter to soften, and cover the entire filet with it. Or melt the butter quickly in a large skillet, and roll the filet in it so that the butter gets all over the beef. Salt and pepper to taste (we add an extra dash of pepper).

Roast for 5 minutes in a very hot oven (at least 500 degrees). Remove from the oven, and reduce temperature to 400 degrees. Sprinkle the shallots over the filet, return the meat to the oven, and roast for 25 to 30 minutes. This should produce a roast that is a little more cooked than rare, a bright pink. (Roast longer if you want it done more.) Let it sit for a few minutes before serving.

TO PREPARE THE SAUCE:

> *4 tablespoons butter*
> *1 tablespoon Dijon mustard*
> *⅓ cup Madeira*
> *⅓ cup Cognac or brandy*
> *1 cup fresh tomatoes, cored, blanched, peeled, and chopped fine*

> *1 cup fresh mushrooms, sliced thin*
> *⅓ cup shallots, chopped fine*
> *2 cups Rich Veal Stock (see page 48)*
> *Salt*
> *Pepper, ground fresh*

While the beef is in the oven, prepare this simple and delicious sauce to be served with it. Combine all ingredients in a saucepan, and bring them to a boil. Just barely simmer for 20 minutes. Put the sauce through a food mill, and serve it separately.

We serve the filet in one piece, without the strings, of course. Garnish with a touch of green: a parsley sprig, a sprinkle of dried parsley, several watercress leaves, or whatever is on hand. We slice this at the table because it's such a mouth-watering delight to see the roast opened and the pink slices of very tender beef pile up.

TENDERLOIN OF BEEF: SLICES, SPICES, AND SPIRITS

SHALLOTS AND SHERRY   SERVES 6

5 *tablespoons butter*	3 *tablespoons Cognac or brandy*
12 *slices beef tenderloin, 2 to 3 ounces each*	6 *tablespoons dry sherry*
1 *cup mushrooms, sliced*	½ *teaspoon green peppercorns, bruised (see page 232)*
2 *tablespoons shallots, onions, or scallions, chopped very fine*	*Juice of ½ lemon*
2 *tablespoons all-purpose flour*	½ *cup heavy cream*
1 *cup Rich Beef or Veal Stock (see pages 46, 48)*	*Salt*
	Paprika (optional)

In a large skillet, heat 3 tablespoons butter, and sauté the tenderloin slices quickly, not longer than 1 minute on each side. (This is important because the slices will be returned to the skillet to cook with the sauce.) Remove, and keep the meat warm.

Add the mushrooms to the skillet, and cook them for several minutes; they should be on the crisp side. Transfer to a small bowl, and set aside.

In the same skillet, add the shallots or onions or scallions (we remember using leeks once, sliced extremely thin, they were good, too), and sauté them for 2 minutes, or until they are softened. Remove skillet from heat, and set aside.

In a small saucepan, melt remaining 2 tablespoons butter; and when it is bubbling, add the flour, and blend well with a small wire whisk. Slowly add the stock, and keep stirring. Cook for several minutes until you have a smooth, thick sauce. Add this to the skillet with the shallots, and reheat.

Add the Cognac or brandy, sherry, green peppercorns, lemon juice, heavy cream, and salt. Blend well, and simmer for 3 minutes.

Carefully place the tenderloin slices and mushrooms into the skillet, and spoon the sauce overall. Bring to a boil over high heat, immediately remove from heat, and serve.

Arrange slices (over rice would be nice) on a large serving platter. The slices should overlap, accordion-style. Pour the sauce over all, and sprinkle liberally with paprika.

POT ROAST IN THE ITALIAN STYLE

TOMATOES AND RED WINE SERVES 6

3-pound eye round of beef
Salt
Pepper, ground fresh
2 tablespoons all-purpose flour
1 tablespoon olive oil
1 tablespoon butter
2 garlic cloves, chopped fine
1 onion, chopped fine
2 cups dry red wine, good quality
3 cups ripe tomatoes, cored, blanched, peeled, and chopped fine (or use canned Italian plum tomatoes)

1 cup tomato sauce or purée (homemade or canned, but purée, not paste)
½ teaspoon dried sage
⅛ teaspoon dried oregano
⅛ teaspoon dried thyme
2 bay leaves
2 tablespoons fresh Italian parsley, chopped very fine (or 1 teaspoon dried)

Ask your butcher to remove excess fat from the eye round and to tie it for you so that it won't lose its shape in cooking. Mix the salt, pepper, and flour together, and pat this mixture all over the eye round liberally.

In a large, heavy casserole, heat the oil and butter, and brown the meat well on all sides. The flour will burn somewhat, but we think this process helps seal in the meat juices. Add the garlic and onion, and cook for about 2 minutes, stirring. Then add the wine, and allow to cook, uncovered, for 15 minutes.

Add the tomatoes, tomato sauce or purée, sage, oregano, thyme, and bay leaves. Cover the casserole, and simmer for 2½ hours. After 2 hours, test meat for doneness. The sauce should be somewhat thickened; if you want it thicker, uncover casserole during last 30 minutes of cooking. We do not strain the tomato-wine sauce, but depending on amount of fat in casserole, we try to defat. You can skim off the fat with a spoon, or if you cook the pot roast ahead of time and cool it; the fat will rise to the top and solidify (just as it does when you make stock).

To serve, remove meat from casserole, and set on a plate. Remove strings, put pot roast on an attractive platter, pour sauce over it, and sprinkle the roast with chopped fresh Italian parsley.

A great accompaniment for this is pasta, any kind, cooked *al dente*, with a little butter (not much), and some grated Parmesan cheese. There'll be enough tomato-wine sauce on each person's plate to combine with the pasta. You won't be bored selecting the pasta. There's *cavatelli, conchigliette, maruzze, maruzzelle, ditali, ditalini, farfalle, farfalloni* (we hope you sometimes choose these "big butterflies"), *fettucine, fettuccelle* (*tagliolini*), *fusilli, mafalde, rigatoni, spaghetti, vermicelli,* and very many more *maccheroni*. Or how about making some of your own *pasta fresca all'uovo?*

MOZZARELLA MEAT LOAF IN THE FAMILY STYLE

MOZZARELLA AND BREAD   SERVES 8

2 pounds ground chuck
2 links Italian sausage, removed
  from casings and crumbled
2 eggs, lightly beaten
2 small onions, chopped fine
2 tablespoons parsley, chopped
  fine (or 1 teaspoon dried)
1 garlic clove, chopped fine
½ cup grated Parmesan, Romano,
  or Locatelli cheese
2 cups mozzarella, ¼-inch cubes

5 pieces Italian bread, soaked in
  ¾ cup milk for 5 minutes and
  squeezed dry
3 tablespoons canned tomatoes
  (or 1 fresh tomato, blanched,
  cored, peeled, seeded, and
  chopped)
2 teaspoons salt
  Pepper, ground fresh
½ cup fresh bread crumbs

In a large bowl, combine the ground chuck with the sausage; add the eggs, onions, parsley, garlic, Parmesan cheese, mozzarella, bread, and tomatoes. Add the salt and some pepper to taste.

On a flat surface, roll the meat mixture in the fresh bread crumbs, and put it into an oiled 11-by-3 baking pan. Bake in a preheated 350-degree oven for 1½ hours. Remove the pan from the oven, and transfer the meat loaf to a serving platter.

In addition to the great combinations in the meat loaf, the loaf itself produces another great combination if it is accompanied by Peppers and Tomatoes al Gennaro (see page 327). It's great with any salad dressed with oil and vinegar, or try it with Fresh Minted Cucumbers (see page 318). You will have the ideal combination, especially if you are a meat-and-potatoes person, if you serve it with Potatoes and Garlic, Cream, and Cheese (see page 330).

POT ROAST IN THE ORIENTAL STYLE

GINGER AND SOY SAUCE   SERVES 6 TO 8

2 tablespoons all-purpose flour
1 tablespoon curry powder
1 teaspoon salt
½ teaspoon pepper, ground fresh
2 tablespoons peanut oil
    4-pound round tip roast
⅓ cup soy sauce
⅓ cup honey
⅓ cup dry sherry

¼ cup water
2 tablespoons fresh ginger,
    chopped very fine
2 tablespoons cornstarch
1 cup cooked wild rice (optional)
1¼ cups toasted almond slivers
    (optional)

Combine the flour, curry powder, salt, and pepper, and mix well. Put mixture on a large piece of wax paper, and roll the beef round in it to coat it completely. (Stand the roast on its ends to coat them.)

In a heavy saucepan or Dutch oven, heat the oil, and sear the pot roast until it is browned all over. Remove the meat, and pour off the oil and fat.

Using the same saucepan, add the soy sauce, honey, sherry, water, and ginger, and blend. Place the meat back in the saucepan, cover, and cook over low heat for 3 hours or longer, until the pot roast is done. Turn the meat several times while it is cooking so that all sides cook in the sauce and spices.

Remove the meat when it is done. Pour the cooking liquid into a 2- or 4-cup measure; after a minute or two, the fat will rise to the top so that you can remove it with a spoon. To prepare 2 cups of sauce, add enough water to the cooking liquid to measure 1½ cups. Pour this back into the pan. Combine the cornstarch with ½ cup cool water, blend, and add to other liquid, stirring constantly. Reheat, bring to a boil, and simmer for several minutes until sauce thickens. Strain the sauce, adjust seasoning if necessary, and if you wish, add 1 cup cooked wild rice and ¼ cup toasted almond slivers.

To serve, spoon 3 tablespoons of sauce over the meat, and serve the rest separately.

CALF'S BRAINS IN MADEIRA

MADEIRA AND LIGHT CREAM   SERVES 3 TO 4

TO PREPARE THE BRAINS:

> *2 pairs calf's brains*
> *9 tablespoons salt*
> *20 tablespoons white vinegar*
> *5 cups water*

Put enough water in a bowl to cover the brains, and add 3 tablespoons salt and 6 tablespoons vinegar. Soak the brains for 2 or 3 hours; change the water 2 additional times, and add 3 tablespoons salt and 6 tablespoons vinegar with each soaking. Very carefully remove the skin and membrane.

In a medium-size saucepan, bring to a boil 5 cups water and the 2 remaining tablespoons vinegar. Add the brains, cover, and simmer for 20 minutes. Drain carefully, and rinse in *cold* water. Repeat this rinsing a few times. Wipe the brains dry, and cut into good-size cubes (about 1½ inches).

TO MARINATE THE BRAINS:

> *1 egg, lightly beaten*   *1 tablespoon fresh parsley,*
> *2 tablespoons light cream*   *chopped fine*
> *¼ cup Madeira*   *1 garlic clove, chopped fine*
> *1 teaspoon salt*   *Pepper, ground fresh*
> *⅓ teaspoon paprika*

Combine these ingredients, add the brains, and marinate for 1½ hours.

TO COOK THE BRAINS:

> *4 to 5 tablespoons butter*
> *½ cup fresh bread crumbs*
> *1 lemon, cut in wedges, seeds removed*

Heat the butter in a large skillet. Dip each piece of brain in the bread crumbs, and sauté on each side for 2 or 3 minutes, or until brown. Put the pieces of brain on paper to drain.

Serve the cooked brains with lemon wedges.

OXTAIL RAGOUT

ROSEMARY AND MADEIRA   SERVES 6

TO BROWN THE OXTAILS:

6 pounds oxtails, jointed
2 tablespoons butter
Salt
Pepper, ground fresh

Wipe the oxtails clean with a tea towel, and butter each side. Sprinkle with salt and pepper to taste, place the oxtails in a shallow baking tray, and brown well on each side under the broiler. (There should be about 6 inches between the meat and the broiling unit.) Be careful not to char the meat.

TO COOK THE OXTAILS:

⅓ cup all-purpose flour	*2 bay leaves*
4 tablespoons butter	*½ teaspoon dried rosemary*
3 medium-size onions, sliced fine	*½ teaspoon dried thyme*
3 large garlic cloves, chopped fine	*2 cups beef stock or broth*
6 carrots, in ¼-inch slices	*½ cup Madeira*

When the oxtails are cool enough to handle, sprinkle some flour over both sides, or dip them in flour. Shake off the excess, and set them aside.

In a large, covered saucepan, melt the butter, add onions and garlic, and sauté until light brown. Put the oxtails in the saucepan, and add the carrots, bay leaves, rosemary, thyme, and beef stock. Cover, and bring to a boil. Remove the cover, and skim off any foam. Cover again, and simmer slowly for about 2½ hours, or until the oxtails are tender. Remove the cover, add the Madeira, and allow the alcohol to cook away (about 10 minutes). Remove the saucepan from the heat. Do *not* cover until the ragout is cool; then cover and refrigerate. The fat will solidify; it can then be removed.

Reheat slowly. If you would like a thicker sauce, add some beurre manié little by little until you achieve the consistency you want.

((7))

Double Pork Chops, Filled and Flambéed, and More Pork

THE pigsty is now a quasi-scientific laboratory. Improvements in pig breeding, hygiene, shipping, and spoilage control have been responsible for making pork available all year long. Sold fresh, pickled, cured, smoked, or rendered, it's a popular food all over the world; it is probably the meat most often cooked in China. Pork can be found in one form or another in most American homes at any given moment, although we in the United States consume only half as much pork as beef.

The U.S. Department of Agriculture grades pork as U.S. No. 1, U.S. No. 2, and U.S. No. 3. Hogs are usually prepared for market when 5 or 6 months old. The flesh of hog, pig, or swine is white or the palest of pinks. (This is by courtesy of the butcher, who drains the blood for black puddings.) At its best, pork is young, its meat firm and fine grained, and its fat white. Legs and loins of pork are the two key cuts of the hog. Pork belly, which produces bacon and salt pork, is universally known, as are pigs' feet. And pork shoulders, marketed as picnic shoulders, Boston butts, and hocks, are popular, too. You can buy and cook almost every part of a pig. Chitterlings (intestines) and tails are only two examples of the surprising parts that go into the cuisines of many countries.

A whole loin of pork divides into a full loin half and a full rib half. From the center of the whole loin come the rib and loin center cuts. The last word in pork roast is the *center-cut loin*; it is the tenderloin of the hog and weighs 3 to 4 pounds. The *center-cut rib* is excellent, too; but because it doesn't contain the tenderloin, the meat doesn't go as far. A crown roast of pork is made from the center rib cuts.

Two good cuts for roasting are the *full loin half* and the *full rib half*. Either of these cuts (and we suggest that you ask your butcher to bone it) can be used in preparing our roast loin recipes. A delicious cold combination is loin of pork served with potato salad and gherkins or other pickles. In our family, pork loin was often combined (hot this time) with potatoes and onions and a sprinkle of tomatoes, the vegetables being added at the appropriate moment during the cooking. And when the roast was almost done, fresh peas were added to the roasting pan, and sometimes mushrooms or boiled Brussels sprouts. We've seen six, eight, or ten apples cooking along with the roast. A special combination for us was (and still is) roast pork with kidney beans. We also enjoy serving four to six people a rack of pork in the Danish style (a loin stuffed with apples and prunes, braised in white wine, and served with preserved currants).

Center-cut loin and *rib chops* are expensive, but they're excellent in quality, especially the loin chops because they contain part of the tenderloin. These chops can be cut, cooked, and served single or double. We present an easy, tasty way to prepare double chops (Double Pork Chops Filled and Flambéed). Pork chops can be cooked with any of a number of vegetables; they are especially good with potatoes, onions, sauerkraut, or Brussels sprouts. They can be prepared in the Milan style by salting and peppering them, coating them with egg and bread crumbs, and cooking them in clarified butter. An easy method of preparation is to marinate the chops in oil, vinegar, salt, pepper, garlic, thyme, and bay leaf for 1 hour, brown them on both sides, and finish off cooking them in the oven (add vegetables, too).

Spareribs come from the breast of pork; one slab can contain up to thirteen ribs. We avoid large slabs of ribs and try to get slabs weighing less than 3 pounds. With these, there is less waste because of bone, and we find the meat is tenderer. Spareribs are often at their best when they have been marinated in any one of a variety of sauces made with soy sauce, honey, fruit juices, and so on and then grilled. We've always used spareribs (second choice only to homemade pork sausage) as a flavoring agent and as a cooked meat with vegetables, in casseroles, and in pasta sauces. Spareribs with Steamed Savoy Cabbage is one of our favorite combinations.

We find it hard to believe that the *sausages* of ancient times were plain and unspiced, but it's true that not until the Middle Ages were herb, spice, and meat combinations developed that were the forerunners of the modern sausage. The Romans, who were fond of sausage, called it *salsus*, which is "salted" in Latin; that was about all they added to the sausage meat. The sausages that have become famous took their names from the cities of their origin: frankfurter from Frankfurt, bologna from Bologna, and wienerwurst from Vienna. Our recipe for Angela's Homemade Pork Sausage combines coarsely chopped fresh lean pork meat with fennel, salt, pepper, and paprika (and hot pepper if one wants it). In our family, we have always hand-minced the sausage because we believe that using a machine would break down the cells of the meat and thus destroy some of the flavor. We were quite pleased recently to read that Roger Lamazère, who runs one of the best restaurants in Paris, was heard to say the same thing. We are never without sausage because it's one of the best foods to keep in the refrigerator or freezer; with it, you can always pull together a meal on short notice. Slice it, fry it, and add it to an omelet (Frittata con Salsiccia, see page 140) or just serve it sliced and pan-fried as an appetizer, something to nibble on. We've combined it with chicken and beef meatballs in Casserole Ratatouille. We've brought it together with broccoli (Sausage and Broccoli) and with green beans in a tomato sauce (Fagiolini Verdi con Salsicce al Gennaro). And with eggs, lots of them, we've made a Torta di Salsiccia. Roman, yes! Unspiced, no!

SPARERIBS WITH STEAMED SAVOY CABBAGE

RED PEPPER FLAKES AND GARLIC   SERVES 6

1 *medium-size fresh savoy cabbage*	2 *racks spareribs, cut into 6 sections* (*see Note*)
2 *tablespoons salt*	½ *teaspoon dried red pepper flakes*
¼ *cup olive oil*	*Salt*
2 *cloves garlic*	*Pepper, ground fresh*

When buying the savoy cabbage, test for freshness. Be sure it feels firm and crisp. (If it's soggy and droopy, avoid it.) Remove the outer green leaves, and core the cabbage. Cut the head into 6 wedges. (They will seem large to you, but they will shrink during cooking.) Put the wedges in cool water with 2 tablespoons salt, and allow to stand for 30 minutes to 1 hour.

In a large covered saucepan, heat the olive oil. Cut 1 garlic clove in half, and brown it lightly in the oil. With a wooden spoon, push down on the garlic pieces to extract some juice. Discard the garlic. Brown the sparerib sections well, 1 or 2 pieces at a time. (They will cook with the cabbage for at least an additional 30 minutes, but they should be fairly well cooked before the cabbage is added.)

Move the bowl or pan with the cabbage wedges close to the saucepan containing the spareribs. Lower the heat, and with your hands, transfer the wedges, 2 or 3 pieces at a time and dripping wet, to the sparerib pan. Do this carefully, for the water added to the hot oil and sparerib grease will spatter furiously. (It's important *not* to drain the cabbage completely when transferring to pan because the water cuts the strong oil and sparerib grease.)

Cover the saucepan, and cook over high heat for about 10 minutes. Remove the cover, and stir the ingredients. This will be easier to do as the cabbage cooks and softens. Keep the pan covered, and simmer and steam until the cabbage is tender (20 to 25 minutes). During the cooking, mince the second garlic clove, and add it to the saucepan, along with the red pepper flakes. Taste for seasoning and add salt and fresh ground pepper as needed.

This must be served hot and is perfectly wonderful with a crusty bread.

Note: There should be enough for 4 ribs per serving. Try to avoid the prepackaged ribs, for you want to get small, meaty ribs.

CASSEROLE RATATOUILLE

GREEN PEPPERS AND EGGPLANT   SERVES 6 TO 8

8 tablespoons olive oil
2 large onions, sliced fine
2 large cloves garlic, chopped fine
2 green peppers, cored, seeded,
  and cut into thin strips
4 zucchini, unpeeled, ends
  removed, and sliced thin
1 large eggplant, unpeeled, ends
  removed, cut in half lengthwise,
  sliced thin
6 pieces chicken (breasts, thighs,
  or whatever)

6 Italian sweet or hot sausages
  (your preference)
12 meatballs
6 fresh tomatoes, cored, blanched,
  peeled, and chopped coarse (or
  2-pound can Italian plum
  tomatoes, well drained)
1 tablespoon oregano
1 teaspoon sugar
Salt
Pepper, ground fresh

TO PREPARE THE MEATBALLS:

½ pound ground chuck
2 slices of French or Italian bread,
  moistened with ½ cup milk
  and squeezed dry
1 tablespoon parsley, chopped
  fine

2 eggs, lightly beaten
¼ cup grated Parmesan cheese
Salt
Pepper, ground fresh
3 tablespoons vegetable oil

Put all the ingredients in a bowl, and mix them with your hands. Shape the mixture into 12 balls, and in the skillet brown them on all sides in the vegetable oil. Do *not* overcook; they will cook further in the casserole.

You can brown these meatballs ahead of time and just add them to the casserole when you are assembling and layering the other ingredients, or you can brown the beef balls with the chicken and sausage.

TO PREPARE THE CASSEROLE:

Heat 4 tablespoons olive oil in a large skillet, and add the onions, garlic, and peppers. Cook them for 8 to 10 minutes, or until they are softened. Remove from the skillet, and set aside. Sauté the slices of zucchini and eggplant, and add 1 tablespoon olive oil to the skillet, as needed, while you sauté. Drain the slices on paper towels and set them aside.

Sauté the chicken pieces and sausage (and meatballs, if you have not browned them ahead of time), adding oil as necessary. Assemble in a large casserole by adding layers of zucchini-eggplant-onion mixture, tomatoes, chicken, sausage, meatballs, salt and pepper to taste, sugar and oregano. Cover the casserole (aluminum foil will do), and bake in a preheated 375-degree oven for 45 to 60 minutes.

TORTA DI SALSICCIA
(Sausage and Egg Pie)

SAUSAGE AND EGGS   SERVES 6 TO 10

TO PREPARE THE DOUGH:
> 1¾ *cups all-purpose flour*
> 6 *tablespoons butter*
> *Pinch of salt*
> 5 *tablespoons cold water*

In a medium-size bowl, add the flour, butter, lard, and salt. Mix very gently with your fingers. Add the water a little at a time, and keep mixing until it forms a ball. Dust with flour, wrap the dough in wax paper, and chill for 1 hour.

TO PREPARE THE FILLING:

2 *pounds Italian sausage*	3 *tablespoons grated Parmesan,*
12 *eggs*	*Romano, or Locatelli cheese*
2 *tablespoons parsley, chopped*	*Salt*
fine	*Pepper, ground fresh*

Remove the casing from the sausage, and in a large skillet, brown the meat. (As a rule, there is enough fat in the sausage, so you don't need to add any to the skillet.) Remove from heat.

Beat the eggs in a bowl; add the parsley, cheese, and salt and pepper to taste. Add the sausage, and mix well. Set aside.

Roll out half the dough to fit the bottom of an 8-by-8-by-2-inch pan. Pour the sausage and egg mixture into this pie shell, and then roll out the remaining dough for the top crust.

Bake in a preheated 350-degree oven for 1 hour, or until the top crust is golden. Remove from oven, and let cool before slicing.

This dish can be served for lunch with a tossed salad, or the pie can be cut into small wedges and served as an appetizer.

DOUBLE PORK CHOPS FILLED AND FLAMBEED

COGNAC AND ROSEMARY   SERVES 4

TO PREPARE THE FILLING:

2 *tablespoons butter*

2 *tablespoons shallots, chopped fine*

1 *inner celery stalk, including leaves, chopped fine*

1½ *cups bread cubes (soft), about ½ inch in size*

2 *tablespoons fresh parsley, chopped (or 1 teaspoon dried)*

1 *teaspoon salt*

Pepper, ground fresh

½ *teaspoon dried rosemary leaves*

3 *tablespoons Calvados (or dry sherry, dry vermouth, or dry white wine) (optional)*

In a heavy skillet, heat 2 tablespoons butter, and cook the shallots and celery for about 10 minutes. Then add the bread cubes, and cook them until they brown lightly. Remove the skillet from the heat, and add the parsley, salt, pepper, rosemary, and Calvados (or a substitute, if you wish). Mix well with a rubber spatula or wooden spoon. Fill each of the pork chops, packing the pockets as fully as you can. If you need to fasten the opening, use toothpicks, but cut off their ends so that no wood protrudes.

(Trimming the toothpicks allows the meat to come into direct contact with the skillet. Of course, you will have to remove the toothpicks before you serve the chops, but this is easily done with a small pair of pliers.)

TO PREPARE THE CHOPS:

4 tablespoons butter
4 loin rib pork chops, center cut,
  2 inches thick, each with a
  pocket
4 tablespoons Cognac, warmed
2 tablespoons shallots, chopped
  fine

½ pound mushrooms, sliced thin
2 tablespoons Dijon mustard
Salt
Pepper, ground fresh
Dried rosemary

In a heavy, covered skillet, heat 2 tablespoons butter, and brown the chops well on all sides. Measure 2 tablespoons of warmed Cognac, and sprinkle over the chops. Ignite the Cognac, and allow it to burn off completely. Cover the skillet, and let the chops cook at a bare simmer for about 45 minutes. During this time, turn the chops over once.

After 45 minutes, add the shallots, mushrooms, and mustard to the skillet. Cover the skillet, and continue simmering for about 30 minutes, or until the chops are done.

When the chops are thoroughly cooked, transfer them to a serving platter. Salt and pepper the mushroom mixture to taste in the skillet, and add the remaining Cognac. Increase the heat, and with a rubber spatula, stir the contents of the skillet to deglaze it as much as you can.

Pour this sauce between the chops; do *not* cover them with it. Garnish the chops by sprinkling a little dried rosemary over them after you've poured the sauce onto the platter.

PIGS' FEET IN GELATIN IN THE SOUTHERN ITALIAN STYLE

FRESH MINT AND VINEGAR   SERVES 8

4 whole pigs' feet (3 to 4
  pounds), split in half
1 tablespoon salt
2½ cups cooking liquid

2½ cups white vinegar
20 small fresh mint leaves
1 dried hot chili pepper, cut into
  very small pieces

Wash the pigs' feet well in cool water. Put the 8 halves in a heavy saucepan, and add enough water to cover them. Add salt, and bring to a boil. Cook them until tender (1½ to 2 hours, depending on their size and weight). It's difficult to describe the state of doneness of a pig's foot! We usually test by sticking a fork into the skin and meat, as far as it'll go. It should enter easily.

Remove the feet from the liquid, and set them aside. Then measure 2½ cups of the cooking liquid, and strain it through several layers of cheesecloth. Put the strained liquid in a clean saucepan, and add the white vinegar, mint leaves, hot pepper, and cooked feet. Bring to a boil, and continue boiling for 3 minutes. Remove from the heat. Transfer to a bowl or any dish deep enough to allow the liquid to cover the feet.

Place the bowl in the refrigerator for several hours, until the liquid gels. The gelatin will not be clarified, but don't be concerned; the flavor is all there. (You *can* clarify the liquid, but we're not convinced it's worth the time and trouble. This is Italian soul food, not *haute cuisine*.) This dish will keep in the refrigerator for several weeks.

This may be served as a buffet item or as an appetizer. It is excellent picnic fare, too.

SAUSAGE AND BROCCOLI

LEMON AND BROCCOLI   SERVES 4

> 1 bunch fresh broccoli
> 2 tablespoons salt
> ⅓ cup olive oil
> 4 links Italian pork sausage, kept
>   whole, or Angela's Homemade
>   Pork Sausage (see page 260)

> 3 cloves garlic, halved
> ⅓ cup dry vermouth
> Juice of 1 lemon

Cut the broccoli into spears ½ to 1 inch thick and 4 inches long. (Be sure that each spear is part stalk, part flower.) Clean it, and let stand in cold water (with 1 tablespoon salt) for 30 minutes. Boil 2 quarts water, add 1 tablespoon salt, add the washed broccoli spears, and *undercook* them.

In another saucepan, heat the olive oil, and cook the sausages until they are brown on all sides. Remove them to a serving platter.

In the same saucepan, add the garlic pieces, and cook until light brown (not too dark, or the garlic will be bitter). Press down on the garlic pieces with a spoon or fork to extract juices. Discard the garlic. Then add the broccoli, toss it in the oil until good and hot, and transfer to the sausage platter.

Add the vermouth to the saucepan, and cook down by approximately half; pour this over the broccoli. Sprinkle the broccoli with lemon juice, and serve.

ROAST LOIN OF PORK WITH PEARS

PEARS AND CHESTNUTS   SERVES **6**

TO PREPARE THE PORK:

2 slices bacon
4-pound loin of pork (see Note 1)
1 teaspoon salt
1 medium-size onion, chopped coarse
1 carrot, sliced very thin
1 celery stalk, including leaves, sliced thin

1 sprig fresh thyme (or ½ teaspoon dried)
1 bay leaf
½ cup plus 2 tablespoons Madeira
½ cup Brown Sauce (see page 93)

Cook the bacon in a roasting pan on top of the range until the slices are crisp. Remove the slices, and reserve for another use. (Cooked bacon will keep in the refrigerator a week or more. It'll get soggy, but can be recrisped in the oven.) Salt the pork loin, and place it carefully in the bacon fat in the roasting pan. Add the onion, carrot, celery, thyme, and bay leaf. Cook for about 15 minutes, or until the meat is well browned on all sides. Add ½ cup of the Madeira, and the Brown Sauce, and cover the roasting pan with foil. Place in a preheated 350-degree oven, and roast for 1 hour. Check occasionally, and stir the vegetables in the sauce. At the end of the hour, remove the foil, and continue to roast for an additional 40 minutes.

Remove the pork loin from the oven, and transfer to a serving platter. Put the sauce through a fine sieve and press to extract as much juice as possible. Discard what remains in the sieve. Again on top of the range, deglaze the pan over fairly high heat by adding 2 tablespoons Madeira and scraping the pan with a rubber spatula. Put this through the sieve, also. Pour the sauce over the pork loin.

TO PREPARE THE PEARS AND CHESTNUTS:

   6 pears
   ¾ cup sugar
   Juice of 2 lemons
   1 pound fresh chestnuts (or ½ pound dried chestnuts or 1-pound can whole chestnuts, unsweetened) (see Note 2)
   ½ cup honey

While the pork is roasting, core and peel the pears. In a saucepan that will hold the pears close together in one layer, combine the sugar and lemon juice. Place the pears on top of this mixture, and add just enough water to cover the pears. Bring to a boil, and simmer the pears for about 10 minutes. Do *not* overcook; keep them *al dente*. Remove the pears from the syrup, cut them in half lengthwise, and set aside.

If you are using fresh chestnuts, cut a cross, about ½ inch long, on the *flat* side of each chestnut. Place the chestnuts on a baking sheet, and bake them in a moderate oven (350 to 375 degrees) for 15 minutes, or until the crisscross edges of the cuts curl back. (Our grandfather, in charge of chestnuts for as long as he lived, covered the chestnuts at this point with several tea towels or a bath towel. He claimed this helped the inner skin to come off more easily.) Peel off both skins while the chestnuts are hot. If you didn't take Grandfather's advice and you still have some inner peel on the chestnuts, drop them in boiling water for about 2 minutes, and peel off remaining skin, loosening the edge of the skin with a paring knife. When the chestnuts are peeled, simmer them in water until they are tender. (Depending on the size and freshness of the chestnuts, this will take 30 minutes or longer.) Do *not* allow the chestnuts to break apart. When tender, drain, and dry them.

Put the honey in a large skillet, and when it is hot, add the pear halves and chestnuts. Cook over low heat until the pears become glossy and the chestnuts are glazed. With a slotted spoon, transfer the pears and chestnuts to the serving platter, arrange them around the pork roast.

We like slicing the roast at the table, spooning a little sauce alongside each serving, and adding 1 or 2 pear halves and several chestnuts.

Note 1: A tenderloin of pork is a delicious cut of meat; we enjoy it as much as a filet mignon or a filet of veal. The center-cut loin is the last word in roast pork, but it has to be stretched to serve 6 people. For 6 or 8 people, we usually buy the full loin half; it is cheaper than the center cut. Ask your butcher to bone it completely for you; the exceptionally lean loin will then make a regal roast.

Note 2: If you are using dried chestnuts, soak them in water (be sure they are completely covered), and let them sit for 5 to 6 hours or overnight. Drain them; then simmer them in fresh water until tender. Drain, dry, and glaze, as with fresh chestnuts.

If you are using canned whole chestnuts, drain, dry, and glaze, as with fresh chestnuts.

FAGIOLINI VERDI CON SALSICCE AL GENNARO
(Sausage with String Beans)

TOMATOES AND STRING BEANS   SERVES 4 TO 6

⅓ cup olive oil
2 large links Angela's Homemade Pork Sausage (see page 260), cut into ¼-inch slices (or Italian pork sausage)
2 cloves garlic, chopped fine
1 pound fresh green string beans, ends removed, kept whole
2 tablespoons fresh basil, chopped (or 1 teaspoon dried)

1 celery stalk, including leaves, sliced fine
2 cups fresh tomatoes, cored, blanched, peeled, and chopped coarse (or canned plum tomatoes), use as little liquid as possible
Salt
Pepper, ground fresh

In a medium-size, covered saucepan, heat oil, and sauté the sausage slices on both sides until well browned. Add the garlic, and cook it until it begins to brown slightly. (This will take only 2 or 3 minutes.) As soon as the garlic turns color, add the beans, basil, celery, and tomatoes. Cover, and bring to a boil. Lower the heat, and simmer until the beans are cooked *al dente* (approximately 30 minutes). Salt and pepper to taste.

We often make a luncheon of this, especially if the string beans have just been picked and brought in from the garden. This recipe will serve 3 or 4 as a main dish for lunch or 6 if served as a vegetable.

Fennel

Fennel is used both as a flavoring agent and as a vegetable. Although it is only now gaining popularity in the United States, England, and other places, it has always been a favorite in Italy. Fennel, the source of anise flavoring, is sometimes called *sweet fennel*, sometimes *Roman fennel*. It grows profusely in Italy, France, Greece and other European countries. Modern Italians make as much fuss over fennel as the ancient Romans did. The Florentine *finocchiona* is a salami flavored with fennel; one is likely to find fennel served as a vegetable in restaurants; even the seed combines with fish, soups, and sausage.

If we remember correctly, we tasted fennel before we tasted celery. At an early age, we learned a great combination of food was slices of fresh fennel dipped in olive oil, heavily seasoned with salt and freshly ground pepper. It's a good *crudité* with cocktails (don't fret over the olive oil; it's a reliable stomach liner). In our family, we couldn't live without fennel seed because it is a basic ingredient in Angela's Homemade Pork Sausage, and Angela's Homemade Pork Sausage is appetizer, main dish, flavoring agent for soups, pasta, sauces, and vegetables. Small packages of fennel seed come to us from Italy several times a year. What did our octogenarian Aunt Margaret bring us when she came to visit last year? A bag of fennel seed!

ANGELA'S HOMEMADE PORK SAUSAGE

FENNEL AND PAPRIKA

This is a very old family recipe. In our home this sausage was made several hundred pounds at a time. It was an annual family event in which everyone participated. Some of the sausage was eaten fresh as soon as we finished making it; the rest was kept for weeks in the refrigerator or ice box to be used as needed, which was several times a day. The aroma of sautéeing sausage seemed to be with us always. It was always added to tomato and other sauces for spaghetti, macaroni, ravioli, manicotti, *cavatelli*, lasagne, and all the other pastas.

It was cooked with vegetables and therefore added bounce to escarole, broccoli, Brussels sprouts, and cabbage. It was used to stuff chickens, capons, turkeys, and other birds, bringing forth the comment: "Why doesn't my stuffing taste like this?" It pocketed chops, flank steaks, and rollatini and added special flavor to meats that were roasted, stewed, and braised. It was fried with peppers and roasted with potatoes (liberally sprinkled with oregano). When pan fried it was (and still is) the basis of our favorite quick meal for sometimes unexpected company.

It was eternally on hand because it was put up in tens of jars, the sausage first dried, then packed into the jars filled with homemade lard (fat rendered from the sausage meat). We went to great lengths to explain, sometimes in an apologetic tone, the family sausage-making ritual to non-Italian friends (who, when they visited, would see sausage links hanging from poles competing for space with the drying pasta), but we knew that both the men and the women of the family took pride in the amount and the quality of the riches stored away in the family's *salsiccia* bank.

3-pound pork butt, as lean as possible	*½ teaspoon pepper, ground fresh*
1½ tablespoons salt	*2 yards sausage casing, soaked*
1 teaspoon fennel seed	*in ½ cup orange juice for*
1½ tablespoons paprika	*several hours or overnight*

Cut the meat into thin strips; then cut these strips by hand into the smallest pieces possible. Place the cut meat into a large bowl, and keep it cold for ease in handling. Add the salt, fennel seed, paprika, and pepper, and mix well.

Thoroughly wash the casing in lukewarm water, and fit it over a sausage funnel. (Approximately 1 yard of the casing should fit over the cone of the funnel.) Tie the end of the casing (the 1 or 2 inches of casing overhanging the funnel cone) with strong string, and feed the sausage meat into the funnel with your thumb. As the casing fills, puncture it with a needle to release air. (During filling, rotate and puncture the casing every few inches.) The casing should be firmly packed; if it is too loose, use your hand directly on the casing to pack it more fully. Tie the casing with string each 5 inches or so to form the individual sausage links. If the casing breaks, stop funneling, tie the casing at the break, and start again from the beginning.

This sausage may be kept in the refrigerator *uncovered* for 3 weeks; it may be kept frozen for 1 month.

PORK SAUSAGE WITH RISOTTO

WHITE WINE AND RICE   SERVES 6

2 tablespoons olive oil
6 links Angela's Homemade
   Pork Sausage (see above)
   (or 12 if store-bought)
1 cup dry white wine (or ⅔ cup
   dry vermouth and ⅓ cup
   water)
5 tablespoons butter
2 small onions, chopped fine
2 cups rice, uncooked

Salt
Pepper, ground fresh
4¼ cups Rich Chicken Stock or
   broth (see page 49)
4 tablespoons grated Parmesan
   cheese
4 teaspoons fresh flat Italian
   parsley, chopped fine (or 2
   teaspoons dried)

In a large skillet, heat the oil, and sauté the sausages until they are browned on all sides. Pour off the fat, and discard (or keep for another use). Pour ½ cup wine (or dry vermouth mixture) over the browned sausages, and cook over low heat until they are well done.

Melt 3 tablespoons butter in another skillet, add the onions, and cook until they turn pale yellow. Add the rice, and mix it well so that the butter coats the rice. Add pinches of salt and pepper to taste (go lightly because the stock or broth may be salty). Add the stock and remaining ½ cup wine (or vermouth and water), cover the skillet, and cook until the rice is done. (The rice should be dry and not overcooked.) Stir in the Parmesan cheese, remaining 2 tablespoons butter, and parsley.

Transfer the risotto to a serving platter, and top with the cooked sausages. This dish may be served with a brown or a tomato sauce. We enjoy the sausages and risotto plain, with a big green salad.

A SHOULDER OF PORK WRAPPED AROUND FRESH FENNEL AL VAGNINI

FENNEL AND GARLIC   SERVES 8 TO 10

5-pound pork shoulder, boned
3 garlic cloves, chopped fine
2 tablespoons fresh basil, chopped
fine (or 1 teaspoon dried)
Salt

Pepper, ground fresh
3 fresh fennel stalks, bulb portion
removed (see Note)
Pork rind (large enough to wrap
around the rolled shoulder)

Flatten out the pork shoulder, with the smoother side of the meat facing downward. Pick over the meat, removing any excess fat and pieces of cartilage that may have been missed by your butcher. Wipe the meat clean with paper towels or a tea towel. Sprinkle the garlic and basil over the rougher surface of the pork (which should be facing upward). Salt and pepper to taste.

Wash, trim, and dry the fennel stalks, and lay them crosswise at the narrow end of the meat. If you use fennel seed instead, sprinkle it over the meat as you did the garlic and basil.

Beginning with the smaller end, roll the meat, holding the fennel stalks tightly in place. Make as tight a roll as you can, and tie with kitchen string at 1-inch intervals along the roll. Cover the roll with a layer of pork rind, tying it in several places so that it won't fall off. (This bastes the meat during the cooking.)

Place the wrapped pork roll on a rack in a preheated 325-degree oven. Put a baking pan into the oven *below* the roast to catch the drippings from the pork roast and the rind. (Do *not* put the roast in the pan; this is an important point and, in our view, is the secret of this dish.) Cook for approximately 2½ hours, or a little longer if you wish. Remove the roast from the oven, take off the rind, and put the roast on a serving platter.

A great combination is peeled whole potatoes, carrots, and onions roasted in the pan catching the pork drippings. Depending on the size of the vegetables, cooking time will take 1 to 1½ hours.

This roast is also excellent served cold. When you carve it, hot *or* cold, the slices may crumble or break up, especially if they are very thin. Don't be overly concerned about this; all the flavor is still there. But do pay some attention to arranging these broken slices in a pleasant form on the individual plates.

Note: Fresh fennel is now available in many supermarkets; it's gaining in popularity in home gardens as well. The whole stalk (which resembles a celery stalk if the large, bulbous end is removed) is attractive as cooked in this dish. If you can't get fresh fennel, use 1 teaspoon dried fennel seed. What you lose in appearance will *not* be lost in flavor.

ROAST LOIN OF PORK ALLA LUISA

HONEY AND SOY SAUCE   SERVES 8

½ cup honey
¼ cup white vinegar
2 tablespoons fresh ginger,
   chopped fine (or 2 teaspoons
   powdered)

1 cup fresh pineapple, chopped
   fine
½ cup soy sauce
4-pound loin of pork (see Note)

Combine the ingredients to make the marinade, and marinate the loin of pork in the refrigerator overnight (the pork should marinate for no less than 12 hours, up to 24 hours). Remove the pork from the refrigerator 2 hours before cooking to allow it to reach room temperature.

Place the pork in heavy-duty foil with approximately 1 cup of the marinade. Save the rest of the marinade; you will need it later for basting. Seal the foil securely, and place the pork in a roasting pan in a preheated 325-degree oven for 3 hours. During the last 30 minutes of cooking, open the foil carefully, pour in the remainder of the marinade, and baste frequently.

Allow the pork to rest for 15 or 20 minutes before slicing and serving. We usually put the whole roast on a serving platter, arrange vegetables around it, and slice it at the table. This roast is excellent served with tiny boiled potatoes, in their skins, with butter, salt, and freshly ground pepper.

In addition to the pork roast and potatoes, serve a casserole of 8 apples (cored, peeled, and sliced) with ⅓ cup sugar, 3 tablespoons butter, and

½ teaspoon nutmeg. Cook this for 45 minutes in a moderate oven (350 degrees). For the last 10 minutes, put the apples under the broiler to brown them nicely.

Note: For ease in carving, have your butcher remove the bottom of the chine bone. Some butchers crack the bone to make carving easier, but we prefer the loin completely de-boned.

A VARIATION WITH MADEIRA

MADEIRA AND BROWN SUGAR   SERVES 8 TO 10

½ cup Madeira
½ cup brown sugar
1½ teaspoons orange zest,
  chopped fine

½ cup fresh orange juice
Pepper, ground fresh

Place the loin of pork in a shallow roasting pan, and roast in a pre-heated 325-degree oven for 1 hour.

In the meantime, combine the Madeira, brown sugar, orange zest, and orange juice in a saucepan, and cook over medium heat for 5 minutes to allow the sugar to dissolve. When the roast has cooked for 1 hour, pour this sauce over the loin. Baste every 15 minutes and roast for 2 more hours. Remove the roast to a platter, and let it stand for 20 minutes before serving.

We bring the roast to the table, surrounded by accompaniments, and slice and serve it at the table. This roast develops a lovely glaze, and it's attractive to look at. A great combination with this roast is Angela's Broccoli di Rape (see page 307).

((8))

Veal Cubes in Saffron, Tomato, and Wine Sauce and Other Versatile Veal Dishes

S CHNITZEL à la Holstein is a good descriptive title because it tells us that the schnitzel (a Viennese veal scallop, perhaps copied from the scallopine alla Milanese) comes from a young dairy cow such as the Holstein. Most veal as we know it is very young beef; the animal is usually 2½ to 3 months old and fed exclusively on milk. Veal is an expensive meat, but it has little fat or marbling; we think it's one of the most delicious meats, and we're mystified by the low consumption of it in the United States. (We've been told that the per capita consumption of veal is less than 3 pounds a year. On the other hand, can you believe that American restaurants feature veal cutlet dishes. But in our experience, ably think of veal primarily in terms of cutlets. This is understandable because cutlets are very popular in the United States, and most Italian-American restaurants feature veal cutlet dishes. But in our experience, cutlets are seldom served in American homes; one might be offered veal chops, but never, in our recollection, a rack, a breast, or a shoulder of veal. And what a pity.

The Department of Agriculture grades veal for sale as prime, choice, and good, but we were taught to buy veal by its color. The fat (what little there may be) should be white, never yellowish. The lean meat should be the palest of pinks; in fact, it should really seem white with a slight pink overcast. *Plume de Veau* is not a government grade; it is a registered name for veal produced by one of the largest meat dealers in the country. And although it is expensive, it is some of the finest veal available.

A veal carcass is just like a beef carcass, but it is butchered differently. It is cut in half crosswise, into a foresaddle and a hindsaddle. The most desirable cut from the foresaddle is the *rack*; this can be made into rib chops or cut into scallops. It can also be bought whole to roast as a rack of veal or to be made into a crown roast. Other foresaddle cuts are the shoulder, neck, and breast. The *shoulder* (also known as *chuck* of veal and similar to chuck of beef) is usually prepared without the bone for roasting; shoulder and *neck* meat may also be cut into stew pieces. The *breast* of veal may be braised with or without the bone and made with or without a pocket. In our family, breast of veal was traditionally roasted with bones intact and with a pocket, which was stuffed with bread crumbs, parsley, Parmesan cheese, raisins, eggs, salt, and pepper. But our presentation of it in this chapter (Breast of Veal with Rosemary) is both boneless and pocketless. We simply place a stuffing over the boned breast and roll it.

From the veal's hindsaddle come the leg of veal, loin, and flank. The *leg* is a popular cut and is butchered in a variety of ways. It can be boned and tied for roasting (although you wouldn't get the whole leg because it's too large). The upper half of the leg resembles a ham with the bone in it. The *shank* (or lower part) of the leg can be cut crosswise into pieces about 1½ inches. A typical Italian dish is *ossobuco*, in which the shinbones are cooked in wine with vegetables and flavored with parsley, lemon rind, garlic, and anchovy filets. The Italians make this delicious dish more festive by serving it in great combination with risotto, usually dressed in butter and grated Parmesan cheese. The marrow inside the shinbones is considered a delicacy, and marrow forks are provided with the *ossobuco* to dig it out.

The *loin*, the filet mignon of veal, is kept whole. We think it's one of the finest cuts of meat, yet we rarely see it on restaurant menus or have it in friends' homes. In this chapter, we present it moist-cooked in a brown sauce with braised chestnuts (Mignonette of Veal with Braised Chestnuts). It may seem foolish to moist-cook such an expensive and elegant cut of meat, but the taste is superb. Filet of beef can be cooked in the same manner.) You usually see the loin in markets cut into chops about 1 inch thick. Although they are expensive, they are popular and make excellent eating. In this chapter, we present loin chops in combination with chicory, Cognac, and cream (Chops, Chicory, Cognac, and Cream).

Cutlets can also be cut from the *flank* of veal, but it is generally accepted that flank cutlets are not very desirable. As a rule, flank meat is ground for the veal patties you see in those neatly wrapped plastic packages.

Veal *cutlets* (which are *not* veal scallops) are often sold in slices almost ½ inch thick. There is no bone, no fat, and no waste. And they are not really prohibitively expensive when you take that into consideration. Veal *scallops* (*scaloppine* in Italian and *escalopes de veau* in French) are similar to cutlets, but they are cut in very thin slices. The most expensive veal cutlets and scallops come from the rib and loin, but beautiful and tender cuts also come from the leg.

To call veal versatile seems to us to understate the case. Veal, like chicken, is extremely adaptable. It can be sautéed or stuffed, breaded or braised, rolled or roasted, cubed or curried, stewed or skewered, floured and fried. The Germans prepare thin slices of veal, sautéed and combined with chanterelles (their famous *Pfifferlinge* found in the famous Black Forest) for a dish called *Geschnetzeltes Kalbfleisch*. The Italians created *Vitello Tonnato;* the whitest slices of veal from the loin are braised and then seduced by a tuna sauce. The dish is accented with capers, and for extra pleasure, one may add slices of pimiento or artichoke hearts. Another interesting Italian preparation is presented at the New York restaurant Il Monello; they call it *Bocconccini di Vitello.* Morsels of veal from the filet are sautéed in butter and flamed with Belgian mandarine; more butter is added, along with some white wine, a dash of demiglace, and lemon juice. This combination gives the veal a touch of sweet and sour. The French, of course, have their *blanquette de veau à l'ancienne,* combining flour, butter, a white stock enriched with egg yolks and cream and accented with lemon juice and nutmeg. This is not too different from their veau fricassee, in which the veal is first seared, rather than browned, in butter. An unusual French preparation involves sautéeing thin slices of veal with mushrooms and Cognac, covering them with a cream sauce, and capping the dish with slices of baked apple. This is then lightly browned under the broiler to comᵖlete *escalopes de veau Normande.* Veal and apples seem to have an affinity for each other. La Caravelle, the famous New York restaurant, combines veal chops with Calvados (apple brandy). Veal is great in combination with the orange, too; veal pieces are browned in clarified butter and stewed slowly with veal stock, white wine, onions, shallots, carrots, parsley, and fresh orange juice. The liquid is than strained and reduced, and julienne strips of orange peel are added.

The Swiss national dish—well, almost—is *émincés de veau:* sautéed strips of veal cloaked in a white wine and herb sauce.

We've chosen some of our favorite veal preparations for this chapter, including four scaloppine dishes. There are many advantages to scaloppine: They are easy to prepare and can be done at the last few minutes; they're not fatty, although they are almost always cooked in butter; they're so tender that they can be cut with a fork; they freeze well and thaw quickly. We think they are truly elegant. They are splendid combination here with hazelnut butter and in a green peppercorn sauce. They are also great with vegetables: fried green peppers and with fresh green peas.

SCALOPPINE IN THE MILANESE STYLE WITH FRIED ITALIAN PEPPERS

GREEN PEPPERS AND PARMESAN CHEESE   SERVES 6

TO PREPARE THE PEPPERS:

3 tablespoons olive oil
2 small garlic cloves, halved
1½ pounds green Italian peppers, wiped clean, cored, seeded, and cut into ¼-inch lengths

Salt
Pepper, ground fresh

In a large skillet, heat 3 tablespoons olive oil. When it is hot, add the garlic pieces, and brown them lightly. As the garlic cooks, press down on each piece with a wooden spoon to extract some garlic juice. When they are done, remove and discard the garlic pieces. Add the pepper slices, and fry them until they are softened (they should be soft but not mushy) and somewhat charred. Salt and pepper to taste. Transfer the peppers to a serving platter, and keep them warm.

TO PREPARE THE VEAL:

1½ pounds scaloppine of veal, cut from the leg in thin slices (less than ¼ inch thick)
⅓ to ½ cup all-purpose flour
Salt
Pepper, ground fresh
⅓ cup olive oil
6 tablespoons butter

3 eggs
¼ cup cool water
2 cups fresh bread crumbs
¼ cup grated Parmesan cheese (or Romano)
2 whole lemons, each cut lengthwise into 6 wedges, seeded and cored

The veal slices should be very thin; pound them until they are about 4 by 6 or 5 by 7 inches each. (There will be 7 to 9 slices of this size in 1½ pounds.) Cut each slice into 2 or 3 pieces so that each scaloppine is now 2 by 3 or 3 by 3 inches.

Put the flour on a dinner plate, and dredge each piece of veal. (We find the easiest way to do this is to pick up the piece of veal at one corner with the thumb and index finger, covering as little meat as possible with the fingers. Brush the piece of veal against the flour quickly and gently on one side, then on the other, and shake the veal over the flour plate in quick, short strokes to remove any excess flour.) Lay the floured pieces of veal on wax paper. As soon as the pieces are floured (we usually start flouring them only minutes before we're ready to cook them), sprinkle them with salt and pepper to taste.

In the same skillet, heat half the oil and butter. While this is heating, combine the eggs and water and beat lightly; also combine the bread crumbs and Parmesan cheese. Put the egg and the crumb-cheese mixtures in large plates or wide soup bowls, and place them close to the skillet. Pick up the floured veal, one piece at a time, dip it into the egg, then into the crumbs, and place it in the skillet. Repeat this until the skillet has one layer of veal pieces. Cook each piece 2 or 3 minutes on each side. When this batch is completed, coat and cook the next batch. Transfer the cooked pieces to the serving platter on which you have put the fried peppers. Arrange the lemon wedges on the platter, and serve hot.

VEAL CUBES IN SAFFRON, TOMATO, AND WINE SAUCE

SAFFRON AND TOMATOES   SERVES 4

2 pounds boneless veal shoulder (or breast), cut into 1½-inch cubes

2 tablespoons all-purpose flour

1 teaspoon salt

Pepper, ground fresh

2 tablespoons olive oil (or vegetable oil)

2 tablespoons butter

1 faggot (or bouquet garni): 2 celery stalk pieces, 3 inches long, tied with string to form a cylinder, filled with sprigs of parsley, thyme, and rosemary and 1 bay leaf (see Note)

1 cup shallots (or onions) chopped

1 large clove garlic, chopped fine

2 cups fresh tomatoes, cored, blanched, peeled, and chopped (or canned plum tomatoes)

½ cup dry white wine (or ¼ cup dry vermouth and ¼ cup water)

1 cup Rich Beef Stock or broth (see page 46)

1 teaspoon saffron strands

Put the veal cubes, flour, salt, and pepper to taste in an 11-by-14 plastic bag. Hold the bag closed with one hand, hold the bottom of the bag with the other, and shake it vigorously to coat the veal.

Heat the oil and butter in a large skillet, add the veal cubes in batches, and sauté until they are light brown. As the pieces brown, remove them to a covered, ovenproof baking dish. Add the faggot to the casserole.

In the same skillet, combine the shallots, garlic, and tomatoes, and cook for 10 minutes. Add this tomato mixture to the veal.

Still using the same skillet, combine the wine, stock, and saffron. Mix these ingredients well over high heat, and scrape the sides of the skillet clean. Pour this liquid over the contents of the casserole, cover, and bake in a preheated 350-degree oven for 1½ hours.

If you wish to serve a starch with this, we suggest rice instead of noodles. Cook the rice dry; there is adequate sauce in the veal dish, and it is not meat to be soupy.

Note: Whatever happened to the term *faggot?* We're sure it's been replaced by *bouquet garni.* The traditional faggot was made of a sprig of thyme, several sprigs of parsley, and a bay leaf tied together with a piece of string. We like to put these herbs between 2 pieces of celery. You may substitute 1 tablespoon each of dried parsley, thyme, and rosemary and 1 bay leaf for the faggot.

A VARIATION: VEAL CUBES BAKED IN A PIE

SAFFRON AND TOMATOES   SERVES 4

Prepare the recipe for Veal Cubes in Saffron, Tomatoes, and Wine Sauce as described, but reduce the cooking time by 30 minutes. Transfer the contents to a shallow (and attractive) baking dish (10 to 12 inches wide and about 2 inches deep).

Make a pâté brisée (see page 150). Roll out the pastry to a circle at least 15 inches wide, and use a pizza or ravioli cutter to cut a circle at least 1 inch large than the size of the baking dish or casserole (using the cover of the baking pan as a guide). Cover the pie, and make your favorite crust edge. Use remaining dough to make several lattice strips, and cut some leaves or other shapes to decorate the top of the piecrust. Prick the crust in several places to make steam openings, and bake the pie in a preheated 375-degree oven for 30 to 40 minutes, or until crust is brown.

VEAL SCALLOPS IN A GREEN PEPPERCORN SAUCE

GREEN PEPPERCORNS AND CREAM   SERVES 4

TO PREPARE THE VEAL:
> *1 pound scaloppine of veal, cut from the leg in thin slices*
> *(less than ¼ inch thick)*
> *⅓ cup all-purpose flour*
> *Salt*
> *4 tablespoons butter*

The scallops should be very thin and about 4 by 6 or 5 by 7 inches after pounding. There will be 4 or 5 slices of this size in 1 pound. Cut each slice into pieces 2 by 3 or 3 by 3 inches.

Put the flour on a dinner-size plate, and dredge each piece of veal. (Brush the piece of veal against the flour quickly and gently on one side, then on the other. Shake the piece of veal over the plate in quick, short strokes to remove any excess flour. Lay the floured pieces of veal on wax paper. Perform this entire operation as quickly as possible. (We usually start doing this only a minute or so before heating the butter.) As soon as all the veal is floured, sprinkle the pieces with salt to taste. (Do *not* add pepper; the green peppercorns will add enough spice.)

In a large skillet, heat the butter, and brown the veal pieces in batches (2 to 3 minutes on each side). (Do only as many pieces as you can fit in the skillet in one layer without overlapping them.) As each batch is done, transfer the slices to a large, warm serving platter.

TO PREPARE THE SAUCE:

¼ *cup dry white wine (or 3 tablespoons dry vermouth combined with 1 tablespoon water)*
½ *cup heavy cream*
2 *tablespoons green peppercorns, drained and crushed (see Note)*
1 *tablespoon Dijon mustard*
1 *tablespoon fresh parsley, chopped (or 2 or 3 sprigs)*

In the same skillet in which the veal pieces were cooked, add the wine, and clean the pan by scraping and stirring constantly with a rubber spatula. The wine will cook away rather quickly, and the sauce will thicken. Add the cream and bruised peppercorns, bring the mixture to a boil, and remove it from the heat. Blend in the mustard (still using the spatula), and pour the sauce over the veal. Clean the pan completely of sauce (there's little of it, and none should be wasted).

Sprinkle the chopped fresh parsley overall, or lay 2 or 3 sprigs fresh parsley alongside the veal slices. Serve immediately.

Note: It's easy to crush the peppercorns in a mortar and pestle; it takes only a couple of strokes. The idea is to *bruise* them, *not* purée them. Or you can wrap them in a tea towel, handkerchief, or several layers of cheesecloth, and pound them once or twice with a food mallet, empty wine bottle, or small, heavy skillet. Set them aside.

A VARIATION: VEAL SCALLOPS IN HAZELNUT BUTTER

BUTTER AND HAZELNUTS   SERVES 4

Brown the pieces of veal as directed, and keep them warm.

TO PREPARE THE SAUCE:
> *6 tablespoons sweet butter*
> *3 tablespoons blended hazelnuts*
> *3 tablespoons fresh lemon juice*
> *Sprig of parsley (or 1 tablespoon fresh parsley, chopped)*

In a skillet or saucepan, heat the sweet butter, and add the pulverized hazelnuts. (This can be prepared ahead of time if you have a food processor that makes flavored butters. Combine butter and hazelnuts according to the directions provided by the manufacturer.) Blend well, and heat the mixture. Add the lemon juice, blend well, and pour over the cooked scaloppine.

Garnish with a sprig of fresh parsley or 1 tablespoon of chopped fresh parsley. The great combination here is the mixture of butter and hazelnuts, and it becomes greater if the dish is accompanied by broiled tomatoes (halves or slices), simply salted and peppered.

BREAST OF VEAL WITH ROSEMARY

ROSEMARY AND WHITE WINE   SERVES 6

TO STUFF THE VEAL:
½ cup shallots, chopped
½ cup fresh parsley, stems removed, chopped (or 1 tablespoon dried)
1 celery stalk, including leaves, chopped coarse
1 carrot, scraped, cut lengthwise into thin strips, and then cut into tiny pieces
1 tablespoon fresh rosemary (or 1 teaspoon dried)

Several tablespoons Rich Chicken Stock (if needed) (see page 49)
3- to 4-pound breast of veal, boned (see Note)
Salt
12 paper-thin slices capocollo (or Genoa salami)

If you have a food processor (such as a Cuisinart), combine and blend the shallots, parsley, celery, carrot, and rosemary. Process them to the consistency of crunchy peanut butter. (Do *not* overblend.)

If you have a blender, combine these same ingredients, and blend. If the mixture is too dry, add 1 or more tablespoons stock, but do *not* make a soupy mixture, and do *not* overblend. (You can also do this by hand with the aid of a chopper.)

Spread the veal out on a flat surface, boned side up. Salt the veal breast, and then cover it with the crunchy vegetable mixture. Leave a margin of bare meat on all side; this will make it easier (and neater) to roll. Place the slices of capocollo (or salami) over the vegetables. Roll up the breast, beginning with the narrower end, and tie it crosswise at 1-inch intervals and then lengthwise once.

TO COOK THE VEAL:

2 tablespoons butter
2 tablespoons olive oil
1 teaspoon fresh rosemary (or ½
teaspoon dried)
1 cup dry white wine
1½ cups Rich Chicken Stock (see
page 49)

2 tablespoons beurre manié
(equal parts flour and butter,
mixed until completely
blended)

In a heavy, enameled saucepan, large enough to hold the rolled veal breast comfortably (or a Dutch oven or anything similar with a cover), heat the butter and oil, and brown the veal roll on all sides. When the veal is fully browned, add the rosemary and wine, and simmer, *uncov-*ered, 25 to 30 minutes. During this cooking time, baste the roll with the pan liquid (but remember that the wine will be cooking away). Add 1 cup stock, and cover the pan. Lower the heat as much as you can (but maintain a slow simmer), and cook for an additional 1½ hours. Baste every 15 minutes or so.

When the veal roll is done, transfer it to a serving platter. Remove and discard the string.

Add remaining stock to the pan, and deglaze it over high heat. Add the beurre manié, a little at a time, until you achieve a slightly thickened sauce. Pour 2 or 3 tablespoons sauce over the veal roll; then sprinkle on some fresh or dried rosemary. Serve the remaining sauce in a bowl or gravy boat. Slice the roll, and pass the sauce, or add a little to the individual servings. But do *not* cover the veal slice completely with the sauce.

Note: This tasty preparation is made from one of the least expensive cuts of veal. A breast of veal may be prepared with or without a pocket. In this case, no pocket is necessary because the stuffing is simply placed over the breast, which is then rolled. But be sure to ask your butcher to bone the breast.

A SHOULDER OF VEAL, SEASONED AND STUFFED

ONIONS AND CARROTS   SERVES 6 TO 8

TO STUFF THE VEAL:

½ cup fresh parsley, chopped (or 1 tablespoon dried)
1½ cups bread crumbs
1 tablespoon Marsala
2 small cloves garlic, chopped fine
1 tablespoon fresh tarragon (or 1 teaspoon dried)

1 teaspoon salt
1 teaspoon pepper, ground fresh
2 tablespoon butter, melted
4-pound shoulder of veal, boned (see Note)

In a large bowl, mix all the stuffing ingredients. Place the veal, unrolled, on a flat surface. Spread the stuffing evenly over the veal. Roll the veal, and tie it neatly, first lengthwise and then at 1-inch intervals along the roll, to help keep its shape as it cooks.

TO ROAST THE VEAL:

6 whole carrots, scraped, ends cut off
6 small potatoes, peeled and halved
3 onions, halved
3 stalks celery, including leaves, cut diagonally into 2-inch slices

2 cups Rich Chicken Stock (see page 49)
1 cup dry vermouth
Salt
Pepper, ground fresh
1 tablespoon tapioca starch
½ cup water

Arrange the vegetables in a 10-by-15 baking dish, and place the veal roll on top of them. Add 1 cup stock and ½ cup vermouth to the baking pan. Sprinkle with salt and pepper to taste.

Roast in a preheated 425-degree oven for 30 minutes. Baste the veal with the pan liquid several times during this period of cooking. Then cover the veal with tin foil, and reduce the heat to 350 degrees. Continue roasting for 1½ hours, basting every 20 minutes or so. Add the remaining 1 cup stock and ½ cup vermouth as necessary.

Transfer the veal and the vegetables to a large serving platter. Mix the tapioca and water, and set it aside. Put the baking pan on the stove top, and bring the sauce to a boil. Scrape the pan clean of all the brown bits with a wooden spoon or spatula, add the tapioca starch, and stir constantly. Thin this sauce with more water if necessary to achieve the desired consistency.

Serve the veal and vegetables, and pass the sauce in a separate bowl.

Note: Ask your butcher to bone the veal shoulder and prepare it for roasting. Tell him you plan to stuff it, and have him roll and tie it for you. (Study his tied roll carefully; it should be your model when you retie the stuffed, rolled veal.) Of course, the veal has to be untied and unrolled so that it can be stuffed, so we usually ask the butcher for more string to retie it.

VEAL BIRDS IN WHITE WINE

MUSHROOMS AND WHITE WINE   SERVES 6

TO PREPARE THE FILLING:

2 thin slices bacon
½ cup onion, chopped fine
1 clove garlic, chopped fine
¼ cup shallots, chopped fine
1 tablespoon fresh tarragon, chopped fine (or 1 teaspoon dried)

1 cup bread crumbs
1 tablespoon fresh parsley, chopped fine (or 1 teaspoon dried)
2 eggs
Salt
Pepper, ground fresh

Sauté the bacon slices in a skillet; when they are done, remove them, and set them aside to drain. In the same skillet, cook the onion, garlic, shallots, parsley, and tarragon for about 5 minutes. Add the bread crumbs. Crumble the bacon, and add it, too.

In a bowl, lightly beat the 2 eggs; salt and pepper them to taste. Add the bread and bacon mixture to the eggs, and blend well.

TO PREPARE THE VEAL:

6 *thin veal scaloppine,*
  approximately 4½ by 8 inches
3 *tablespoons butter*
½ *cup onion, chopped fine*
1 *clove garlic, chopped fine*
¼ *cup shallots, chopped fine*
1 *teaspoon fresh tarragon,*
  chopped fine (or ½ teaspoon
  dried)

½ *cup white wine*
3 *cups Rich White Wine Sauce*
  (see page 99)
¼ *pound mushrooms, sliced thin*
1 *teaspoon lemon juice*
  Parsley, chives, paprika or
  pepper, ground fresh
  (optional)

Place the scaloppine on a flat surface; as you spread each scallop, put the narrower end closer to you. Divide the filling among the scaloppine, and spread it evenly over each piece. (The back of a spoon or a rubber spatula is helpful; use your hands, too). Roll each scaloppine, beginning with the narrower end, and secure it with a 6- to 8-inch wooden skewer. (Think of fastening two pieces of paper with a straight pin.)

In a large skillet, heat 3 tablespoons butter, and sauté the veal birds until they are lightly browned all over. Remove them, and set them aside.

In the same skillet, cook the onion, garlic, shallots, and tarragon for 5 minutes. Transfer this mixture to a covered casserole large enough to hold all 6 birds in one layer. Over relatively high heat, deglaze the skillet with the white wine. (Use a rubber spatula for this.) As soon as the bottom of the skillet is scraped clean, add this liquid to the casserole. Also add the white wine sauce and the veal birds to the casserole. Cover the casserole, and bake it in a preheated 350-degree oven for 45 minutes.

While the birds are baking, wipe the mushrooms clean with a damp paper towel or tea towel, cut them into *very* thin slices, and toss them in the lemon juice. When the veal has baked for 45 minutes, add the mushrooms to the casserole, stir gently to blend them into the sauce. Bake an additional 15 minutes, and serve hot.

This dish looks and tastes especially good served over cooked rice. Put the cooked rice on a large, decorative oval platter, and line the birds up in a row on the rice, as though they were sitting on a telephone line. Cover with the sauce and sprinkle with parsley, chives, paprika, or black pepper, or whatever you prefer to serve as an accent. Please don't forget this important little touch.

SCALOPPINE E PISELLI
(Veal Scallops with Fresh Green Peas)

MARSALA AND PROSCIUTTO   SERVES 6

1½ *cups fresh green peas*
½ *pound mushrooms, wiped*
   clean with a damp tea towel,
   and sliced thin
   Juice of ½ lemon
1¼ *to 1½ pounds veal cutlets, cut*
   from the leg, sliced thin
   (about 6 large slices)
2 *tablespoons olive oil*
2 *tablespoons, plus ½ cup,*
   butter
2 *heaping tablespoons fresh*
   parsley, chopped (or 1
   teaspoon dried)

2 *heaping tablespoons shallots,*
   chopped
1 *teaspoon fresh thyme (or ½*
   teaspoon dried)
¼ *pound prosciutto, sliced paper-*
   thin, cut lengthwise into
   ¼-inch strips and then into
   ¼-inch cubes (or capocollo)
½ *cup Marsala*
   Salt
   Pepper, ground fresh

Place the fresh peas in a saucepan of boiling water, and cook them for 3 to 5 minutes. (The peas should be only half cooked; they will cook further when they are added to the veal.) Remove the peas from the heat, drain them, and set them aside.

In a small bowl, combine the sliced mushrooms and lemon juice; toss the slices to coat them with the juice. (The mushrooms will probably absorb the juice, so don't worry if you see little of it left in the bottom of the bowl.) Set the mushrooms aside.

Pound the cutlet slices until they are about ¼-inch thick. Then cut them in half or in thirds to make the scallops.

In a large skillet, heat 1 tablespoon each oil and butter, and sauté the scaloppine for a little less than 1 minute on each side. (Do this in batches. There should be only one layer of scallops, with some space between the pieces, in the skillet at any one time.) Add the remaining 1 tablespoon oil and 1 tablespoon butter as needed. Transfer the sautéed veal pieces to a warm plate.

In the same skillet, heat ½ cup butter slowly. Add the parsley, shallots, thyme, prosciutto (or capocollo), mushrooms, and peas. Stir well with a wooden spoon or rubber spatula, and return the veal pieces to the skillet. Increase the heat to high, add the Marsala, and cook for 5 minutes. Add just a little salt, but be liberal with the freshly ground pepper. To serve, arrange the veal slices in a row on a large oval platter (be sure they overlap), and pour the sauce overall.

For a great variation on this dish, substitute snow peas, cut into julienne strips, for the green peas. Unlike the peas, the snow peas do not have to be cooked ahead of time. Just add them with the parsley, shallots, and so on.

VEAL SHANKS LIMONE

LEMON AND THYME   SERVES 4

Veal shanks cooked in this way are a typical Italian dish. (Tomatoes are often added.) *Ossobuco,* as it is called in Italy, may be served with a sprinkling of anchovy filets, but we omit them here because we think the cooked-down wine and stock are salty enough. The dish is combined with lots of parsley (among other vegetables), but we use the parsley simply as a bright green garnish (it's beautiful with the lemon rind) and accent the thyme instead. The resulting bouquet and flavor *è fantastico*—even more so if combined with a risotto. Be daring. Truffle your risotto, and sprinkle it liberally with grated Parmesan cheese.

4 veal shanks, cut into 1¾- to
  2-inch thick slices
4 tablespoons peanut oil
4 tablespoons butter
2 large cloves garlic, chopped
  fine
3 celery stalks, including leaves,
  sliced fine
2 medium-size onions, sliced
  fine
3 carrots, scraped and sliced
  fine

1½ cups dry white wine
2 cups Rich Beef Stock (see
  page 46)
2 teaspoons fresh thyme (or 1
  teaspoon dried)
4 tablespoons lemon zest, diced
  very fine
Salt
Pepper, ground fresh
2 tablespoons fresh parsley,
  preferably flat Italian type,
  chopped

Be sure your butcher saws through the bones.

In a heavy, covered saucepan large enough to hold the shanks in one layer (or a large Dutch oven or enameled iron saucepan), heat the oil and butter. Add the veal shanks, brown them well on all sides (15 to 20 minutes); they should be a deep, rich brown. (This is an important step, so *don't* underplay it. The shanks won't brown once you add the rest of the ingredients.)

Then add the garlic, celery, onions, and carrots. Move the shanks to the side of the pan, stacking them, or remove them from the pan. Stir the vegetables to brown them partially (about 10 minutes). Rearrange the shanks in one layer, cover them with the vegetables, and add the wine, stock, thyme, and 2 tablespoons lemon zest. Salt and pepper to taste. Cover, and cook at a low simmer for 1½ to 2 hours. (Veal shanks are served well cooked and tender to the point that the meat can be separated from the bone with a fork.) After about 45 minutes, turn the shanks over, stir the vegetables, and baste (if necessary). When they are done, transfer the shanks to a serving platter, and keep them warm.

Turn the heat to high, and boil the sauce until it is somewhat reduced and the thickness you prefer. Pour this sauce over the cooked shanks. Sprinkle the remaining 2 tablespoons lemon zest and the chopped parsley overall, and serve the dish (we hope) with risotto.

An important part of this dish is the marrow inside the bones. You'll be particularly elegant (as well as practical) if you supply marrow forks with which your guests can dig out the marrow. If you don't have such forks, don't worry; other utensils can be used to remove the marrow.

MIGNONETTE OF VEAL WITH BRAISED CHESTNUTS

CHESTNUTS AND BUTTER   SERVES 8

2 cups dried chestnuts	2 cups chicken stock
2 tablespoons butter	Juice of ½ lemon
5-pound filet of veal (see Note)	2 tablespoons lemon zest, chopped
Salt	fine
Pepper, ground fresh	2 tablespoons parsley, chopped
3 cups Brown Sauce (see page 93)	fine

Soak the chestnuts overnight at room temperature in cool water to cover; change the water two or three times. Add ½ teaspoon salt to the water for *each* soaking.

In a very large, heavy, covered casserole, melt the butter. Add the veal filet, salt and pepper it to taste, and brown it well on all sides (20 to 30 minutes). Add the sauce, and slowly bring it to a boil. Cook the veal, covered, at the lowest simmer possible for 2 hours. Check every 15 or 20 minutes to be sure sauce is not thickening or sticking to the bottom of the casserole.

While the veal is simmering, drain the chestnuts. Put them into a medium-size saucepan. Cover them with fresh water, and bring to a boil. Lower the heat, and simmer the chestnuts for about 1 hour. To test for doneness, taste one; it should be rather underdone, chewable but noticeably raw. Drain the chestnuts, and put them back in the saucepan. Add the stock, and cook for an additional 30 to 40 minutes. Set aside.

Transfer the filet to a large serving platter, and remove the strings. Strain the chestnuts, and arrange them around the filet. Add the lemon juice to the sauce. Strain the sauce and pour it over the filet. Garnish with the chopped lemon zest and parsley.

When you serve this meat, cut it into slices about 1 inch thick at the table. It is extremely tender, so don't be concerned if it falls apart. Add 5 or 6 chestnuts and a generous spoonful of sauce to each serving.

Note: Have the butcher wrap the filet in a little fat and tie it with string.

CHOPS, CHICORY, COGNAC, AND CREAM
(Some of our favorite things)

COGNAC AND CREAM   SERVES 6

TO PREPARE THE CHICORY:
1 pound fresh chicory (see Note)

Separate the chicory leaves and wash them in cold water; wash the leaves a second time to get rid of all the sand. Drain the chicory, and cut the larger leaves in half or thirds (the pieces should be about 2 inches long, uncooked). Set aside until ready to cook.

TO PREPARE THE CHOPS:

6 tablespoons butter
6 veal loin chops, cut thick (at least ½-pound each)
Salt
Pepper, ground fresh

¼ cup, plus 2 tablespoons, shallots, chopped fine
¼ cup Cognac
1½ cups heavy cream

In a heavy skillet large enough to hold the chops in one layer, heat the butter. While it is melting, salt and pepper the veal chops to taste on both sides. When the butter is bubbling, place the chops in the skillet, and cook them for about 20 minutes. (Move them around with a wooden spoon to keep them from sticking, and check them for brownness.) When the chops are done on one side, turn them over, and cook the other side for 20 minutes. Transfer them to a baking pan, and put in a warm oven (200 to 250 degrees) while you make the sauce (about 5 minutes).

Into the same large skillet, put ¼ cup shallots, and cook them for 2 to 3 minutes, stirring constantly with a wooden spoon or rubber spatula. Pour in the Cognac, and ignite it. Tilt the skillet sideways, and move the liquid all around in the pan. Use the wooden spoon or rubber spatula to deglaze the skillet. Then add the heavy cream, and cook the sauce over high heat for about 5 minutes, until it has thickened somewhat. Taste the sauce for seasoning, and adjust it to your taste.

TO COOK THE CHICORY:

> 2 cups Rich Chicken Stock (see page 49) (or veal or beef stock)
> 1 teaspoon sugar
> ½ teaspoon grated nutmeg (or powdered)
>   Salt
>   Pepper, ground fresh

While the chops are cooking, bring the stock to a boil in a large saucepan. Add the chicory, stir well, cover the pan, and cook until tender (about 10 minutes). Drain the chicory into a bowl (do *not* squeeze it dry), and add the sugar, nutmeg, salt, and pepper. Mix well.

Arrange the cooked chicory on a large serving platter. Place the veal chops on top of the chicory, and pour the cream sauce overall. Do not cover the chops completely with sauce; cover half of each chop, and if there's sauce left over, pour it between the chops. Be sure to scrape all the sauce out of the skillet and onto the serving platter. Sprinkle 2 tablespoons chopped raw shallots overall.

Note: Do not confuse chicory with endive. What is called chicory in the United States resembles a head of lettuce or escarole; it has crinkly leaves, dark green on the outside, yellow and white inside. (Endive looks like a small white banana without a curve and without a peel.) In England, this vegetable is called endive. In the United States, endive is Belgian endive; and in Belgium, where endive is grown in tremendous quantity, it is called *chicorée de Bruxelles.*

((9))

A Leg of Lamb, Simply Wined and Potted, and Other Lamb Preparations

WE visited the Dutchess County Fair in Rhinebeck, New York, only once, but it was an unforgettable trip because it put us in the sheep business. There were two irresistible ewes and a lovelorn ram, all blue-ribboned, registered Hampshire sheep. We bought them at bargain prices from Martin Simnacher, neighbor, friend, and sheep adviser, who helped us get started. It didn't take many years to build a flock of sixty registered sheep. The ewes were given names like Allessandra, Bathsheba, Cassandra, Desdemona, Elisabetta, and Fiona. The rams were Antony, Brutus, Caesar, and Dominic. The gestation period of a ewe is five months, and many of our ewes lambed twice a year, usually delivering twins. Once a ewe was serviced, we had to separate her from her ram. We learned an easy way to recognize when separation was necessary. Rams in service were belted and buckled with mating blocks on their undersides. The blocks were made of colored wax (in decorator colors—lampblack, Venetian red, azure). When Antony, wearing azure, had serviced Allessandra, there would be a smear of azure on Allessandra's backside. Cassandra was impossible; her rump bore marks of blue, red, and black!

A Greek family living in New York came frequently on early Sunday mornings to buy black baby lambs; usually only a month or so old. (Hampshires are born black; their wool turns white in about three months.) During our sheep-raising period, we never ate lamb; we grew so fond of our flock, we could never slaughter them. It was difficult enough to sell them.

For reasons too complicated to explain, we had to sell the flock. After all was signed, sealed, and just about delivered, we learned that the purchase was made in the name of a cemetery! (Sheep are used to keep the cemetery lawn trimmed.) It took us months to get back in the swing of preparing tasty lamb dishes.

If you buy a leg of lamb at a supermarket (or anywhere else for that matter), be sure it is no larger than 8 pounds. Ideally, it should be between 4 and 6 pounds, because weight is an indication of the youthfulness of the lamb. Lamb, or *spring lamb*, as we see it advertised, is less than one year old, usually between four and seven months old. When it is one year old, it is a *yearling*, either a ram or ewe. Even though spring lamb is available fresh in the spring and summer months, you can buy frozen spring lamb in the fall and winter months. Better still, buy it in spring and summer, when it is most plentiful, and freeze it yourself. Lamb from New Zealand and Australia is excellent. For a number of years, we visited the British Virgin Islands, and it was there that we first enjoyed frozen New Zealand lamb. Hothouse lamb (and very young lamb, under ten weeks of age) is a gourmet delicacy.

Like veal, lamb is butchered in half crosswise first to produce a *foresaddle* and a *hindsaddle*.

The rack, chuck, breast, and foreshanks are all cut from the foresaddle. The *rack* is an exquisite cut of meat, competing for tenderness and flavor with the loin (from the hindsaddle). A crown roast of lamb is made with two racks. The rack of lamb is comparable to the portion of beef that gives us rib roasts and rib sections. Like the first cuts or prime ribs, the first cut of racks is special, too. *Chuck* comes from the shoulder and neck of the lamb. Chuck is to lamb what it is to beef, but because the lamb is slaughtered at an earlier age than its beef counterpart, the meat is tenderer. Lamb *shanks* come from the front legs of the lamb, and although they can be roasted, we prefer them braised and moist-cooked. Our Aunt Mary made an especially good meat and tomato sauce for pasta, distinguished by the addition of a lamb shank. *Breast* of lamb can be delicious if it is boned, stuffed, rolled, and roasted or moist-cooked.

The *loin* of lamb, from the hindsaddle, gives us the equivalent of tenderloin, porterhouse, and filets mignons. It usually is cut into chops, which can be beautifully broiled with a touch of rosemary or oregano and garlic. The part of lamb with the most meat is the leg, and it is very popular in the United States. Its popularity has increased since charcoal grilling has gained in favor. Kabobs cut from a leg of lamb can be skewered, spiced, grilled, and garnished easily and tastily.

When lambs' tails are docked (cut off), the animals appear neater and blockier, more attractive to the market. We have uncovered a recipe for lambs' tail pudding, which is a traditional British country dish. Lambs' tails, docked in spring, are gathered, skinned, washed, and stewed until the meat, fat, and cartilaginous bones form a mass. This mass is then mixed with batter and potatoes and baked in the form of a pastry. (Lamb's testicles may not be substituted.)

Lamb, like other meats, combines well with goose liver and truffles. When it is enveloped in pastry, it is *à la périgourdine*. A great combination results if the young lamb is seasoned with butter and lemon, roasted on a spit, and served with a mint sauce. Or stuff a milk-fed baby lamb with rice to which lightly sautéed pieces of the animal's heart, liver, kidneys, and sweetbreads are added.

Lamb *shoulders* can be boned and stuffed with forcemeat, then tied, lardooned, and cooked with carrots, onion, faggots, and white wine. Or braise a shoulder after stuffing it with ham, bread crumbs, onion, and garlic.

There are many ways to combine lamb stew cuts (boned and cut from the neck and shoulder) with sauces. For example, brown the cubes, and combine them with white wine and tomato purée, deglazing the pan to which the lamb cubes were cooked or boiling down heavy cream with butter. Browned lamb cubes can be topped with a mixture of chopped shallots, parsley, tarragon, and lemon juice combined with the meat juices. In this chapter, we present lamb cubes cut from the leg or shoulder (Lamb, Cubed and Casseroled, in a Satisfying Stew).

Noisettes or *medallions* of lamb come from the loin or rib, weigh just several ounces each, and are trimmed to look like small filets mignons or tournedos. They are delicious and expensive and make some great combinations. Almost always sautéed in butter, they combine well with mushrooms, artichoke hearts, asparagus spears, Béarnaise sauce, potato balls, ham, grilled tomatoes. Madeira sauces, horseradish sauces, fried eggplant cubes, or rice pilaf. One of our favorite combinations involves sautéeing the noisette in butter (we like it medium rare for this), placing the lamb piece on top of a thin slice of toasted Italian or French bread, and serving it with steamed Brussels sprouts cooked in olive oil and garlic.

Legs of lamb are best prepared roasted, pot-roasted, or braised. One famous and great combination is to roast it, coated thickly with bread crumbs and chopped parsley. The only sauce it needs is its own juices. We add some finely chopped garlic to the mixture of parsley and bread crumb to make it a greater combination. Or just roast it plain and serve it with a mint sauce.

Our leg of lamb is roasted and merged with mint and ginger (Leg of Lamb à l'Orange, in this chapter), a second leg of lamb is braised with basil and olive oil (A Leg of Lamb, Simply Wined and Potted, also in this chapter).

Lamb chops, cut either from rib or loin, are grilled, broiled, sautéed, roasted, or braised. One distinguished preparation calls for braising the whole loin, allowing it to cool in its own juices, cutting the loin into chops, and glazing them in aspic jelly. Often, the chops are dipped in egg and bread crumbs mixed with parsley, other herbs, and truffles and sautéed in butter and oil. Chops can be combined with mushrooms, ham, potatoes, foie gras, shallots, or onions. We bring our lamb chops into unison with oregano and garlic in an old family recipe, Agnello Arrosto (also in this chapter).

LAMB, CUBED AND CASSEROLED, IN A SATISFYING STEW

GARLIC AND RED WINE   SERVES 4 TO 5

3 tablespoons olive oil
3 garlic cloves, whole
2½ pounds lamb leg or shoulder,
    cut into 1½-inch cubes
2 cups fresh tomatoes, chopped
    (or canned plum tomatoes)
1 teaspoon sugar
1½ teaspoons salt
1 teaspoon fresh basil, chopped
    fine (or ½ teaspoon dried)

½ teaspoon thyme
½ cup dry red wine
3 carrots, cut into 1-inch slices
1 cup lima beans, fresh or frozen
3 medium potatoes, cut into
    1-inch cubes
Pepper, ground fresh

In a heavy, covered 3-quart casserole, heat the oil, and add the garlic and lamb cubes, a few at a time. Sauté the lamb until brown. Skim off any fat in the casserole. Then add the tomatoes, sugar, salt, basil, thyme, and wine. Bring to a fast boil, reduce the heat, cover the casserole, and simmer for 1 hour.

Add the carrots and fresh limas, and cook for 10 minutes. Add the potatoes, and cook for 20 minutes, or until the vegetables are done. (If you're using frozen limas, cook them according to the directions on the package, and add them at the very end, just to heat them through for a few minutes.) Add the freshly ground pepper, and serve the stew with crusty Italian bread.

A LEG OF LAMB, SIMPLY WINED AND POTTED

BASIL AND OLIVE OIL   SERVES 6 TO 8

6-pound leg of lamb	*4 tablespoons fresh or frozen basil,*
4 or 5 garlic cloves, halved	*chopped (or 2 teaspoons dried)*
1 cup dry white wine	*Salt*
2 tablespoons olive oil	*Pepper, ground fresh*

With a small, sharp knife, make small incisions (evenly spaced) in the lamb, and insert a garlic half in each cut. Place the lamb in a Dutch oven, and add the wine. In a small dish or bowl, make a paste with the oil and basil; spread this paste on top of the lamb. Add salt and pepper to taste. Marinate the lamb for at least 2 hours (or overnight) in the refrigerator.

Bring the lamb to room temperature, cover the Dutch oven, and place it in a preheated 500-degree oven for 30 minutes. Then lower the heat to 325 degrees, and continue cooking for an additional 2 hours for a medium done roast. (For pinker meat, cook only an additional 1½ hours. For well-done meat cook an additional 2½ hours.) Keep the Dutch oven covered during entire cooking time except when you check the lamb and baste it every 15 minutes. Remove the garlic pieces before serving.

LEG OF LAMB A L'ORANGE

GINGER AND MINT   SERVES 6

*1 cup fresh orange juice
(approximately 2 oranges)
¼ cup soy sauce
¼ cup honey
1 tablespoon fresh mint, chopped
fine (or ½ teaspoon dried)
1 tablespoon fresh ginger,
chopped fine (or ½ teaspoon
powdered)*

*5½-pound leg of lamb, boned
and tied
3 garlic cloves, slivered
1 teaspoon salt
Pepper, ground fresh*

To make a marinade for the lamb, combine the orange juice, soy sauce, honey, mint, and ginger, and mix well.

With a small, sharp knife, cut openings evenly spaced in the skin of the meat, and insert a garlic sliver in each cut. Set the lamb in a baking pan, and pour the marinade mixture over it. Place the orange halves reserved from the juiced oranges on both sides of the meat. Scoop some of the marinade mixture into the orange halves. Marinate the lamb for 2 hours or more at room temperature, basting every 30 minutes.

Remove the lamb from the marinade, and wipe it dry. Reserve the marinade mixture. Place the orange halves in a shallow baking pan. Place a rack over the oranges and put the lamb on the rack. Salt and pepper the lamb, and place it in a preheated 450-degree oven for 15 minutes. Then cook at 350 degrees for 2½ hours. Brush the lamb with the marinade every 15 minutes. Remove the garlic slivers and orange halves before serving.

Note: Save the orange half shells after you have extracted the juice from them; they will be marinated and cooked with the lamb.

AGNELLO ARROSTO
(Roasted Lamb Chops)

OREGANO AND GARLIC   SERVES 4

3 tablespoons olive oil
8 shoulder lamb chops, 1½ inches
  thick
1 teaspoon oregano
1 teaspoon fresh or frozen basil,
  chopped fine (or ½ teaspoon
  dried)
1 teaspoon fresh parsley, chopped
  fine (or ½ teaspoon dried)
1 garlic clove, chopped fine

5 potatoes, peeled and cut into
  ¼-inch-thick slices
1 teaspoon salt
½ teaspoon sugar
¾ cup fresh or canned tomatoes,
  peeled, seeded and chopped
1 cup canned peas
2 tablespoons grated Parmesan
  cheese

Cut away most of the fat from chops. Oil a roasting pan with 1 table-spoon olive oil. Place the chops in the pan, and top each one with oregano, basil, parsley, and garlic. Add the potatoes to the pan alongside the chops. Add the salt and sugar to the tomatoes, and pour them over the chops and potatoes. Sprinkle 2 tablespoons olive oil on top of the chops and potatoes. Bake in a preheated 350-degree oven for 35 to 40 minutes.

For the last 5 minutes, add the peas mixed with cheese on top of potatoes.

Remove the chops and vegetables with a slotted spoon onto a large platter and serve immediately.

HERBED, ROASTED RACKS OF LAMB

BASIL AND BAY LEAVES   SERVES 6

TO MARINATE THE LAMB:

3 *cloves garlic, halved*

1 *tablespoon fresh tarragon,*
chopped fine (or 1 teaspoon
dried)

1 *tablespoon fresh or frozen basil,*
chopped fine (or 1 teaspoon
dried)

¼ *cup dry white wine (or dry*
vermouth)

2 *racks of lamb, trimmed neatly,*
fat scored

Combine the ingredients for the marinade, and mix them well. Place the racks of lamb in a pan just large enough to hold them, and pour the marinade over the meat. Allow to marinate at least 4 hours (or overnight, as we do) in the refrigerator. (If you marinate the lamb overnight, allow it to come to room temperature before you roast it.)

TO ROAST THE LAMB:

¼ *cup onions, chopped*

¼ *cup carrots, chopped*

¼ *cup celery, chopped*

12 *small potatoes, peeled and dried*

2 *bay leaves*

Salt

Pepper, ground fresh

Transfer the racks to a roasting pan, fat side up, and roast them in a preheated 450-degree oven for 15 minutes. Remove from the oven. Lift up the racks or move them aside in order to add the onions, carrots, and celery to the pan. Place the racks of lamb on top of these vegetables. Surround the lamb with the potatoes, and pour the marinade over the meat. Place 1 bay leaf on each rack. Salt and pepper liberally overall.

Reduce the oven heat to 350 degrees, and roast 1 hour or longer, depending on how well done you prefer lamb.

Cooked racks of lamb are attractive to look at and should be brought whole to the table. Each rack will adequately serve 3 people and we like to carve double chops for each person. Herbed Roasted Racks of Lamb are superb in combination with Potatoes in a Charlotte Mold (see page 328).

LAMB WITH AN APRICOT GLAZE

APRICOTS AND GINGER   SERVES 6 TO 8

1 cup apricots
½ cup sugar
½ cup orange juice
1 tablespoon fresh ginger,
    chopped (or ginger powder)
Salt
Pepper, ground fresh
5-pound leg of lamb

3 garlic cloves, sliced in half
    lengthwise
1 teaspoon fresh or frozen basil,
    chopped (or ½ teaspoon
    dried)
½ cup sherry
½ cup Madeira

In a small saucepan, cook the apricots, sugar, orange juice, and ginger until thickened. Put through a sieve, and set aside.

Trim the excess fat from the lamb, and wipe dry. With a sharp knife, make small incisions (evenly spaced) in the lamb, and insert a piece of garlic with the basil into each cut. Salt and pepper the lamb and place it on a rack in a roasting pan, and pour the sherry over the meat. Put ½ cup water in the bottom of the roasting pan. Cook for 1 hour in a preheated 350-degree oven.

Spread some of the apricot sauce on the top of the lamb, and roast 2 hours longer (30 minutes per pound), basting the lamb with the remaining sauce every 20 minutes or so. (When done, the lamb will have a lovely glazed look.) Remove the lamb to a platter, and let it stand for 20 minutes before slicing.

Meanwhile, remove as much of the fat as you can from the roasting pan. Put the pan on top of the stove, and pour the Madeira into the pan; with a whisk, mix well over medium heat. Allow this to simmer for about 10 minutes, whisking frequently. Strain, and serve with the lamb.

ROAST LEG OF LAMB WITH ANCHOVY SAUCE

ANCHOVIES AND LEMON   SERVES 8 TO 10

5- to 6-pound leg of lamb
2 garlic cloves, cut into 4 pieces
  crosswise
1 teaspoon dried rosemary
2 teaspoons fresh ginger root,
  chopped (or 1 teaspoon
  powdered)
1 tablespoon salt

Pepper, ground fresh
¾ cup dry vermouth
6 anchovy filets, chopped fine
2 tablespoons lemon zest,
  chopped fine
2 tablespoons shallots (or scal-
  lions) chopped fine

Wipe the leg of lamb clean with a tea towel, and with a small, sharp paring knife, cut 8 little pockets in the skin of the lamb. (Space the pockets evenly over the top of the leg.) Insert a piece of garlic into each slit.

In a mortar, combine the rosemary, ginger (fresh or dried), salt, and pepper to taste, and grind to a smooth paste with a pestle. (This is quite easy to do, but in case the herbs are too dry, add a few drops of vermouth to help create the paste.) Spread this paste all over the meat after you have set the leg of lamb, fat side up, on a rack in a roasting pan.

Place the lamb in a preheated 325- to 350-degree oven, and cook for 2 to 2½ hours, basting with the vermouth and pan juices every 15 minutes or so. When the leg of lamb is done, remove it from the oven and take out the garlic pieces. Transfer the roast to a serving platter, and allow it to sit for about 15 minutes before carving it.

Pour all the pan juices into a 1-cup measure. Skim off as much fat as you can. You should have 1 cup defatted pan juice; if you don't, add some hot water to make up the difference. (If by chance you have more than 1 cup, reserve the extra pan juices for another use. However, this is unlikely because the vermouth will have cooked away.) Pour the pan juices back into the roasting pan, add the anchovies, and cook on the stove top over medium heat until the anchovies are blended into the sauce. (This should take only 3 or 4 minutes.) Add the lemon zest and shallots or scallions. Bring just to the boil, remove from the heat, and serve sauce separately with the slices of lamb.

SKEWERS OF LAMB, PINEAPPLE, PEPPERS, AND OTHER THINGS

PINEAPPLE AND PEPPERS   SERVES 4

2 *pounds lamb shoulder, cut into*
   1½-inch cubes
10 *small onions, whole, parboiled*
   for 5 minutes
1 *fresh pineapple, skinned, cored,*
   and cut into 1½-inch cubes
   (see Note)
3 *Italian green peppers, cored,*
   seeded, and cut into 2-inch
   cubes
10 *small cherry tomatoes*

½ *cup soy sauce*
2 *tablespoons olive oil*
2 *garlic cloves, cut crosswise into*
   4 pieces
1 *teaspoon fresh or frozen basil,*
   chopped (or ½ teaspoon dried)
1 *tablespoon fresh ginger root,*
   peeled, grated, and ground (or
   ½ teaspoon powdered ginger)
Pepper, ground fresh

Mix all the ingredients listed above in a large ceramic or glass bowl. Add the lamb cubes, and marinate in the refrigerator overnight. (This is an important step; the time for marination should be from 12 to 24 hours.) Remove from the refrigerator to allow the lamb and other ingredients to come to room temperature before grilling. (This will take about 2 hours.)

On 10-inch skewers, alternate the lamb cubes, pineapple, green peppers, onions, and tomatoes. Place the skewers over the charcoal about 4 inches from the flame, and brush frequently with the reserved marinade. Turn the skewers often, and cook for 15 minutes, or until the lamb is done to your taste. This dish can also be cooked under the broiler.

Note: You will need about 16 pieces of pineapple; reserve the rest for another use. If you substitute canned pineapple, the taste will be significantly altered. You really should make every effort to use fresh pineapple cubes for this dish.

A GALANTINE OF LAMB

MARSALA AND PISTACHIOS   SERVES 10

TO MARINATE THE LAMB:

5-pound leg of lamb, boned
1½ cups of Marsala
1 teaspoon dried rosemary

Ask your butcher to bone the leg of lamb for you. Our butcher sews the
leg by tacking it in places with string: the overall effect is a somewhat
oblong-shaped piece of meat with one of the narrower sides open in order
to take the stuffing. Also have the butcher grind the salt pork, veal, and
pork together.

Wipe the lamb clean with a kitchen towel, and put it in a large bowl
or pan. (Do *not* use an aluminum pan; choose one of glass, earthenware,
or enameled metal.) Pour the Marsala over the meat, and sprinkle the
meat with the rosemary. (Before you add the rosemary, rub it between
the palms of your hands to pulverize it, or grind it in a mortar with a
pestle.) Allow the lamb to marinate in the refrigerator overnight, or for
at least 12 hours. Turn the meat several times during the marination.
Remove the meat from the refrigerator, and allow it to come to room
temperature (about 1 hour) before stuffing and cooking it. Reserve the
marinade.

TO PREPARE THE FILLING:

¼ pound prosciutto, chopped fine   *½ pound lean veal, ground fine*
¼ cup pistachio nuts, shelled   *½ pound lean pork, ground fine*
1 truffle, preferably black,   *1 tablespoon orange zest,*
  chopped fine   *chopped fine*
¼ cup Marsala   *Salt*
¼ pound salt pork, ground fine   *Pepper, ground fresh*

While the meat is reaching room temperature, combine the prosciutto,
pistachios, truffle pieces, and Marsala, and allow this mixture to marinate for 2 or 3 hours. Then combine this with the ground salt pork,

veal, and pork. Add the orange zest and salt and freshly ground pepper to taste, and mix well. Stuff the boned leg of lamb. (We usually find it necessary to secure the opening after the lamb has been stuffed; this can be done easily by sewing it.)

The key step in preparing this galantine is to tie the meat properly. The cloth you use may be cheesecloth, a torn sheet, or a large kitchen towel, but be sure it's one large piece. Spread out the cloth on a flat surface, and put the narrower end of the leg at one edge of the cloth; there should be at least 6 inches of cloth on each side of it. Enclose the meat in the cloth, tightening the cloth as you go along. When it is fully rolled, secure the cloth with a safety pin, sew it, or tie it in 2 or 3 places. Tighten the cloth at each end, and tie each end with string as tightly as you can. You will end up with an odd-shaped sausage, but the meat will be encased (like sausage meat).

Put the wrapped lamb in a large, heavy, covered saucepan. Pour in the reserved marinade, and add just enough water to cover the meat. Also add about 1 teaspoon of salt to the water. Cover the saucepan, and bring to a boil. Then lower the heat, and simmer for 2 hours. Remove the meat from the water, and allow it to cool for 15 or 20 minutes.

Unwrap the cooked lamb, and rinse the cloth in fresh cool water several times. Rewrap the meat, in the same way as before, being absolutely sure to tie the cloth as tight as you can. Put the wrapped meat on a flat platter or tray, and weight it down. (You'll have to improvise this, but one of the easiest ways is to put another plate or platter on top of the meat and top that with a heavy can of juice, an iron, or whatever.) It will have to remain weighted in the refrigerator until the following day.

Remove the weights, strings, and cloth. Slice thin, and garnish with a sprig of parsley or watercress. This galantine makes an excellent buffet dish because it can be prepared well ahead of time and requires no last-minute care.

((10))

Potatoes in a Charlotte Mold, Eggplant Oval Puffs, and Other Vegetables

THERE'S tragedy in a meal if a cook selects a prime piece of meat, cooks it *par excellence*, and then serves a stale, overcooked, tasteless mishmash of vegetables with it. Americans, as a rule, fit this description. On the other hand, we've rarely eaten poorly prepared vegetables in Europe or in the homes of Americans with European backgrounds. And by no means do the Europeans walk away with the blue ribbons. Chinese and Japanese vegetable preparations are even better.

On a recent trip to Rome, we decided to stay in a new hotel on the outskirts of the city. The setting was an upper-class area of new apartment houses. In the middle of all this chic, we found a square block of vegetable, meat, and fish stands—everything bright and fresh and attractively displayed. This surprise occurs in America, too. You can find fresh vegetables in U.S. supermarkets, but you will have to check and recheck the plastic packs. Fortunately, really fresh vegetables are available in many open-air shops across the country. We encourage you to seek fresh, young vegetables wherever and whenever you can.

Throughout this book, we make comments about the quality of

vegetables and other foods whenever we feel it necessary to do so. If you want to know more about spinach, look in the Index. Carrots? Cauliflower? Look in the Index. It won't be as good as having Nonna Beatrica or Mamma Angela at your side, but you'll get some of their *consiglio* ("advice").

If we had to choose one family of foods to live with for the rest of our lives, we would choose vegetables. There are so many vegetables and so many ways to cook them. Moreover, we can't think of more beautiful things to *look* at. What can compare with the shape, color, or gleam of a bright red tomato; a smooth-as-silk, deep purple *aubergine*; the pure white mound of a mushroom; a bunch of carrots, with their fernlike ends; lacy celery hearts; fresh, pale green dandelion leaves; a majestic artichoke; a family of garlic cloves; the regal leek; the beauty and mystery of the inner rings of an onion?

Our choice of vegetables as *the* food is also based on the fact that all the essentials of a balanced diet can be found in vegetables. There are proteins, carbohydrates, fats, minerals, and vitamins. These elements vary in amount from one vegetable to the next, but in no other food group is there more complete nourishment.

Meat and potatoes are only the beginning of great combinations. All kinds of vegetables combine with all kinds of meat, fish, poultry, game, pastas, and eggs. And, of course, vegetables combine wonderfully with each other. What about cool green salads composed of various lettuces, each with its own color, texture, and taste. The combination may be elaborated by adding basil or tarragon, parsley or peppers. Or add new beet leaves or sorrel or the palest blush of a nasturtium bud. Think of fresh garden peas with butter, fresh corn on the cob with butter and salt. We love navy beans with molasses, sweet potatoes with brown sugar, leeks with lemon, asparagus with hollandaise, carrots with cream. And then there's the combination of thin slices of Spanish onions and oranges.

Here are some combinations for which we have not included full recipes. You can read between the lines and cook them anyway:

Shred zucchini, add salt, and cook it in sour cream, dill, and paprika.

Combine boiled potatoes with some lemon juice, butter, sugar, salt, freshly ground pepper, and finely chopped lemon zest. An interesting way to prepare this is to put the mixture through a potato ricer.

Combine a casserole assortment of zucchini, string beans, potatoes, and whole eggs. Just break the eggs open over the vegetables in the baking pan. Season this with Parmesan cheese, garlic, basil, parsley, salt, and fresh ground pepper, and sprinkle fresh bread crumbs overall.

Heat chick peas, sliced scallions, and slivers of roasted red peppers in one of the oil and vinegar dressings given on pages 359–364.

Instead of spinach, broccoli, and cheese soufflés, use butternut squash or another squash variety, such as Hubbard, and accent it with curry or ginger. With 3 eggs, you'll need about 1½ cups of cooked squash.

Stir-fry snow peas in peanut oil with some salt, sugar, and several table-spoons of Rich Chicken Stock (see page 49).

We think you'll like our vegetable combinations we present in this chapter. Rollatini di Melanzano are thin slices of eggplant filled with ricotta, basil, and shallots, rolled, and then baked in a sauce of tomato and roasted red pepper. Our Chestnut Purée is combined with fennel. And because we enjoy our lentil soup with lots of celery, our lentil purée is, of course, combined with celery. Our broccoli-rape cooked and then combined with garlic and olive oil, has to be made at home; we've never seen it as restaurant fare. This is true, too, of Peppers and Tomatoes al Gennaro. Although we have included Angela's Stuffed Artichokes (page 10) with appetizers, this dish can be served as a vegetable, too. Mamma Angela, tired of meat stuffings, as we often are, stuffs her artichokes with bread crumbs, parsley, garlic, and the barest hint of pork sausage.

CARCIOFI QUARTATI
(Artichokes in Quarters)

OLIVE OIL AND LEMON   SERVES 4

4 medium-size artichokes
2 tablespoons olive oil
1 tablespoon butter
1 garlic clove, chopped fine
1 tablespoon fresh tarragon,
chopped fine (or ½ teaspoon
dried)
1 tablespoon fresh parsley,
chopped fine (or 1 teaspoon
dried)

Juice of 1 lemon
1 cup Rich Chicken or Veal Stock
(see pages 49, 48)
Salt
Pepper, ground fresh

Clean and prepare the artichokes (see page 9). Be sure to dry the artichoke quarters with paper towels or a tea towel; otherwise they will not sauté properly.

In a large, covered skillet or saucepan, heat the oil, butter, garlic, tarragon, parsley, and lemon juice. Add the artichoke quarters, and sauté them, uncovered, for about 5 minutes. Add the stock and bring it to a boil. Lower the heat, cover, simmer for 12 to 15 minutes, until the artichokes are tender. Be sure to turn them once during this period. (Do *not* overcook the artichokes.)

Most of the liquid in the skillet will cook away; the artichokes will have absorbed some of the liquid, too. Salt and pepper to taste, and serve hot.

Asparagus

There are many varieties of asparagus. The best known are the French *Argenteuil*, white; the *German* and *Belgian*, white; the *Italian* or *Genoa*, purple; and the commonly found *green* asparagus. The battle between green and white asparagus enthusiasts continues, and the argument will probably go on ad infinitum. Actually, both kinds are delicious.

If you grow your own asparagus, you know what fresh quality is like. There is almost nothing more delicious than fresh-picked asparagus boiled immediately and served even faster, with a spoonful of butter. If only there were a chain of gardens to sell asparagus in the come-pick-your-own fashion. Most people, alas, have to depend on the local grocer or supermarket. We think it's best to avoid plastic-wrapped bunches; buy asparagus loose if you can, so that you can look it over carefully. The lower portion of the stem should be whitish with pink overtones, and the stem should be fairly smooth. Pick up a stalk. It should be firm, not limp.

Home grown or "store boughten," asparagus is simply cooked.

There are two things to do to help any asparagus stalk taste better:

Hold the stalk horizontally with both hands; bend it by moving your hands downward (or upward) to the point where it snaps or breaks in two. Discard the lower part of the stalk, and keep the upper portion for cooking. (We keep the bottom stalks and use them in soups and stocks for flavor, but they're too fibrous for eating plain.)

Use a vegetable peeler to peel the lower part of the usable stalk, just as you would peel a potato, carrot, or cucumber.

Although they grow out of the ground, asparagus are often filled with sand and grit. Soak them in cool, salted water for 30 minutes or longer, then rinse them several times before cooking. Stand the bunch upright in a narrow, deep pan, and add boiling water up to the beginning of the flower portion. (The tips cook by steaming.) We use a 6- or 8-cup coffee percolator, which is an ideal cooking utensil for asparagus. The percolating cup unit is removed, of course, and the cover is put on. This process rarely takes more than 10 minutes, less if the asparagus are really fresh and if you like them *al dente*.

A 2-pound bunch of fresh asparagus can be stretched to serve six people, but it's better for four.

ASPARAGUS, MAMMA ANGELA'S STYLE

ASPARAGUS AND EGGS   SERVES 6

1 cup vegetable oil (or peanut or corn oil)	2 eggs, well beaten
	Salt
18 medium-size asparagus stalks	Pepper, ground fresh
1 cup all-purpose flour	1 to 1½ cups fresh bread crumbs

Heat the oil in a large, heavy skillet. While the oil is heating, roll each asparagus stalk in the flour, and shake off any excess. Dip the stalk in the beaten egg, to which you've added salt and freshly ground pepper to taste. Next, roll the stalk in the bread crumbs. Put the stalk in the hot oil, and cook it until lightly browned (about 5 minutes) on all sides. (Do *not* overcook the stalks; they should be *al dente*.)

This dish is easy to prepare if you set up for it properly. Keep the scraped asparagus stalks in iced water until you are ready to use them. Dry the stalks, and have three plates lined up in a row: one for the flour, one for the eggs, and one for the bread crumbs. Follow an assembly-line routine: While the first stalk is cooking in the oil, prepare the next one and add it to the oil; and so on. They cook quickly and are at their best if eaten just as soon as they are done. However, they will keep in a warm oven for up to 1 hour; place them on a baking tray, making sure that the stalks are not touching.

ASPARAGUS IN THE FLEMISH STYLE

BUTTER AND LEMON   SERVES 4 TO 6

2 pounds white asparagus,   2 tablespoons fresh parsley
    canned or fresh (see Note)   chopped fine (or 1 teaspoon
½ pound butter, melted   dried)
2 tablespoons fresh lemon juice   Salt
4 hard-boiled eggs, chopped fine   Pepper, ground fresh

Heat the canned or bottled white asparagus in their own juice (or cook fresh green stalks according to the instructions on page 302). Drain the stalks, and arrange them in a neat stack on a napkin-covered plate to dry them completely. (Fold the sides of the napkin across the asparagus and then fold the ends or flaps up and over to keep the asparagus covered and warm.) The asparagus are attractive served this way.

Combine the butter, lemon juice, chopped egg, parsley, and salt and pepper to taste, and serve this sauce at room temperature in a separate dish.

Note: French, Belgian, and German asparagus, all white, can be found fresh in specialty markets, but they are expensive. This is one time we suggest that you give in and buy canned or bottled imports—big, fat, juicy asparagus, and very tender. You can, of course, use the fresh green American variety in this recipe.

Beans

One could almost write the history of man by examining his use of the bean. We've always been fascinated with the use of the uncooked bean in ancient Rome: The Romans, in their elections, voted pro with a white bean and con with a black one. Bean-bags may be temporarily out of vogue as toys, but what about that decorator fashion, the bean-bag chair? Broad bean or butter, soy or string, fava or French—beans grow all over the world, in endless varieties. Who has not eaten haricot, kidney, navy, or pinto beans?

PUREED FLAGEOLETS WITH THE FLAVOR OF BRITTANY

ONIONS AND SALT PORK   SERVES 8

1 pound French dried beans
  (flageolets) (or 1 pound dried
  white beans)
3 cups water
¼ pound salt pork, in one piece
1 large carrot, cut into ½-inch
  slices
1½ cups onions, chopped coarse
2 garlic cloves, chopped fine
1 bay leaf
3 sprigs fresh thyme, chopped
  fine (or 1 teaspoon dried)
1 cup fresh tomatoes, cored,
  blanched, peeled, and
  chopped coarse (or canned
  plum tomatoes, drained)

4 tablespoons butter
  Salt
  Pepper, ground fresh
½ cup soda or salt cracker
  crumbs
2 shallots, chopped fine
4 tablespoons fresh parsley,
  chopped fine (or 2
  teaspoons dried)

Rinse the *flageolets* (or white beans) in a colander, and remove any that are darkened or blemished, or any foreign matter you may find.

Rinse the beans again under running water several times. Put them in a large saucepan, cover them with water (about 1 inch over the top of the beans), and let them soak overnight at room temperature. (If you don't have time to soak the beans overnight, bring them to a fast boil. Remove the saucepan from the heat, cover it, and set it aside for 1 hour.)

If you have soaked the beans overnight, drain them, return them to the saucepan, and add 3 cups water. (If you preboiled them, they will have absorbed the water.) But if any water is left, drain the beans, and return them to the saucepan. Add 3 cups fresh water.) Add the salt pork, carrot, onions, garlic, bay leaf, thyme, and tomatoes. Bring these ingredients to a boil, and simmer for about 1 hour; then remove the salt pork, and set it aside to cool. Continue simmering the beans for an additional 50 minutes to 1 hour, or until they are cooked through and very tender. (The total cooking time for the beans over low heat will be about 2 hours. This does *not* include the 1 hour cooking time if you preboil the beans rather than soak them overnight.) Discard the bay leaf. If during the cooking time, all the moisture is cooked off, add a little hot water. (But do *not* add too much liquid. The beans will be puréed, and they should have a thick consistency.)

When the salt pork is cool enough to handle, cut it into ¼-inch cubes, and sauté them in a skillet until lightly browned. Set aside.

When the beans are cooked, put them through a food processor, 2 cups at a time. (If you use a blender, blend about 1 cup at a time, and be sure *not* to overblend.) Put the puréed beans in a shallow baking dish or casserole. Salt and pepper to taste.

Use a rolling pin to crush enough soda (or salt) crackers to make about ½ cup of crumbs. (Roll hard and steadily so that the crumbs will be fine.) Combine the crumbs, shallots, salt pork pieces, and parsley; sprinkle this mixture over the top of the puréed beans, and dot with butter. If the purée needs reheating, heat in a 400-degree oven for 15 minutes. If not, put the dish under the broiler only until the crumbs take on a bit of color and the butter is melted.

Flageolets fantastiques. Fagioli fantastici! They are fabulous and we can't help getting carried away.

BLACK-EYED PEAS AND SALT PORK

BLACK-EYED PEAS AND SALT PORK
SERVES 4 TO 6

1 pound dried black-eyed peas
1½ quarts water
¼ pound salt pork, cut into
  ¼ inch cubes
¼ teaspoon hot red pepper flakes
1 slice bacon

2 medium-size onions, chopped fine
1½ cups chicken stock or broth
1 cup rice, uncooked
Salt (if needed)

Put the dried black-eyed peas in a colander; wash and drain them, and pick them over to remove any foreign-looking matter. Then put them in a bowl, add 1½ quarts water, and let them soak overnight at room temperature. (Some packers provide instructions for quicker cooking of dried peas. These instructions are dependable, so take advantage of them if you're short of time.)

The next day, put the peas (and the water they soaked in) in a heavy, covered saucepan. Add the salt pork cubes and pepper flakes, cover the pan, and cook slowly for 20 minutes.

While the peas are cooking, fry the bacon until it is well done, remove it from the skillet, and set it aside to drain. Sauté the onion in the bacon fat until it turns pale yellow. In a separate saucepan, bring the stock to a boil. Crumble the bacon slice, and add it to the black-eyed peas, along with the onion, boiling stock, and raw rice. Cover the saucepan, and continue to simmer over low heat until the rice is cooked. (This will take no longer than 20 minutes if everything was at the boiling point when you added the rice.) Adjust seasoning. (We doubt you'll want more pepper, but you may wish a dash more salt.)

This dish may be served with pork; we also like it with lamb, the white meat of chicken or turkey, or a simple omelet and salad at lunchtime. Splendid combinations all.

ANGELA'S BROCCOLI DI RAPE

GARLIC AND OLIVE OIL   SERVES 4 TO 6

4 cups cooked broccoli di rape   *1 dried hot chili pepper*
   (*see Note*)   (*optional*)
¾ cup cooking liquid   *Salt*
⅓ cup olive oil   *Pepper, ground fresh*
1 clove garlic, chopped fine

Wash the *broccoli di rape* well and cut off the ends. Remove the strings on the larger stalks just as you would on a large celery stalk. Cut the larger *broccoli di rape* leaves in half. If you are not ready to cook them, let them stand in cool water.

In a large saucepan, bring 2 or 3 cups of water to a boil. Add 1 teaspoon salt and bring the water to a rapid boil. Add the *broccoli di rape* and cook them until they are just tender (*not* beyond the *al dente* point). Depending on the size and freshness of the stalks, this will take 5 to 10 minutes.

Remove them from the boiling water immediately and transfer them to a bowl. A fork or slotted spoon works best for this. Reserve about ¾ cup of the water in which the *broccoli di rape* were cooked.

In a large saucepan, heat the olive oil, and sauté the garlic until it turns pale yellow. (Do *not* let it brown.) Add the hot chili pepper (if you wish). Now add the cooked *broccoli di rape* and ¾ cup of its cooking liquid. You must do this *very* carefully because the hot oil will sizzle and splatter as you add the liquid. Bring to a boil, and remove from the heat. (Do *not* overcook.) Add salt and pepper to taste. Serve immediately.

Note: Broccoli di rape is a bitter-flavored cousin of broccoli. The stalks are thin and long and the leaves resemble those of regular broccoli. But *broccoli di rape* do *not* have the large, tightly closed heads of broccoli; instead, they have tufts of flowerets here and there throughout the stalks.

Although our family has served *broccoli di rape* for as long as we can remember, we're unable to describe the origin of this tasty green vegetable. We are not among those who believe it derives from the turnip or mustard green. Nonetheless, you should try preparing it in

Angela's style. To add to the confusion about its origin, it is marketed under the names of *broccoli rape, broccoli rabe, rapini, rappini* and even *raab*. Combined with olive oil, garlic and red pepper it is simply superb.

Cauliflower

When you buy cauliflower, select a white head, with tightly packed flowers and fresh green leaves. If the flesh has discolored, the flowers have spread, or the leaves have grayed, you'll have a tough, chewy vegetable to deal with.

We remove the leaves and scoop out most of the stalk. This is done by turning cauliflower upside down, carving with a paring knife into the center stalk, and removing the bulk of it. Don't cut too deeply, or you'll end up with flowerettes instead of a whole cauliflower. We always put the cleaned head in salted cool water for at least 30 minutes. According to old family folklore, this was the way to rid the head of worms.

A WHOLE CAULIFLOWER, SAUCED AND CRUMBED

LEMON AND CREAM   SERVES 6

1 medium-size fresh head of
    cauliflower, whole
4 tablespoons butter
4 tablespoons all-purpose flour
2 cups Rich Chicken Stock or
    broth (see page 49)
Salt

Pepper, ground fresh
2 egg yolks
Juice of 1 lemon
½ cup heavy cream
⅓ to ½ cup fine bread crumbs
Paprika

Prepare the cauliflower head as described in the preceding paragraph; be sure to soak it, head down, in cool salted water. If the head bobs above the water, weight it down with a plate or anything that will keep it submerged.

Cook the cauliflower, head up, in boiling salted water until tender (about 20 minutes, depending upon the size of the head). (Do *not* overcook; if you do, the cauliflower will break into pieces as you remove it from the boiling water.) Test for doneness by inserting a fork into a thick stalk section. It should be *al dente*.

While the cauliflower is cooking, prepare the sauce. Melt the butter in a saucepan, add the flour, and whisk constantly to blend well. Cook for 2 minutes; then slowly add and blend in the chicken stock. Add salt and pepper to taste. When all is blended, lower the heat. In a bowl, beat the egg yolks with the lemon juice. Carefully beat in the heavy cream. Stir about ⅓ cup of the hot sauce into the egg yolk and cream mixture, and then stir this into the hot remaining sauce. Bring the sauce just to the boiling point. When the cauliflower is done, drain it. (We do this by first pouring off the water into a colander and then emptying the head into the colander.) Transfer the head, stalk end down, to an ovenproof platter. (The cauliflower will be very hot, but you will be able to handle it if you use kitchen toweling and lift it with both hands.)

Pour the sauce over the cauliflower head; do this slowly so that the sauce penetrates the head as much as possible. Sprinkle the bread crumbs over the head and some paprika, too. Place this under the broiler until the bread crumbs brown. Serve immediately.

A SAUCE VARIATION:
Add 1 teaspoon curry powder and 2 tablespoons finely chopped fresh ginger (even candied ginger will do) to the saucepan after the butter and flour have been blended. (It is important to cook the curry powder with the roux.) Follow the remaining steps to complete the sauce.

CAULIFLOWER, SCALLIONS, AND RED PEPPERS IN THE CHINESE STYLE

SCALLIONS AND RED PEPPERS   SERVES 4 TO 6

1 head fresh cauliflower	1 tablespoon soy sauce
2 tablespoons fresh ginger root	1 tablespoon rice wine (or dry
4 scallions	sherry)
1 sweet red bell pepper (or 2	½ teaspoon cornstarch
fresh red cherry peppers)	1 tablespoon cool water
⅓ cup Rich Chicken Stock or	2 tablespoons peanut oil
Broth (see page 49)	

Select, clean, and soak the cauliflower head as described in the introduction to these recipes. Cut the head into 1-inch flowerettes. If the stalks are thick, pare them down with a swivel vegetable peeler, or cut them back with a small sharp knife (as you might whittle). Put the flowerettes in a salad drier, and twirl them dry; then wrap them in a tea towel. Set aside.

Cut several thin slices from a piece of fresh ginger root, peel the slices, and dice them as fine as you can (less than ⅛-inch cubes). Set aside.

Wash and dry the scallions, removing the outer layers if necessary. Slice them crosswise as thin as you can; include the green portion if it is tender. Set aside.

Wash and dry the pepper(s), and remove the stem(s) and seeds. Cut the pepper lengthwise into ¼-inch strips and then into ¼-inch dice. Set aside.

In a small bowl, combine the stock (or broth), soy sauce, and rice wine (or sherry), and set aside. Dissolve the cornstarch in the water, and set aside. (We apologize for all the "set asides," but as you know, that kind of preparation is an essential part of the Chinese style. There's nothing odd in *doing* it, just in *writing* about it.)

And now for cooking all the "set asides." It is not absolutely necessary to cook this dish in a wok (you *can* use a large skillet), but we're doing this in the Chinese style, so we'll assume a wok. (We prefer the wok; in fact, we use it for many things unknown to Chinese cookery.)

Pour the oil into the wok, and bring it to a high heat (but do *not* let it smoke. Add the ginger pieces, and toss them constantly until they turn amber. Add the scallions and peppers, and stir-fry them until they are heated through (which should take only a couple of minutes). (We use a pair of chopsticks and stir constantly.)

Now divide the cauliflowerettes into 4 portions (do this visually). Add 1 portion at a time, and toss quickly to get some of the oil on each piece. Repeat, stirring constantly, until all the cauliflower is in the wok.

Add the mixture of stock, soy sauce, and wine to the wok. It should come to a boil quickly because the wok is very hot. Turn the heat down somewhat (if you need to), and add the cornstarch. Cook over high heat for several minutes, and keep tossing or turning the cauliflower and other vegetables to coat them with the sauce.

Vegetables prepared in the Chinese style should be *undercooked*. Serve immediately.

PUREE OF CELERY AND LENTILS

CELERY AND LENTILS   SERVES 8 TO 12

1½ *quarts water*
  1 *medium- to large-size celery*
    head
  1 *pound lentils*
  ½ *pound potatoes, peeled and*
    cut into ½-inch cubes
  2 *small onions, chopped coarse*
  1 *large or 2 small garlic cloves,*
    chopped fine
  1 *bay leaf*

Salt
Pepper, ground fresh
  (*preferably white*)
1 *cup* (*approximately*) *light*
  cream
6 *tablespoons butter*
½ *cup fine bread crumbs*
1 *tablespoon grated Parmesan*
  cheese

Pour the water into a large, heavy saucepan, and set aside.

Separate the celery stalks, wash them well, and scrape off the stringy outer layer of the larger outside stalks. (It's easy to do this with a vegetable peeler.) Cut the stalks, including the leaves, crosswise into thin slices (less than ¼-inch thick), and put them into the saucepan with the water.

Put the lentils into a colander; wash and drain them, picking them over to remove discolored or odd-looking lentils or foreign matter. (We always seem to find something that doesn't belong there no matter how good the lentil packer.) Add the lentils to the saucepan.

Add the potatoes, onions, garlic pieces, bay leaf, and salt and pepper to taste. Bring these ingredients to a boil, and simmer for 35 to 40 minutes, or until the lentils and potatoes are done. We usually remove several lentils and 2 pieces of potato and test their "mashability.")

When the vegetables are cooked, drain them, and put them through a food mill. Whip them in an electric mixer or blender, or put them through a food processor in batches. Add the cream and butter, and blend these well into the purée. (Add less or more cream to obtain the consistency you wish.) Test for seasoning, and add more salt and pepper if you want.

Put the purée in a baking dish. (We find the classic white French-type soufflé dish, which comes in many sizes, useful and attractive. Sprinkle the purée with the bread crumbs and Parmesan cheese. Reheat in a hot oven (400 degrees) for 10 to 15 minutes, and serve.

Celery and lentils are always tasty in combination, and lentil soup is more delicious if you add 1 or 2 cups of celery pieces to it.

Chestnuts

It is only natural that two lands of great cuisines, Italy and France, are the main exporters of the *castagna*, the *marron*, the chestnut. This sweet brown nut is extremely popular in both countries, and like the almond, it can be boiled, mashed, roasted, and blended. No wonder it has found its way into kitchens in many other parts of the world. In addition to enhancing turkey and chicken stuffings and dressings, chestnuts may be used in combination with cream, chocolate, and Cognac. Classically, chestnut purées are made with celery; for example, in *marrons braises* (braised chestnuts), they are combined with a bouquet garni, some butter, lots of celery, and a dash of concentrated veal stock. Celery is also an ingredient in the traditional *marrons étuve pour garniture* (which are stewed chestnuts used as a garnish for main dishes). The peeled chestnuts are put in a buttered pan and covered with a white stock (or water), salt, sugar, and celery. They are simmered for almost 1 hour, or until they are tender. In this chapter, we present them combined elegantly with fresh fennel and puréed. (Fennel, as we've said before, is an underutilized vegetable in this country. Whenever we find it in our local supermarket, we buy it and decide what to do with it later. Fennel will keep for several weeks in the refrigerator crisper.) As the Italians say, *incantevole* ("delightful").

CHESTNUT PUREE

CHESTNUTS AND FENNEL   SERVES 8

*3 cups dried chestnuts (or 4
   cups fresh peeled chestnuts)
   (see Note)
5 cups warm water
4 cups Rich Beef Stock or
   broth (see page 46)
1¼ cups fresh fennel, including
   leaves, chopped fine*

*2 pieces lemon zest, each about
   1 by 2 inches
6 tablespoons butter
½ cup heavy cream
Salt
Pepper, ground fresh
1 teaspoon Pernod (optional)*

Soak the dried chestnuts in 5 cups warm water, covered, overnight. Drain them, and remove any parts of the inner reddish skin remaining on the chestnuts. (They will peel off easily after soaking; use a paring knife.) Pick over the chestnuts to remove any blemishes.

Put the chestnuts in a heavy, covered saucepan, and add 3 cups stock (or broth), fennel pieces, and lemon zest, and bring this to a boil. (Use only 3 cups stock to start with. As the chestnuts cook, they will absorb the stock, and you may have to add part or all of the remaining cup.) Cover, and simmer for 1 hour, or until the chestnuts are tender. When the chestnuts are done, remove and discard the lemon peel.

Use a food processor, blender, or sieve to purée the chestnuts. Add the butter and heavy cream, and mix well, until the butter is thoroughly melted and combined. Season with salt and fresh ground pepper to taste, and add the Pernod (if you wish). The purée should be very thick. (To achieve the consistency you wish, add more or less of the heavy cream and the stock.)

Put this mixture in a shallow baking dish, dot with additional butter, and keep it in a warm oven (325 degrees) until it is ready to be served.

Note: Although we prefer to use fresh chestnuts, the dried variety, when cooked in this way, are almost indistinguishable from their fresh friends. Dried chestnuts are easy to work with, and they will save you a lot of time. They can be found in specialty grocery stores across the nation; they are sold loose, by the pound, and are quite inexpensive compared with the imported cans of chestnut purée. If you use canned purée for this recipe, you will need four 8¾-ounce cans to serve eight. Cook the chopped fennel in enough beef stock to cover until very tender. Drain, and purée. Add to the chestnut purée, and heat. Add the butter, cream, salt, pepper, and Pernod (if you wish).

Corn

Corn may be even more American than the proverbial apple pie. It was first carried to Europe by Columbus, but within two generations of his voyage to the New World, the vegetable was known throughout Europe and as far afield as Africa, India, China, and Tibet. Corn is now considered a staple all over the world. The corn plant is hardy as well as practical; every part of it is used for one purpose or another. And an encyclopedia informs us that a crop of corn matures somewhere in the world every month of the year. Corn participates in many great combinations: for example, with lardoons of salt pork to make corn chowder, with green pepper to make corn in the south-of-the-border manner, with eggs to make fritters, and with pimientos to make a salad. You can muffin it, waffle it, and cream it.

The ideal way to cook corn is fresh from the garden. Husk it, and cook it as quickly as you can. But for most of us, this is rarely possible. Fortunately, refrigerating the corn helps keep it fresh for a little while longer. To check for freshness, there's Grandmother's fingernail test: Press a fingernail into a kernel (even if you have to open the husk). If you discover milky drops, your chances that the ear of corn is young and tender are increased.

We think the best way to cook corn on the cob is to combine water and milk in equal amounts to cover the corn and bring the liquid to a boil. Then put the ears of corn into the boiling liquid, cover, and cook for 6 or 7 minutes. And the best way to serve corn on the cob is with softened butter, salt, and pepper.

Corn flour or corn meal is, of course, the basis for corn bread, which is almost as popular as corn on the cob. Corn bread or sticks should be served piping hot, straight from the oven, and smothered with butter.

In this chapter, we offer two of our favorite corn recipes: Corn Custard in the Tara North Style and Corn and Saffron Soufflé.

CORN CUSTARD IN THE TARA NORTH STYLE

2 cups fresh corn kernels (see   *Salt*
  Note)   *White pepper*
3 eggs, room temperature   *3 tablespoons butter, melted*
¼ cup all-purpose flour   *2 cups light cream*

Follow the instructions for cooking fresh corn (page 314). Then scrape enough kernels to fill 2 cups (this may take 5 to 8 ears of corn, depending on size of kernels and ears).

Beat the eggs until the whites and yolks are well blended. Add the corn, and mix well. Then combine the flour with the salt (about 1 teaspoon; less if you're watching your salt) and white pepper (about ½ teaspoon). White pepper is essential here because this custard (or pudding, as others call it) is the palest yellow and white combination; specks of dark pepper would look like strange or foreign matter. Beat the flour, salt, and pepper into the corn and egg mixture, and stir well. Then add the melted butter (be sure it's *not* hot) and light cream.

Liberally butter a baking dish (the 1½-quart size, 7½ by 9 by 3½, is ideal). Pour the corn mixture into this dish, and set it in a larger baking pan. Create a bain-marie by filling the larger pan with warm water up to 1 inch of the top of the smaller baking dish.

In a preheated 325- to 350-degree oven, bake for about 1 hour, until the custard is set. Test for doneness by inserting a clean knife into the center of the baking dish. If it comes out dry and fairly clean, the custard is done; if not, cook a little longer.

This dish can hold for 5 or 10 minutes, but it should be served promptly.

Note: We've often been asked if frozen or canned niblets can be used for this recipe. Our answer is yes, but we always explain that the end product will be somewhat different. This dish is light and tender and requires light and tender kernels—fresh ones, right off the cob. Nevertheless, frozen or canned corn is preferable to the old cobs one finds in some supermarkets.

CORN AND SAFFRON SOUFFLE

> 1½ cups fresh corn kernels
> 6 eggs, separated, room temperature
> 1 teaspoon saffron powder
> 1 teaspoon salt
> 2 egg whites, room temperature

Follow the instructions for cooking fresh corn (page 314). Scrape enough kernels to make 1½ (at least 6 ears of corn, depending on size of kernels and ears).

See comments (on page 315) about substituting frozen or canned corn for fresh kernels.

In a blender, combine the 6 egg yolks, saffron powder, fresh corn, and salt until well blended.

Whip the 8 egg whites until they hold stiff peaks. (Do *not* overbeat; if you do, they will become dry and glossy.) Fold the corn mixture into the egg whites.

Liberally butter a 2-quart soufflé dish, and pour this mixture into it. Bake in a preheated 375-degree oven for 30 to 35 minutes.

You must serve this soufflé at once. And on your way from the oven to the table, dust the soufflé as lightly as you can with an extra sprinkle of saffron powder.

FRESH CRANBERRY MOUSSE

The cranberry is not a vegetable, but it can be served as one. In addition to its lovely color, it has a lovely taste, especially when sweetened with sugar and served in combination with turkey or chicken. This Fresh Cranberry Mousse makes an elegant picture. It is especially effective on a buffet and merits serving any time during the year.

2 *cups fresh cranberries*	4 *egg whites, room temperature*
1½ *cups cranberry juice*	*Healthy pinch of salt*
1½ *cups sugar*	1 *cup heavy cream, whipped*
4 *tablespoons gelatin, unflavored*	*Sugar*

Put the fresh cranberries in a colander, and rinse them several times, discarding any stems, blemished berries, or foreign matter. After the cranberries have been picked over, put them in a heavy saucepan, but reserve 4 or 5 berries for the garnish. Add the cranberry juice, 1 cup sugar, and unflavored gelatin. Cook over medium heat until the cranberries pop (6 to 8 minutes, depending on the amount of heat). When the berries are popped and done, transfer them to a bowl, and put them in the refrigerator to cool for 50 minutes to 1 hour. (The cranberry mixture should cool but *not* set or jell.)

While the cranberry mixture is in the refrigerator, prepare a 1-quart soufflé dish. Make a wax paper collar long enough to go all the way around the dish. Fold the wax paper in half, and oil it lightly. Wrap it around the soufflé dish, and secure it with a rubber band. Set aside.

Whip the egg whites until they are foamy. Add the pinch of salt, and continue to whip them until they form soft peaks, adding the remaining ½ cup sugar, 1 teaspoonful at a time, until it is absorbed. (The egg whites should not be grainy with sugar.)

Remove the cranberry mixture from the refrigerator. Whip the heavy cream, and fold it into the cooled cranberry mixture. Then gently fold in the egg whites. Pour this mixture into the collared soufflé dish, and refrigerate until set (4 to 5 hours).

Remove the dish from the refrigerator, and take off its collar. Roll the reserved whole, uncooked cranberries in sugar, and place them on top of the mousse. This mousse freezes well, so you will have to thaw it for almost 2 hours before serving.

Although the traditional accompaniments are turkey and chicken, this mousse combines well with cold lamb, veal, and pork, particularly when the meat is not sauced.

FRESH MINTED CUCUMBERS

CUCUMBERS AND MINT   SERVES 6

3 small- to medium-size fresh
  cucumbers
2 tablespoons butter
3 tablespoons fresh mint,
  chopped fine (or 1 teaspoon
  dried)
2 pieces lemon zest
  (approximately 1 inch by 2
  inches), cut into thin strips and
  then into ⅛-inch cubes

Juice of 1 lemon
Salt
Pepper, ground fresh

Select firm cucumbers. Cut off the ends of the cucumbers, and peel them with a vegetable peeler. Allow the cucumbers to sit for about 30 minutes in cold water to which 1 tablespoon salt has been added. Drain the cucumbers, and cut them in quarters lengthwise. Remove the seedy portion if necessary (it is almost always necessary to do this unless the cucumbers are very small).

Boil 3 or 4 cups water, and add the cucumber pieces and 1 teaspoon salt. Cook for only 4 or 5 minutes. Drain the cucumbers in a colander, and refresh them under cold water. Put them on a tea towel, and dry them well.

In a skillet, heat the butter, add the cucumber pieces, and sauté them for 3 to 4 minutes, just until they are heated through. Transfer them to a serving plate.

Add the mint, lemon zest, lemon juice, and salt and pepper to the skillet, and with a rubber spatula, combine these ingredients with the butter over very high heat. (This will take less than 1 minute.) Pour this sauce over the cucumbers, and serve immediately.

Eggplant

Known for thousands of years as the *mala insana* (the raging apple), eggplant was always soaked in salt and cold water to remove its insanity. We salt and drain it, not because we fear its poisonous drippings, but because we want it to be less bitter. Every recipe we have with eggplant as an ingredient requires salting and draining, and the importance of this process is directly related to the size of the eggplant. That is, the larger the vegetable, the more essential the process.

We prefer buying smaller-sized eggplants, and we look for vegetables with the lovely green, capelike bracts and stem firmly attached. If the bracts are loose, it is likely that the vegetable has aged and started to spoil. The eggplant should also be firm. An eggplant that is beginning to shrivel is easy to recognize; don't buy it. We like to see seeds that are snow white. (Of course, there is no way to check the whiteness of the seeds in the shop, but you *can* check the stems and bracts.)

The eggplant, aubergine, or *melanzana* is versatile. It can be cooked cubed, sliced, julienned, halved. It can be puréed, sautéed, creamed, baked, and grilled. An international star, it is prepared *à la grecque, à la turque, à la portugaise, à la catalane,* and *à l'italienne.* And although eggplant can be cooked either peeled or unpeeled, we almost never remove its beautiful skin. It's great in combination with onions, tomatoes, peppers, butter, olive oil, salt, and fresh ground pepper.

EGGPLANT CUBES, PEPPERED AND PUFFED

EGGPLANT AND EGGS   SERVES 6 TO 8

> 2 medium-size eggplants   3 eggs, well beaten
> 2 tablespoons salt   ¼ cup milk
> ½ cup all-purpose flour   1 cup vegetable oil (or corn or
> 1 teaspoon salt   peanut oil)
> Pepper, ground fresh

Select fresh, firm eggplants; they should be young and tender and not too seedy. Wipe them clean with kitchen toweling, and slice off both ends. (Do not peel the eggplant.) Lay each eggplant on its side, and cut it into 1-inch slices. Lay each slice flat, and cut it into 1-inch strips; then cut the strips into 1-inch cubes. Put all the cubes in a colander, sprinkle with 2 tablespoons salt, toss the cubes, and let them stand in the colander for about 40 minutes. The eggplant cubes will release some juice, so put the colander in a sink or over a plate to catch the liquid.

In a plastic bag, combine the flour, 1 teaspoon salt, and a liberal amount of fresh-ground pepper. (Do *not* substitute preground pepper.) Add the eggplant cubes, close the bag, and shake it vigorously to coat each cube with the seasoned flour. Cut or tear open the sack, and place it next to your stove top area.

Combine the eggs and milk in a flat-type bowl, and beat until blended. (This bowl, too, should be next to the stove.)

In a large skillet, heat the oil. (It should be hot but *not* smoking.) Take several floured eggplant cubes, dip them into the egg mixture, and put them in the skillet. Fill the skillet with the eggplant, but be sure to leave about ½ inch between cubes. Turn the cubes as they brown and puff on each side (about 2 minutes). Cook the eggplant in batches and put on paper towels to drain. Although the cubes cook quickly and are best eaten right away, they will keep in a warm oven for about 30 minutes.

The crisp outer texture in combination with the soft inner quality of the eggplant cubes, all piping hot, makes this a delectable dish. These cubes are an excellent accompaniment for a simple roast, filet mignon, a fish salad, and other things. And they are especially good served with cold foods.

EGGPLANT OVAL PUFFS

EGGPLANT AND PINE NUTS   SERVES 6

1 medium- to large-size egg-plant (about 1 pound)	½ cup milk
1 tablespoon butter	¼ cup fresh parsley, chopped (or 1 teaspoon dried)
1 tablespoon olive oil	½ cup grated Parmesan cheese
1 medium-size onion, chopped fine	½ cup pine nuts
	Salt
2 celery stalks, including leaves, chopped fine	Pepper, ground fresh
	2 eggs, lightly beaten
2 cups fresh Italian or French bread, cut into ½-inch cubes	½ cup fresh bread crumbs
	⅓ cup vegetable shortening

In a large saucepan, bring 1½ quarts water to a boil.

Select a firm, fresh eggplant, wipe it off or wash it (if necessary), and cut off the ends. With a swivel-type peeler, peel or scrape the eggplant.

Slice it crosswise into ½-inch slices, and cut these slices into ½-inch cubes. Put all the cubes in a colander, salt them liberally, and allow them to rest for 20 to 30 minutes. Add the cubes to the boiling water, cover the saucepan, and remove it from the heat. Leave the cubes in the hot water, covered, for 10 minutes. Then drain them, and set them aside.

In a skillet, heat the butter and oil, and add the onion and celery pieces. Sauté them for about 10 minutes, until the onion softens somewhat. But the celery should still be crisp.

Moisten the bread cubes with the milk, and squeeze them. (Do *not* squeeze them too dry; they should be moist, but not dripping wet.)

In a large bowl, combine the eggplant, bread, onion and celery mixture, parsley, Parmesan cheese, and pine nuts. Season with salt and freshly ground pepper to taste, and mix well. Add the lightly beaten eggs, and mix well. (It really is best to do this with your hands.)

Put the bread crumbs on a large sheet of wax paper. Put your palms in the bread crumbs, and shape a portion of the eggplant mixture (about 1 heaping tablespoonful) into an oval puff (the shape of an egg, but smaller). You should end up with 12 puffs. (It may be easier to flatten the mixed ingredients into the shape of a pie and divide the pie into 12 portions before you shape the ovals.) Press your hands in the bread crumbs before you mold each oval, and press your hands lightly around the mixture to bring the ingredients together (as you do when making hamburgers or meatballs).

Heat the vegetable shortening until it is hot, and cook 6 puffs at a time, browning them well on all sides. When each puff is done, transfer it to a paper towel to drain.

These rich, delicious puffs can be served as a light luncheon dish (2 per person) with a fresh green salad, lightly dressed. They are great in combination with cold meats, leg of lamb, or roast chicken. They are especially good served in place of stuffing with roast chicken, capon, or turkey.

EGGPLANT FARCIE

EGGPLANT AND TOMATOES   SERVES 8 TO 12

1 *large or 2 small eggplants*
2 *tablespoons salt*
2 *small- to medium-size zucchini*
8 *tablespoons butter*
2 *large onions, chopped coarse*
  (*about 1½ cups*)
2 *cloves garlic, chopped fine*
3 *stalks celery, including leaves,*
  strings removed, chopped
  coarse (*about 1 cup*)
2 *long Italian green peppers,*
  seeded and chopped coarse

4 *large fresh tomatoes, cored,*
  blanched, peeled, and cubed
  (*about 2 cups*)
4 *tablespoons fresh basil,*
  chopped (*or 1 tablespoon*
  dried)
2 *tablespoons fresh thyme,*
  chopped (*or 1 teaspoon*
  dried)
Pepper, ground fresh
1½ *cups bread crumbs*
2 *tablespoons oil*

Wash and dry the eggplant(s). Cut off (and discard) the ends, but do *not* peel the eggplant(s). Cut them into ¾-inch-thick slices, and then cut each slice into ¾-inch cubes. (You should have about 5 cups of eggplant.) Place the eggplant cubes in a colander and sprinkle them with salt.

Wash and dry the zucchini. Cut them in quarters lengthwise, but do *not* peel them. Scoop out the pulp (if the zucchini are very small, this won't be necessary), and cut the zucchini quarters into ¾-inch cubes. (You should have about 4 cups of zucchini.) Add the zucchini cubes to the eggplant in the colander, toss them together, and allow them to drain for 1 hour.

In a large saucepan, melt 4 tablespoons butter, and cook the onions for 5 minutes, or until they are softened. Add the garlic, and cook for 2 more minutes. Add the eggplant, zucchini, tomatoes, basil, thyme, and fresh ground pepper to taste. Stir, and cook over high heat for 5 minutes.

Use 2 tablespoons butter to grease an 8-by-12-by-2-inch baking dish. Sprinkle the bottom of the dish with ½ cup bread crumbs. Fill the baking dish with the eggplant mixture, or *farcie*. Top with the remaining 1 cup bread crumbs, and dot with the remaining 2 tablespoons butter and the oil. Bake in a preheated 400-degree oven for 30 to 40 minutes, until the *farcie* is cooked through and bubbling.

This dish can also be served as a luncheon entrée. Garnish the top with fresh-grated Parmesan cheese. It is especially delicious in combination with a slice of country ham or cold chicken or turkey, and it's very good indeed with outdoor-grilled beef or lamb kabobs.

ROLLATINI DI MELANZANE
(Stuffed and Rolled Eggplant Slices)

BASIL AND RICOTTA

SERVES 8

Two 1-pound eggplants
½ cup olive oil
Salt
Pepper, ground fresh
2 cups ricotta
3 tablespoons shallots, chopped fine (or onions)
1 large garlic clove or 2 small cloves, chopped fine
2 tablespoons fresh basil, chopped (or 1 teaspoon dried)

1 teaspoon dried oregano
½ cup grated Parmesan cheese
1 cup tomato sauce (see page 128)
½ cup roasted peppers, diced (see page 13)
3 tablespoons fresh parsley, chopped (or 1 tablespoon dried)

Select fresh, firm eggplants. Wash them, and cut off both ends, but do *not* peel. Stand each eggplant on its wider end, and cut into thin slices lengthwise; they should be no thicker than ¼ inch, thinner if you can manage it. You should get 6 to 9 slices, depending on the thickness of the eggplant. (Do not use first and last slices because they will be mostly skin.) Put the slices on a large baking pan or sheet, and use a pastry brush to cover both sides of the slices with olive oil. Salt and pepper each slice to taste. Put the baking pan under the broiler (about 6 inches from the unit), and broil the slices for about 5 minutes on each side. (Do *not* overcook the slices; if you do, they will tear when you roll them.) All slices will not fit on the baking sheet at one time, so you'll have to broil them in batches. Set the broiled slices aside.

In a bowl, combine the ricotta, shallots (or onions), garlic, basil, oregano, Parmesan cheese, and salt and pepper to taste. Mix well.

Lay the eggplant slices on a clean, flat work surface, and distribute the ricotta mixture (about 1 tablespoon per slice) among them. (Use up *all* this stuffing mixture.) Spread the mixture over the slices. Roll each slice, starting with the narrower end.

Combine the tomato sauce and roasted peppers, and bring to a boil. Spoon 3 tablespoons of this sauce over the bottom of a baking pan or casserole. Set the rolled eggplant slices side by side in the pan, and cover them with the remaining sauce. Cover the baking pan or casserole with a lid or tin foil, and bake in a preheated 350-degree oven for 30 minutes.

Sprinkle the *rollatini* with parsley, and serve hot.

RATATOUILLE WITH FRESH FENNEL

FENNEL AND EGGPLANT   SERVES 6

2 *small eggplants*
4 *small zucchini*
¼ *to* ⅓ *cup olive oil*
2 *medium-size onions, sliced fine*
3 *cloves garlic, chopped fine*
4 *Italian green peppers, washed,*
  cored, fibers and seeds removed,
  and cut into thin strips
1 *head fennel, including leaves,*
  sliced fine
2 *cups chopped fresh tomatoes,*
  cored, blanched, peeled, and cut
  into ½-inch cubes (or canned
  plum tomatoes, drained)

2 *tablespoons fresh basil,*
  chopped (or 1 teaspoon dried)
6 *sprigs fresh parsley, stems*
  removed, chopped fine (or 1
  teaspoon dried)
Salt
Pepper, ground fresh

Wash and dry the eggplants. Cut off (and discard) the ends, but do *not* peel the eggplants. Cut them into thin slices, and salt them lightly. Place the slices in a colander.

Wash and dry the zucchini. Cut off (and discard) the ends, but do *not* peel the zucchini. Cut them into thin slices, and salt them lightly. Add the zucchini slices to the eggplant slices in a colander, and allow the vegetables to drain for 20 to 30 minutes.

Dry the eggplant and zucchini slices with a tea towel or paper towels.

In a large skillet, heat a small amount of the oil. (Do *not* add much; the eggplant slices will absorb it quickly as they cook.) Sauté the eggplant slices. (Do *not* worry if they are lightly scorched.) Set them aside to drain. Then add the zucchini slices, and sauté them. Add a little oil if necessary during the sautéeing, but do *not* overdo this. Set the slices aside to drain.

In the same skillet, add a little more oil, and sauté the onions and garlic for about 5 minutes. (Do *not* burn the garlic.) Add the peppers, fennel, tomatoes, basil, and parsley.

In a covered casserole, arrange a layer of eggplant slices and then a layer of zucchini slices. Spoon some of the tomato and fennel mixture over the slices. Add salt and pepper to taste. Repeat the layers of eggplant and zucchini. Top with the remaining tomato and fennel mixture. Salt and pepper to taste. Cover, and bake in a preheated 325- to 350-degree oven for about 1 hour. We prefer this ratatouille somewhat overcooked to allow the wonderful flavors time to combine.

Zucchini is a rather liquid vegetable, so do *not* add any liquid other than what is called for in the recipe.

PUREE OF GREEN BEANS AUX ECHALOTES

GREEN BEANS AND SHALLOTS   SERVES 6 TO 8

2 pounds fresh green beans
½ pound potatoes, peeled and
   cut into chunks
8 tablespoons butter
½ pound shallots, chopped
   coarse
1 teaspoon fresh tarragon,
   chopped (or ½ teaspoon
   dried)

½ cup heavy cream
Salt
Pepper, ground fresh
¼ cup fine fresh bread crumbs
2 tablespoons grated Parmesan
   cheese

Remove the ends from the fresh green beans, and wash the beans well. Pick them over, discard poor ones, and remove any blemishes with a paring knife. Drain the beans, and put them in a large, covered saucepan. Add enough water to cover the beans, and bring to a boil. Turn down the heat, cover the saucepan, and let the beans simmer until *al dente*. (They will make a better purée if they are slightly underdone.) Add about ½ teaspoon salt to the simmering beans for the last 3 or 4 minutes of cooking time. Drain the beans, and set them aside.

While the beans are cooking, boil the potato chunks in a small saucepan until they are soft enough to mash. (When you add the potatoes to the boiling water, add ½ teaspoon salt, too.) Drain, and set aside. In a large skillet, melt 2 tablespoons butter, and sauté the shallots until they are softened. (Be careful not to scorch them.)

Use a food processor (such as a Cuisinart) or a food mill set to the finest grind.

If you are using the processor, put the steel knife in the work bowl, and add about ¼ each of the green beans and shallots and some of the tarragon. Process until completely smooth. Remove the purée, and repeat with the remaining beans, shallots, and tarragon.

Heat the heavy cream until hot but *not* boiling. Add the hot cream, 3 tablespoons butter, and the potato chunks to the work bowl; run the machine just long enough to blend the potatoes (only 3 to 4 *seconds*). Combine the potato mixture by hand with the puréed beans and shallots, and stir in the remaining butter. Put all this purée in a shallow casserole or baking dish; salt and pepper to taste.

Combine the bread crumbs and grated Parmesan cheese, sprinkle over the purée, and place in a hot oven (350 degrees) until the purée is heated through.

If you are using a *food mill*, put the beans, shallots, tarragon, and potatoes through the mill separately or together. Heat the cream, add it to the purée, and mix thoroughly. Add the remaining butter (in this case, 6 tablespoons) and salt and pepper to taste, mix well, and arrange the purée in a casserole or baking dish. Follow the rest of the procedure in the preceding paragraph.

This casserole comes from oven to table. It is excellent in combination with roasted or broiled chicken, pork, or slices of cold meat.

PEPPERS AND TOMATOES AL GENNARO

PEPPERS AND TOMATOES   SERVES 6

⅓ cup, plus 1 tablespoon, olive
  oil
2 garlic cloves, chopped very
  fine
3½ cups fresh tomatoes, cored,
  blanched, peeled, and
  chopped coarse (or canned
  plum tomatoes)
1 teaspoon salt
1 tablespoon fresh basil
  chopped (or 1 teaspoon dried)

1 large Italian sausage (¼
  pound) cut on a slant into
  ¼-inch slices
2 pounds Italian green peppers,
  seeded and quartered
2 onions, sliced (about 1 cup)
Pepper, ground fresh
⅓ cup dry red wine (or Madeira)
  (optional)

Heat 1 tablespoon olive oil in a large skillet, add the garlic, and sauté until lightly browned. Add the tomatoes, 1 teaspoon salt, and basil. Cook over medium heat for 30 minutes.

While the tomatoes are cooking, heat the remaining ⅓ cup olive oil in another skillet, and brown the sausage slices well on both sides. Transfer the slices with a slotted spoon to the tomato mixture in the other skillet.

Reserve the oil in which the sausage cooked in the skillet, add the peppers, and toss them well. Sauté the peppers for about 5 minutes, then add the onions, and cook for another 20 minutes, or until vegetables are softened and slightly charred. Add them to the tomato mixture, and cook for an additional 5 to 10 minutes. Adjust the salt and pepper to taste. Add ⅓ cup red wine or Madeira (if you wish) to the skillet after the peppers and onions have cooked. Deglaze the pan, and add the liquid to the tomato and pepper mixture before the last 5 or 10 minutes of cooking.

POTATOES IN A CHARLOTTE MOLD

ONIONS AND PARMESAN CHEESE   SERVES 6 TO 8

8 medium-size potatoes, whole   ½ cup heavy cream (optional)
    and unpeeled   ½ cup sour cream (optional)
1 tablespoon shortening   1 teaspoon paprika (optional)
2 tablespoons salt   ½ cup grated Parmesan cheese
10 tablespoons butter   Salt
4 large onions, chopped fine

With your hands, rub the shortening over the potatoes. Sprinkle the potatoes all over with salt, and place them in a pie plate or another baking pan. Cover the potatoes with a sheet of foil, and bake in a preheated 400-degree oven for 1 to 1¼ hours, or until they are done. (Test for doneness by piercing the largest potato with a knife or fork.)

While the potatoes are baking, add 2 tablespoons butter and the chopped onions to a large skillet or saucepan. Cook them slowly, until they turn pale yellow. (Do *not* scorch the onions; if you do, they make unsightly specks in the potato mold.) Set the onions aside.

Remove the potatoes from the oven. Take each potato, hold one side with a potholder, cut the potato in half on the long side, and remove as much of the potato as you can from its jacket. (Or if you wish, just peel them. Either method seems to work easily.) Put the potato pulp in a baking dish, and mix it well with 6 tablespoons butter. Season to your taste with salt, and keep warm. (If this mixture cools, set the baking pan in the oven to warm it up again.)

With the remaining 2 tablespoons butter, grease a 1½ quart charlotte mold. (Use the *full* 2 tablespoons.) Fill one-third of the mold with some of the warm potato mixture, and pack it tightly into the mold. (The best way to do this is to press down on the mixture with your fingers, but you can also use a rubber spatula or wooden spoon.) Arrange a layer of about one-third cooked onions on top of the potatoes. Add another layer of potatoes, filling the mold two-thirds full. Add another layer of onions. Repeat the procedure with the remaining potatoes and onions, making a third double layer. Place the charlotte mold in a preheated 350-degree oven, and leave it there for 5 minutes, just until the butter used for greasing the mold melts.

While the mold is in the oven, combine the creams, scald them, add the paprika, and mix well with a whisk. Remove the mold from the oven and turn it out onto an ovenproof platter. (Run a knife inside the rim to help loosen the potatoes.) Cover the mold with the cream and paprika mixture. Sprinkle Parmesan cheese over the entire mold. (Be sure to get Parmesan on the *sides* of the mold.) Put the mold under the broiler for several minutes to melt the cheese before serving.

The cream mixture may be omitted, especially if other dishes on your menu are creamy. In that case, turn the mold out onto an ovenproof platter, sprinkle all over with the Parmesan cheese, and run the mold under the broiler to melt the cheese.

LULU'S POTATO PIE WITH HAM, NO LESS

PARMESAN CHEESE AND ONIONS
SERVES 8

3 pounds potatoes (7 or 8 large ones)
½ cup grated Parmesan, Romano, or Locatelli cheese
½ cup cooked ham, chopped fine
¼ cup Italian parsley, chopped fine

½ cup onions, chopped fine
2 eggs, lightly beaten
Pepper, ground fresh
2 tablespoons olive oil (or vegetable oil)

Bake the potatoes in a preheated 350-degree oven for 1 hour. When they are done, let them sit for 20 minutes, or until they are cool enough to handle. Remove the skins, and put the potatoes through a food mill, a few at a time, Transfer the potatoes to a large bowl, and add the cheese, ham, parsley, onions, and eggs. Mix well with a wooden spoon. Add the freshly ground pepper, and mix again, making sure all ingredients are well blended.

Put the oil in an 8-by-8-by-2-inch pan; make sure all sides are coated well. Add the potato mixture, and pat it firmly into the pan. (Don't be afraid to use your hands.) Bake in a preheated 350-degree oven for 50 minutes, or until the top is golden. Remove to a rack, and let cool at least 30 minutes before slicing.

Serve this dish warm or cold. If you cut Lulu's Potato Pie into 2-inch squares, you will have 16 pieces, but you will serve only eight people with them because everyone seems to want a second serving of the pie.

POTATOES WITH GARLIC, CREAM, AND CHEESE

POTATOES AND GARLIC   SERVES 8

6 large baking potatoes (about 2 pounds), peeled and quartered	*6 tablespoons butter*
	¼ cup grated Parmesan cheese
1½ cups heavy cream	*Salt*
1 large clove garlic (or 2 small cloves), minced	*White pepper, ground fresh*

Put the potato quarters in a large, heavy saucepan, and cover them with water. Add about 1 teaspoon salt, and bring to a boil. Simmer the potatoes until they are tender (about 30 minutes, depending on the size of the potatoes and the heat under the pan). (We usually test for tenderness by forking a potato.) Drain the potatoes in a colander, transfer them to a baking pan, and put them in a preheated 375-degree oven for several minutes to dry them out.

In a small saucepan, heat the cream, garlic, and 4 tablespoons butter, but do *not* let the mixture boil.

In the meantime, put the potatoes through a food mill or a heavy-duty electric mixer with a wire whisk. (A food processor can be used, but the potatoes will have to be processed with the cream and butter according to the manufacturer's instructions.) Add the mixture of hot cream, garlic, and butter to the potatoes, and blend well. Add the Parmesan cheese by sprinkling it in, and combine it with the potato mixture. Now salt and pepper as you wish. (Be sure to use *white* pepper. Black pepper specks would spoil the appearance of this dish.)

Arrange the potato mixture in an attractive baking dish (a shallow one, if possible). Smooth the top with a rubber spatula, but don't try to smooth it too much; the spatula strokes should be clearly visible. Dot the top with the remaining 2 tablespoons butter, and run the dish under the broiler for 1 or 2 minutes, until the butter melts and the top is golden.

Serve this while it is hot.

RISO CON SALSICCIE
(Rice with Sausages)

SAFFRON AND SAUSAGE   SERVES 4 TO 6

2 tablespoons olive oil
3 links Italian sausage, casings
  removed
1 clove garlic, whole
½ cup onions, chopped fine
2½ cups Rich Beef Stock or
  broth (see page 46)

1 cup long-grain rice, uncooked
Healthy pinch of saffron
Salt
Pepper, ground fresh
Grated Parmesan, Romano,
  or Locatelli cheese

In a 2-quart casserole, heat the oil, and brown the sausage meat and garlic. Press down on the garlic clove with a wooden spoon to extract some juice. Discard the garlic. Transfer the browned meat to a bowl, and set aside.

In the same casserole, brown the onions lightly. Add the stock (or broth), rice, sausage meat, saffron, and salt and pepper to taste. Cover the casserole, and bake in a preheated 350-degree oven for about 35 minutes.

Serve hot, and pass the grated cheese.

FRESH SUMMER SQUASH

MINT AND HONEY　　　　　　　　　　　　　　SERVES 4 TO 6

> 4 cups summer squash (about　　Salt
> 　1½ pounds)　　　　　　　　Pepper, ground fresh
> 4 tablespoons butter
> ½ cup honey
> 4 tablespoons fresh mint,
> 　chopped (or 1 tablespoon
> 　dried)

Wash the squash, and cut off the ends. (Do *not* peel the squash.) Slice them very thin.

Butter a 9-by-9-by-3 glass baking dish (or something equivalent). Arrange the squash slices in the baking dish in layers, dotting each layer with butter, honey, mint, and salt and pepper to taste.

Cover the baking dish with foil, and bake in a preheated 350-degree oven for 30 minutes, or until the squash is *al dente*.

Serve hot. This dish is easy and exquisite. *Queste coccozelle si sciolgono in bocca* ("these squash will melt in your mouth").

BAKED WHOLE TOMATOES WITH PESTO

TOMATOES AND BASIL　　　　　　　　　　　　SERVES 6

> 6 medium-size fresh tomatoes　　¼ cup grated Parmesan cheese
> 1 clove garlic, minced　　　　　½ teaspoon salt
> 1 cup fresh basil leaves, stems　　½ to ¾ cup olive oil
> 　removed　　　　　　　　　1 tablespoon butter
> ¼ cup pine nuts

Wash the tomatoes, and cut out the stem openings. Spear this opening with a fork, and plunge each tomato into boiling water for 1 minute or less, remove the tomato and peel off the skin. Be careful not to puncture the tomatoes when you core and peel them; they must be whole in the sense that the pesto will stay inside. Slice off the bottoms of the tomatoes (if necessary) so that the tomatoes will stand erect when stuffed.

Put the basil, pine nuts, Parmesan cheese, salt, and oil in a blender or food processor, and blend until the pesto is smooth. Fill each tomato with 1 tablespoon of the pesto.

Select a baking dish large enough to hold the tomatoes without touching. Butter the dish, and place the tomatoes in it. (Don't forget to leave space between them.) Bake them, uncovered, in a preheated 400-degree oven for 20 to 30 minutes. (We prefer these tomatoes underdone.)

This dish can also be prepared and served cold. Fill each raw tomato with 1 tablespoon of pesto, and serve. If you prefer less tomato, cut the peeled tomatoes into ¾-inch slices, place 1 teaspoon of the pesto in the middle of each slice, and serve. If you don't use all the pesto, don't worry. Leftover pesto freezes well.

Grandpa and Zucchini

"Questi zucchini che crescono in terra, fanno stare anche a me in terra." This sentence is difficult to translate, but its meaning is something like this: "These zucchini that grow on the ground, will also keep me on the ground." We heard this sentence mumbled by Grandpa all summer long, for as long as he was with us. Unlike every other member of the family, including second and third cousins, he didn't appreciate zucchini because it was filled with water. According to Grandpa, a diet of zucchini would leave him weak. Nevertheless, zucchini was a staple in *our* household, summer and winter. *Courgette, Italian marrows, Italian squash, zuchetti, courgeon,* or *coccozelle*—call it what you will, zucchini is one of our favorite vegetables. (We grew up calling it *coccozelle,* and Grandpa called *us coccozelle* whenever we did not learn a lesson, understand a moral, or excel in a sport.)

As versatile as the potato, the zucchini is a special vegetable because it combines beautifully with so many other foods. For example, prepared *à l'indienne,* zucchini simmer in butter with salt and curry and are covered with *una salsa besciamella. À la niçoise* calls for flouring the zucchini and sautéeing them in oil, then combining them with tomatoes and onions that have also been cooked in oil.

If you layer them in an *au gratin* dish, combine them with rice cooked in stock and tomatoes, and add onions, garlic, and parsley, you will have *courgettes à la Provençale*. Originally in the south of France, and now in many other parts of the world, zucchini is also prepared with a stuffing of risotto flavored with Parmesan, garlic, and tomato purée, topped with bread crumbs, a sprinkle of oil and chopped parsley, and for the gourmet, 1 or 2 tablespoons of a good meat sauce. Zucchini can also be stuffed with meat, bread, or raisins. They combine to make bread (A Summertime Bread, see page 339), soup (Zucchini and Corn Soup, see page 88), and salads (Zucchini Salad with Capocollo, see page 365). The Creoles are known to turn them into jam by browning them in fat, stirring and cooking all the while, salting, and allowing most of the cooking liquid to evaporate until the mixture turns to an amber color.

Actually, we've never tasted a poor zucchini dish, and recipes in abundance are everywhere, so there is no point in repeating them. But in this chapter, we present several zucchini dishes that we've adapted or created: Zucchini Pudding in the Tara North Style, Ratatouille with Fresh Fennel, a zucchini pudding brought *a tavola* in a skillet (Zucchini in a Skillet), and A Mold of Zucchini, which combines zucchini with mushroom duxelles. We hope you'll enjoy them.

ZUCCHINI PUDDING IN THE TARA NORTH STYLE

ZUCCHINI AND CREAM   SERVES 6 TO 8

2 cups zucchini (about 4 medium-size zucchini)	¼ cup fresh basil, chopped fine
1 tablespoon salt	3 eggs, room temperature
1 fresh hot green or red pepper, chopped fine	¼ cup all-purpose flour
	2 tablespoons butter, melted
	2 cups light cream

Wash the zucchini, and cut off the ends, but do *not* peel. If the zucchini are small, grate the whole vegetable; if they are large, grate only the outside portion. (Cut them in half lengthwise, and remove the seeds.) Grate the zucchini, using the shredding side of a grater. As you grate the zucchini, transfer it to a colander, and add some salt. Each time you add more grated zucchini to the colander, add more salt. Let the liquid drain from the zucchini for about 30 minutes. With your hands, press down on the zucchini gratings in the colander to remove as much liquid as possible. Transfer the zucchini to a bowl.

Add the chopped pepper and basil to the bowl, and toss it with the zucchini.

Beat the eggs well, and stir them into the zucchini mixture. Then add the flour, and stir again. Add the melted butter and cream.

Pour this mixture into a buttered 1½-quart glass or ceramic baking dish, and place the baking dish in a pan of hot water, forming a bain-marie. Bake in a preheated 325-degree oven for 1 hour, or until done.

The end product will be a custard most delicately flavored with fresh zucchini. Serve within 10 minutes or it will begin to sink.

ZUCCHINI IN A SKILLET

ZUCCHINI AND ONIONS

SERVES 6 TO 8

3 cups fresh zucchini (3 medium-
 to large-size zucchini)
1 tablespoon salt
2 tablespoons butter
2 medium-size onions, chopped
 fine
2 small cloves garlic, minced
2 green Italian peppers, chopped
 fine

2 red cherry peppers, chopped
 fine
6 egg whites, room temperature
2 whole eggs
3 tablespoons olive oil (or
 vegetable oil)
½ cup grated Parmesan cheese

Wash and dry the zucchini. Cut off the ends, but do not peel. Cut each zucchini in half lengthwise. (If they are large, with mature seeds, removed seeds by scooping or cutting out.) You can cut the halves in half again, but be sure the pieces are large enough to hold when you grate them. Most graters have a shredding side; use it to grate the zucchini. Put the shreds in a colander, add salt, toss, and set aside to drain for at least 30 minutes. After 30 minutes, press down on the zucchini with your hands to remove as much liquid as possible.

Heat the butter in a large skillet or saucepan. Add the onions, and cook them over moderate heat until they are softened (about 5 minutes). Then add the garlic and green and red peppers. Stir, and cook for 5 minutes. Transfer this mixture to a large mixing bowl, add the drained zucchini, and mix well.

Beat the egg whites and whole eggs together thoroughly, and combine them with the vegetable mixture.

Heat the oil in a 10-inch covered skillet (preferably the black iron type), and add the zucchini and egg mixture. Cover the skillet, and cook over medium heat for at least 10 minutes. Continue cooking until the underside is lightly browned. (Use a rubber spatula to lift the edge of the zucchini mixture and view the underside.) Add the Parmesan cheese, and place the skillet under the broiler to melt the cheese.

This dish is served in the skillet (which will be extremely hot and must be handled with care). Freshly made hot cornsticks are a great combination with this.

A MOLD OF ZUCCHINI

ZUCCHINI AND MUSHROOMS   SERVES 10 TO 12

TO PREPARE THE ZUCCHINI:
> 4 cups fresh zucchini (2 to 2½ pounds)
> Salt

Buy or pick small fresh zucchini. Wash and dry the whole zucchini, and cut off the ends. (Do *not* peel the zucchini.) If the zucchini are tiny, grate them in their entirety; if they are larger, cut them in half lengthwise, scoop out the seeds, and then grate. Put the gratings in a colander, salt liberally, and let them sit in the colander for at least 30 minutes to drain off as much liquid as possible.

TO PREPARE THE DUXELLES:
> ½ pound fresh mushrooms   ¼ cup onion, chopped fine
> 1 tablespoon butter   Salt
> 1 tablespoon olive oil   Pepper, ground fresh

We always wipe mushrooms with a moistened tea towel or paper towel, and we cut off about half of each stem (freeze these stem pieces for stockpot use). Chop the mushrooms, including the remaining stem parts, and squeeze them dry by wringing them in a tea towel. (This is practice for squeezing the zucchini gratings, which you'll be doing in a few minutes.)

In a skillet, heat the butter and oil, and sauté the mushrooms and onions until they are almost dry. Add salt and pepper to taste, and set aside.

Now squeeze the zucchini gratings (it's all right to use the same tea towel you used for the mushrooms). Put the squeezed zucchini in a large bowl, and add the cooked mushrooms.

TO PREPARE THE MOLD:

4 whole eggs	2 tablespoons fresh basil,
2 egg yolks	chopped (or 1 teaspoon dried)
½ cup heavy cream	1 teaspoon dried oregano
½ cup fresh fine bread crumbs	4 tablespoons butter, melted
½ cup grated Parmesan cheese	and cooled

In another bowl, beat the whole eggs and egg yolks together. Pour in the cream, and mix well. Add the bread crumbs, Parmesan cheese, basil, oregano, and the melted butter. (Remember, the butter *must* be cooled; otherwise, it will cook the eggs.)

Combine the egg mixture with the zucchini and mushrooms, and pour this into a generously buttered 1½-quart ring mold. Create a bain-marie by placing the mold in a larger pan and filling the larger pan with enough warm water to reach halfway up the ring mold. Put this in a preheated 325-degree oven and bake until the mold is set (about 45 to 50 minutes).

Remove the ring mold from the pan of water, and loosen the edges of the baked mold by running a knife along both inside edges of the pan. Place the serving platter over the ring mold, and invert. (Do this quickly, and use both hands.) Serve right away.

((11))

Some Breads, Biscuits, Pizzas,
and Rolls

O N E of our earliest remembrances is helping our grandmother carry pans full of dough to the local baker at 3:30 P.M. every Wednesday of every week. At 5:30 P.M., we would help her carry home delicious hot loaves of bread, enough to last a week. The Italian women in our neighborhood (and we've learned in the years since then that other Italian women in other Italian neighborhoods did the same) went to and fro to bake the week's supply of homemade bread, just as our grandmother did.

Those Wednesday afternoons were some of the happiest times of our lives. Twenty or thirty women, usually clad in black, were all at the baker's at the same time. We can remember Zia Maria, Maria-Antonio, Maria Giuseppe, Maria Michele, Isabella, and of course, our grandmother Beatrice. The baker always knew *her* bread as it came out of the oven because it was the best.

The bakery, in a brownstone basement in the old multiethnic Clinton community on New York City's West Side, was a warm and pleasant place for us and our brothers and sisters. The baker, barely distinguishable from the big loaves of Italian bread, for he was always heavily floured himself, was perennially cheerful. We often wondered how his white face could always smile in the midst of the magpie chattering of all those women but some time ago, we concluded that the smell of freshly baked bread will usually bring out the better side of anyone. We can see the baker now, sliding the loaves into the oven on his long-handled wooden peel. He was loyal, tireless, patient, a good listener. And if we remember correctly, he charged only a penny a loaf for baking. No one we know today makes loaves of bread of the size that *Signora Beatrice e le altre signore* made in those days.

Nevertheless, if anyone eats poor bread today, we think he has only himself to blame. Flour can provide more protein, more iron, more vitamin B_1 and nicotinic acid than any other single food item. Sick people, people on diets—all people should know that bread is good for health (especially, but not exclusively, whole-grain bread) and that it still is one of the best bargains in spite of the inflated cost of flour, yeast, and eggs. Bread *is* food, and it is probably the one food that combines with almost every other.

A SUMMERTIME BREAD
(Zucchini Bread with Basil and Chives)

BASIL AND ZUCCHINI   MAKES 2 LOAVES

We call this a summertime bread because it is best when you've plenty of fresh zucchini, fresh basil, and fresh chives. Of course, you can make it with frozen or dried basil and chives, but it will be a different loaf. We suggest you make it in the summertime or early fall and freeze the loaves.

2 cups zucchini
2 cups all-purpose flour
1 teaspoon salt
1 tablespoon baking soda
½ teaspoon baking powder
3 eggs, room temperature
1 cup sugar
1 cup liquid vegetable oil (or ½ stick margarine and 7 tablespoons vegetable shortening melted to make 1 cup)

4 tablespoons fresh basil, chopped fine
4 tablespoons fresh chives, chopped fine

Wash the zucchini, cut off the ends, but do *not* peel them. Unless the zucchini are very small, quarter them lengthwise, and cut out the seed portion. (If the zucchini are small, just grate them as they are.)

Sift the floor, salt, baking soda, and baking powder together.

Beat the eggs and sugar until they are smooth and thick. Add the shortening (if using melted shortening, be sure it's cool first).

Add the zucchini, chives, and basil to the egg mixture. Then add the flour mixture, and stir until smooth.

Grease and flour two 5-by-9-by-2½ loaf pans. Pour the batter into the pans, and bake in a preheated 350-degree oven for 50 to 60 minutes, until done.

Cool the loaves in their pans for 10 minutes. Turn them out on a rack, and cool some more, or eat the bread hot.

CHEESE AND DILL BREAD

CHEDDAR CHEESE AND DILL   MAKES 1 LOAF

2½ cups all-purpose flour
1 tablespoon sugar
1 egg, room temperature
½ teaspoon salt
1½ tablespoons butter, melted,
   lukewarm
½ cup milk, lukewarm
1 envelope active dry yeast (or
   1 cake compressed yeast
   dissolved in ¼ cup of
   lukewarm water)

½ cup grated Cheddar cheese
¼ teaspoon dill weed
   Small amount egg yolk and
   water

In a large bowl, sift the flour and sugar together. Make a well in the center, and add the egg, salt, butter, milk, and yeast. Mix well with a wooden spoon until the dough leaves the sides of the bowl. Turn the dough out onto a lightly floured board, and knead it for 10 minutes, or until the dough is smooth.

Put the dough in a buttered, medium-size bowl. Be sure the dough is shielded from any drafts, and cover it with a dampened towel. Let it rise until it is double in bulk (about 2 hours). When it has doubled, transfer the dough onto a lightly floured board, and punch it down, adding the cheese and the dill. Put the dough back into the buttered bowl, and let it rise again (about 1½ hours).

When the dough is ready a second time, turn it out onto a floured board, and shape it to fit a buttered 9-by-5-by-3 loaf pan. Let the dough rise again (about ½ hour). Brush the top of the dough with the egg and water mixture. Bake it in a preheated 350-degree oven for 45 or 50 minutes, or until golden. Cool the loaf on a rack.

A SPECIAL SPOON BREAD

COUNTRY HAM FAT AND WHITE CORN MEAL   SERVES 8

5 cups milk	*1½ tablespoons rendered fat from*
1¼ cups white corn meal, stone	*a country ham (or pork*
ground if possible	*sausage fat or bacon fat)*
1 teaspoon salt	*5 egg yolks*
1½ tablespoons butter	*5 egg whites*

In the top of a double boiler, scald the milk, and slowly add the corn meal and salt. Stir this mixture frequently, and cook it until it is smooth and thick (15 to 20 minutes). Move the pan off the heat, and add the butter and country ham fat or its substitute. Mix this well, and allow the mixture to cool (about 5 minutes).

In a bowl, beat the egg yolks well, and add them to the cooked corn meal mixture.

In another bowl, beat the egg whites until they are stiff, and fold them into the corn meal and egg yolks.

Then butter a shallow, 2-quart baking dish (and in this case, please be *liberal* with the butter), and pour the batter into it.

Bake this special spoon bread in a preheated 350-degree oven for about 35 minutes. Before you remove it from the oven, it should be browned and puffed. Serve it right away.

WHOLE-WHEAT BREAD WITH HONEY

4 cups whole-wheat flour *5 cups lukewarm water*
½ cup instant potatoes *6 tablespoons shortening*
½ cup nonfat dry milk *½ cup honey*
2 tablespoons salt *7 cups all-purpose flour*
2 packages (¼ ounce each)
active dry yeast

Mix the whole-wheat flour, instant potatoes, dry milk, and salt, and set aside.

Sprinkle the yeast in 1 cup lukewarm water, and set that aside. Mix the shortening, honey, and 4 cups lukewarm water.

Add the whole-wheat flour mixture to the shortening mixture, and mix until smooth. Then add the yeast mixture, and blend well.

Add the flour, 1 cup at a time, and stir until the dough leaves the sides of the bowl. (Don't worry if all 7 cups are not used; add the rest of the flour, if necessary, while kneading.)

Turn the dough onto a lightly floured board, and knead it until it is smooth. Place the dough in a lightly greased bowl, turn the dough over to grease the top. Cover, and let it rise in a warm place until it has doubled in bulk (2 to 3 hours).

Divide the dough into three equal parts. Cover with a tea towel, and let rest 4 or 5 minutes.

Shape three loaves, and place them in greased 5-by-9-by-2½ loaf pans. Let them rise again, covered with a tea towel.

Bake in a preheated 400-degree oven for 50 minutes to 1 hour.

MS. JANE WALSH'S BREAD WITH CHOPPED
SHALLOTS AND COTTAGE CHEESE

SHALLOTS AND COTTAGE CHEESE   SERVES 6 TO 8

1½ *tablespoons dry yeast*
¼ *cup lukewarm water*
1 *cup cottage cheese, creamed*
4 *tablespoons shallots, chopped*
   fine
1 *tablespoon butter, softened*
2 *tablespoons sugar*

1 *teaspoon salt*
¼ *teaspoon baking soda*
1 *egg, unbeaten*
2¾ *cups all-purpose flour*
   Softened butter and coarse
   salt

Combine the yeast and lukewarm water, and allow the yeast to soften.

In a large bowl, combine the creamed cottage cheese, shallots, butter, sugar, salt, baking soda, and egg, and mix well. Add the softened yeast, and mix well again.

Add the flour, ½ cup at a time, to form a rather stiff dough, beating well after each addition. (If you don't use all the flour and have approximately ¼ cup left over, don't fret; you can use a little of it on your hands when you punch down the dough.) Leave the dough in this bowl. Cover it well, and put it in a warm spot, away from drafts, and wait until it doubles in bulk (1½ to 2 hours, or longer). (It may seem unusual *not* to knead a dough, in this case, it is not necessary. All you have to do is mix the dough well with a wooden spoon as you add the flour, and then just leave it in the bowl to rise.) When it has doubled, punch the dough down a little, and transfer it to a liberally buttered baking pan (1½ to 2 quarts). Again allow the dough to double. Then place it in a preheated 350-degree oven, and bake it for 45 to 50 minutes, until it has a golden glow.

At this point, quickly brush or rub the top with softened butter, sprinkle the top with coarse salt, and leave the bread in the oven for 10 minutes. Be absolutely sure to turn off the oven at the moment you butter and salt the top of the loaf. Remove from the baking pan within minutes after you have removed it from the oven. After it has cooled, this bread may be frozen.

A LOAF OF ORANGE BREAD

SWEET BUTTER AND ORANGE   MAKES 1 LOAF

2½ to 3 cups all-purpose flour   *1 envelope active dry yeast (or*
2 tablespoons sugar   *1 cake compressed yeast*
1 egg, room temperature   *dissolved in ¼ cup lukewarm*
½ teaspoon salt   *water)*
2 tablespoons sweet butter,   *½ cup fresh orange juice, room*
* melted and cooled*   * temperature*
1 teaspoon orange zest, grated

In a large bowl, sift together 2½ cups flour and the sugar. Make a well
in the center, and add the egg, salt, butter, orange zest, and yeast. Mix a
little with a wooden spoon, adding the orange juice, a bit at a time.
Keep mixing until the dough leaves the sides of the bowl. Turn the
dough out onto a lightly floured board, and knead for 10 minutes, or
until the dough is smooth.

Put the dough in a buttered, medium-size bowl. Be sure the dough is
out of any drafts; cover the dough with a tea towel. Let it rise until it
is double in bulk (about 2 hours). Then punch the dough down, and
let it rise again until double in bulk (about 1½ hours).

When the dough is ready, turn it out onto a lightly floured board,
punch it down, and shape it to fit a 9-by-5-by-3 buttered loaf pan. Let
the dough rise again (about ½ hour). Bake the bread in a preheated
350-degree oven for 45 to 50 minutes, or until it is golden. Cool on a
rack.

PANE ITALIANO DELLA MAMMA
(Mother's Italian Bread)

YEAST AND SUGAR   MAKES 3 LOAVES

8 cups all-purpose flour   *1½ cups lukewarm water*
1 tablespoon sugar   *2 tablespoons vegetable oil*
1 tablespoon salt   *1 piece fresh yeast, a little larger*
2 eggs, room temperature   * than a 1-inch cube (see Note)*
½ cup milk

In a large bowl, combine the flour, sugar, and salt. Make a well in this flour mixture.

In a separate bowl, mix the eggs, milk, water, vegetable oil, and yeast. Add this to the flour mixture, and mix until the dough can be turned onto a floured board. Knead for 10 minutes. Add more flour, lightly, if necessary, while kneading. Let the dough rise in a buttered bowl, covered with a tea towel, in a warm place until it is double in size (about ¾ hour if fresh yeast is used, otherwise 1½ hours). Punch it down.

Divide the dough in three. Shape each third into a loaf 12 to 14 inches long, and place the loaves on a greased, large cookie sheet. (You may get only 2 on a sheet, depending on sheet and oven size.) Let them rise again (about 45 minutes).

Bake the loaves in a preheated 350-degree oven for 50 to 60 minutes, until they are done.

Note: Mamma insists on fresh yeast. She says that fresh yeast is quicker to use and is better in bread making. We have substituted 2 packages of dry yeast in place of her "cake of yeast," and it has done well, but everyone we know claims to be able to pick out Mamma's bread among all others.

PANE ITALIANO DELLA FIGLIA
(Daughter's Italian Bread)

YEAST AND SUGAR   MAKES 2 LOAVES

2 envelopes active dry yeast (or   2 eggs, room temperature
2 cakes compressed yeast   1½ teaspoons salt
dissolved in ¼ cup lukewarm   2 teaspoons sugar
water)   1½ cups lukewarm water
5 to 5½ cups all-purpose flour

Dissolve the yeast in the lukewarm water, and set it aside.

In a large bowl, add 5 cups flour. Make a well in the center, and add the eggs, salt, sugar, and yeast. Mix a little with a wooden spoon. Add the lukewarm water, a little at a time, mixing until the dough leaves the sides of the bowl.

Turn the dough out onto a lightly floured board, and knead for 15 minutes, or until the dough is smooth. Butter a large, warm bowl, and let the dough rise in it until it is double in bulk (about 1½ hours). (Be sure the dough is covered with a towel and away from any drafts.)

When the dough has doubled, punch it down, and let it rise again until double in bulk (about 1 hour). When the dough is ready, turn it out onto a lightly floured board, and cut it in half. Roll each half back and forth until it is 12 to 14 inches long. Place the loaves on a flat tray (or two flat trays). With a razor blade, make two slanted slashes in the middle of each loaf. Let the loaves rise again for about 20 minutes. Bake in a preheated 350-degree oven for 50 minutes, or until it is golden. Cool on a rack.

This bread is delicious when served warm. It freezes well for three to four weeks, but no longer, or it will be somewhat dry when thawed.

ITALIAN WHOLE-WHEAT BREAD

WHOLE WHEAT AND SUGAR   MAKES 2 LOAVES

3½ cups whole-wheat flour
2 cups all-purpose flour
2 eggs, room temperature
2 teaspoons salt
2 teaspoons sugar
2 tablespoons melted shortening

2 envelopes active dry yeast (or
2 cakes compressed yeast
dissolved in ¼ cup lukewarm
water)
1½ cups lukewarm water

In a large bowl, sift together 3½ cups of whole-wheat flour and 1½ cups all-purpose flour (reserving the other ½ cup for kneading). Make a well in the center, and add the eggs, salt, sugar, shortening, and yeast. With a wooden spoon, mix a little, adding the lukewarm water, a bit at a time. Keep mixing until the dough leaves the sides of the bowl. Turn the dough out onto a lightly floured board and knead for 15 minutes, or until the dough is very smooth.

Put the dough in a large, buttered, *warm* bowl; cover it with a large, clean cloth or towel; and keep it away from any drafts. (To warm the bowl, fill it with hot water. Leave the water in it until you are ready to put the dough in it; then empty the bowl, and dry it. It will butter easily because of its warmth.) Let the dough rise until it doubles in bulk (about 1½ hours). Then punch the dough down, and let it rise until double in bulk again (about 1 hour).

When the dough is ready, turn it out onto a lightly floured board, and cut it into two equal pieces. Roll each piece back and forth until it is 12 to 14 inches long. Place the loaves on a flat oven tray. With a razor blade, make slashes to form 2 slanted lines in each loaf. Let the loaves rise again (about ½ hour).

Bake the loaves in a preheated 350-degree oven for 50 minutes or until they are golden. Cool them on a rack.

This bread is delicious when served warm. It freezes well for three or four weeks, but no longer, or it will dry out when thawed.

DIANA BUCHANAN'S BUTTERMILK BISCUITS

BUTTERMILK AND BAKING POWDER   MAKES 12 TO 16 BISCUITS

> 2 cups all-purpose flour
> 1 teaspoon salt
> 4 teaspoons baking powder
> 2 tablespoons vegetable shortening, melted
> ¾ to 1 cup buttermilk

Put the flour in a large bowl, and make a well in the center. Add the salt, baking powder, melted vegetable shortening, and buttermilk. (Do *not* add all the buttermilk at once; add ¾ cup now, a little at a time, and more later if you need it.)

Mix all the ingredients with a wooden spoon. When they are thoroughly combined, turn the mixture out onto a lightly floured board. Knead the mixture only until a dough is formed. (Do *not* knead too much.) Roll out the dough immediately, and with a 2½-inch biscuit cutter, cut out biscuits as close to one another as you can. Grease a baking pan or sheet, and transfer the biscuits to it. Combine the leftover dough, shape it, and cut more biscuits.

Bake the biscuits in a preheated 400- to 425-degree oven for 10 to 15 minutes, until they are done and lightly browned. Serve immediately.

These biscuits freeze well and can be reheated in foil.

DIANA BUCHANAN'S YEAST ROLLS

MILK AND SUGAR   MAKES 40 TO 50 ROLLS

½ cup sugar	*6 cups all-purpose flour*
1 teaspoon salt	*2 eggs*
1 cup milk, scalded	*2½ packages (¼ ounce each)*
½ cup shortening, melted	*active dry yeast dissolved in*
(made of equal parts butter	*⅔ cup lukewarm water*
and vegetable shortening)	*Butter or shortening*

In a large bowl, combine the sugar and salt, and add the milk. (The milk should not be boiling, and it's all right if it is only lukewarm.) Stir well with a large, strong wooden spoon. Add the shortening, and combine well. Add 2 cups flour, 1 cup at a time, and stir with the wooden spoon to combine each cupful with the other ingredients in the bowl. Add 1 egg (no need to beat it first) to the bowl, and combine; add the second egg, and stir well. Add the yeast mixture, and continue beating with a circular motion. Add more flour, ½ cup at a time, until 4 to 4½ cups of flour are used, or until the dough in the bowl can be kneaded.

Flour a board, and empty the dough out of the bowl onto it. Clean the bowl and wooden spoon by adding some flour and working out the dough clinging to them. Knead dough for at least 10 minutes, adding flour as necessary to keep the dough from sticking, until it is smooth. Roll it into a ball, cover it with a tea towel or bowl.

Warm a large, deep bowl (see page 346), and grease it. Place the ball of dough in the bowl, and cover it with a towel. Allow the dough to rise to at least double its bulk. Keep this in a warm place (we usually put the bowl in an unheated oven and keep the oven door closed).

When the dough has doubled, turn it onto a lightly floured work surface. Cut the dough in half. Set one half aside, and keep it covered with a bowl or tea towel. Roll the other half into a large circle, about ½ inch thick. Using a 2½-inch biscuit cutter, cut circles in the dough as close to one another as possible. Remove the excess dough, combine it into a ball, and set it aside under the tea towel. On each circle of dough, mark a straight line across the circle with a knife, just as if you were going to cut the circle of dough in half. Fold over the half, and make a thumb impression at the curved edge of the semicircular-shaped roll. (This will resemble a Parker House roll.) Place each roll on a baking or cookie sheet, leaving 1 inch of space between the rolls on all sides. Cover with a tea towel, and allow to rise for 1 hour.

Roll out the other half of the dough, and repeat this procedure. Fill another baking sheet, cover, and allow to raise for 1 hour.

Combine leftover dough, roll it out, and make more rolls.

Bake the rolls in a preheated 400- to 425-degree oven for about 15 minutes, or until they are deliciously browned.

Serve them as hot as you can, with lots of butter. These rolls freeze exceptionally well and also keep well unfrozen for several days. Reheat them in foil. We make one tray for eating now and one for the freezer. With every mouthful, we are eternally grateful to Diana Buchanan for one of life's simplest and greatest pleasures.

ITALIAN BREAD ROLL ALLA VERDURA

SWISS CHARD AND PARMESAN CHEESE   SERVES 8 TO 12

TO PREPARE THE DOUGH:
½ recipe Pane Italiano della Mamma (page 344)

Combine the ingredients according to the instructions on page 344, and put the dough in a warm, buttered bowl to rise. When the dough has doubled in size (it's almost impossible to give an exact timing for this, but you'd better count on about 2 hours), punch it down.

Using a rolling pin and a little extra flour (to prevent sticking), roll out the dough to a circle about 18 inches in diameter. (This may seem large to you, but it isn't; when the dough is rolled with the ends tucked under, you'll have a filled loaf roll about 15 inches long.)

TO PREPARE THE FILLING:

2 cups Swiss chard (see Note)	*1 clove garlic, chopped fine*
3 tablespoons vegetable oil	*½ cup grated Parmesan cheese*
2 onions, chopped fine	*Pepper, ground fresh*

Cook the Swiss chard *al dente* in as little water as possible. Drain by putting the greens in a strainer and pressing them against the strainer. (Don't be afraid to squeeze the greens with your hands.) Chop the greens. (Do this by hand, not in a blender.) Measure 2 cups of the Swiss chard, and set it aside.

In a skillet, heat the vegetable oil, add the onions and garlic, and sauté them until the onions begin to turn color (about 5 minutes). (Do *not* overcook, and do *not* allow the garlic to brown too much.)

At this point, and with the Swiss chard cooked and measured, you're ready to roll.

Spread the Swiss chard mixture over the dough as evenly as possible, stopping ½ or ¾ inch from the edges. (A rubber spatula will be helpful for this.) Sprinkle Parmesan cheese overall, and then grind fresh pepper to taste over the greens.

Roll the dough, jelly-roll fashion, as tightly as you can. When the roll is completed, tuck each end under with the seam side underneath. Place the loaf on a greased cookie sheet, or grease any other flat-surfaced piece of equipment that fits in your oven. Cover the loaf with a cloth, and allow it to rise for 45 minutes to 1 hour.

Before you put the loaf in the oven, you *can* brush it with a mixture of egg and water or with milk. This gives the loaf a richer texture, and is worth the effort. With or without this addition, the bread roll will develop a warm, light brown color.

Bake the loaf in a preheated 350-degree oven for 50 minutes to 1 hour, or until it is done. Remove the loaf from the oven, and allow it to cool for 15 to 20 minutes before you attempt to slice it.

Cut the loaf into 1-inch slices (approximately), and serve with butter. This bread roll may be eaten hot or cold; most people seem to prefer it warm to hot.

Note: Other greens, such as spinach, kale, and broccoli flowerettes, can be used in place of Swiss chard.

Pizza Pie and Pizza Rustica, Funiculi, Funicula!

Pizza pie as we know it in America is essentially the Neapolitan pie in the mariner's style. It consists of a yeast dough spread into a pie shape and dressed with tomatoes, oregano, garlic, salt, and pepper. It has been said that this pizza pie is the triumph of the poor Neapolitan over poverty, for these ingredients are fairly inexpensive in Naples. Today's version of the pizza is hardly what one can call inexpensive and is surely no one's triumph over poverty; pizza pies are almost always dressed with more costly items, including sausage, mozzarella, Parmesan cheese, prosciutto and other ham pieces, mushrooms, olives, and mussels.

The pizza pie improvisations run wild, but then Italians must be Italian even if they are second- or third-generation Americans. In this chapter, we present a version that is perhaps somewhere in between. Pizza in Lulu's style combines basil with oregano, which is delightful, especially when the basil is fresh and finely chopped. We also combine some Parmesan with lots of mozzarella cheese, but *per favore*, do not add the mozzarella until the last few minutes of cooking.

A lesser known Italian pie, really much less known in this country than the pizza pie, is the pizza *rustica*. Because it is an Italian pie, there are as many versions of pizza *rustica* as there are of pizza. The pizza *rustica* we've included in this chapter (Pizza Rustica Colomba) is, as you might guess, an old southern (Italian, that is) recipe (adapted for American products) that is still being made by our mother, Angela (born 1898), and was made by our paternal grandmother, Maria (born 1859), who claimed it was made by her mother, Rosaria (born 1817), who claimed her mother, Elizabetta (born 1795), made it, and so on ad infinitum.

PIZZA WITH PORK RENDERINGS IN THE COUNTRY STYLE

FENNEL AND PORK   SERVES 8 TO 12

TO PREPARE THE PORK RENDERINGS:
> 1 *pound pork butt*
> ¼ *cup water*
> ½ *teaspoon dried fennel*

Cut the fat and some lean meat into enough very small pieces to measure 2 cups. In a medium-size skillet, sauté the pork renderings (*cracklings*) in the water until browned (about 15 minutes). When they are done, cool them completely, and add the fennel. Put in a medium-size bowl, and set aside.

TO PREPARE THE PIZZA:

3 to 3½ cups all-purpose flour	*1 teaspoon salt*
1 envelope yeast (or 1 cake fresh	*1 cup warm water*
dissolved in ¼ cup lukewarm	*1 tablespoon lard*
water)	*1½ tablespoons sugar*
1 egg, lightly beaten	

Put 3 cups flour in a large bowl (reserving ½ cup), and make a well in the center. Add the egg, salt, and yeast. With a wooden spoon, mix the dough, adding the warm water a little at a time, until the dough leaves the sides of the bowl. Turn the dough onto a floured board, and knead it for 10 minutes, or until it is very smooth.

Warm and butter a medium-size bowl; let the dough rise in it (covered and away from drafts) for about 1 hour, until doubled in bulk. Then turn the dough out onto a well-floured board, and flatten it out to a circle about 10 inches in diameter. Add the pork renderings and half of the reserved ½ cup flour, and knead until well combined. (It is important to keep adding the remaining flour while kneading; in this way you will keep the dough from sticking to your hands.)

Grease a 14-inch pizza pan, put the dough on it, and shape the dough into a flat round. Let the dough rise again (about ½ hour). Then spread the dough out on the tray, and pat it evenly with the palm of your hand, working it toward the outer edge of the tray. Take 1 tablespoon lard, and spread it on top of the dough. Sprinkle 1½ tablespoons sugar overall. Let the dough rise again (½ hour).

Bake in a preheated 350-degree oven for 1 hour, or until the top is nicely browned. This is a sauceless but very tasty pizza. It should be eaten while it is still warm.

PIZZA RUSTICA COLOMBA

HAM AND CHEESE   SERVES 16 TO 24

TO PREPARE THE PIZZA FILLING:

2 pounds boiled ham, cut into
  ½-inch squares
1½ pounds Italian sausage, sweet,
  sliced thin
2 cups grated mozzarella
2 cups grated Parmesan cheese

12 eggs, lightly beaten
¼ pound prosciutto, cut into
  ½-inch squares
1 tablespoon fresh, flat Italian-
  type parsley, chopped
½ teaspoon pepper, ground fresh

Pan-fry the sausage slices for about 10 minutes. Then mix all these ingredients together, and set aside.

TO PREPARE THE PIZZA CRUST:

3 cups all-purpose flour
4 eggs, lightly beaten
Pinch of salt

3 tablespoons water
3 tablespoons vegetable oil
1 egg, lightly beaten

In a large bowl, add the flour, and make a well in the center of the flour. Add the eggs, salt, water, and oil, and mix carefully. Cover the bowl, and let the dough rest for about 10 minutes. Then knead it for 10 minutes. Cut the dough in two, with one piece slightly larger than the other. Roll each piece separately to fit an 8-by-11-by-2-inch pan (or a 10-inch round pan 2 inches deep), lining the pan with the larger piece. Prick the bottom dough with fork tines, and add all the filling mixture. Cover the pie with the smaller piece of dough, pricking it with a fork. Seal the top dough to the bottom by brushing the lightly beaten egg on the rim of the bottom pastry and the rim of the top pastry and pressing them together with your thumb (or follow whatever method of joining a top crust to a bottom crust you prefer). Brush the top of the pie with the remaining beaten egg.

Bake the pie in a preheated 350-degree oven for about 1 hour, until the crust is quite brown. This pizza *rustica* may be frozen for 1 month.

PIZZA IN LULU'S STYLE

TO PREPARE THE DOUGH:

2½ to 3 cups all-purpose flour   *½ to ¾ cups warm water*
1 egg, room temperature
1 teaspoon salt
1 envelope yeast (or 1 cake
yeast, dissolved in ¼ cup
lukewarm water

Put 2½ cups flour in a large bowl, and make a well in the center. In a small bowl, mix the egg, salt, and yeast. Pour this into the flour well. With a wooden spoon, mix well, adding the warm water a little at a time, until the dough leaves the sides of the bowl. Turn the dough out onto a lightly floured board, and knead for 10 minutes, or until the dough becomes smooth. Warm and butter a medium-size bowl, and let the dough rise in it (covered and away from drafts) until it is double in bulk (1 to 1½ hours). Punch the dough, and let it rise again (about 1 hour).

Butter a 12- or 14-inch pizza pan well. Work the dough in the pan by flattening and shaping it to fit the pan, making sure you push it to the outer edge and create a rim. Let the dough rest for 15 minutes.

TO PREPARE THE TOMATO SAUCE:

1 tablespoon olive oil   *1 tablespoon fresh basil,*
1 clove garlic, chopped fine   *chopped fine (or 1 teaspoon*
1½ cups fresh tomatoes, cored,   *dried)*
blanched, peeled, and chopped   *1 teaspoon salt*
fine (or canned plum tomatoes   *1 teaspoon dried oregano*
with as little liquid as possible)

In a skillet, heat the oil, and cook the garlic for 1 minute. Add the tomatoes, basil, salt, and oregano, and cook for 10 minutes. Set aside.

TO ASSEMBLE THE PIZZA:

1 recipe tomato sauce
2 tablespoons grated Parmesan, Romano, or Locatelli cheese
Pepper, ground fresh

2 tablespoons olive oil
1 whole mozzarella (1 pound), sliced thin

Spread the tomato sauce over the dough in the pizza pan. (A large spoon or rubber spatula will be helpful.) Sprinkle the grated cheese over the dough, and be somewhat liberal with the freshly ground pepper. Dot the pizza with 2 tablespoons oil.

Bake in a preheated 375-degree oven for 45 to 50 minutes, or until the rim of the pizza is lightly and nicely browned. Then remove the pizza from the oven for only 1 or 2 minutes, just long enough to spread the mozzarella slices over the pizza. Return the pizza to the oven immediately, and allow it to remain for about 5 minutes, until the mozzarella has softened but not lost its shape.

Serve this pizza hot. It will make a generous meal for four.

((12))

Green Salads, Buffet Salads, Other Salads, and Salad Dressings

THE salads we like best are fresh greens tossed with an oil and vinegar dressing. If the ingredients are of prime quality, and if the salad is properly made, the experience of eating it can be sublime. The combinations of greens and dressings are legion. In this chapter, we've given you our basic oil and vinegar dressing and thirty-eight variations; we could have gone on a lot longer, but you no doubt have your own favorites.

It's obvious that salads are excellent as main dishes at luncheons or late suppers, Sunday brunches, and buffets. If a salad is your main dish, it should be served with bread of some kind. Hot white bread or rolls make a wonderful combination, but so do whole-wheat toast, French or Italian bread, Jewish rye, and black bread. And what about croissants? Brioches? Corn sticks or corn bread, muffins, or even spoon bread? Main dish salads may call for meat, chicken, turkey, shrimp, lobster, or any fish. The meat may be smoked or boiled, roasted or raw. For example, julienne slices of smoked turkey and almost any other smoked meats are excellent in the many variations of chef's salads. Boiled beef vinaigrette makes a delicious late or Sunday supper meal, and poached poultry can be used in many salad ways. Leftover roasted meats and baked fish have a place in salads, and raw meats and fish can make daring yet delicious offerings for the buffet table. Although the Italian preparation of thin sliced raw beef with a spicy sauce (the dish called *carpaccio*) is usually served as an appetizer, we have served it as a buffet item with wonderful results. Use the leanest top round, and slice it paper-thin. As in the case of slicing or cubing meats for Chinese dishes, we suggest that you have the meat very cold, even partially frozen; this facilitates the slicing. The sauce we use is our basic oil and vinegar dressing, but we use a champagne vinegar (a white vinegar will do in place of the red wine vinegar; this has more to do with the color of the sauce than with the taste); then we add anchovies, capers, onion, Dijon mustard, and gherkins, blending all these ingredients in our food processor for only 1 second (the sauce should be grainy). Serve the meat and sauce separately.

Ceviche preparations, with raw fish, can be sensational. Most ceviches are marinated overnight, which makes the rawness disappear. Combine fresh scallops with lime juice, chopped scallions, finely chopped garlic, a bay leaf, and some red pepper flakes to your taste, toss well, and refrigerate overnight. We've used striped bass, too, cut into ½-inch cubes, with excellent results.

An interesting dish combines cooked *calamari* (squid) and *conchiglie or scungilli* (conch) with Kalamata olives in an herb dressing.

Main dish salads accompanied by bread, toast, rolls, or biscuits combine well with wine—so serve it. Big buffets or special suppers may call for a baked ham, roast turkey or filet, a galantine, a pâté, and a salad; or the meats can be preceded by a soup, in which case don't repeat the essential ingredients of the soup in the salad. A perfect conclusion to a lunch or supper of soup, salad, bread, and wine is cheese and fruit. One of our favorite desserts after a hearty salad is orange slices combined with orange zest cooked in syrup, with Cognac or brandy poured overall.

Salad combinations may include cucumbers, chicory, celery, and chick peas. Or they may feature beans, broccoli, beets, and bulgar. An interesting, tasty and combination of food is a bulgar salad known as *tabbouleh*. Bulgar is soaked in cool water, drained well, and mixed with chopped scallions, chopped mint, chopped parsley, olive oil, lemon juice, and salt and pepper. Our touch to *tabbouleh* is to add finely chopped fresh tomatoes, not too ripe.

When making green salads, we avoid iceberg lettuce, which we find tasteless. The best greens for a simple, plain salad are arugola and Bibb. Romaine, Boston, chicory hearts, and watercress are surely second best, sometimes as good as the first. In the country, Mamma Angela picks dandelion sprouts as soon as they appear, and they make salads in a class by themselves. Combine different greens—spinach with endive, endive with romaine, romaine with chicory, and so on—they taste better and look better. Give a special touch to your green salad by adding several slices of fresh raw mushrooms, slivers of fresh red peppers, or several ripe olive halves.

Fresh vegetables (some cooked, some raw) make beautiful salads: artichokes, zucchini, asparagus, tomatoes, broccoli, scallions, green beans (wax, limas, and kidneys, too), lentils, beets, celery, and cauliflower (try it with mushrooms, walnuts, and a piquant dressing), peas, onions, potatoes. One *truc* (trick) with cukes is to slice them very thin and put them in cold water with several teaspoons of salt—guaranteed to prevent the hiccup. Endive is magnificent; so are mushrooms, and so are leeks vinaigrette.

Use small, uncooked zucchini for salads. Do not peel them; just cut off the ends, and slice them thin. Add some thin slices of fresh green pepper and scallions, and toss with one of the oil and vinegar dressings. (This salad should be refrigerated with dressing for 40 or 50 minutes; see page 359.)

Fruits fare well in salad combinations. The best apples to use in salads are Delicious and Cortland; to make them crisp and keep them white, place them in salted water. Drain and dry them before combining them with other ingredients. Peaches and pineapple, apricots and avocados are also salad makers. When using bananas, be sure to toss them, after slicing, in lemon juice to keep them from turning brown.

For stuffing with salad, use cucumber cups, avocado halves, whole tomatoes, half tomatoes, pears, prunes, peaches, melons, and mushrooms. For molded salads, try cherries and cranberries.

An entire discipline of salad devotes its attention to figs, dates, and prunes. Some people prefer a simple bed of sliced radishes in various cream dressings; some dote on eggs and their versatile salad styles. Other schools of salad are aspics, timbales, mousses, macédoines.

There is no end to the variety of salads. We're usually guided by what is available in the markets and what we have in the pantry or refrigerator. When fruit and vegetables are at their best, vary your menu, and accent the salad accordingly. Without question, a great and simple pleasure is to pick several just-ripe tomatoes; wash, core, blanch, and peel them; slice them in any fashion; dress them with oil, vinegar, salt, and pepper; and sprinkle them liberally with fresh chopped basil. Extend this principle to other vegetables (asparagus, broccoli, leeks, cauliflower, green beans, beets, and so on) when they are to be had this fresh in your garden, a neighbor's garden, or the local vegetable market. When fruit and vegetables are not so fresh, accent the potato, meat, and fish salads.

Salad Dressing

As good as salad ingredients may be, a salad will only be as good as its dressing. Much has been written about ways to prepare dressings ahead of time and about how to treat lettuce leaves with an oil and vinegar dressing and keep them in the refrigerator for several hours. Even though such advice has appeared in cookbooks of some distinction, we simply don't believe it. Olive oil (and other oils) will solidify if refrigerated. How can that make a tasty salad?

To make a good salad, the lettuce, vegetable, or whatever should first be washed and well drained. Among today's variety of kitchen equipment, there are several plastic salad spinners that accomplish this in an exemplary way. The washed and spun-dry greens should be refrigerated *without* dressing for about 3 hours. The greens should be taken out of the refrigerator only minutes before they are to be dressed and served. But oil and vinegar salad dressings should never be refrigerated. (The only exception to this is when oil and vinegar dress vegetables such as cauliflower, beets, or green beans and several hours of marination are required so that the vegetables can absorb the dressing. Even in these cases, however, the salad should be removed from the refrigerator in sufficient time to allow it to come to room temperature before it is served.) We start our dressing in a salad bowl by combining the garlic and vinegar and allowing them to marinate for 1 hour. We then add the other ingredients just before serving time.

OIL AND VINEGAR DRESSING

OLIVE OIL AND VINEGAR   MAKES ABOUT ½ CUP

TO PREPARE THE BASIC DRESSING:

> *1 garlic clove, cut into 4 or 5 pieces*
> *2 tablespoons wine vinegar*
> *6 tablespoons olive oil*
> *½ teaspoon salt*
> *Pepper, black or white, ground fresh*

Put the garlic pieces and vinegar in a salad bowl, stir well, and allow to stand for at least 1 hour, or as long as 4 hours.

Do not add any other ingredients until you are ready to dress the salad, which should be just a few minutes before serving. Then press the garlic pieces against the side of the bowl with the back of a spoon, and discard them. Add the oil, salt, and pepper to taste.

Add the cold, crisp lettuce leaves, just out of the refrigerator, toss until fairly well coated, and serve within minutes. Contrary to what one reads and hears about "beating the salad to death"—we suppose this comes from the French *fatiguer la salade* ("tire the salad, or toss it very well") —we believe in simply tossing it, and rather briefly and lightly at that. If the leaves are dry and crisp, there'll be no difficulty in coating them with the salad dressing with only three or four tosses, depending on the amount of salad.

There are hundreds of ways to vary this dressing. Some of our favorite combinations follow:

OIL AND VINEGAR DRESSING 1: BASIL
Add 2 tablespoons fresh basil, chopped fine (or ½ teaspoon dried), to the basic dressing.

OIL AND VINEGAR DRESSING 2: TARRAGON
Add 1 tablespoon fresh tarragon, chopped fine (or ½ teaspoon dried), or substitute 2 tablespoons tarragon vinegar for the wine vinegar.

OIL AND VINEGAR DRESSING 3: OREGANO
Add ½ teaspoon dried oregano to the basic dressing.

OIL AND VINEGAR DRESSING 4: THYME
Add 1 tablespoon fresh thyme, chopped fine (or ½ teaspoon dried).

OIL AND VINEGAR DRESSING 5: PARSLEY
Add 1 tablespoon fresh parsley, chopped fine (or ½ teaspoon dried).

OIL AND VINEGAR DRESSING 6: MUSTARD
Add 1 teaspoon Dijon mustard to the basic dressing and mix well.

OIL AND VINEGAR DRESSING 7: LEMON JUICE
Add 1 teaspoon fresh lemon juice to the basic dressing.

OIL AND VINEGAR DRESSING 8: MUSTARD AND LEMON JUICE
Add 1 teaspoon Dijon mustard and 1 teaspoon fresh lemon juice.

OIL AND VINEGAR DRESSING 9: SHALLOTS
Eliminate the garlic. (No marination is necessary.) Combine 2 tablespoons fresh shallots, chopped fine, with all the other basic ingredients.

OIL AND VINEGAR DRESSING 10: ONION
Substitute 2 tablespoons onion, chopped fine, for the garlic, and marinate for 30 minutes.

OIL AND VINEGAR DRESSING 11: SCALLIONS
Add 2 tablespoons scallions (white and pale green parts only), sliced fine.

OIL AND VINEGAR DRESSING 12: LEEKS
Add 2 tablespoons leeks (white part only), sliced fine.

OIL AND VINEGAR DRESSING 13: CELERY LEAVES
Add 2 tablespoons celery leaves, chopped fine (or ¼ teaspoon dried celery seed).

OIL AND VINEGAR DRESSING 14: MUSHROOMS
Add ¼ cup fresh mushrooms, sliced fine, to the basic dressing. Marination is not essential, but the mushrooms *may* be marinated for 30 minutes to 1 hour.

OIL AND VINEGAR DRESSING 15: TRUFFLES
Add a truffle, black or white, chopped fine, to the basic dressing.

OIL AND VINEGAR DRESSING 16: PAPRIKA
Add ½ teaspoon paprika.

OIL AND VINEGAR DRESSING 17: CHILI PEPPER
Add ¼ teaspoon dried red pepper flakes.

OIL AND VINEGAR DRESSING 18: VEGETABLE OIL
Substitute 2 tablespoons vegetable oil for 2 tablespoons olive oil.

OIL AND VINEGAR DRESSING 19: LIME
Add 1 teaspoon fresh lime juice.

OIL AND VINEGAR DRESSING 20: LEMON OR ORANGE ZEST
Add 1 teaspoon lemon or orange zest, chopped fine, to the basic dressing.

OIL AND VINEGAR DRESSING 21: ANCHOVIES
Add 1 or 2 anchovy filets, chopped fine (or ½ teaspoon anchovy paste).

OIL AND VINEGAR DRESSING 22: WALNUTS
Add 4 tablespoons walnuts, chopped coarse.

OIL AND VINEGAR DRESSING 23: PINE NUTS
Add 4 tablespoons pine nuts to the basic dressing.

OIL AND VINEGAR DRESSING 24: CAPERS
Add 1 tablespoon capers, squeezed dry.

OIL AND VINEGAR DRESSING 25: CREAM
Substitute 6 tablespoons light cream for 6 tablespoons olive oil in the basic dressing.

OIL AND VINEGAR DRESSING 26: NUT OIL
Substitute 2 tablespoons nut oil (such as walnut oil or peanut oil) for 2 tablespoons olive oil in the basic dressing.

OIL AND VINEGAR DRESSING 27: EGG YOLKS
Add 2 hard-boiled egg yolks, rubbed through a sieve.

OIL AND VINEGAR DRESSING 28: BACON
Add 2 tablespoons crumbled crisp bacon bits.

OIL AND VINEGAR DRESSING 29: BACON FAT
Substitute 4 tablespoons bacon fat for the olive oil in the basic recipe.

OIL AND VINEGAR DRESSING 30: HORSERADISH
Add 2 tablespoons grated horseradish (if fresh, 1 tablespoon).

OIL AND VINEGAR DRESSING 31: CURRY
Combine 1 tablespoon shallots, onions, or scallions, chopped fine, with 1 teaspoon curry powder, and cook this mixture for several minutes in 1 tablespoon hot oil (1 of the 6 tablespoons of oil in the basic dressing). Add this to the other basic ingredients.

OIL AND VINEGAR DRESSING 32: CROUTONS
Omit the garlic clove. (No marination will be necessary). Dry out 1 slice of bread, or toast it; rub some fresh garlic into it. Cut the bread into ½-inch cubes, and add them to the basic dressing when you combine it with the lettuce.

OIL AND VINEGAR DRESSING 33: OLIVES
Add 4 tablespoons black or green olives (pits removed), chopped fine. Cured black olives are especially good in this variation.

OIL AND VINEGAR DRESSING 34:
PIMENTO OR ROASTED PEPPER
Add 4 tablespoons pimiento or roasted pepper, chopped fine.

OIL AND VINEGAR DRESSING 35: CHIVES
Add 2 tablespoons chives, chopped fine.

OIL AND VINEGAR DRESSING 36: PARMESAN
Add 1 tablespoon grated Parmesan cheese to the basic dressing at the time you dress the salad.

OIL AND VINEGAR DRESSING 37: DILL
Add 1 tablespoon fresh dill, chopped fine (or ½ teaspoon dill weed).

OIL AND VINEGAR DRESSING 38: SUGAR

There are those who decry the use of sugar in an oil and vinegar dressing. The classic French vinaigrette decidedly, declaratively, and defiantly eliminates it (as it does garlic, except in the hands of those wise and good cooks in Provence), but we think one of the tastiest oil and vinegar dressings calls for some sugar—although very little, to be sure. We believe the following addition to the basic oil and vinegar dressing is excellent for green salads. (The next time you mix a green salad, make two dressings, this one and the basic one, and see for yourself.) Add ⅛ teaspoon superfine granulated sugar (or regular sugar) to the garlic and vinegar, marinate for at least 1 hour. Add the other ingredients, and follow the basic recipe.

A SALAD IN THE NEAPOLITAN STYLE

ANCHOVIES AND BLACK OLIVES   SERVES 6

1 *medium-size cauliflower head*   1 *tablespoon capers, drained*
1 *teaspoon salt*   1 *recipe Oil and Vinegar Dressing*
18 *black olives, pits removed, cut*   3 *(see page 360)*
   into ¼-inch bits
6 *anchovy filets, washed and*
   dried well, cut into ¼-inch
   pieces

In a large saucepan, bring some water to a boil. Cut the cauliflower head into flowerettes, discarding heavy stems and any leaves. Make flowerettes uniform in size; they should be no longer than 1½ inches in length or width. Add about 1 teaspoon salt to the water as it reaches the boil; then add the cauliflower pieces. Cook them until they are *al dente* (about 10 minutes). (Do *not* overcook them.) Drain immediately, and run the flowerettes under cold water to stop further cooking. Dry them in a kitchen towel and put them in a large bowl. Add the olives, anchovies, capers and dressing, and toss gently.

It is best to make this salad ahead of time (to allow the cauliflower to absorb the dressing) and refrigerate it. Remove it from the refrigerator at least 30 minutes before serving to allow the dressing to reach room temperature, and toss again.

ZUCCHINI SALAD WITH CAPOCOLLO

CAPOCOLLO AND ZUCCHINI   SERVES 6

6 small whole zucchini (no
thicker than 1½ inches)
⅓ cup shallots, chopped fine
1 teaspoon fresh tarragon,
chopped fine (or ½ teaspoon
dried)
¼ pound capocollo, sliced thin
and cut into ¼-inch pieces
(see Note)

¼ cup fresh red pepper, chopped
fine (or canned pimiento)
½ to 1 cup basic Oil and Vinegar
Dressing (see page 360)
Salt
Pepper, ground fresh

In a saucepan large enough to cook the whole zucchini, bring some water to boil. Wash the zucchini, and add them to the water. Cook them until they are tender (only about 5 minutes). (They should be *al dente*; do not make squash of them.) Drain the zucchini, and when they are cool enough to handle, cut off the ends and slice them thin. Put the slices in a large clean bowl. Add the chopped shallots, tarragon, capocollo pieces, red pepper (or pimiento), and half the salad dressing. Toss gently, add more dressing to your taste, and adjust the salt and pepper. (Some capocollo is *piccante*, so watch the amount of pepper you add.)

This salad may be assembled and dressed ahead of time and refrigerated for as long as overnight to allow the zucchini to absorb the dressing. But remember, you must remove the salad from the refrigerator 30 to 60 minutes before serving, allow it to reach room temperature, and toss it again.

Note: Capocollo is a highly spiced pork butt, cured in the form of a thick (4 to 5 inches) sausage. It is sliced thin, like salami, and can be consumed as a cold cut or in combination with other food where a ham flavor is desired. Capocollo can be bought at most delicatessens.

A RICE SALAD WITH VEGETABLES AND FLAVORED WITH TUNA

RICE AND TUNA   SERVES 6 TO 8

4 cups cooked rice
2 cups cooked carrots
2 cups cooked cauliflower buds
1 medium-size fresh red pepper,
cored, seeded, and cut into
¼-inch cubes
1 medium-size fresh green pepper,
cored, seeded, and cut into
¼-inch cubes

7-ounce can tuna fish, drained
and flaked
1 cup Oil and Vinegar Dressing 3
(see page 360)

Cook the rice, drain it, and allow it to cool (or use leftover rice). Scrape the carrots, cut off the ends, and cook the carrots whole in boiling salted water; allow them to cool and cut them into cubes. (You can also cube the carrots first and then cook them.) To cube the carrots, cut them lengthwise into 4 lengths, and then cut these strips crosswise into cubes approximately ¼-inch in size. Do *not* cook the red and green peppers. Cook the cauliflower buds until *al dente*; drain them well, and dry them in a tea towel.

Be sure that all the cooked vegetables are thoroughly cooled. Then combine all the ingredients, starting with ½ cup of the Oil and Vinegar Dressing. Mix by hand in order to determine when the ingredients are bound together by the dressing (they should be able to be mounded on a platter), and add more dressing as necessary.

Adjust the seasoning to taste, adding more salt and pepper or a dash of lemon juice (if needed).

Mound the salad on a bed of lettuce leaves, and garnish with some chopped parsley or 1 or 2 sprigs of watercress.

This salad may be assembled and dressed ahead of time to allow the vegetables to absorb the dressing. Refrigerate, but be sure to remove the salad 1 hour before it is to be served. If you refrigerate the salad, leave it in a bowl so that you can toss it once again after it's out of the refrigerator. Allow it to come to room temperature. It can be arranged on a serving platter and garnished 15 to 30 minutes before serving.

INSALATA DI CAVOLO CINESE
(Salad of Chinese Cabbage)

CHINESE CABBAGE AND PURPLE ONIONS   SERVES 10 TO 12

*5 cups Chinese cabbage,
chopped fine*
*2½ cups young, small zucchini,
unpeeled, ends removed*
*1½ cups young, small cucumbers,
partially peeled, ends removed*
*1 large green pepper, cored
and seeded*

*1 large red pepper, cored and
seeded*
*3 medium-size purple onions,
sliced thin in full rings*
*½ cup fresh parsley, chopped fine
(or 2 teaspoons dried)*
*Oil and vinegar dressing
(see below)*

Cut the zucchini, cucumbers, and red and green peppers into ½-inch cubes. Put all the vegetables in ice-cold salted water, and allow them to stand for about 1 hour. Drain and spin-dry in a plastic salad spinner. (You can't use a woven wire salad basket because of the small pieces of vegetables.) You can also drain them in a colander and pat them dry with kitchen towels. In any case, combine the dry vegetables with oil and vinegar dressing (we suggest Dressing 6 or Dressing 7, see page 361). You will need approximately 1 cup salad dressing (depending on how wet you want your salad). It is best to assemble this salad just before serving.

When the salad is dressed, turn it out on a round or oval platter, and mound it so that it resembles a melon mold; garnish with more chopped parsley or strips of red and green pepper. This salad is good for a buffet supper.

A SALAD OF SQUID RINGS

LEMON AND OIL   SERVES 6 TO 8

TO PREPARE THE SQUID:

4 cups water
2 teaspoons salt
1 bay leaf
*2 pieces lemon zest, about 1 by 2
inches each*

*2 pounds fresh or frozen whole
squid, washed and cleaned
(see page 211)*

In a saucepan, combine the water, salt, bay leaf, and lemon zest, and bring this to a boil. Add the squid. Cook over medium heat for 10 to 15 minutes, until the squid are tender. Halfway through this cooking time, add the tentacles. Drain the squid, and put them in cold water to stop them from cooking further. Drain again, and cut the squid bodies into thin rings, approximately ¼ inch wide. Chop the tentacles into ½-inch pieces. Set all the squid pieces aside. Cover them completely.

TO PREPARE THE SALAD AND DRESSING:

1 garlic clove, quartered

½ teaspoon sugar

¼ cup fresh lemon juice

⅓ to ½ cup olive oil

¼ cup fresh green pepper, chopped fine

1 medium-size red or purple onion, sliced very thin

2 inner celery stalks, including leaves, sliced fine

2 tablespoons fresh flat Italian parsley, chopped fine

Salt

Pepper, ground fresh

While the squid is cooking, combine the garlic, sugar, and lemon juice in a large bowl, mix well and allow to stand for 30 minutes or longer. With a wooden spoon, press the garlic pieces against the side of the bowl to "bruise" them and thereby extract some of the juice; then discard the garlic pieces. Add the olive oil, and mix well. Then add the green pepper, onion, celery, parsley, salt and pepper to taste, and the squid rings and chopped tentacles. Mix well, and serve.

This salad goes well on a buffet table and is sure to be a conversation piece. It's especially good with pastas, casserole dishes, roasts, and so on. It can also be served as an appetizer or first course; arrange several spoonfuls on a washed and dried Boston lettuce leaf, a group of arugola leaves, or inner chicory leaves.

A VARIATION:

An interesting variation is to add freshly cooked peas instead of, or in addition to, the green pepper. Use 1 cup peas (or a little less), increase the amount of olive oil and lemon juice, and adjust the seasoning to taste.

FRESH FINOCCHIO SLICES IN SALAD

FENNEL AND OLIVE OIL

SERVES 6

3 large heads fresh fennel	*2 tablespoons red wine vinegar*
1 garlic clove, quartered	*6 tablespoons olive oil*
⅛ teaspoon superfine granulated	*½ teaspoon salt*
sugar (or regular sugar)	*Pepper, ground fresh*

Wash and dry the fennel, and remove any blemished outer leaves. Slice each head of fennel as thin as possible. If the stalks are tender, use the portion immediately above the bulb. (To test for tenderness, simply taste a piece.) Separate the slices; if you're not ready to dress the salad, put the slices in the refrigerator (tied in a plastic bag).

In a large bowl, marinate the garlic with the sugar and vinegar for at least 1 hour. Press the garlic pieces against the side of the bowl to extract what juice and flavor you can, and discard them. Add the oil, and whisk briskly until the dressing becomes cloudy. Add the salt and pepper (use a liberal amount of pepper in this case).

Toss the dressing and fresh fennel slices just before serving. The fennel may or may not be arranged on lettuce leaves, whichever you prefer.

HOMEMADE PICKLED MUSHROOMS

OLIVE OIL AND LEMON

SERVES 6 TO 8

1 pound fresh white medium-size	*2 tablespoons fresh parsley,*
mushrooms	*chopped fine (or 1 teaspoon*
1 cup olive oil	*dried)*
½ cup fresh lemon juice	*¼ teaspoon celery seed*
1 bay leaf	*1 teaspoon salt*
1 tablespoon fresh thyme,	*Pepper, ground fresh*
chopped fine (or 1 teaspoon	
dried)	

Wipe the mushrooms clean with a tea towel or a damp paper towel, and trim the stem neatly so that they are all the same size. (Cut-off stems can be frozen for the stockpot.)

Combine all the ingredients, and allow them to marinate overnight. Toss and coat with the juices as frequently as possible. (Don't make this an ordeal. If you're at all like us, and you probably are, you'll be in the kitchen a hundred times before tomorrow evening's meal; so each time you're there, give the mushrooms a toss.) We usually divide the mushrooms and sauce in two sterilized ball jars with covers, and shake them with vigor and love.

One of the easiest foods to "cook," these mushrooms are simply served on toothpicks or on a bed of fresh watercress, arugola, or Bibb lettuce. Any leftover sauce can be reused by adding clean, fresh mushrooms with the stems cut off; you can add to the sauce in the same proportions given above.

POTATO SALAD IN THE FAMILY STYLE

MAYONNAISE AND ONION   SERVES 6 TO 8

2 pounds potatoes, unpeeled and
cut in large pieces (see Note)
1 medium-size onion, chopped
fine
1 medium-size green pepper,
cored, seeded, and chopped fine
2 celery stalks, including leaves,
chopped fine
1 tablespoon fresh parsley,
chopped fine (or 1 teaspoon
dried)

¼ cup olive oil
3 tablespoons white vinegar
2 tablespoons sugar
1 cup mayonnaise, homemade
if possible
2 teaspoons salt
Pepper, ground fresh
Chopped fresh parsley (or
paprika or hard-boiled eggs,
sliced, and dried parsley)

In a large saucepan, boil the unpeeled potatoes until they are just tender. (Do *not* overcook them; if you do, they will be mushy when dressed.) Allow the potatoes to cool, and carefully peel off their skins. In a large bowl, combine the onion, green pepper, celery, parsley, and potatoes, and mix gently. Refrigerate for 1 hour.

In a medium-size bowl, combine the oil, vinegar, sugar, mayonnaise, salt, and fresh ground pepper to taste, and blend well. Pour this over the potato mixture, and mix well with two wooden spoons. Better still, mix gently with your hands.

Cover the bowl with foil, and refrigerate the potato salad for at least 2 hours.

To serve, mound the potato salad on a platter. Sprinkle some chopped fresh parsley on top of the mound, or sprinkle some paprika overall. Another attractive way to decorate this salad is to make a strip of overlapping slices of hard-boiled egg down the center of the mound and then to sprinkle a thin line of dried parsley down the center of the egg slices.

Note: We use new potatoes or waxy small red potatoes because they hold their shape better when dressed.

Endive

We can't remember the last time we were served endive in someone's home, and we rarely see it on American restaurant menus. This great Continental favorite deserves to be more popular here. Some endive is grown in the United States, but the quality of the Belgian variety is considered superior.

The vegetable is usually 4 to 6 inches long and 1 to 2 inches wide; its many leaves are white to pale yellow, fitted close together and tapering to a point. One pound of endive usually produces 4 individual pieces of vegetable, enough for 4 servings. The calorie count per serving is under 20.

Endive makes many great combinations. A *roulade au jambon* combines a cooked and chilled endive with a slice of ham and chopped aspic. Most often, it is served au gratin. An unusual appetizer presents half an endive, raw, filled with a combination of steak tartare and Roquefort cheese.

Europeans treat endive with the same versatility that Americans treat potatoes. It is buttered, braised, and béchameled; it is souped, souffléed, and tossed in salads; it is puréed, Parmesaned, and sprinkled with pepper.

ENDIVE VINAIGRETTE

TO PREPARE THE ENDIVE:

> 6 *individual pieces Belgian endive* (*approximately* 1½ *pounds*)
> 1 *teaspoon salt*
> 2 *tablespoons lemon juice*
> ½ *cup water*
> 3 *tablespoons butter*

Wash the endives, and be sure to rinse *between* the outer leaves. Drain the endives well. In a skillet with a tight-fitting cover (or a shallow, wide saucepan with a cover), arrange the endive pieces, one next to the other. Sprinkle with salt, and add the lemon juice, water, and butter. Cover the pan, and cook over very low heat for almost 1 hour. After 25 to 30 minutes, turn each endive so that the other side will cook in the juices.

You can also bake these in a preheated 325- to 350-degree oven, covered, for 1 hour. Check every 15 minutes to be sure the endives don't stick to the pan. If the liquid has evaporated, add a little more water.

When the endives are done, remove them from the cooking vessel, and drain them. Chill them thoroughly, and cut each endive in half lengthwise. Arrange the halves side by side, cut side up, and let them cool.

TO PREPARE THE SAUCE:

> 2 *tablespoons wine vinegar*
> ½ *cup olive oil*
> 2 *tablespoons fresh shallots, chopped fine*
> Salt
> *Pepper, ground fresh*

The sauce should be made just before serving, but have all the ingredients ready in advance. Put the vinegar in a bowl, and add the oil. Whisk constantly until the dressing becomes cloudy. Add the shallots and then the salt and fresh ground pepper to taste. Stir again, pour or spoon the sauce over the endive halves, 1 tablespoon or more per pair, and serve.

The vinaigrette sauce can be varied, for example, by adding Dijon mustard or tarragon. (See the various oil and vinegar combinations, pages

360–364.) But don't get carried away about varying the dressing because the important combination here is endive and shallot.

CURRIED CHICKEN SALAD

CURRY AND MAYONNAISE   SERVES 6 TO 8

TO PREPARE THE CHICKEN:

3 *whole chicken breasts, split*   6 *black peppercorns, whole*
   (*about 3 pounds*)   1½ *teaspoons salt*
2 *carrots, chopped coarse*   2 *bay leaves*
2 *celery stalks, chopped coarse*   3 *cups water* (*approximately*)
1 *onion, sliced*

In a large, covered saucepan (about 4 quarts), combine the chicken breasts, carrots, celery, onion, black peppercorns, salt, bay leaves, and just enough water to cover these ingredients. Bring to a boil; then lower the heat, and simmer, covered, for about 30 minutes, or until the chicken is tender. (Do *not* overcook the chicken.) Remove the chicken from the broth. (Save the broth for another use.) Remove the skin and bones from the chicken, and cut the meat into 1-inch chunks.

TO PREPARE THE SALAD:

½ *cup celery, including tender*   1 *teaspoon curry powder*
   light green leaves, sliced thin ¾ *teaspoon salt*
½ *cup tart apples, unpared, cored,* ⅛ *teaspoon white pepper, ground*
   and diced   *fresh*
½ *cup fresh green pepper,*   ¼ *cup almond slivers* (*optional*)
   chopped fine   *Curry powder* (*or paprika*) *and*
2 *tablespoons onion, chopped fine* *parsley* (*or watercress*), *or hard-*
¾ *cup mayonnaise*   *boiled eggs and dried parsley*
3 *tablespoons light cream*

In a large bowl, combine the chicken pieces, celery, apple, green pepper, and chopped onion. Set aside.

In a small bowl, combine the mayonnaise, cream, curry powder, salt, and white pepper, mix well, and add to the chicken mixture. Add the almond slivers (if you wish). Toss well, and refrigerate until it is thoroughly chilled.

Mound the salad on an oval platter *without* a base of lettuce leaves. Then garnish in one of these ways: Sprinkle very lightly with curry powder (or paprika), and add a sprig of parsley (or watercress). Or make a strip of overlapping hard-boiled egg slices down the center of the mound, and then carefully sprinkle a thin line of dried parsley flakes down the center of the egg slices.

A SALAD OF TRUFFLES

TRUFFLES AND PINE NUTS   SERVES 6

*8 to 10 truffles, about ¾ inch in
    diameter*
1 teaspoon butter
*6 rounded tablespoons pine nuts
    (or slivered almonds)*

*6 inner leaves Boston or Bibb
    lettuce, fully formed*
4 tablespoons walnut oil
1 tablespoon lemon juice

Drain and dry the truffles; slice them paper-thin.

Melt the butter and brown the pine nuts in it.

Wash and dry the lettuce leaves. Place 1 lettuce leaf on each of 6 salad plates. Combine all the other ingredients, and divide them among the lettuce leaves.

STRIPED BASS SALAD

FISH AND TARRAGON   SERVES 6 TO 8

TO PREPARE THE DRESSING:

1 garlic clove, quartered
¼ teaspoon sugar
3 tablespoons white wine vinegar
1 tablespoon Dijon mustard
⅓ cup peanut oil

⅓ cup olive oil
Juice of ½ lemon
Salt
Pepper, ground fresh

In a large bowl, combine the garlic, sugar, and wine vinegar, and let this stand for about 1 hour. With a wooden spoon, press the garlic pieces against the side of the bowl to extract more garlic juice; then discard the garlic pieces. Add the mustard, and beat constantly with a wire whisk to blend. Add the two oils, and blend well. Add the lemon juice, and mix again. Add the salt and pepper to taste, and mix well.

TO PREPARE THE SALAD:

2 cups striped bass, cooked, boned, and cut into ½- to 1-inch chunks (see Note 1)

1 cup fresh green peas, cooked (see Note 2)

¼ cup celery hearts, including tender light green leaves, chopped fine

½ cup shallots, chopped fine (or scallions or onions)

¼ cup carrot shavings, about 1 inch long, made with a vegetable peeler

1 tablespoon capers, drained

1 tablespoon fresh tarragon, chopped fine (or 1 teaspoon dried)

1 tablespoon fresh parsley, chopped fine (or 1 teaspoon dried)

Salt

Pepper, ground fresh

You can cook filets of striped bass or cook a whole fish and filet it yourself. (Do *not* overcook the fish; it should be tender and flaky.) Add the cooked fish, cooked peas (they *must* be a brilliant fresh green), celery, shallots, carrots, capers, tarragon, and parsley. Add salt and pepper to taste. Mix lightly; try not to break up the fish pieces too much. When mixed, taste for seasoning, and add more salt and pepper if you wish.

This salad may be served on lettuce leaves, but our way of serving it is on shells made of *pâté brisée*. These are easy to make if you have 12 or 16 sea shells, some perhaps, that you use for Coquille St. Jacques or our Coquille Beatrice. Make a good pastry (see page 150), and cover 6 or 8 clean shells as you would fill a pie plate. Place another shell on top of each pastry-filled shell, and press them together lightly. With a small, sharp knife, clean the edges of the shells by cutting or scraping off the excess pastry. Bake the shells in a preheated 375-degree oven for about 15 minutes. Separate the shells, and allow the crust to cook, uncovered, in the base shells only, until light brown. When done, remove the shells from the oven, and allow them to cool on a rack.

We usually make 2 shells per person, fill the bottom shell with the salad, and place the second shell on top, arranged in to look as if the shell is actually open, with the salad filling showing. This is an elegant luncheon dish arrangement, sure to "make conversation"—or at least prompt a chorus of *ahs, oohs,* and *oh, mys.*

Note 1: Any white fish can be substituted for the bass. You can use cod or red snapper, for example. Let freshness and price help determine your fish purchase.

Note 2: You can also use frozen peas, but avoid canned peas for this recipe. They are usually too soft and mushy and they lack color. The fish is soft and combines better with crisp peas.

((13))

Condiments, Chutneys, Preserves, and Pickled Eggplant

WE'D rather smell bread baking than almost anything. But one smell that runs a close second is that of cooking relishes, pickles, chutneys, and preserves. We can't explain the appeal of home-made jams, jellies, and marmalade; perhaps it is that the aromas of pickling and preserving carry one back home—to the southwest or the southeast, to India or Indiana, to Milwaukee or Milano, to Toronto or Tallahassee. Bring our Purple Plum Chutney to the table (recipe in this chapter), and the extravagant compliments will be loud and clear.

The word *condiment* is derived from the Latin *condire*, meaning "to season or pickle." Salt and pepper, vinegar and mustard, herbs and ginger are only some of the world's great condiments. Anything that adds piquancy to food can be considered a condiment. Our Pickled Egg-plant in the Mediterranean Style (in this chapter) adds relish to food and stimulates the appetite. We think it should replace the coleslaw in the little white pleated-paper cup on sandwich plates.

As with all other foods, the combinations are infinite. There are Chinese hundred-year eggs pickled in ashes, tea, lime, and salt and *sen ya tain,* which are brine-cured duck eggs. Combinations of vegetables or fruits are endless, too. And let's not forget the pickled walnut. One thing we remember with great pleasure was the chutney served by Madame Saucourt at Le Mas des Serres in St. Paul de Vence in France. It was made of mangoes, plums, pineapples, papayas, sour cherries, ginger root, and other goodies and served with chicken curry.

APRICOT AND CANTALOUPE CHUTNEY

APRICOT AND CANTALOUPE   MAKES 6 TO 8 PINTS

1 *pound dried apricots*
1 *chili pepper (or ½ teaspoon dried red pepper flakes)*
2 *cups currants, dried*
1 *teaspoon ground cloves*
1 *teaspoon ground nutmeg*
2 *tablespoons salt*
2 *tablespoons mustard seed*
¼ *cup fresh ginger, chopped fine (or crystallized ginger)*
3 *large cloves garlic, chopped fine*

4½ *cups cider vinegar*
1 *pound dark brown sugar*
4 *medium-size onions, chopped fine*
3 *medium-size cantaloupes*
½ *cup fresh orange juice*
2 *tablespoons orange zest, chopped fine*

Wash and dry 8 pint-size jars, and sterilize them by whatever method you prefer. Keep the jars hot (in boiling water) until you are ready to fill them.

Dice the apricots into ½-inch pieces, cut the chili pepper into small bits, and put both in a large bowl. Add the currants, cloves, nutmeg, salt, mustard seed, ginger, and garlic. Set this aside.

In a large, heavy saucepan, combine the cider vinegar and brown sugar, and bring to a boil over moderate heat. Then add all the ingredients in the bowl to the saucepan. Bring this mixture to a gentle simmer, and cook uncovered for 45 minutes.

Meanwhile, put the chopped onions in a bowl (use the one you used for the apricot mixture). Skin and seed the cantaloupes, and cut them into ½-inch cubes. Add them to the onions. Then add the orange juice and orange zest.

When the apricot mixture has simmered for 45 minutes, add the cantaloupe mixture, and simmer uncovered for an additional 45 minutes.

Fill the jars, cap them, and clean them by wiping them with a damp sponge or kitchen towel or by running them under warm water. Store the jars in a cool, dark place for about 6 weeks. After 6 weeks the chutney is ready to be served.

PURPLE PLUM CHUTNEY

GINGER AND PLUMS   MAKES ABOUT 4 QUARTS

9 cups Italian plums (about 3
* pounds)*
4 apples
½ cup onions, chopped
2 tablespoons lemon zest,
* chopped fine*
½ cup raisins
½ cup dried currants
1 cup cider vinegar

1 cup water
1½ cups sugar
1 teaspoon salt
½ cup fresh ginger root, chopped
* fine (or preserved ginger)*
1 teaspoon whole cloves
4 cinnamon sticks, each about
* 1½ inches long*

Wash 4 quart-size jars, and sterilize them. Keep the jars hot until you are ready to fill them. (If you would rather use smaller jars, you will need to prepare 8 pint jars for this recipe.)

Cut the plums in half, and remove the pits. Peel and core the apples, and cut each one into 8 pieces. In a large bowl, combine them with the onions, lemon zest, raisins, and currants. Put this aside.

Combine the vinegar, water, sugar, salt, and ginger root in a large saucepan. Tie the cloves and cinnamon sticks in a cheesecloth bag, and add the bag to the saucepan. Bring to a boil, and boil for 3 minutes.

Now add the mixture of fruits and vegetables to the saucepan, and cook slowly for 30 to 45 minutes, until the mixture thickens.

Remove and discard the spice bag. Pour or ladle the hot chutney into the hot, sterilized jars, and seal them immediately. The chutney should be stored for at least 4 weeks in a dark, dry, cool place before use.

CHESTNUTS IN RUM

CHESTNUTS AND RUM   MAKES ABOUT 3½ PINTS

6 cups water
2 pounds dried chestnuts
 (4 cups) or 2 pounds fresh
 (6 cups) (see page 258)
2 pounds dark brown sugar
1 cup water

1½ cups light rum
½ orange, sliced very thin
2 tablespoons fresh ginger,
 chopped fine (or preserved
 ginger)

Have your 4 pint-size jars washed, sterilized, and ready.

Bring 6 cups water to a boil in a heavy saucepan. Add the chestnuts, and cook them, covered, for 1 hour. Drain the chestnuts, and remove their skins, if any.

In another saucepan, combine the brown sugar, 1 cup water, 2½ cups rum, orange slices, and ginger, and bring this mixture to a boil, but do *not* cook it. Remove the saucepan from the heat *immediately*.

Put the chestnuts into the sterilized jars, and pour the hot syrup over them, leaving ½ inch of space at the top of the jars. Cover the jars tightly. These chestnuts do not have to be stored for any length of time; you can use them right away. They may be served cold, or as a hot sauce.

BRANDIED FIGS

FIGS AND BRANDY   MAKES ABOUT 2 QUARTS

5 pounds sugar
2 cups water
12 cloves, whole
4 cinnamon sticks
1 lemon, seeds and ends removed,
 sliced very thin

2 tablespoons preserved ginger,
 chopped fine (or 2 tablespoons
 fresh ginger, grated)
24 large fresh figs
½ cup brandy

Have 4 pint-size or 2 quart-size jars washed, sterilized, and ready to be filled.

In a large saucepan, combine the sugar, water, cloves, cinnamon sticks, lemon slices, and ginger pieces. Cook over very low heat until the sugar is melted (about 10 minutes.)

Carefully add the figs (they bruise easily), and continue to cook slowly for about 45 minutes, or until the figs become transparent.

There should be enough (and maybe a little more) to fill the 2 quart jars. With a slotted spoon remove the figs from the saucepan, and place them in the sterilized jars. Divide the cloves, cinnamon sticks, lemon slices, and ginger pieces equally between the jars. Add ¼ cup brandy to each jar, and fill the jars with the spice syrup. Cover and seal the jars. Allow them to stand at least one month, though you will probably enjoy looking at them for longer.

PICKLED EGGPLANT IN THE MEDITERRANEAN STYLE

EGGPLANT AND VINEGAR   MAKES 4 PINTS

> *12 cups eggplant shoestrings*
> *(about 3 medium-size egg-*
> *plants)*
> *4 tablespoons salt*
> *4 cups white vinegar*
> *2 tablespoons sugar*
>
> *½ cup olive oil*
> *2 chili peppers, chopped fine*
> *½ cup chives, chopped fine*
> *4 cloves garlic, halved*
> *2 tablespoons oregano*

Wash, sterilize, and dry your canning jars.

Peel the eggplant with a vegetable peeler, cut off and discard the ends, and lay the eggplant on its side. Cut it into ¼-inch-thick slices; then put a few slices together, stack them up, and cut them into ¼-inch strips. (This is what we call *shoestring style*; others call it *match style* or julienne.) Put these eggplant shoestrings in a colander, salt them, toss them, and set them aside for 30 minutes. (Put something under the colander to catch the drippings, or put the colander in the sink.)

In a large saucepan, bring the vinegar and sugar to a boil. Add the eggplant pieces, and boil for 5 minutes. (Do *not* overcook.) Drain the eggplant, and reserve the vinegar.

Add the oil, chili peppers, chives, and oregano to the eggplant mixture, and toss well. Fill the sterilized jars, leaving ½-inch space at the top. Press the eggplant mixture to the bottom of the jar to release its juice. If more juice is needed, add 1 or 2 tablespoons of the reserved vinegar mixture. Add 2 pieces of garlic to each jar, and seal tightly. This should be stored in a cool, dark place for 4 weeks before it can be used.

We use lots of this pickled eggplant. It adds excitement to any anti-pasto; it can be served as a first course, with or without lettuce; and it's great in combination with hot or cold slices of beef, poultry, pork, veal, or lamb. Add it to chef's salads; place it next to grilled burgers; include a large plateful in your next buffet.

Nectarines and Apricots

Flushed with red, the nectarine, a variety of the peach, is nectar of the Gods when picked fresh and served as a dessert fruit, especially in fra-grant combination with a chilled sauternes. It is also popular as a major ingredient in jams and preserves. In this chapter, we combine it with apricots.

We've never heard of peeling an apricot, and this, to us, makes the apricot a special food. One of the most ancient of fruits, it is grown extensively in California, Australia, France, Hungary, and the Middle East. Dried apricots, a popular food all over the world, are a great com-bination with other foods, as they prove in our Nectarines alla Caramel.

NECTARINES ALLA CARAMEL

NECTARINES AND APRICOTS   MAKES ABOUT 2 QUARTS

6 pounds small-size fresh   *¼ cup Grand Marnier liqueur*
  nectarines, not too ripe   *½ cup honey*
1 cup dried apricots   *6 cups sugar*
¼ cup water

Wash 2 or 3 quart-size canning jars, and sterilize them.

Blanch and carefully peel the nectarines; do *not* remove the pits.

Chop the apricots into ½-inch squares (you should have 1 cup).

Combine the water, Grand Marnier, and honey, and pour this mixture into a baking pan large enough to hold the nectarines in a single layer side by side. Sprinkle 3 cups sugar over this liquid, and then arrange the nectarines in the pan. Sprinkle the dried apricot pieces overall, and cover with the remaining 3 cups sugar.

Bake in a preheated 250- to 275-degree oven for about 3 hours, until a caramel syrup has been formed. During the baking, turn the nectarines several times so that each is completely covered with and baked in the syrup.

Carefully put the caramelized nectarines into the sterilized jars, and divide the syrup equally, leaving ½-inch space at the top of the jars. If the nectarines can be consumed right away, no storage is necessary.

FRESH PINEAPPLE CHUTNEY

PINEAPPLES AND DATES   MAKES 4 TO 5 PINTS

1 *fresh medium-size pineapple*	2 *cups dates, pitted and chopped*
½ *cup fresh ginger root*	1 *cup currants, dried*
4 *tablespoons lemon zest*	1 *teaspoon red pepper flakes*
3 *cups light brown sugar*	½ *teaspoon ground allspice*
3 *cups cider vinegar*	1 *teaspoon salt*

Wash and sterilize the canning jars.

Lay a fresh pineapple on its side, and with a large, sharp knife, cut off both the end with the leaves and the bottom end. Stand the pineapple bottom end up, and cut it in half; cut each half in half. Stand up one quarter on its thicker end, skin side facing left, hold the top with one hand, and slice the core out with one stroke. Do this for each quarter. Lay each cored quarter lengthwise, skin side down, and with a small, sharp knife, cut the meat away from the skin (as you would with a half grapefruit or half avocado). Discard the skins. On a clean surface, slice the pineapple quarters lengthwise into ⅔-inch slices, and then cut these into ⅔-inch cubes. There should be 3 to 4 cups of cubes, depending on the size of the pineapple. If you have more than 4 cups, reserve the extra fruit for another use.

Use a vegetable parer to peel the fresh ginger root and lemon. (Try to peel the lemon without getting much of the white pith.) Chop both the ginger and the lemon zest fine.

Combine all the ingredients in a heavy, enameled saucepan, and bring the mixture to a boil quickly over high heat. Cook the mixture at a lively boil, stirring frequently, until it thickens (about 50 minutes).

As soon as the chutney has thickened, ladle it into pint-size canning jars. Secure the tops with lids. When the jars are sealed and cool enough to handle, run them under warm water to wash away any syrup on the outsides. This chutney may be served as soon as it has cooled, or it may be stored for several years if properly sealed.

A FIG PRESERVE

FRESH FIGS AND FILBERTS   MAKES ABOUT 5 PINTS

5½ cups sugar   *1 lemon, ends removed, sliced*
1¾ cups water   *fine*
3 tablespoons lemon zest,   *3 cups filberts, skinned, halved,*
*   chopped fine*   *   and toasted*
5 pounds purple figs, sliced thick *½ cup Cognac (or brandy)*

Combine the sugar, water, and lemon zest in a heavy saucepan, and cook over low heat for 5 minutes, or until the sugar is completely dissolved. Then add the figs and lemon slices, and simmer for 20 minutes.

Let this mixture stand, covered, overnight.

Bring the fig mixture to a simmer again, and cook it for an additional 20 minutes, until it thickens. Add the filberts and Cognac (or brandy). Cook 1 minute more.

Pour or ladle the mixture into the sterilized jars, and seal the jars. This preserve may be consumed right away or stored for future use. Brandied fruits, however, develop a better flavor if stored for a minimum of 4 weeks.

A PEACH-AND-ALMOND CONDIMENT WITH
CHAMPAGNE VINEGAR

PEACHES AND ALMONDS   MAKES ABOUT 3 PINTS

4 or 5 fresh peaches	*⅔ cup brown sugar*
4 tablespoons fresh lemon juice	*⅔ cup almonds, slivered and*
4 tablespoons lemon zest,	*toasted*
chopped fine	*½ cup fresh ginger root, peeled and*
1 cup golden raisins	*chopped fine (or preserved*
½ cup water	*ginger)*
½ cup champagne vinegar	*1 large fresh sweet red pepper*

Wash and dry 3 or 4 pint-size canning jars, and sterilize them.

Blanch and peel the peaches. Cut them in half, and remove the pits.

Cut the peach halves into 1-inch cubes (you should have about 3 cups).

The red pepper should be seeded and chopped fine (you need ½ cup).

Combine all the ingredients in a heavy, enameled saucepan, stir well, and bring to a boil. Lower the heat. Allow the peach and almond mixture to simmer slowly for 40 minutes, or until it becomes as thick as you want it.

Fill the sterilized jars, and store them in a cool, dark place for 4 weeks.

QUINCES AND APPLES IN A SPICED SYRUP

HONEY AND QUINCES   MAKES ABOUT 3 PINTS

2 pounds quinces, not overripe	*3 tablespoons fresh ginger,*
Quince seeds	*chopped fine (or crystallized*
1 pound firm apples	*ginger)*
1 tablespoon lemon juice	*3 tablespoons lemon zest,*
2 cups white vinegar	*chopped fine*
1 cup cooking liquid	*2 cinnamon sticks, broken in*
1 cup honey	*pieces*
2 cups sugar	*12 whole cloves*

Wash and dry 3 pint-size canning jars, and sterilize them in whatever manner you prefer.

Wash the quinces, and peel and core them. Reserve the seeds. Cut the quinces into slices, and put them in a saucepan. Cover them with boiling water (just barely), and cook them over moderate heat until they are tender. Test them with a fork; they should be *al dente*. (Do *not* overcook them.) Drain the slices, but reserve 1 cup cooking liquid.

Wipe the apples with kitchen toweling, peel and core them, and slice them. Put the apple slices in a bowl, add the lemon juice, and toss them. (This will keep them from discoloring.) Set aside.

In a heavy saucepan, combine the white vinegar, 1 cup cooking liquid (from the quinces), honey, sugar, ginger, and lemon zest. In a square of cheesecloth, tie the broken cinnmaon sticks, cloves, and quince seeds into a bag; add this to the vinegar and honey mixture. Bring to a boil, and cook for several minutes, until the sugar is dissolved. Add the tender quince slices and raw apple slices, and simmer until the quince slices turn clear.

Remove and discard the spice bag. Fill the hot, sterilized jars with the boiling quince and apple mixture. Cover the jars with tops, and seal them right away. The mixture can be eaten immediately, even while hot, but improves in flavor if stored for a minimum of 4 weeks.

((14))

Sweets: Cakes, Cheesecakes, Crepes, Pies, Tarts, and More Sweets

D ESSERTS, without question, one of the great and abiding riches of the table, can no longer be thought of as "food for the Gods" because every man and woman has laid claim to them. Who has not eaten apple pie? Who has not eaten ice cream?

Recipes for desserts fill pages of entire books. Cakes with frostings, fillings, and icings compete with cookies, custards, and crepes. There are soufflés and sauces galore and pies, pastries, and puddings from every part of the world. With today's modern kitchen equipment and appliances, every family can present a gelatin, cream, or frozen dessert. And everyone can bombe! And mousse, too.

Cake alone, not to mention other desserts, is a pillar in the construction of our culture. There's the birthday cake, the Valentine cake, the Easter cake, the Christmas log, the wedding cake, the anniversary cake, the "welcome home" cake, the "congratulations" cake, and the "bon voyage" cake. And there's Sister Mary's Ricotta Cake (in this chapter), which is an unusual combination of ricotta and orange and lemon zest baked in a pastry. You could call this a pie, but we think of it as cake because it's baked in a cake pan, not a pie plate.

Although we grew up thinking of fresh, uncooked fruit as synonymous with dessert, we know that fruit cooked with other foods produces happy marriages of flavor and aroma. The Empress Josephine's sweet tooth was assuaged by bananas and rum Creole, Nero's wife craved strawberries on a bed of rose petals, and Cardinal Wolsey insisted on strawberries with fresh thick cream. Fruit is everywhere, in every season. And fruits go into cakes, pies, soufflés, puddings, and every compote. There's strawberry shortcake, blueberry pie, and apricot mousse. Here are just a few great combinations: oranges and coconut, peaches and wine, cherries and Cognac, apples and ginger and nutmeg and cinnamon, bananas and rum, pineapple and kirsch, strawberries and cream, pears and chocolate, prunes and port. And in this chapter, we combine prunes with Madeira (Prunes Steeped in Madeira).

The great combinations are limitless. Imagine a sherbet combined with Armagnac and capped with a giant prune macerated in Armagnac. And we recently heard of hazelnut ice cream covered with chocolate shavings and set in a crown of meringue. One evening, we may combine goat cheese and warm crackers for dessert; the next night, the treat may be a *haselnuss torte* (a cake batter combined with ground hazelnuts, layered with buttercream, with more nuts on top). One of our favorite duets is bourbon and chocolate, presented in this chapter in Cocoa Roll à la Bourbon.

We won't engage in debates over who discovered or really invented ice cream or whether puddings should be served at the beginning rather than at the end of a meal. We think the importance of desserts is indelibly written in history. It is a fact, for instance, that there is a recipe for an ice cream dessert in the handwriting of Thomas Jefferson. (Is this one of the reasons Americans are the greatest ice-cream consumers in the world?) But ice cream alone, even in its many masks, is not sufficient to satisfy the world's appetite for sweets. So let's move on to cakes, cheesecakes, and crepes, to pies, tarts, soufflés, and perhaps some prunes.

As Alvin Kerr once said, "Bread may be the staff of life, but dessert is its cloak of elegance." Dessert represents the culmination of the cook's arduous labors. It comes to the table as his or her consummate achievement and as a tribute to good friends and warm friendships.

Almonds

Although they are mentioned in the Bible and were cultivated in Western Europe countries during the Renaissance, almonds were not introduced and grown in the United States until just before the Civil War.

But the "Greek nuts," as the Romans called almonds, are among the front runners in popularity today. They can be blanched, toasted, salted, fried, boiled, ground, peppered, and used in many dishes, ranging from soups to desserts. Classic combinations pair the almond with trout and chicken stuffing. In this chapter, we present them with cream (Almond Cream Meringue Pie), and with ginger (Almond Ginger Roll) in desserts worthy to be gifts to take to kings.

ALMOND GINGER ROLL

ALMONDS AND GINGER   SERVES 8 TO 12

8 egg yolks
6 tablespoons sugar
1 tablespoon ground ginger
8 egg whites
¾ cup almonds (4 ounces),
* ground (or walnuts or filberts)*
3 or 4 tablespoons confectioners'
* sugar*

1½ cups heavy cream
2 tablespoons sugar (optional)
3 tablespoons preserved ginger,
* chopped fine*
6 slices preserved ginger

In a large bowl, beat the egg yolks until they form a ribbon when the beater is raised. While you are beating the yolks, gradually add the sugar, a spoonful at a time; then add the ground ginger.

In another bowl, beat the egg whites to stiff points. Fold the egg yolks into this mixture. (Do *not* overfold.) Slowly fold in the ground almonds. Set aside while you prepare the baking sheet.

Grease a 10-by-15 jelly-roll pan with shortening. Line the pan with wax paper, and then apply more shortening to the top of the wax paper.

Pour the soufflé mixture into the prepared jelly-roll pan, and spread it evenly. (A rubber spatula is excellent for spreading the mixture and cleaning out the bowl.) Bake in a preheated 350-degree oven for 30 to 35 minutes, until the cake's color is "light toast."

When the cake is done, remove the pan from the oven, place a damp cloth over it, and allow the cake to cool completely. Remove the cloth, and sprinkle with confectioners' sugar.

Place another piece of wax paper (large enough to hold the cake) on a flat surface. Sprinkle some confectioners' sugar on the wax paper, and turn the cake out onto it. Peel off the paper on which the cake was baked, taking care not to tear the cake.

Whip the heavy cream, and add 2 tablespoons sugar (if you wish). Add the preserved ginger pieces, and spread this cream mixture over the cake.

Roll the cake, jelly-roll fashion (from the long side). Use the wax paper as a guide in rolling the cake by lifting up the paper and pushing forward. When the roll is completed, move it to a serving plate, seam side down.

If you are ready to serve, sprinkle the roll with more confectioners' sugar. If not, cover the roll with wax paper or plastic wrap, and refrigerate it. Just before serving, sprinkle it with confectioners' sugar. Garnish by crisscrossing two thin slices of preserved ginger in three places on top of the roll.

AN ITALIAN CAKE FOR ANY FAMILY

ANISETTE AND LEMON   SERVES 12

TO PREPARE THE SPONGE CAKE LAYERS:

1 cup cake flour	*½ cup cold water*
¾ teaspoon baking powder	*1 cup granulated sugar, sifted*
¼ teaspoon salt	*1 teaspoon vanilla extract*
2 eggs, room temperature	*½ teaspoon lemon extract*

Sift the flour, baking powder, and salt together in a bowl.

Separate the eggs; place the whites in a small bowl and the yolks in a large bowl with the cold water. Beat the egg yolks and water with an electric beater, a whisk, or whatever, until the yolks are fluffy and tripled in volume. During this process add the sifted sugar, a spoonful at a time. Continue beating until the yolks form a heavy ribbon when the beater is lifted and the mixture is thick enough to mound slightly (about 10 to 15 minutes). Stir in the flavorings. Add the flour mixture *all at once* and fold it in with a rubber spatula.

Beat the egg whites until they form moist, stiff peaks when the beater is raised. Then, with a rubber spatula, fold them into the yolk mixture until completely blended.

Pour the cake mixture into two round 8-inch layer pans lined (bottoms only) with liberally buttered wax paper, and bake in a preheated 350-degree oven for 25 to 30 minutes, or until done.

Remove the pans from the oven, and invert them on a cake rack until the cakes have cooled; then lift off the pans, and peel off the wax paper.

TO PREPARE THE FILLING:

⅓ cup semisweet chocolate pieces
¾ cup granulated sugar
1 pound ricotta
½ teaspoon powdered cloves
2 tablespoons anisette liqueur
2 tablespoons fresh lemon zest, chopped fine
2 tablespoons fresh orange zest, chopped fine

Melt the chocolate in the top of a double boiler over hot water. Stir in the sugar, and beat until well blended. Add the ricotta, powdered cloves, anisette, and lemon and orange zest.

TO ASSEMBLE THE CAKE:

2 cake layers
4 tablespoons sweet vermouth
1 recipe ricotta filling

Split the cake layers crosswise to form 4 layers. Place 1 layer, cut side up, on a cake plate. *Carefully* sprinkle the cut side with 1 tablespoon vermouth. Then spread with one-third of the filling. Repeat this procedure with the next 2 layers. Top with the last layer, and sprinkle with the remaining 1 tablespoon vermouth. Chill the cake for 4 or 5 hours.

THE FINAL TOUCH:

1 cup heavy cream, whipped
1 tablespoon sweet vermouth

When it is time to serve the cake, beat the heavy cream until it forms stiff peaks. Fold in the sweet vermouth. Decorate the cake with this mixture as you wish. You may frost the sides and pipe on (with a pastry tube) rosettes or garlands or anything you wish. We simply spread the cream over the top and sides and smooth it, but not too evenly.

Chocolate

For centuries, chocolate, a product of the cacao bean, has held first place as temptress *à la table*. Nearly any dieter will admit his or her complete helplessness in the presence of almost any chocolate dessert. The cultivation of the cacao bean dates back to the Aztecs in Mexico and to Isabella's Spain, but chocolate as we know and use it was developed by the Swiss and Dutch in the late nineteenth century. Roasted cacao beans are milled; chocolate liquor is produced from this and poured into molds that yield slabs of rich brown chocolate. Chocolate liquor also produces ground cocoa, the basis of that comforting winter drink. Who hasn't experienced the delight of hot fudge sauce on chocolate ice cream, or of the torten, pies, *pots de crème*, cream puffs, bombes, mousses, candies, cakes, cookies, and other fabulous desserts that owe their appeal to chocolate or cocoa. Chocolate is one of the greatest combiners, blending happily with almost any food. In the following recipe (Cocoa Roll à la Bourbon), it appears in a gingham frock with black lace thoughts, desirous of a merger with bourbon, cream, and cocoa.

COCOA ROLL A LA BOURBON

BOURBON AND CHOCOLATE   SERVES 6 TO 10

6 eggs, separated (see Note)	*3 tablespoons bourbon*
1 cup sugar	*3 tablespoons cocoa powder*
6 ounces dark sweet chocolate	*1 cup heavy cream*

Beat ¾ cup sugar and all the egg yolks until they form a ribbon when the beaters are raised. Slowly melt the chocolate in the top of a double boiler, just until it is smooth. Add the bourbon to the chocolate, and mix well. Allow this to cool until it is lukewarm; then blend it into the yolk mixture.

Beat the egg whites until they are stiff, and blend them into the mixture of yolks and chocolate.

Butter a cookie sheet (about 9½ by 13½ inches). Cover the bottom of the pan with wax paper, and butter the wax paper. Spread the mixture evenly over the wax paper, using a spoon, spatula, or large knife.

Bake in a preheated 350-degree oven for 10 minutes. Then reduce oven heat to 300 degrees, and bake for 5 minutes, until it is done (check for doneness by the ordinary methods: toothpick comes out dry, cake springs back from touch, whatever you prefer). (Do *not* overcook.)

Remove the cookie sheet from the oven, and cover the top with a cloth or tea towel wrung out in cold water. When the cake is cool, remove the cloth, and loosen the roll from the baking sheet. Dust the top of the cake with 1½ tablespoons cocoa powder. Turn the cake out onto another piece of wax paper, and carefully peel off the buttered wax paper from the bottom, being careful not to tear the cake.

Whip the heavy cream with the remaining 1½ tablespoons cocoa powder and ¼ cup sugar. Spread this mixture evenly over the cake, and roll it up à la jelly roll.

The roll may be decorated with a dusting of cocoa powder (1 additional tablespoon) or a dollop or two of whipped cream. This cake will keep well in the refrigerator for up to 3 days; it can also be frozen.

Note: When you separate eggs, do it while the eggs are cold; it will be easier that way. Then allow both yolks and whites to come to room temperature. (Whites will increase more in volume if they are beaten when warm.) You should always test eggs for freshness. There are several ways to do this: Put it in a deep bowl filled with warm water. If it sinks, chances are it is fresh; if it floats, its freshness is in doubt. Or, in a dark room, hold an egg over a candle flame or light bulb. Look through the shell, and if the yolk and white appear clear, that's a good sign of freshness; if they seem cloudy, the egg may be stale. But the most accurate test for freshness is to break each egg, and put it in a small dish or bowl before adding it to others in any given recipe. If an egg is spoiled, you'll know immediately because of its bad smell.

A MOCHA CHEESECAKE

COCOA AND CHOCOLATE   SERVES 12 TO 20

TO PREPARE THE CRUST:

2 cups chocolate cookie crumbs
½ teaspoon cinnamon
¼ cup butter, melted
2 tablespoons butter

Combine the crumbs, cinnamon, and melted butter, and blend well. Grease a 9-inch springform pan with 2 tablespoons butter. Then press the crumb mixture against the sides and bottom of the pan. (Do this with your hands.) Refrigerate for 1 hour to set the crust.

TO PREPARE THE FILLING:

1 teaspoon instant coffee	*8 ounces semisweet chocolate*
1 teaspoon vanilla extract	*¾ cup sugar*
1 teaspoon water	*3 eggs*
2 tablespoons cocoa powder	*1½ pounds cream cheese, softened*
¼ cup butter, melted	*3 cups sour cream*

In the top of a double boiler, combine the instant coffee, vanilla, and water, and mix until the coffee is dissolved. Add the cocoa, melted butter, and chocolate, and melt over moderate heat. Stir until smooth. Remove from heat.

Beat the sugar and eggs until they form a ribbon when the beaters are raised, and add the cream cheese, bit by bit. Then add the lukewarm chocolate mixture, and beat slowly until well blended. Gradually add the sour cream.

Pour this batter into the chilled crust, and bake in a preheated 350-degree oven for 50 minutes. Remove the pan from the oven (even though the filling will be liquid-looking), and let it stand for 30 minutes. Then refrigerate the cake until it is firm (about 2 hours). Before serving, decorate with dollops of whipped heavy cream (forced through a pastry bag) along the outer edges of cake and a chocolate tidbit atop each dollop. Or add one large dollop of cream in the center, and place a chocolate tidbit on top.

Serve with whipped heavy cream, unsweetened, on the side. (Serving this rich cake with more cream may sound lavish, but the combination is excellent because the plain heavy cream cuts the rich mocha flavor. Together they're mouth-watering.) This cheesecake, so easy to prepare, holds up well and can be stored in the refrigerator for 1 week or longer.

CASSATA DI CAFFE E CIOCCOLATA

COFFEE AND CHOCOLATE   SERVES 12 TO 16

TO PREPARE THE CRUST:

1 cup plain chocolate wafers, crushed
1 cup graham crackers, crushed
½ cup butter, melted
2 tablespoons butter

Combine the first three ingredients, and blend well. Grease a 10-inch springform pan with the 2 tablespoons butter, and press the crumb mixture against the bottom and sides of the pan. (Be sure to get a good layer of crumbs on the bottom and at least halfway up the sides of the pan, but it is not necessary to have the mixture cover the sides completely.) Refrigerate the crust for at least 1 hour before filling.

TO PREPARE THE WHITE FILLING:

¾ tablespoon unflavored gelatin
½ cup, plus 2 tablespoons, cool water
½ cup sugar
1 teaspoon almond extract

1 pound whole-milk ricotta
¾ cup heavy cream, whipped
3 tablespoons sliced almonds, toasted

Add the gelatin to the cool water to soften it (this will take several minutes). Add the sugar and almond extract, and combine well. Bring this mixture to a boil, and simmer slowly until the sugar and gelatin are completely dissolved.

Transfer the gelatin mixture to a large bowl, add the ricotta, and whip it until smooth. Blend in the whipped cream and toasted almonds, and set aside while you work quickly to prepare the mocha filling.

TO PREPARE THE MOCHA FILLING:

¾ *tablespoon unflavored gelatin*	1 *pound whole-milk ricotta*
2 *tablespoons cool water*	¾ *cup heavy cream, whipped*
½ *cup sugar*	
4 *ounces semisweet chocolate*	
½ *cup hot strong coffee (or ½ cup*	
boiling water mixed with 4	
tablespoons instant coffee)	

Add the gelatin to the cool water, and allow it to soften.

Add the chocolate to the hot coffee, and stir it until it melts.

Add the sugar and chocolate-coffee mixture to the softened gelatin, and blend well. Bring this to a boil, and simmer slowly, until the sugar and gelatin are completely dissolved.

Transfer the gelatin mixture to a large bowl. Add the ricotta to it, and whip the mixture until it is smooth. Add the whipped cream, and blend until the mixture is one even color.

Fold together the white and mocha fillings. (Do *not* overmix. The point is to obtain a swirl of the two colors.) Pour the mixture into the crumb crust, and refrigerate for at least 4 hours, or even overnight.

Before you remove the springform, loosen the *cassata* around the edge with a small knife of metal spatula. Keep the *cassata* on the pan's base. Sprinkle the top with cocoa powder, shaved chocolate, or some chocolate wafer crumbs.

Oranges

Our grandmother would not buy oranges unless the fruit and vegetable vendor would allow her to dig into the orange rind with her thumbnail. It wasn't always that she would utter *"ha sapore"* ("it has flavor"). Often, we remember the vendor saying, as patiently as he could, *"Per favore, Signora Beatrice, non toccate gli aranci"* ("Please, Signora Beatrice, don't touch the oranges"). We're quite sure she would be against buying plastic-wrapped fruit. When you buy oranges, pay attention to the skins. They should be thin and unblemished. And if the skin is a bright orange color, that usually means the orange is ripe and flavorful.

ORANGE CAKE IN THE GRAND MARNIER STYLE

ORANGE AND LEMON   SERVES 8 TO 10

TO PREPARE THE CAKE:

1 cup butter, room temperature
1 cup sugar
4 egg yolks, room temperature
1 cup sour cream
2 tablespoons orange zest,
  chopped fine

2 cups all-purpose flour
1 teaspoon baking powder
1 teaspoon baking soda
4 egg whites, room temperature

Cream the butter and sugar until well blended. Add the egg yolks, sour cream, and orange zest. Beat until light and fluffy and until a ribbon is formed when the beaters are raised. (Combining the butter and sugar is especially easy if you use a regular or heavy-duty electric mixer, as is the bringing of the yolk mixture to the ribbon stage. Of course, you can also do this by hand.)

In a large bowl, sift together the flour, baking powder, and baking soda. Stir this into the butter and sugar mixture. Beat the egg whites until stiff, but not dry, and fold them into the mixture.

Pour this batter into an oiled (use vegetable oil) and floured 9-inch tube pan. Bake in a preheated 325-degree oven for 1 hour. Remove the cake, and let it sit for 15 to 20 minutes. When the pan is cool enough to handle, very carefully loosen around the edge of the cake with a sharp knife, and invert the cake onto a cake platter.

TO PREPARE THE SYRUP:

Juice of 1 orange
Juice of 1 lemon
¾ cup sugar
Pinch of salt
¼ cup Grand Marnier liqueur

In a small pot, gently boil the orange juice, lemon juice, sugar, salt, and Grand Marnier until the mixture becomes syrupy (about 5 minutes).

Pour this syrup slowly over the cake, and let it soak in. Serve with some seeded orange slices and whipped cream alongside. This cake will keep in the refrigerator for about 1 week if it is wrapped carefully in foil.

SISTER MARY'S RICOTTA CAKE

RICOTTA AND ORANGE   SERVES 8 TO 10

TO PREPARE THE PASTRY:

1½ cups all-purpose flour	1 egg yolk
¼ teaspoon salt	2 tablespoons ice-cold water
6 tablespoons butter (see Note)	
2 tablespoons shortening (other than butter) (see Note)	

Place the flour, salt, butter, and shortening in a large bowl, and blend these ingredients with your fingertips or a pastry blender (the pastry arm of a heavy-duty electric mixer works wonders here) until mixture is crumbly and looks like coarse meal. In a small bowl, beat the egg yolk and water, and blend this into the flour mixture just until the dough is pulled together. (If you have to add a few more drops of cold water to achieve this, do so, but do *not* overmix the dough.) Flour your hands, and quickly shape the dough into a flattened ball. Wrap it in wax paper, and refrigerate it for 30 minutes or longer.

Roll out the dough into a piece ⅛ inch thick and approximately 12 inches in diameter. Line a round 9-by-1½-inch cake pan with the dough. (Do *not* precook.)

TO PREPARE THE FILLING:

1½ pounds ricotta	1 tablespoon vanilla extract
2 tablespoons orange zest, grated	⅓ teaspoon salt
2 tablespoons lemon zest, grated	4 eggs
¼ cup flour	1 cup sugar

In a large bowl, combine the ricotta, orange zest, lemon zest, flour, vanilla, and salt. Blend these ingredients thoroughly, and set them aside.

In an electric mixer, beat the eggs slowly until foamy. Add the sugar, and mix until the yolks form a ribbon when the beaters are raised. Stir the beaten eggs into the ricotta mixture, and blend until smooth. Pour the filling into the pastry-lined cake pan. Bake the cake in a preheated 350-degree oven for 50 to 60 minutes, or until the filling is firm and the pastry is golden brown.

Cool the cake on a rack for 30 minutes; then remove it from the pan, and leave it on the rack until completely cooled.

Note: An easy way to proceed is to use stick butter. Cut the equivalent of 6 tablespoons into quarters lengthwise and then into tiny squares; do this on wax paper. Then measure the shortening and cut it into ¼-inch pieces, again on wax paper. Put the butter and shortening back into the refrigerator (on the wax paper) until you are ready to blend the pastry. Refrigerating the pieces is important; don't neglect this step.

GATEAU DU CIEL WITH SAUCE MAGDALENE
(Heaven Cake)

SUGAR AND EGG WHITES   SERVES 8 TO 10

TO PREPARE THE CAKE:

1 cup all-purpose flour	½ teaspoon cream of tartar
1¼ cups sugar	Healthy pinch of salt
8 egg whites	1 teaspoon almond extract

Combine 1 cup flour and ½ cup sugar, and sift into a bowl.

In another bowl, beat the egg whites until they are foamy. (A heavy-duty mixer would be ideal for this.) Add the cream of tartar, and beat for about 30 seconds. Then add the salt and almond extract. (We add the salt and the extract while the heavy-duty beater is going. If you're using an eggbeater or a whisk, it's more difficult to do this.) Add the remaining ¾ cup sugar, 1 tablespoon at a time. Stop beating. Add the flour and sugar by sprinkling a few tablespoons at a time (or put flour and sugar back into the sifter, and sift again) over the egg whites. When about one-third of the flour mixture is sprinkled, fold it into the egg whites. (As we've said again and again, a rubber spatula works wonders here.) Repeat the sprinkling or sifting of the flour mixture and the folding into the egg whites until all the flour mixture is blended.

Pour this mixture into a 9-inch tube pan. (Do *not* oil, butter, or grease the pan.) Bake the *gâteau* in a preheated 350- to 375-degree oven for 30 minutes or a little longer, until it is done. (One way to test for doneness is to touch the cake lightly with your fingers; if it springs back, it's baked.)

Remove the tube pan from the oven, and turn it upside down on a wire rack. Allow the cake to cool; then remove it from the pan with the the help of a knife or metal spatula.

TO PREPARE THE SAUCE MAGDALENE:

4 egg yolks	*¼ cup Grand Marnier liqueur (or*
½ cup sugar	*Cointreau, kirsch, mirabelle, or*
1 cup milk, scalded	*eau de vie de poire William)*
Healthy pinch of salt	*1 cup heavy cream, whipped*

In the top of a double boiler, combine the egg yolks and sugar, and beat constantly with a wire whisk until the yolks are thickened. (Do *not* let yolks curdle. A way to prevent them from curdling is to lift the top saucepan out every now and then and to keep the water in the bottom saucepan at a simmer rather than a raging boil.) Add the scalded milk and salt, and stir constantly until the sauce resembles light cream. Remove the top saucepan from double boiler. Add the liqueur, and blend well. Set the pan in the refrigerator to cool the sauce.

Just before serving, whip the heavy cream and fold it into the chilled liqueur sauce.

We serve this cake (with some powdered sugar dusted over it) and its sauce separately. Pass the bowl of sauce, and let your guests help themselves.

A CASHEW CHEESECAKE

CASHEW NUTS AND CREAM CHEESE   SERVES 10 TO 16

4 eggs, room temperature
1¾ cups sugar
½ cup heavy cream
32 ounces cream cheese (2
   pounds), room temperature
1 teaspoon vanilla extract
3 teaspoons kirsch

8 ounces cashew nuts (1½ cups),
   whole or broken
2 tablespoons butter
½ to ¾ cup graham cracker
   crumbs
Confectioners' sugar

Combine the eggs, sugar, heavy cream, softened cream cheese, vanilla, and kirsch in a mixing bowl, and whip with an electric mixer until smooth. (A heavy-duty mixer with a wire whisk beater accomplishes this in several minutes.)

Place the nuts in the container of a food processor (such as a Cuisinart), and blend until the mixture is smooth and pasty. (The nuts may also be broken with a rolling pin and then ground in batches with a mortar and pestle or crumbled in a blender.) Add the nuts to the cream cheese and eggs, and whip again until all is smooth.

Butter an 8-inch round metal baking pan (2 or 3 inches deep) heavily with 2 tablespoons butter. Then coat it thickly with the graham cracker crumbs. Remove excess crumbs by tapping the pan and turning it upside down. Fill the pan with the cream cheese batter, and tap it gently on a counter or tabletop to level the mixture. Then place the pan in a bain-marie. The cake pan should *not* touch the sides of the larger pan, and it should sit in 1 inch of water. Bake in a preheated 325-degree oven for 2 hours. Then turn off the heat, and leave the cake in its water bath in the oven, with the door closed, for 1 additional hour. Lift the cake pan out of the water bath, and let it rest on a rack for 2 hours. To remove the cake from the baking pan, hold a cake stand tightly against the pan, and turn them over in one motion. (A large plate or a serving tray may be used instead of a cake stand.)

Sprinkle the cheesecake with confectioners' sugar, and serve. This rich, moist cake will easily serve 16 people. It keeps well in the refrigerator for as long as 1 week.

A BASIC DESSERT CREPE

EGGS AND MILK   MAKES 24 CREPES

6 eggs
2 cups milk
¾ cup all-purpose flour
¾ teaspoon salt
½ cup butter (1 stick)

Mix the eggs, milk, flour, and salt with a whisk until well beaten. (Use a blender if you have one, but mix only half the batter at one time. This will take only 4 or 5 seconds per batch.) Then allow the batter to stand for at least 1 hour (more standing time will not hurt).

Clarify the butter by melting it in a skillet and removing the foam that comes to the top, or filter the melted butter through cheesecloth. (A tablespoon makes easy work of scooping off the foam.)

Brush a crepe pan or a skillet (7 to 8 inches wide) with a little clarified butter. Heat the pan, and then add 3 tablespoons of the batter to coat the entire bottom of the pan. (You accomplish this by moving the skillet in a swirling motion.) You may have to adjust the amount of batter slightly. All you want is a thin layer of batter that covers the bottom completely (it's all right if the layer runs up the side by ⅛ inch or so). Cook the crepe on one side to a light brown; then cook the other side.

Crepes may be stacked and covered with foil, plastic wrap, or a tea towel; better yet, *wrap* the stack completely in a tea towel. This will prevent the crepes from drying out before you are ready to fill them. (It is *not* necessary to put wax paper or foil between the crepes. We can't understand where this wasteful and time-consuming procedure originated. Our crepes don't stick together; yours shouldn't either. They peel off, one from the next, easily, so why layer them with wax paper or anything else.)

CREPES WITH COOKED PEARS

PEARS AND GINGER   SERVES 6

TO PREPARE THE FILLING:

3 *pears, peeled, cored, and sliced*   4 *tablespoons candied ginger,*
    fine   *chopped fine*
1 *apple, peeled, cored, and sliced*   *Juice of ½ lemon*
    fine   *Pinch of salt*
1 *cup sugar*

Combine the pears, apple, sugar, ginger, lemon juice, and salt in a small, heavy saucepan. Cook over low heat for about 45 minutes until the mixture becomes soft, thick, and jamlike.

TO PREPARE THE CREPES:

12 *Basic Dessert Crepes* (*see page 402*)
 2 *tablespoons sugar*
 2 *tablespoons candied ginger, chopped fine*
 4 *tablespoons ground filberts*

Lay out the crepes on a flat working surface, and place 1 heaping tablespoon of the pear mixture on each crepe, spreading it evenly with the base of the spoon. If any pear mixture is left over, add a little more to each crepe. Fold the crepes in quarters lengthwise, and arrange them in a shallow baking dish. (Arrange the crepes so that they overlap; they will look better that way.) Sprinkle the sugar, candied ginger, and ground nuts over the crepes, and bake them in a preheated 375-degree oven for 10 minutes.

TO PREPARE THE SAUCE:

½ *cup sugar*
½ *cup butter*
 Juice of 1 lemon
¼ *cup mirabelle* (*or brandy or kirsch*)

Combine all the ingredients, and bring the mixture to a boil. Pour the sauce into a serving bowl, and add it to the hot crepes as they are individually served.

CREPES LIMONE

SUGAR AND LEMON   SERVES 4 TO 6

TO ASSEMBLE THE CREPES:

12 *Basic Dessert Crepes (see page*   ¾ *cup sugar*
   402)   3 *tablespoons lemon zest,*
12 *tablespoons heavy cream*   *chopped fine*
  (*about ¾ cup*), *whipped*   3 *tablespoons butter*

Arrange the crepes on a flat working surface, and place 1 tablespoon whipped cream in the center of each. Using the back of the spoon, spread the cream over most of the crepe, leaving a 1-inch border uncovered all around. Fold the crepes in quarters lengthwise (or roll them, if you prefer), and arrange them in a large iron skillet or shallow baking dish. Sprinkle the crepes with the sugar and lemon peel, and dot with butter. (Be sure you sprinkle the sugar carefully all over the crepes.) Place the crepes under the broiler, until the sugar melts and starts to brown. (But do *not* let the sugar turn into brittle.)

TO PREPARE THE SAUCE:

½ *cup butter* (1 *stick*)
½ *cup brandy*
½ *cup orange liqueur*
4 *tablespoons lemon juice*

Combine all the ingredients in a saucepan, bring to a boil, and remove from the heat at once. (Do *not* allow the sauce to continue to boil.) Pour the hot sauce over the crepes quickly, and serve immediately.

MIRABELLE MERINGUE PIE

CREAM AND MIRABELLE   SERVES 8 TO 10

TO PREPARE THE PIE SHELL:

4 *egg whites, room temperature*   ¼ *teaspoon vanilla extract*
  Pinch of cream of tartar   ¾ *cup granulated sugar*
  Pinch of Salt   1 *tablespoon vegetable oil*

Beat the egg whites until they are frothy (about 1 minute). Add the cream of tartar, and beat a little more (1 minute). Then add the salt and vanilla, and continue beating while you add the sugar, ½ teaspoon at a time, until the whites form shiny, firm peaks when the beaters are raided. (If you use a heavy-duty mixer, this entire process should take no more than 5 minutes at a speed between medium and high.)

Pour the vegetable oil into an ovenproof 9- or 10-inch glass pie plate, and spread it over the plate. (We find a paper towel helpful for this.) Be sure to oil the top of the rim. With a rubber spatula (really the only utensil to use for this), scrape the meringue out of the mixing bowl and into the oiled pie plate. Just mound the meringue in the plate; it will look like a snow-covered mountain. Then, beginning at the center of the mound, push the meringue to the outer edge of the pie plate in sweeping motions with the spatula, as if you were making a well in a mound of flour. You should end up with a piecrust edge of meringue, 1 to 1½ inches thick and 1 to 1½ inches high, on the rim of the plate.

Bake the meringue shell on the middle shelf of a preheated 200-degree oven for at least 2 hours. When it is done, cool the shell on a wire rack.

TO PREPARE THE FILLING:

> *4 egg yolks, room temperature*
> *½ cup granulated sugar*
> *1 tablespoon fresh lemon juice*
> *3 tablespoons of mirabelle*
> *1 cup heavy cream, whipped*

Combine the egg yolks and sugar in the top of a double boiler, mixing well with a small wire whisk. Heat the yolk mixture over moderate heat, *stirring all the time*. (The egg must not be allowed to curdle or thicken against the sides of the pan; use the whisk to stir all the yolk mixture all the time.) If you think the egg is cooking too quickly, lower the heat; better still, lift the top pan out of the bottom one for about 15 seconds, using one hand to lift as you keep whisking with the other. Depending on the intensity of the heat, you will cook and whisk for 5 to 10 minutes, until the yolk mixture is the thickness of mayonnaise and just as smooth. (This is *most* important because if the mixture is thinner—the consistency of heavy cream, for example—the filling will not solidify after it has cooled.)

When the right thickness is reached, remove the pan from the heat. Add the lemon juice immediately, keep stirring, and then add the mirabelle. Mix this well, and set it aside to cool. (To speed up the cooling, wet a sponge or a folded towel in cold water, and place it under the pan. Beat the heavy cream until it forms peaks when the beaters are raised. Use a rubber spatula to fold the cooled egg mixture into the whipped cream, and blend until the mixture is one even color. Transfer this filling mixture to the cooled meringue shell. (Again, the rubber spatula is essential.) Refrigerate for at least 3 hours before serving. The following variations all follow the same basic procedure used to prepare our Mirabelle Meringue Pie, but in each case, the filling features a delicious new combination.

1. ALMOND CREAM MERINGUE PIE

ALMONDS AND CREAM   SERVES 8 TO 10

Substitute 1 tablespoon almond extract for the 3 tablespoons mirabelle. When the pie has cooled, toast ¼ cup almond slivers in 1 teaspoon melted butter until lightly browned, and sprinkle them on top of the pie.

2. BLACK CURRANT CREAM PIE WITH CASSIS

CASSIS AND BLACK CURRANTS   SERVES 8 TO 10

Soak ¾ cup dried black currants in 4 tablespoons crème de cassis for several hours. Substitute 3 tablespoons cassis for the 3 tablespoons mirabelle. When you are ready to serve the pie, strain the currants, and sprinkle them over the top of the pie.

3. MOCHA MERINGUE CREAM PIE

COCOA AND COFFEE   SERVES 8 TO 10

Combine 3 tablespoons crème de cacao, 1½ tablespoons instant coffee, and 1½ tablespoons cocoa powder in the top of a double boiler, stirring until the coffee and cocoa are dissolved and the mixture is well blended. Add this to the filling in place of the 3 tablespoons mirabelle. A few minutes before you serve the pie, sprinkle cocoa powder over the meringue crust edge. (Do *not* overdo this.)

4. ORANGE ZEST MERINGUE PIE

COINTREAU AND CREAM   SERVES 8 TO 10

Substitute 3 tablespoons Grand Marnier or Cointreau liqueur for the 3 tablespoons mirabelle. You may wish to add 2 drops each red and yellow food coloring (but *no more* than that) to the yolk mixture after adding the lemon juice and liqueur; this will give the filling a pale orange tint. When the pie has cooled, decorate it with 6 to 8 thin slices of orange zest in whatever arrangement pleases you most.

5. CHOCOLATE CREAM MERINGUE PIE

CRÈME DE CACAO AND CHOCOLATE   SERVES 8 TO 10

Substitute 3 tablespoons crème de cacao for the mirabelle. Add 3 ounces melted semisweet chocolate to the yolk mixture after the lemon juice and liqueur have been added.

6. CREME DE MENTHE CREAM PIE

CRÈME DE MENTHE AND CREAM   SERVES 8 TO 10

Substitute 3 tablespoons crème de menthe liqueur for the 3 tablespoons mirabelle. You can also add 1 drop green food coloring (if you wish). If you have a sprig of fresh mint, add a piece to the center of the pie just before serving.

7. PRALINE CREAM PIE IN MERINGUE SHELL

PECANS AND BOURBON   SERVES 8 TO 10

To prepare a praline powder, caramelize 1 cup sugar and adding 1 cup chopped pecans and a dash of salt. Butter a cookie sheet, and pour the praline mixture onto it. Allow the mixture to cool and harden, break it in pieces, and put it through a blender. (Do *not* overblend.) Substitute 3 tablespoons bourbon whiskey for the 3 tablespoons mirabelle. Fold in the praline powder as you blend the yolk mixture with the whipped cream.

8. RUM RAISIN MERINGUE PIE

RAISINS AND RUM   SERVES 8 TO 10

Soak ½ cup raisins in 4 tablespoons light or dark rum for about 1 hour. Strain the raisins, and sprinkle them over the bottom of cooked and cooled meringue shell before adding the filling. Substitute 3 tablespoons light or dark rum for the 3 tablespoons mirabelle.

9. RASPBERRY MERINGUE PIE

RASPBERRIES AND FRAMBOISE   SERVES 8 TO 10

Substitute 3 tablespoons framboise for the 3 tablespoons mirabelle. You may also wish to add 1 drop red food coloring to the yolk mixture after adding the lemon juice and framboise; this will give the filling a pale pink tint. After the filling has solidified (3 to 4 hours in the refrigerator), place fresh whole raspberries at 1-inch intervals around the edge of the filling, next to the meringue crust edge.

CHOCOLATE PIE A LA BOURBON

CHOCOLATE AND BOURBON   SERVES 8 TO 10

TO PREPARE THE PASTRY:

1 cup all-purpose flour
½ teaspoon salt
¼ cup pecans, chopped (see Note)
2 tablespoons butter, cut into bits (see page 399)

2 tablespoons shortening (other than butter), cut into bits (see page 399)
3 to 4 tablespoons ice-cold water
½ cup whole filberts (or pecan halves)

Mix the flour, salt, chopped pecans, butter, and shortening with a pastry blender (or blend with the pastry arm of a heavy-duty electric mixer), until the mixture resembles oversized corn meal.

Add 3 tablespoons water, and stir the mixture *as little as possible*. Using your hands, bring the pastry together to form a ball (add more water only if *absolutely* necessary to bring the dough together).

Roll the dough out on a floured surface, line a 9- or 10-inch pie plate with it, and prick the entire pastry with a fork. Bake in a preheated 450-degree oven for 10 to 12 minutes, until light brown. Remove the crust from the oven, and allow it to cool before filling it. Add the whole filberts (or pecan halves) to the bottom of the pie shell, and set aside.

TO PREPARE THE FILLING:

1-ounce square semisweet chocolate (or chocolate bits)
1 cup semisweet chocolate bits
¼ cup bourbon whiskey
3 egg yolks

3 egg whites
¼ teaspoon cream of tartar
2 tablespoons confectioners' sugar
1½ cups heavy cream, whipped

Combine both chocolates and the bourbon in the top of a double boiler, and melt the chocolate. Set this aside to cool.

Whip the egg yolks until they are really thick and form a ribbon when the beaters are raised. Then add the cooled chocolate mixture to the yolks and continue beating until well blended.

Beat the egg whites and cream of tartar, add the sugar, and continue beating until the egg whites are stiff. Fold them into the chocolate mixture. Fold in two-thirds of the whipped cream, and pour this mixture into the pie crust. Chill the pie for 2 hours or longer.

Serve the remaining whipped cream as a topping for each pie serving. (Do *not* spread this cream over the whole pie.) This is such a rich dessert that servings should be smaller than usual.

Note: The easiest, quickest way to chop the pecans is in a blender.

Strawberries

One of the dismal things the world of food has to offer is the overripe, blemished strawberry. There's nothing quite as unpleasant as handling a wet, leaky, moldy berry; we know we just don't like it. Then there is the half-red, half-green strawberry with a very hard spot; we don't appreciate that either. But when a berry is fresh, firm, bright red, and topped with a sprightly green cap, there is nothing more stunning. One of the most beautiful sights in the world is a large bowl of really fresh strawberries. And one of the greatest combinations is fresh strawberries with fresh, cold, thick cream.

But these versatile fruits combine so well, so deliciously with many other foods, too. With oranges, they become *à la maltaise*; with raspberries, they are *cardinal*; with kirsch and rice, they are *fraises Condé*. They blend well with pineapple and in Bavarian creams, with pastry and in compotes, with port and in ice creams. Strawberries are ideal in jams, liqueurs, soufflés, cheesecakes, and mousses. We love them all.

Two of our favorite strawberry combinations (featured in this chapter) are with bourbon and with sour cream. Iris Compitello's Fresh Strawberry Pie in the Southern Style was created by Iris and Joe, a great combination unto themselves, and it joins strawberries with sour cream. Strawberry Pie in the Carolina Style, inspired by brother Jerry of New York, South Carolina, and Kentucky and his ninth-generation Kentucky wife, Boone, is a monument to magnificent fresh strawberries and fresh thick cream in happy combination with bourbon.

IRIS COMPITELLO'S FRESH STRAWBERRY PIE
IN THE SOUTHERN STYLE

SOUR CREAM AND CREAM CHEESE   SERVES 8

TO PREPARE THE PIE CRUST:

> 1 cup all-purpose flour
> 6 tablespoons sugar
> 6 tablespoons butter, room temperature
> 1 egg yolk

Combine these ingredients, and press them into a pie pan with your fingers. Bake in a preheated 375-degree oven for 15 minutes. Remove the crust from the oven, and set it aside to cool.

TO PREPARE THE FILLING:

> 3-ounce package cream cheese softened
> 3 tablespoons sour cream
> 1 to 1½ quarts fresh whole strawberries, hulled

> 3 tablespoons sugar
> 3 tablespoons cornstarch
> ½ cup water
> 1 cup heavy cream, whipped

Beat the cream cheese and sour cream until they are blended, and spread this mixture over the cooled pie shell.

Add whole strawberries on top of the cream mixture, but put enough soft berries to make 1 cup in a blender. In a saucepan, mix the sugar and cornstarch, water, and blended berries. Cook this mixture over low heat until it thickens; then simmer it for 1 minute, and set it aside to cool. Pour the cooled sauce over the berries in the pie shell, and refrigerate the pie until thoroughly cooled.

Top the pie with the whipped cream, and serve.

STRAWBERRY PIE IN THE CAROLINA STYLE

STRAWBERRIES AND BOURBON   SERVES 8

¾ *cup sugar*
1 *tablespoon unflavored gelatin*
3 *eggs, separated, at room*
   temperature
¾ *cup bourbon whiskey*
½ *cup pecans, chopped*
½ *cup heavy cream, whipped*

1 *cooked rich pastry pie shell* (*see*
   page 398)
1 *cup heavy cream*
2 *cups fresh whole strawberries*
   (*see Note*)
Powdered sugar

Combine 3 tablespoons sugar with the gelatin, and mix well. Set this aside.

Whip the egg yolks until they are thick, and *slowly* add the bourbon. (This must be done *very* slowly because alcohol has a strange effect on yolks: If it is added too quickly, it almost cooks them.)

In the bottom part of a double boiler bring some water just to the boil, and then lower the heat. In the top part of the double boiler, combine the yolk mixture with the sugar and gelatin. Cook the mixture over hot (not boiling) water, stirring constantly, until it is thick enough to coat a spoon (about 10 minutes). (It is *most* important to stir this mixture constantly, and we think the best utensil to use is a rubber spatula because you can really clean the sides of the pan with it.) Be very watchful while you are doing this. If the heat is too high, or if the water boils, the yolks will cook around the side of the pan. Don't allow that to happen. When the mixture is the proper thickness, remove the top pan from the double boiler, and set it aside to allow the mixture to reach room temperature.

Now whip the egg whites, and when they are fully foamed, add the remaining sugar, 1 teaspoon at a time, beating constantly until the whites form stiff, glossy peaks when the beaters are raised. Fold this into the cooled yolk mixture. Add the chopped pecans and whipped cream. (Remember, the yolk mixture must be cooled first. If the cream is added to the yolk mixture while it is still warm, the cream will break down.) Pour the filling mixture into the cooked, cooled pie shell, and refrigerate until it is set (about 2 hours).

Whip the 1 cup remaining cream, and spread it evenly over the filling. Then arrange whole, unblemished strawberries on top of the cream, placing the berries as close together as you can, to cover the surface completely. Place the berries stem side down until you get to the very center of the pie. Place 3 or 4 stemmed berries stem side up in the center.

We like to dust the berries lightly with powdered sugar just before serving but we don't sugar all of them. We start dusting at the outer edge of the pie but leave the center berries unpowdered.

Note: As you wash and dry the berries, select 3 or 4 that have beautiful green caps and stems, and save them to decorate the center of the pie.

Brazil Nuts

In their natural state of growth, Brazil nuts are tangerinelike segments of a larger container that resembles a coconut in shape and weight. There may be a dozen nuts closely fitted into a 4-pound casing. They are catastrophic for the calorie counter, but they can be used in countless ways. One of their more unusual and delicious combinations is with brandy, in our Brandied Brazil Nut Tart (below). Brazil nuts, ground, form the basis of a piecrust that is filled with an uncommonly smooth concoction of brandy and cream.

BRANDIED BRAZIL-NUT TART

BRAZIL NUTS AND BRANDY   SERVES 8

TO PREPARE THE PASTRY:

> *1 cup Brazil nuts, ground*
> *2 tablespoons all-purpose flour*
> *4 tablespoons sugar*
> *¼ teaspoon salt*
> *3 tablespoons butter, melted*

In a bowl, completely blend all the ingredients, and press this into a 9-inch tart or quiche pan, covering the bottom and sides. Bake the pastry in a preheated 375-degree oven for 10 to 15 minutes, until it is golden. Remove it from the oven, and set it on a rack to cool. Then remove the shell from the pan.

TO PREPARE THE FILLING:

> *4 egg yolks, room temperature*
> *½ cup sugar*
> *1 tablespoon lemon juice*
> *3 tablespoons brandy*
> *1 cup heavy cream, whipped*

In the top of a double boiler, combine the egg yolks and sugar, and cook over simmering water, stirring constantly with a wire whisk until the mixture thickens to the consistency of mayonnaise. (This is important; if the yolks and sugar are undercooked, the filling will not solidify.) Remove the top saucepan from the heat, add the lemon juice, and stir well. Add the brandy, and stir again. Allow the yolk mixture to cool to room temperature.

Whip the heavy cream until it forms stiff peaks when the beaters are raised and fold it into the cooled yolk mixture. Pour the filling into the pastry shell, and refrigerate the tart until it is set (at least 2 hours).

This tart will keep nicely overnight. When you are ready to serve it, decorate it with rosettes of whipped cream, or toss some ground Brazil nuts on top.

MOUSSELINE DE MARRONS IN A TART
(Chestnut purée)

CHESTNUTS AND COGNAC   SERVES 8 TO 12

TO PREPARE THE PASTRY:

> *12 tablespoons butter, room temperature*
> *6 tablespoons vegetable shortening, room temperature*
> *½ cup water, ice cold*
> *½ teaspoon salt*
> *1½ cups all-purpose flour*

Combine the butter and shortening, and whip them until they are smooth. (The wire whisk arm of a heavy-duty electric mixer is excellent for this, but any electric mixer will serve, as will a whisk or wooden spoon.) Add the water (we combine ice cubes and water and let them sit), salt, and flour, and mix until a dough is formed. Pat it into a rounded shape, wrap it in wax paper, and refrigerate it for 1 hour. (We almost always double this recipe, use what we need, and freeze the remainder. It will also keep, unfrozen, in the refrigerator for almost 1 week.)

Lightly flour a pastry board or work surface, and roll out the chilled dough until it is quite thin (about ⅛ inch thick). Flour the underside and topside of the dough if necessary as you roll it out. Fold the circle of dough in half, pick it up, and lay it over a 10-inch tart pan. (Be careful not to tear the dough. Press it into the pan so that it covers the bottom and sides. Run the rolling pin over the top of the pan to cut off the excess pastry. Prick the pastry with a fork, cover it with foil, and fill the pan with raw rice, raw beans, or aluminum foil bits to keep the shell from puffing up during the baking and losing its shape. Bake the tart in a preheated 400-degree oven for 8 to 10 minutes. Then remove all filler material, prick the pastry with a fork, and put it back into the oven until it is lightly colored (about 10 minutes). Place the pastry shell on a rack, and allow it to cool completely before adding the filling.

TO PREPARE THE MOUSSELINE:

8¾-ounce can chestnut purée (see Note 1) · ¼ cup Cognac · 1 tablespoon unflavored gelatin · ¼ cup water, lukewarm, with a pinch of salt · ¼ cup honey · 1 cup heavy cream, whipped · Chocolate shavings (or curls) (see Note 2)

Put the chestnut purée and Cognac in a blender for several seconds, until it is thoroughly mixed. (If you don't use a blender, combine and blend these ingredients in the bowl of an electric or hand mixer.)

Soften the gelatin in the salted water, and add the honey. Bring this mixture just to the scalding point, and remove it from the heat. Combine it with the chestnut purée, mix well, and allow it to cool. (This will take about 30 minutes. The purée is cold to start with.)

Whip the cream, and fold it into the cooled chestnut mixture. Fill the cooled tart shell, and refrigerate it for 2 hours or more, until the filling is set.

Decorate with a few chocolate shavings or curls. This rich dessert should be served in rather small portions.

Note 1: We use Clément Faugier's Purée de Marrons Nature.

Note 2: Choose the sweetness of chocolate that you prefer.

CARAMEL TARTS A LA BELLEVUE

DAMSON PLUM PRESERVES AND VANILLA   SERVES 6

⅔ cup butter
⅔ cup damson plum jelly (or preserves)
3 eggs
⅔ cup sugar

1½ tablespoons vanilla extract
Salt
12 individual tart shells (see page 414) (see Note)
½ to 1 cup heavy cream, whipped

Melt the butter and jelly in the top of a double boiler and allow the mixture to cool.

Whip the eggs and sugar until the mixture forms a ribbon when the beaters are raised, and add it to the melted, cooled, jelly. Add the vanilla and salt to taste, and mix well. Pour mixture into the tart shells. (Fill the shells as full as possible. The filling puffs up during cooking, but it will subside to a gummy consistency as it cools.) Bake the tarts in a preheated 350-degree oven for 30 minutes, or until the pastry browns. Remove the tarts from the oven, and allow them to cool. Serve them with whipped cream.

Note: Divide the pastry into 12 equal parts. Roll out and place in 3-inch tart shells. If you use frozen pastry shells, brush them with milk, and bake them in a preheated 350-degree oven for about 10 minutes. Allow them to cool before filling.

Macadamia Nuts

The macadamia nut is underrated, especially for dessert purposes. We think it has a finer flavor and aroma than most other nuts. Why is the supply of these nuts so limited? (The only significant production of macadamias is in Hawaii.) We think macadamias are fantastic in combination with maple syrup, and so we offer you next our Maple Macadamia Pie. We're sure you will thoroughly enjoy its moist coconut consistency. Also in this chapter you'll enjoy our Macadamia Tarts with Fresh Peaches Cooked in Champagne.

MAPLE MACADAMIA PIE

MAPLE SYRUP AND MACADAMIA NUTS   SERVES 6 TO 8

1 pastry shell for bottom of 8- or 9-inch pie plate (see page 414)
1 cup macadamia nuts, chopped (see Note)
1 cup coconut, shredded
3 eggs, room temperature

¼ cup sugar
1 cup maple syrup
¼ teaspoon salt
6 tablespoons butter, melted and cooled

Line the pie plate with the pastry, and make a pastry edge. Arrange the macadamias in one layer over the unbaked pie shell, covering as much of the pastry as you can. Sprinkle the shredded coconut over the nuts, and refrigerate the pie shell.

In a large bowl, lightly beat the eggs. Add the sugar, maple syrup, salt, and melted butter. Mix well, and pour into the pie shell.

Bake the pie in a preheated 400-degree oven for 15 minutes. Lower the heat to 350 degrees, and bake for an additional 20 or 25 minutes, until the filling is custardlike. (If the top browns too quickly, cover it with a sheet of foil.) Insert a knife to test for doneness.

The filling will rise substantially, but it will fall to the level of the pie plate as it cools. This pie is best served lukewarm with a dollop of ice-cold whipped cream.

Note: Most macadamia nuts are sold in airtight jars, and they are usually whole. The best way to prepare the nuts for this pie is to place them on a chopping block and cut each nut in half. Macadamias are tender and may break into more than two pieces as you are cutting them, but don't fret about that.

Peaches

Nonno, as we called our grandfather, was a peach specialist. He was the family member responsible for buying peaches, and it was his delight to plunge slices of them in red wine and eat them at almost any time of day. He said that we should never buy peaches that have no fragrance. We always had tasty peaches in our house, and the attar of peach filled the air. When you shop for peaches, remember that you should be able to smell them. Forget the beautiful skins: it is the odor that counts.

MACADAMIA TARTS WITH FRESH PEACHES COOKED IN CHAMPAGNE

PEACHES AND CHAMPAGNE   SERVES 8

TO PREPARE THE TART SHELLS:

> *1 cup all-purpose flour*
> *1 stick butter*
> *2 tablespoons confectioners' sugar*
> *½ cup macadamia nuts, salted, chopped fine*

Combine the flour and sugar, and cut in the butter with a knife or pastry blender. (This may also be done with the pastry arm of a heavy-duty electric mixer. If you use one, cut the butter into ¼-inch squares, and add it slowly to mixer, as you do in *pâté brisée.*)

Add the chopped nuts. (Do *not* overblend.) Combine this mixture in the palms of your hands, and form it into a ball. Wrap it in wax paper, and chill it for at least 1 hour.

Divide the pastry into 8 parts, and press each part into a 3-inch tart pan. Bake the tarts in a preheated 400- to 425-degree oven for 8 to 10 minutes. Cool the tart shells, remove them from their baking pans, and set them aside.

TO PREPARE THE FILLING:

> *4 fresh peaches*   *4 cloves, whole*
> *2 tablespoons lemon juice*   *½ cup heavy cream, whipped*
> *¼ cup sugar*   *8 macadamia nuts, whole*
> *1 cup champagne*

Parboil the peaches in boiling water to remove their skins. Cut the peaches in half and combine them with the champagne, sugar, lemon juice, and cloves. Bring this mixture to a simmer, and cook the peaches until *al dente*. (Do *not* overcook them.) Remove the peaches from the heat, and cool them in this sauce. (You can cook the peaches several days ahead of time and store them in a container in the refrigerator.)

Place 1 peach half into each tart shell. Top each shell with a good dollop of whipped cream, and top it all off with a whole macadamia nut. Serve immediately.

ITALIAN CHRISTMAS PASTRIES

HONEY AND SUGAR

MAKES MORE THAN 100 PASTRIES, BUT THEY GO LIKE HOTCAKES

7 cups flour
1 teaspoon salt
2 teaspoons baking powder
12 eggs

3 tablespoons vegetable oil
6 cups vegetable oil
2 cups honey
Confectioners' sugar

In a large bowl, combine 6 cups flour, salt, and baking powder, and make a well in the center of the mixture. Beat the eggs well, and add them, along with 3 tablespoons oil, to the flour. Mix well. (Use your hands or two wooden spoons. You can also use the pastry paddle arm of a heavy-duty electric mixer.) When the dough is combined, turn it out onto a floured board, and knead it with the reserved 1 cup flour until the dough is very, very smooth (about 20 minutes). (This is an essential step in the procedure, so do *not* cut it short.) If you use the heavy-duty mixer, we suggest you combine the dough in the mixer and then knead it by hand. Let the dough rest for 15 minutes under a tea towel or large bowl.

TO SHAPE THE PASTRY:
If you have a pasta machine, first shape the dough to resemble a loaf about 17 inches long and 3 inches wide. Cut the loaf into 1-inch slices. With a small rolling pin, flatten each piece so that you can put each one through the machine rollers. Pass each piece of dough through the plain rollers of the pasta machine twice. Change the dial setting to

narrow the opening, and pass the dough through 4 or 5 times more, or until the dough is less than ⅛ inch thick. You will have long strips about 30 inches long and 4 inches wide. Place the dough strips on floured wax paper. (Remember that you will need *lots* of room for this.) Cut each strip crosswise and diagonally into 1½-inch-wide pieces. (If you have a ravioli cutter, use it; it will give the pastries a zigzag edge.) Each strip should now be approximately 1½ by 5 inches. Pinch each strip together in the center with thumb and index finger. This gives the pastries a bow shape.

If you don't have a pasta machine, divide the dough into 4 or 8 parts. (You will need a large working surface and a rolling pin at least 26 inches wide to work with 4 parts; 8 parts will, of course, require a smaller rolling pin and work space.) Roll out a dough circle less than ⅛ inch thick, and use a ravioli cutter to cut long pastry strips 4 inches wide; then cut these diagonally into strips 1½ inches wide. Then pinch each piece of dough to give it a bow shape.

TO FRY THE PASTRY:

Use a large roasting pan (14 by 16 by 2 or 12 by 19 by 2½). (It should fit over two burners on your stove top.) You can also use a pan half this size or a large skillet, but the double-size pan will work twice as fast for you. The recipe calls for 6 cups vegetable oil for frying. The key thing to remember is that whatever pan you use, it should be half filled with oil; for example, a 2-inch-deep pan will require 1 inch of oil. (Do *not* use pans deeper than 2½ inches; the extra depth is simply not necessary.)

Heat the oil until it is quite hot but not smoking. (You can test for the right temperature by adding a tiny piece of dough to the oil: If it rises to the top, the oil is hot enough.) Put the pastries into the hot oil, one at a time, leaving some space in between. Use a wooden spoon and fork to turn each pastry so that the other side will cook. The pastry cooks quickly (about 1 minute per side). It is done as soon as it turns a golden color (it will not brown). Because these pastries cook very quickly, you should work assembly-line fashion; by the time you have put the eighth or tenth piece of pastry in the oil, the first one is ready to come out, and so on.

Transfer the cooked pastries to paper toweling. They also cool quickly. Arrange the goodies on an attractive serving platter, or store them in a covered cardboard box; they will keep in a cool place for about 2 weeks. One way to serve these pastries is to stack them in layers and sprinkle them with honey in lines that resemble angel's hair. Or sprinkle them with powdered sugar. These festive-looking treats can be arranged in baskets for giving as gifts. Create whatever Christmas effect you want.

PRUNES STEEPED IN MADEIRA

PRUNES AND MADEIRA   SERVES 6

2 pounds dried prunes	*1 cup sugar*
2 cups Madeira	*1 cup Calvados*
Zest of 1 orange (see Note)	*½ cup heavy cream*

Put the dried prunes, Madeira, and orange zest in a large, covered ceramic or glass bowl, and allow them to stand at room temperature overnight, or for at least 12 hours.

Put the prunes, Madeira, and orange zest in a saucepan, add the sugar and Calvados, and cook slowly until the prunes are tender. Remove the saucepan from the heat, and transfer the prunes to a ceramic bowl, and set them aside to cool.

To serve, put several prunes and several tablespoons of their cooking liquid into individual serving dishes (glass bowls or very large red wine glasses), and add 1 tablespoon *unwhipped* heavy cream. (*Do not* stir or mix in the cream; just ladle it in.)

Note: Whenever using lemon or orange peel, it is important to eliminate as much of the brittle, bitter white pith as you can. We never grate grate lemon or orange rind because grating does not rid the peel of pith. Instead, we scrape the peel. This is easy as pie if you use a vegetable or potato peeler with a swivel blade. With this kind of peeler, you'll leave the pith behind and end up with the lemon or orange zest. (Of course, very skilled hands can accomplish this with a sharp paring knife.) The zest can then be sliced very thin and chopped fine.

COLD CARAMEL MERINGUE SOUFFLE

CARAMEL AND CREAM   SERVES 8 TO 12

TO PREPARE THE MERINGUE:

> 6 egg whites, room temperature
> Dash of cream of tartar
> 1 cup sugar
> 1 teaspoon vanilla extract

Beat the egg whites until they begin to froth; then add the cream of tartar, and whip until the whites form soft peaks when the beaters are raised. Add the sugar, 1 tablespoon at a time, until all the sugar is absorbed and dissolved. Fold in the vanilla. Put the meringue in a lightly oiled pie plate. (Or put it on an oiled cookie sheet in 2-tablespoon portions.) Bake it in a preheated 200-degree oven for 2 hours.

When the meringue is done, remove it from the oven, allow it to cool, and cut or crumble. You will have 4 cups of meringue crumbs.

TO PREPARE THE CARAMEL SAUCE:

> 3 cups sugar
> 1¼ cups water
> 2 tablespoons lemon juice
> 2 tablespoons light rum (optional)

In a heavy saucepan, melt the sugar over low heat, stirring constantly until it turns a light amber. Add the water and lemon juice, and simmer this mixture for 5 minutes. Remove the saucepan from the heat, add the rum (if you wish), and stir to blend. Cool and refrigerate the sauce. You will have 1 cup.

TO PREPARE THE SOUFFLÉ:

> 2 cups milk
> 1 teaspoon vanilla extract
> 6 egg yolks, room temperature
> ½ cup sugar
> 2 envelopes unflavored gelatin

> ½ cup water
> 2 cups heavy cream, whipped
> 1 recipe meringue crumbs
> 1 recipe caramel sauce

Scald the milk. Add the vanilla, remove the mixture from the heat, and let it cool.

Meanwhile, beat the egg yolks well, and add the sugar slowly, a spoonful at a time. Add the cooled milk slowly, and set this mixture in the top part of a double boiler over hot water. Without bringing it to a boil, cook the custard until it thickens.

Soften the gelatin in the water for 5 minutes or so. Be sure it is thoroughly dissolved. (The best way to do this is to set the bowl with the gelatin in it over hot water. Use the bottom of the double boiler you just used to cook the custard.) Then combine the gelatin and custard. When it is cool and *beginning* to set (watch this carefully; if you let the mixture get too firm, it will be difficult to mix with cream), fold in the whipped heavy cream and ½ cup of the caramel sauce and the 4 cups of meringue crumbs.

To make a collar for the soufflé dish (use a 1- to 1½-quart-size dish), cut a sheet of 12-inch wax paper long enough to fit around the dish, allowing a little extra for an overlap. Fold the wax paper in half lengthwise (this will give you a 6-inch-high collar to accommodate the soufflé). Oil one side of the paper with vegetable oil. Wrap the collar around the dish, making sure that the oiled side is inside and the folded edge is up. Secure the collar with a tight rubber band, or tie it with ordinary string.

Pour the mixture into the soufflé dish (with its collar in place). Refrigerate the soufflé for 4 hours or longer, or until it is fully set. The collar should be removed, of course, before serving.

To serve this soufflé, spoon it onto individual plates, and top each portion with 1 or 2 tablespoons of caramel sauce.

FROZEN SOUFFLE LIMONE

LEMON AND EGGS   SERVES 8 TO 10

TO PREPARE THE CRÈME PÂTISSIÈRE:

2 cups milk
4 egg yolks
½ cup, plus 1 tablespoon, sugar
6 tablespoons all-purpose flour
¼ teaspoon vanilla extract

In a small saucepan, scald the milk. Combine the egg yolks and all the sugar, and beat the mixture until it forms a very thick, pale yellow ribbon when the beaters are raised. Slowly add the flour, and mix well. Pour in the milk, a few drops at a time, beating constantly.

When it is thoroughly blended, transfer the mixture to a saucepan or the top part of a double boiler, and cook it until it has thickened to the consistency of mayonnaise. (If you are cooking the mixture over direct heat, stir and beat it constantly with a wire whisk.) Remove it from the heat, and add the vanilla. This will make approximately 1½ cups (a little more than you'll need for the soufflé).

TO PREPARE THE SOUFFLÉ:

1 cup egg whites, room
  temperature
½ teaspoon cream of tartar
1 cup sugar
  Zest from 4 lemons, chopped
  very fine

Juice from 4 lemons
1 cup crème pâtissière
3 cups heavy cream
2 tablespoons sugar

Beat the egg whites until they are frothy. Add the cream of tartar, and beat steadily until the whites begin to form peaks when the beaters are lifted. Add 1 cup sugar, a spoonful at a time, and continue beating until the mixture forms stiff peaks.

Carefully fold in the lemon zest, lemon juice, and *crème pâtissière*. (A rubber spatula is helpful for doing this.)

Beat the heavy cream and 2 tablespoons sugar until whipped. Carefully fold the whipped cream into the egg whites mixture (again using the rubber spatula), and pour all of this into a 1½- or 2-quart soufflé dish fitted with a collar (see page 423). Freeze the soufflé until it is set. If you intend to serve it the same day, allow 6 to 7 hours for freezing. You can also make this a day ahead of time; it freezes well.

RUM SOUFFLE

RUM AND LIME   **SERVES 10 TO 12**

10 eggs, separated, room
temperature
1½ cups sugar
¾ cup lemon juice
¼ cup lime juice
Pinch of salt
2 tablespoons unflavored gelatin

¾ cup rum, light or dark
3 cups heavy cream
2 tablespoons lemon zest,
chopped very fine
2 tablespoons lime zest, chopped
very fine

Beat the egg yolks until they form a ribbon when the beaters are raised. Add 1 cup sugar, a spoonful at a time, and continue beating. (The mixture should be light and smooth, not granular.) Add the lemon and lime juice and salt. Cook the mixture over low heat, preferably in the top of a double boiler, until it thickens. Mix the gelatin with the rum, and add to the hot custard; combine until smooth. Set aside to cool.

Whip the egg whites until they form peaks. Add ½ cup sugar, 1 teaspoonful at a time, while whipping. Whip 2 cups heavy cream also until it forms peaks. Fold the egg whites into the cooled custard, and then fold that mixture into the whipped cream.

Fit a 6-cup soufflé dish with a wax paper collar (see page 423). Fill the soufflé dish with this mixture, and chill it in the refrigerator; it will keep overnight. It may also be frozen with the paper collar in place.

To dress the soufflé, whip the remaining 1 cup heavy cream and carefully spread it over the soufflé. (We think it is more appealing to the eye *not* to cover the entire soufflé with the cream. We like to cover only half of the soufflé with it.) Sprinkle the lemon and lime zest over the soufflé. We have decorated this soufflé with nasturtiums, violets, geranium buds, among others. Use whatever bloom is available on the window sill or in the garden.

FROZEN MAPLE WALNUT SOUFFLE

1 cup sugar	*9 egg whites, room temperature*
⅓ cup water	*½ teaspoon salt*
9 egg yolks, room temperature	*2 cups ground walnuts, plus 4 or*
3 cups heavy cream	*8 walnut halves*
1 cup maple syrup	

Combine the sugar and water in a saucepan (large enough to hold a candy thermometer), and bring the mixture to a boil. Cook until the syrup reaches the soft-ball stage—the candy thermometer should register 240 degrees. (See Notes 1 and 2).

While the sugar and water are cooking, beat the egg yolks until they form a ribbon when the beaters are raised. When the syrup has reached the desired heat, add it *slowly* to the egg yolks, whipping all the time. (This is very easily done if you're using an electric mixer, particularly the heavy-duty type. Just keep beating the yolks at a relatively high speed as you add the hot syrup in driblets.)

Then whip the heavy cream until it forms stiff peaks, and add the maple syrup to it. (Use a rubber spatula to fold these ingredients together; it's quite easy to do.) Pour the egg yolks into this, and fold to blend thoroughly, again using your rubber spatula. Set this mixture aside.

Beat the egg whites until they form stiff peaks. Add the salt, and beat only until it is combined with the whites. Fold in the ground walnuts, and combine this mixture with the mixture of yolks and whipped cream.

Prepare one 2-quart soufflé dish or two 1-quart soufflé dishes (we prefer the two), and fit them with collars (see page 423). (We suggest you use clear-glass soufflé dishes. The see-through soufflé is most appetizing and dramatic when it is brought to the table.) Pour the soufflé mixture into it (them). The soufflé will be quite high, and this is as it should be. Place in the freezer, and freeze overnight.

When you are ready to serve the soufflé (it can come out of the freezer about 15 minutes ahead of time), remove the collar and arrange 4 walnut halves on top of the soufflé (or 4 on each soufflé) to form a crosslike decoration. We serve the two 1-quart glass soufflé dishes on an oval or oblong silver tray. The silver tray is not important, but serving the two together *is*.

Note 1: Syrup normally ranges in temperature from 234 degrees (minimum soft-ball syrup) to 338 degrees (burnt sugar or caramel). This recipe calls for a medium soft-ball syrup.

Note 2: A word about the use of a candy thermometer: To ensure the candy thermometer does not heat too rapidly, first place it in a pan of water and bring the water to a boil over high heat; then transfer the thermometer to the boiling syrup. When the desired temperature has been reached, transfer the thermometer from the syrup back to the hot water to cool gradually.

MOUSSE AUX MARRONS
(Chestnut Mousse)

CHESTNUTS AND RUM   SERVES 6 TO 8

2 *cups milk*

½ *cup sugar*

15½-*ounce can chestnut purée*
(440 *grams*), *unsweetened*

2 *tablespoons unflavored gelatin*

½ *teaspoon almond extract*

¼ *cup light Virgin Islands rum*

4 *egg yolks, room temperature*

Vegetable oil

2 *cups heavy cream*

Two 1-*ounce chocolate squares,*
shaved (*see Note* 2)

Pour the milk into a saucepan, add the sugar, and heat slowly, until the sugar is dissolved. Add the chestnut purée, and blend with a wire whisk until the mixture is smooth. Then add the gelatin, and blend again, stirring frequently with the whisk. Bring this mixture to a boil. Then remove it from the heat, and add the almond extract.

Beat the egg yolks well. Add ½ cup of the cooled chestnut mixture to the egg yolks, and mix well with a wire whisk. Repeat this procedure 3 more times, mixing well with the whisk to blend in each ½ cup of the purée. Using a rubber spatula, empty this into the remaining chestnut purée mixture. Place the saucepan back onto the heat, and cook the mixture slowly for about 10 minutes until it thickens to the consistency of heavy cream. (Do *not* bring it to a boil.) Remove the saucepan from the heat again, add the light rum, and stir it in well. Strain this mixture through a sieve into a large mixing bowl, and allow it to cool.

Whip 1 cup cream, and blend it into the chestnut mixture *before* it begins to set or jell.

Oil a 1½-quart savarin mold, and pour the mousse mixture into it. Place it in the refrigerator, and let it set until firm (about 2 hours).

When the mousse is set, unmold it onto a silver tray, a pie stand, or an attractive serving plate.

Whip the remaining 1 cup cream, and put it into a pastry bag with ½-inch star nozzle. Decorate the mousse by piping the cream around the bottom outside edge or by piling it in the middle of the mold. Add dollops or stars of cream on top of the mold, and sprinkle chocolate shavings overall.

Note 1: We use Clément Faugier's Purée de Marrons Nature.

Note 2: You choose the sweetness of chocolate that you prefer.

CREME BRULEE IN THE TARA NORTH STYLE

ALMONDS AND CREAM   SERVES 6

6 *eggs, separated, room*	½ *cup sugar*
temperature	2 *teaspoons strawberry preserves*
½ *cup, plus 2 tablespoons,*	(*or raspberry, blackberry, or*
confectioners' sugar	*other berry preserves*)
2 *cups heavy cream*	
1 *tablespoon almond extract* (*see*	
Note)	

Beat the egg yolks and half of the confectioners' sugar until the mixture forms a ribbon when the beaters are raised.

Combine the heavy cream and almond extract in a saucepan, and heat just to the boiling point. (Do *not* allow the mixture to boil.) Pour the heated cream *slowly* into the yolk mixture, beating constantly. (Be sure to pour the heated cream slowly, otherwise it may cook the yolks.) Put this into a ceramic, glass, or other nonmetallic ovenproof vessel.

Set the baking dish or pan into a larger pan, and fill the larger pan with warm water, up to 1 inch from the top of the baking dish, forming a bain-marie. Bake the custard in a preheated 300-degree oven for about 1 hour, until it is set. Remove the custard from the oven, and allow it to cool.

Beat the egg whites until they are soft and fluffy. Add the sugar, 1 teaspoonful at a time. Beat until the egg whites form peaks. Spread the egg whites over the cooled custard, and sprinkle the remaining half of the powdered sugar over the top as evenly as you can.

Bake the custard with its topping in a preheated 350-degree oven for 10 to 15 minutes, until the topping is lightly browned. (If you think the topping is browning too quickly, cover it with a piece of foil.)

Decorate with 2 dollops of berry preserves in the center of the meringue, and bring this dessert to the table hot.

Note: A liqueur, such as Grand Marnier, may be substituted for the almond extract. Or you may use orange extract instead.

((15))

Menus: Some Simple, Some Splendid

T H E best meals we have ever had have not been the most luxurious or the most expensive; on the other hand, neither have they been the most elementary in the sense that there was little to eat or that the food was prepared in the easiest way. We quickly admit, as we have often in this book, that nothing ever tastes as good as strawberries at their peak of freshness (served simply with fresh cream) or fresh asparagus spears at *their* peak (cooked *al dente* and served with lots of butter) or fresh corn on the cob at *its* peak (simply boiled, buttered, and salted). But it's a different matter to try to plan a great dinner and rely solely on the fresh strawberries, asparagus, or corn. The important thing to remember is that good menu planning always *includes* what is fresh in the marketplace. Not only are vegetables and fruits less expensive when they are in season; their taste is superior then, too. Meat, fish, and poultry should be fresh, too, and of high quality. Some inexpensive cuts of meat (such as flank steak)—if they can be called that—adapt to interesting combinations and preparations; but there is no such thing as cheap veal, beef filet, or pork loin. Quality meat costs more, and you will have to spend that "something extra" to achieve an outstanding menu.

To be sure, most components of a meal may be prepared ahead of time, but this does not mean that good home cooking can be accomplished in 15 or 20 minutes. Elegant dinners, satisfying suppers, and lovely lunches take time to prepare. We abhor the literature that suggests fancy food for 12 in 20 minutes; this is ridiculous and misleading. Good dinners *can* be prepared easily, however, if you plan, organize, and execute them carefully. With today's refrigerators and freezers, food can be prepared in advance and stored. Keep this in mind as you plan a menu. Can the soup, bread, and soufflé be made and frozen? If so, a large part of your preparation can be accomplished ahead of time.

One school of thought (and a prevalent one at that) claims that the intensity of flavors should increase from the first to the second to the third course and so on throughout the meal. We find this difficult to accept. Can anything follow gazpacho or spicy Chinese spareribs? Of course. We've had rather bland steamed fish after hot spicy hors d'oeuvres and found this exciting. We recall a delicious mild galantine of lamb that followed a more intense duck-flavored lasagne. We believe that contrasts of texture and color are equally as important as sharpness of flavor. We're not suggesting a meal that should feature the most robust flavor first, with each succeeding course decreasing in strength; nor are we suggesting the reverse. You have to consider vigor of flavor along with the other qualities of each food, and this may mean varying the intensities of the different parts of the meal.

Along with these considerations, you should think about hot versus cold food. A piping-hot corn soufflé combines beautifully with thin, cold slices of Smithfield ham; a Salad in the Neapolitan Style (page 364) goes well with hot, bubbling entrée crepes.

A good menu does not overemphasize one ingredient such as vegetable greens, cream, eggs, pastry, or pasta. Serving gnocchi, lasagna, and crepes may be all right for anyone on an egg and flour diet, but we believe a menu should be more varied. Can you imagine spinach and cheese in phyllo pastry as a first course, followed by lamb en croûte, followed by apple turnover?

Unfortunately, one currently popular theory is that of the all-French meal, the all-Italian meal, the theme of "everything must be consistent at any price." We think some of the more interesting meals we have had have featured French, Italian, or some other national food but have usually accented a food from another country as well. For example, the foods in the following combinations are pairs from different national backgrounds, but they fare well together: ratatouille with an American prime rib roast, arugola salad dressed with oil and vinegar and accompanied by corn bread, veal scaloppini with stir-fried snow peas, pasta with a lobster sauce followed by mocha meringue pie. More important than national themes are the flavors, textures, colors, and contrasts of the foods that you bring together to form the menu.

One rule that should be followed: Serve good wines with good food. Don't spend dollars and hours preparing your special and important dinner and then diminish it with poor wine. Not all good wine is overly expensive, so cultivate your liquor dealer as you do your butcher. Before you buy a sale case, buy and sample one bottle; if it's good, then buy the case. Study and plan the wines as you do the rest of the meal. In the menus that follow in this chapter, we have offered wine suggestions. We know you'll enjoy the specific wines mentioned, but if you have difficulty getting them, try another, staying within the general grouping (such as Chambertin) if you can. If the wine suggestion is preceded by an asterisk (*), the wine is expensive. But we've also listed many good inexpensive wines.

Here are some menus to give you practical help and ideas for combining the various recipes in this book. There are six four-star dinners to be prepared at home, twelve menus for special situations, and two buffets. All the courses mentioned appear among the recipes in this volume (except for fruit, cheese, and so forth).

SIX FOUR-STAR DINNERS AT HOME

A dinner for 8: elegant, simple food for city or country dining

Coquilles Beatrice
A Simple Roast Filet of Beef
Eggplant Farcie
Endive Vinaigrette
Crepes with Cooked Pears

Wine: A good Burgundy or Bordeaux, such as *Château Margaux or Château Calon-Ségur, a Chambertin, such as *Clos de la Griotte Chambertin or Gevrey-Chambertin, or a Côte de Nuits.

This dinner will tell people you love them because your careful preparation of it from beginning to end will be evident to everyone. It seems to please both women and men; women are curious about the mystique of the farcie, and the men love the pink, tender, tasty beef. Beatrice in her coquilles is divine; the pears in their crepes sublime.

Prepare the coquilles well ahead of time. Then set them on a large baking tray, and place them in a moderate to high oven; they will take less than 30 minutes to bubble. The filet can be roasted during cocktails and should rest out of the oven while everyone is eating the first course. The sauce in the recipe may be eliminated (it usually is by us because the Eggplant Farcie is spicy, juicy, tasty, and exquisite with the beef *sans la sauce*). The vinaigrette may be made ahead of time, but the dressing must be allowed to reach room temperature before serving. You can finish the crepes *à table,* but prepare them ahead, and simply heat them while you are eating the beef or salad course. This menu offers great combinations of tastes and textures. Try it.

A dinner for family and friends with the egg before the chicken

Eggs in Aspic in the Tara North Style
Uccelletti di Pollo (Rolled Chicken Breasts
    with Prosciutto Stuffing)
Potatoes with Garlic, Cream, and Cheese
Apricot and Canteloupe Chutney
Green salad with an Oil and Vinegar Dressing
Caramel Tarts à la Bellevue

Wine: A dry champagne or a chateau-bottled Bordeaux, such
        as *Grand Vin de Château Latour or Château Prieuré-
        Lichine (Margaux).

If simply and properly made, eggs encased in aspic can be one of the most beautiful foods brought to the table. In making the aspic, you must be sure to clarify the stock, making it crystal clear; it is important for the jellied aspic to glisten when it is served. Carefully follow the directions on pages 25–27; reread them, and you'll find this easy to prepare. It takes a little time, but it can be made a day ahead of time and refrigerated. The chicken breasts can be stuffed, rolled, and even breaded in advance and then placed in the refrigerator until you are ready to cook them. Potatoes with Garlic, Cream, and Cheese are a great combination with the chicken and may also be made ahead of time, but they must be heated through before serving. A chutney—of apricots and canteloupes, for example—is a wonderful accompaniment with the chicken. Don't believe that only white wines are proper with chicken; many red wines are perfect with it, too. Champagne is superb with this dinner and will surely add a special touch and taste, but so will a good estate-bottled Bordeaux. Caramel tarts complete this meal.

A rich and beautiful dinner for very special people

Madeira Mold with Liver Pâté en Gelée
Braciola in Brown Sauce (Beef Birds in Brown Sauce)
Wild Rice
A Salad of Chicory and Escarole
Rum Raisin Meringue Pie

Wine: A Chambertin, such as Gevrey-Chambertin "Clos Saint-
       Jacques," or Clos de Beze.

Worthwhile people deserve a worthwhile dinner. This good meal is fairly easy to prepare and quite simple to serve. It works equally well with 8 or 10 at the dinner table; if you want twice as many, an interesting table arrangement would be to set up four tables, with 4 or 5 friends at each table.

For the latter, you'll need to make the full recipe: two 9-inch molds for the Madeira mold. The molds may be made a day ahead of time or on the morning of your dinner party.

Prepare one braciola per person plus two extras for an emergency. The braciola may be stuffed, rolled, and sautéed the day before; let them sit in the brown sauce overnight, and cook them slowly before guests arrive.

Make the pie(s) the morning or afternoon of your party—and there you are.

Important notes in serving the Madeira molds:

1. Unmold them on a silver tray or an attractive platter. But do *not* unmold them onto lettuce or another garnishing. Bring them to the table uncut.

2. Cut them in wedges at the table, and serve a wedge to each person.
3. Serve toast strips (about 1 by 3½ inches in size) with the molds. They should be golden, not burnt. And it's better if they are warm because the contrast with the cold aspic is exciting.

Only the wild rice and salad require preparation 30 minutes to 1 hour before dinner (but crisp the lettuce leaves for several hours in the refrigerator before combining them with the dressing). Add a green, orange, or white vegetable if you wish, but keep it simple because all the flavor is in the braciola. Often, we serve the salad with the braciola; another vegetable (other than the rice) can be redundant and too filling. Braciola are interesting to serve. What Monsieur Point said about caviar (see page 5) we say about steaks: Serving them is easy cooking. But braciola indicate to your guests that you've taken special care to prepare them. A braciola, piping hot, served with wild rice, is a magnificent sight, and it is tender enough to be eaten with a fork. The sublime flavor will surely enhance your reputation as a cook. Sprinkle the meringue pie with confectioners' sugar, and serve it on a tall cake stand.

An exquisite, easy-to-prepare dinner for V.I.P.s

Smoked Salmon Mousse à la Tara North, with toast
Mignonette of Veal with Braised Chestnuts
Fresh Minted Cucumbers
Crepes Limone

Wine: A white wine from Savoy, such as Roussette de seyssel
or Crepy, or a red Bordeaux, such as Saint Émilion
*Château Ausone or Saint Émilion Château Ripeau.

This exquisite dinner is actually rather easy to prepare. The mousse can be made the day before it is to be served, and so can the dessert crepes, although they must not be sauced until just before serving. The filet of veal is a very special cut of meat. It cooks slowly in brown sauce, which is easy to prepare, especially if you have the sauce on hand in the freezer. This dinner was served to Mr. and Mrs. Saul Maloff of Roxbury, Connecticut. Mrs. Maloff is Dorothy Parker, our attractive, talented, and hardworking editor. (Actually, we served the Mirabelle Meringue Pie in place of the Crepes Limone, but we now think the cream in the mousse and the cream in the pie are excessive.)

A *chic dinner with a Chinese touch, calorie conscious but filling*

Crepes Filled with a Spinach and Cheese Soufflé,
   with Sauce Bâtarde
Chicken Chinoiserie
Snow peas, stir-fried
Oranges Napoleon

Wine: *The ginger in this chicken dish comes on strong and probably will interfere with the taste of a truly good wine. Select a fresh, dry rosé from Provence or a good, dry Sancerre. Or be daring (and chic and sensible, too), and serve ice-cold beer.*

You *must* plan this dinner. It is a taste sensation; it's elegant and easy to prepare—with a little organization. Make the crepes ahead of time, along with the Sauce Bâtarde; the spinach and cheese soufflé filling can be made ahead of time, too. Filling, heating, and saucing the crepes is a last-minute act. The crepes have a delicate flavor and texture; the sauce adds a touch of piquancy. The chicken breasts can marinate 3 hours ahead of time. Sautéeing the chicken and stir-frying the snow peas are also last-minute tasks if you are organized. Both should be cooked after you serve the first course. The chicken is exciting, not just in flavor but in texture. The cornstarch "flouring" creates an extra crispness, fascinating after the soft, smooth crepe. The Oranges Napoleon are a perfectly refreshing dessert after the bite of the garlicky, gingered Chinese-style chicken. They, too, may be made well ahead time.

Sophisticated dining: sole, scallops, shrimp, strawberries, and a sancerre

Cold Eggplant al Panariello
Turban of Sole with Rice, Filled with Shrimp and Scallops,
   in a White Wine Sauce

Asparagus in Mamma Angela's Style
Bibb or Boston lettuce with an Oil and Vinegar Dressing
Diana Buchanan's Yeast Rolls
Strawberry Pie in the Carolina Style

*Wine: A dry white Burgundy, such as *Montrachet, Chas-
sagne-Montrachet (icy cold), or Chablis Grand Cru
"Vandesir," or a Sancerre.*

You can serve an excellent dinner if you use good ingredients, prepare them properly, and pay attention to last-minute details. This elegant dinner is designed to bring together delicious combinations of food; it is also designed to allow the cook to prepare things ahead of time so that little or nothing will interfere with pulling the meal together just before serving.

Prepare the eggplant and the pie on the morning of the day you plan to serve the dinner. Actually, both can be made the day before if you wish. The lettuce should be washed, dried, and refrigerated for several hours. Start to prepare your salad dressing ahead of time, but do not combine it with the greens until just before serving. The asparagus spears can be cleaned and refrigerated in a plastic bag; in fact, they can be prepared with bread crumbs and refrigerated until you are ready to be sauté them. Or they can be cooked 30 minutes to 1 hour ahead of time and kept warm in a slow oven. Because Ms. Buchanan's yeast rolls freeze perfectly, they can be made 1 week ahead of time. Then, when you need them, wrap the frozen rolls in foil, and heat them thoroughly. (The more experienced cook will have no trouble making them in time to serve them exquisitely hot from oven to table.) The magnificent turban of sole also can be started ahead of time. You can prepare the shrimp and scallops early in the day; you can make the white wine sauce in advance, too. The ring mold can be arranged with the fish filets, filled with the rice, and refrigerated until 15 minutes before cooking. But cooking the mold, heating the sauce, and assembling the dish can be done only at the last minute. This is really easy to do, but you must read and reread the recipe so that you'll know what is to be accomplished when and how.

FOOD FOR TWELVE SPECIAL SITUATIONS

A brunch

Baked Eggs for Breakfast
Crepes Filled with Chicken Curry
Prunes Steeped in Madeira

Wine: A Chablis, Pouilly-Fuissé, or Corton-Charlemagne, or
   another dry white wine.

It's usually difficult to provide weekend guests with three meals on
Sunday. Late sleepers, churchgoers, train schedules, crowded highways,
and storm warnings all have an effect on Sunday meals for guests. We
think two Sunday meals are more comfortable for everyone, and here
is one we serve in late morning or at noon, before guests go antiquing,
golfing, or whatever. A late-afternoon or early-evening supper makes the
second meal. This arrangement works well for weekends in the country,
but it can also apply for city dwellers who don't dote on large family
meals at noon on Sunday.

A supper (or a lunch) for people who love to eat

Fish Soup in the Mediterranean Style
Hot, crusty bread
Green salad with an Oil and Vinegar Dressing
Chocolate Pie à la Bourbon

Wine: A Muscadet or a Blanc de Blancs, such as Cartier's,
   which is very inexpensive.

This fish soup is a meal in itself; it is not only nutritious but also really
satisfying. The combinations of fish, herbs, and vegetables are made for
each other. With homemade fish stock (something easy to make), the
fennel, fish, and saffron aromas will penetrate the atmosphere, and
people will be eager to find their way into the kitchen. Be sure to use
really fresh fish filets, and add more if you wish to make a thicker soup.

Lobster is not inexpensive, but because this soup is your main course and it serves 8, the meal is actually not costly. The fish soup can easily be doubled to serve 16. With a big salad, lots of bread, and two pies, you can plan a large supper party. Hot, crusty Italian or French bread is an important accompaniment to the hot soup. You can add a thick slice of bread to each soup bowl (before adding the soup) à la Provence or Neapolitan style, or simply serve hot bread in baskets on the side. Both the soup and the bread (with lots of butter) should be hot. Most people prefer to sit and eat, but because there is no "cutting with knife" in this meal, the service can be most informal. A huge tureen filled with piping-hot soup and baskets of bread can be put on a table, and people can help themselves. Serve lots of chilled wine with the fish soup. The salad should be a separate course, with no wine and with time allowed to clear the palate. The dessert is rich, velvety, and divine. Be sure you have enough soup and pie. People who love to eat will want seconds.

A quiet, relaxed dinner for 2

Crème St. Philbert (Cream of Filbert Soup)
Double Pork Chops Filled and Flambéed
Angela's Broccoli di Rape
Fresh fruit and cheese

Wine: *A well-chilled Meursault, such as Clos de la Baronne;*
a Chablis, such as Chablis Grand Cru Les Preuses; or
a Beaujolais, such as Château de l'abbaye (Fleurie).

And this is an easy way to his or her heart. With a minimum of preparation, this can be one of the more relaxed dinners, allowing you maximum time to stir and sip your Dubonnet, bourbon, or ice-cold dry martinis. If you can arrange a love seat (any old sofa will do) and a small table set for two in front of a mellow fire, you'll have it made. Make the Crème St. Philbert ahead of time, put it in a double boiler, cover it, and keep it on low heat while the fire is crackling. Stuff and sauté the chops ahead of time; cover and cook them slowly while you mix another batch of martinis. (Be sure the Meursault or Chablis is in the refrigerator.) Cook the *broccoli di rape* hours ahead, but leave it underdone because it will cook further when you reheat it. Light the candles, serve the soup and wine. Progress to the chops and *broccoli di rape*. Serve the fruit and cheese in front of the fire. Sit on the floor, add more wine, and glow.

Checkered-tablecloth eating, American style

Chicken Thighs in the Gumbo Style
Lulu's Potato Pie with Ham, No Less
Diana Buchanan's Biscuit
Arugola salad with an Oil and Vinegar Dressing
Praline Cream Pie in a Meringue Shell

Wine: Serve one of America's finest premium wines, a California Cabernet Sauvignon.

Here's a supper that is fun to prepare and fun to serve. It's an extremely low-cost meal for 8, 16, or 24, and it is an excellent combination of tastes. Chicken thighs are succulent parts of poultry, even more so when combined with Creole vegetables and herbs. Lulu's potato pie stabilizes the chicken dish, and because it contains ham, the combination with poultry is great. The gumbo sauce goes with the buttermilk biscuit, and dunking should be allowed. A definite break after the gumbo, potato pie, and biscuit course is essential. Serve the salad separately. The arugola salad, as un-American as it may be, is the perfect rest before the all-American satiny-smooth praline cream pie. The chicken thighs and the potato pie can be made early in the day and reheated before serving. The arugola leaves should be washed and dried several hours ahead of time but not dressed until serving. The biscuits can be made ahead, but they are best when baked just before eating. The dessert can be made a day before.

Dinner theme: "I gotta be me"

Clams Aioli Imperiale
Whole Chicken, en Casserole, en Croûte
Green salad with an Oil and Vinegar Dressing
Cocoa Roll à la Bourbon

Wine: A Fleurie or another new, young Beaujolais, such as
Moulin-a-Vent or La Feuille d'Automne.

If you like clams, chicken, and cream and chocolate desserts, this dinner
is for you. Together, they make a meal with plenty of panache. Clams
are delicious prepared this way. The chicken casserole is a Barnum and
Bailey presentation, easy to do if you follow the step-by-step procedure.
At some point, you may feel as if you're transferring trapezes, but this
is part of the excitement and enjoyment of it all. The cocoa roll can be
made the day before and refrigerated. This is a fabulous meal, providing
great combinations of food for the guests and compliments for the cook.

A lunch in early fall

Butternut Squash Soup with Curry
A Summertime Bread (Zucchini Bread with Basil and Chives)
Green salad with Brie

Wine: a very well chilled rosé from Provence.

When the air is crisp and the sky is blue, after working or walking in
cool, crisp air, a good, hot soup with a touch of spice is perfect. Almost
all the main ingredients—the butternut squash, zucchini, chives, and
lettuce—can come straight from the garden. Both the soup and the
bread can be frozen, so this lunch is still excellent weeks after you've
put the garden to bed for the winter.

A meal for an informal mood

Antipasto
Timballo di Fettucine (Baked and Molded Fettucine)
Baked Whole Tomatoes with Pesto
Pane Italiano della Mamma (Mother's Italian Bread)
Fresh, fresh fruit

Wine: A rosé from the Dolomites or a good Italian wine, such
as Bardolino, Valpolicella, or barolo (Antichi Vigneti
Propri).

This is good food for an informal mood, perhaps a supper with the couple next door. The antipasto can be made early in the day, but the *timballo* should be made just before it is served. And it should be served hot. If you know how to cook spaghetti, you'll have no difficulty making it (although in this case you'll be cooking fettucine). Read and reread the procedure for coating the baking dish; have all the ingredients at hand, and you'll see how easy it is to pull this together. It's an effective dish; when turned out—very stylish. You will enjoy this other way of serving a famous pasta.

A chic and satisfying lunch

Vichyssoise Verte (Asparagus and Leek Soup)
Ms. Jane Walsh's Bread of Chopped Shallots and Cottage Cheese
Rum Soufflé

Wine: A dry Riesling, such as Rauenthaler Baiten, Rüdesheimer Berg Roseneck, or *Bernkasteler Doktor.

This lunch will serve 4, 6, or 8, and it's easy to put together. Everything here can be made ahead of time. The soup and bread freeze extremely well. If the bread is frozen, bring it to room temperature, wrap it in foil, put it in an oven, and heat it thoroughly. You can add salad and cheese if you want a fuller lunch. In the summer, the soup may be served cold, but *always* serve the bread hot.

A good meal in the kitchen

Angela's Stuffed Artichokes
Spaghettini, with Lobster and White Wine in a Fresh Tomato Sauce
Mocha Meringue Cream Pie

Wine: A Muscadet or a Sancerre, such as Ackerman's, from France.

If properly prepared, this menu can be a treat for any lunch or supper. It's simple; it's elegant; it's delicious. Most of all, it's fun to prepare.

The family will love it. We serve it to close friends who like to eat in our kitchen. Cooking pasta is a delight when friends are in the kitchen. People enjoy pasta cooking. The artichokes are prepared ahead of time, as is the pasta sauce. But the sauce, too, can be pulled together just before serving, especially if you have all the ingredients prepared (shallots peeled and chopped and so on). We sip wine and talk between the artichoke and pasta courses, and if you're with people you enjoy, the wait for the pasta won't seem long. A rich, velvety dessert is good in the kitchen, too. This is a hearty meal.

A cozy supper with close friends, any night of the week

Melon or figs and prosciutto
Manicotti with Chicken and Almonds
Arugola salad
Orange Cake in the Grand Marnier Style

Wine: A good white Beaune, such as Clos de l'Écu, or an Italian wine, such as Antinori Orvieto Classico or Soave Bolla.

The manicotti are fairly inexpensive to make, and this should allow you to spend more on a good-quality prosciutto and a just-ripe melon or exquisite, perfect figs. This supper is easy to prepare because the melon or figs and prosciutto require no cooking. The manicotti and sauce can be made ahead and frozen. If they are frozen, thaw the sauce to the point where it can be spooned into a baking dish. Put some sauce on the bottom of the baking dish, arrange the still-frozen manicotti in one layer, and cover them with more sauce. Cover the dish with foil, and bake in a preheated moderate oven for 45 minutes to 1 hour, or until the manicotti are bubbly and heated through. The arugola leaves should be washed, spun-dried, and put in the refrigerator several hours before serving time. Prepare an oil and vinegar dressing, but do not dress the salad until you are ready to serve it. The orange cake may be made the day before or during the day on which it is to be served. It should be served at room temperature or a little on the warm side. A dollop of whipped cream served with each slice is tasty.

For an impromptu and tasty supper

Vermicelli with a Special and Quick Sauce
Salad of greens, including watercress and sliced raw mushrooms
Fruit, cheese, ice cream, cookies

Wine: A white Alsatian wine, such as Hauller's Gewurztram-
iner, Hauler's Sylvaner, or Hauler's Riesling.

Almost everyone has been faced with the task of pulling together a meal
with only a half-hour's notice. Don't fret. One of the best ways to
handle this situation is with an interesting and easily prepared pasta
dish. Pasta, properly prepared and served with a tasty sauce, is not only
welcome but elegant. You will have to have salad greens, mushrooms,
fruit, and cheese on hand to fill out this meal. You may wonder how to
make the sauce; after all, fresh ginger is not that common an ingredient
in most Western kitchens. The answer is simple: Always keep some
frozen. It lasts for months, and you can use what you need when you
need it. A neighbor, Mark Berghold, who is a talented twelve-year-old
chef, telephoned one recent Sunday evening to see if he could borrow
some ginger called for in a Chinese dish he was preparing for his parents,
brother, and sister. It was great to be able to say yes.

For the end of a perfect weekend: A warm, friendly Sunday supper

Prosciutto with Roasted Peppers
Fresh Tomato and Fresh Basil Soup
Hot cornbread
Cassata di Caffé e Cioccolata

Wine: Italian wine, such as barolo, a chianti classico such as
Castello di Brolio or Nozzole; or a red Châteauneuf du
Pape, such as Domaine de Nalys.

If you've had company all weekend (or even if you haven't), you may
not be in the mood to cook up a storm on Sunday evening. This menu
is ideal for such an occasion because it requires little effort, provided
you make the cheesecake several days ahead of time. (We've kept this
cheesecake in the refrigerator for almost a week and it was still moist.)

The Prosciutto with Roasted Peppers is a first course and we suggest serving it with refreshments. Serve the piping hot soup in individual bowls or in a tureen when people are at the table. The cornbread should be piping hot and served with lots of sweet butter.

Cool, smooth cheesecake and a cup of coffee or tea is the perfect climax to this simple, fulfilling meal.

TWO BUFFETS

Buffet Numero Uno

A Casserole of Cream Sherried Shrimp
Sliced roast beef
Frittata "Rafanata" in the Italian Style
Chicken in the Burgundy Style
Zucchini in a Skillet
A salad of greens
Raspberry Meringue Pie

Wine: A good Burgundy, such as Vosne-Romanée, Chorey-Les-Beaune, or Mercurey, or a Cotes-du-Rhone, such as Hermitage.

There's no need to settle for the sliced boiled ham, potato chips, white bread, and pickles sort of buffet. The items in this buffet offer wonderful combinations (the roast beef and the Frittata "Rafanata" are a most special pairing), and although these dishes require some time and effort to prepare, almost everything can be made ahead of time. Remember that the greens for the salad should be washed and dried ahead of time; the only last-minute preparation is dressing the salad. The sherried shrimp and the chicken can be kept in a slow oven, but be careful you don't overcook the shrimp and toughen them. The pie can be made the day before.

Buffet Numero Due

Soufflé Roll with Crab Meat
Torta di Verdura (Swiss Chard, Sausage, and Ricotta Pie)
Chicken Thighs in an Herbed Cream Sauce
Cold Shrimp for a Buffet
A Shoulder of Pork Wrapped around Fresh Fennel al Vagnini
Rollatini di Melanzane (Stuffed and Rolled Eggplant Slices)
Insalata di Cavolo Cinese
Frozen Maple Walnut Soufflé

Wine: A Médoc, such as Chateau du Taillan, *Chateau Bey-
chevelle, or Chateau Talbot.

This buffet is bound to impress your family, friends, business associates, or neighbors at a buffet party in your home. Each preparation is unusual, tasty, and in great combination with every other. The *torta,* the chicken, and the eggplant should be served hot, but they can be made ahead of time and heated through just before serving. The soufflé roll can be made the day before, although we prefer making it on the morning of the day it is to be served. The shrimp and pork can be made the day before. And the dessert can be made several days in advance and kept in the freezer. The salad of Chinese cabbage should be prepared ahead of time, with the dressing added 1 hour ahead of time.

APPENDIXES

WEIGHTS AND MEASURES

1 teaspoon	=	⅓ tablespoon
3 teaspoons	=	1 tablespoon
2 tablespoons	=	1 ounce
4 tablespoons	=	¼ cup
5⅔ tablespoons	=	⅓ cup
¼ cup and 1 tablespoon	=	⅜ cup
8 tablespoons	=	½ cup
¾ cup and 2 tablespoons	=	⅞ cup
16 tablespoons	=	1 cup
2 cups	=	1 pint
16 fluid ounces	=	1 pint
1 pint	=	1 pound
2 pints (4 cups)	=	1 quart
4 quarts	=	1 gallon

EQUIVALENT FOREIGN MEASURES

1 teaspoon	=	5 grams
1 tablespoon	=	14 to 15 grams
1 ounce	=	30 grams
11 tablespoons flour (all-purpose)	=	100 grams
7 tablespoons sugar	=	100 grams
7 tablespoons butter	=	100 grams
1 pound (16 ounces)	=	454 grams
1 cup American	=	8 ounces
1 cup English	=	10 ounces

AVERAGE CAN SIZES

Can Size	Cups	Weight
8 ounces	1	8 ounces
No. 1	1⅓	11 ounces
1½	2	16 ounces
2	2½	20 ounces
2½	3½	28 ounces
3	4	33 ounces

SOME EQUIVALENT MEASURES

Almonds, 1 cup chopped	=	⅘ pound, shelled
Butter, 2 cups	=	1 pound
Chocolate, 1 square	=	1 ounce
Cheese, 5 cups grated	=	1 pound
Corn meal, 3 cups	=	1 pound
Eggs, 5 whole	=	1 cup
Egg whites, 8	=	1 cup (approximately)
Egg yolks, 16	=	1 cup (approximately)
Flour, 4 cups	=	1 pound
1 lemon, juiced	=	2 to 3 tablespoons
Nutmeats, 4 cups chopped	=	1 pound
Pecans, 3 cups chopped	=	2½ pounds, unshelled
Rice, 3 to 4 cups cooked	=	1 cup raw
Sugar, granulated, 2 cups	=	1 pound
Sugar, confectioners', 3⅓ cups	=	1 pound
Sugar, brown, 2⅔ cups	=	1 pound

Food Sources

C = CATALOG AVAILABLE
FMO = WILL FILL MAIL ORDERS

NEW YORK

Balducci's, 424 Sixth Avenue, New York, N.Y. 10011
Fresh fruits and vegetables, cheeses, international smoked meats and fish. FMO

Baur Pastries, Inc., 1232 Lexington Avenue, New York, N.Y. 10028
German-style cakes and pastries.

Mario Bosco's, 263 Bleecker Street, New York, N.Y. 10014
Catechini, Italian wild mushrooms, imported Italian products. FMO

Bremen House, Inc., 200 East 86th Street, New York, N.Y. 10028
European chocolates and candies, smoked meats, wursts, fish products, cheeses, and honey. C, FMO

G. Capecci & P. Pernice, "Salumeria Italian," 26 Carmine Street, New York, N.Y. 10014
Pancetta, biroldi, fresh sausage, and other Italian specialties.

P. Carnevale & Son, Inc., 631 Ninth Avenue, New York, N.Y. 10036
Saucisson à l'ail, pâté, boudin blanc et noir, and Italian sausage products.

Cheese Unlimited, Inc., 1529 Second Avenue, New York, N.Y. 10021
Imported and domestic cheeses, French breads, rolls, and biscuits for cheese. FMO

Empire Coffee and Tea Company, 486 Ninth Avenue, New York, N.Y. 10018
Coffee, tea, appliances, and coffee grinders. C, FMO

Faicco's Pork Store, 260 Bleecker Street, New York, N.Y. 10014
Fresh and dry sausages, sopressata salamis, and all fresh cuts of pork.

Ferrara Pastry Shop, 195 Grand Street, New York, N.Y. 10013
French and Italian pastries, rum cakes and petits babas in jars and tins, and imported Italian confectionery products. C, FMO

Mrs. Herbst's Pastries and Strudels, 1437 Third Avenue, New York, N.Y. 10028
   Strudels, Continental pastries, and cookies. C, FMO
Iron Gate Products Co., Inc., 424 West 54th Street, New York, N.Y. 10019
   Seafood, game, and caviar. C, FMO
D. Lampariello & Son, Inc., 210 Grand Street, New York, N.Y. 10013
   Pasta, tomatoes, and Italian sweets. C, FMO
Maison Glass, 52 East 58th Street, New York, N.Y. 10022
   Caviar (fresh beluga), foie gras, Virginia hams, fresh-roasted nuts, cheese, truffles, marrons, smoked birds (pheasants, turkey, rock Cornish hens, and others), mustards, honeys, jams, teas, soups, and coffees. C, FMO
Maryland Midtown Gourmet, 907 Madison Avenue, New York, N.Y. 10021
   U.S. prime beef, white veal, wild game, and game birds. C, FMO
Middle Eastern Food Center, 380 Third Avenue, New York, N.Y. 10016
   Middle Eastern foods (Iranian, Turkish, Arabic, Greek, and Israeli). FMO
O. Ottomanelli & Sons Prime Meat Market, 281 Bleecker Street, New York, N.Y. 10014
   Italian-style veal roast seasoned with herbs, spices, and prosciutto and wrapped in bacon; crown roast of lamb, selected wild game (quail, partridge, pheasant, wild turkey, and venison).
Paprikas Weiss Importer, 1546 Second Avenue, New York, N.Y. 10028
   Spices, sausages, hams, coffees, nuts, pâtés, cheeses, biscuits, and a multitude of imported canned products. C, FMO
William Poll's Gourmet Shop, 1051 Lexington Avenue, New York, N.Y. 10021
   Caviar, salmon, and cheeses. C, FMO
Poseidon Confectionery Co., 629 Ninth Avenue, New York, N.Y. 10036
   Greek pastries, baklava, phyllo, spinach and cheese pie. FMO
Randazzo's Fish Market, 2340 Arthur Avenue, Bronx, N.Y. 10458
   Fresh fish and seafood.
H. Roth and Son, 1577 First Avenue, New York, N.Y. 10028
   Hungarian paprika, spices, and herbs. FMO
Sahadi Importing Co., Inc., 187 Atlantic Avenue, Brooklyn, N.Y. 11201
   Middle Eastern foods, including spices, olives, dry and canned goods, Turkish delights, and sesame candies. C, FMO

Schaller & Weber, Inc., 1654 Second Avenue, New York, N.Y. 10028
Lachs Schunken, Black Forest ham, Westphalian ham, and bolognas and salamis. **c, fmo**

Tom's Latticini, 41-17 National Street, Corona, N.Y. 11368
Cheeses, cured meats, and olives.

Trinacria Importing Company, 415 Third Avenue, New York, N.Y. 10016
Italian, Indian, and Indonesian foods. **fmo**

Wing Woh Lung, 50 Mott Street, New York, N.Y.
Chinese canned goods and condiments. **fmo**

COLORADO

American Tea, Coffee & Spice Co., 1511 Champa Street, Denver, Co. 80202
Coffee, tea, spices, Usinger sausages, dried fruits, raw nuts, and cheeses. **fmo**

CONNECTICUT

The Cheese Shop, 271 Greenwich Avenue, Greenwich, Ct. 06830
Imported and domestic cheeses, other gourmet products, coffees, and ethnic breads. **c, fmo**

Dimyan's Market, 116 Elm Street, Danbury, Ct. 06810
Arabic and Greek foods. **fmo**

Mystic Seaport Museum Stores, Inc., Mystic, Ct. 06355
Johnnycake meal, buckwheat flour, and hickory-smoked cheese. **fmo**

LOUISIANA

Central Grocery, 923 Decatur, New Orleans, La. 70116
Italian, Spanish, Greek, and Syrian foods. **fmo**

MICHIGAN

Big Ten Party Store, 1928 Packard, Ann Arbor, Mi. 48104
Cheese and specialty meats. **fmo**

NEW JERSEY

Cameron's Market, 162 Kearney Avenue, Kearny, N.J. 07032
Scottish meat pies and beef sausages.

L. A. Champon & Co., Inc., 70 Hudson Street, Hoboken, N.J. 07030
Vanilla beans. **fmo**

OKLAHOMA

Antone's Import Foods, 2606 South Sheridan, Tulsa, Ok. 74129
Middle Eastern, European, and Far Eastern foods.

VIRGINIA

Seven Day Shopping Centre, 2121 Ivy Road, Charlottesville, Va. 22903
Imported specialties of all types, with strong selections from Japan, China, Greece, Italy, Germany, India, Mexico, Spain, England, France, and Scandinavian countries. FMO

WISCONSIN

International House of Foods, 440 West Gorham Street, Madison, Wi. 53703
Foods from Japan, China, Korea, Southeast Asia, India, South America, Africa, and Mexico. FMO

CANADA

The Top Banana, Ltd., 1526 Merivale Road, Ottawa 2, Canada K2G 3J6
Fresh vegetables and fruits for Eastern and Western cooking.
S. Enkin, Inc., 1201 St. Lawrence Boulevard, Montreal 129, Quebec, Canada
Indian, Pakistani, West Indian, Chinese, and Japanese foods. C, FMO

INDEX